A Child's Journey Through Placement

A Child's Journey Through Placement

by Vera I. Fahlberg, M.D.

Perspectives Press
Indianapolis, IN

Perspectives Press
P.O. Box 90318
Indianapolis, IN
46290-0318

Manufactured in the United States of America
Paperback edition, 1994
ISBN 0-944934-11-0

Cover photo used with permission courtesy of Superstock, Inc., New York

Library of Congress Cataloging in Publication Data:

Fahlberg, Vera.
  A child's journey through placement
  by Vera I.Fahlberg.
     p. cm.
Includes bibliographical references and index.
ISBN 0-944934-04-8 cloth; 0-944934-11-0 paper
   1. Foster children--Pyschology. 2. Attachment behavior in children. 3. Foster home care--United States--Case studies.
I. Title
HV875.F143 1991
362. 7' 33' 019--dc20   91-32036
                                         CIP

This book is dedicated both to those children who are currently within the child welfare system and to those who have already completed their journeys— and to their travelling companions.

Table of Contents

Acknowledgements

I offer my thanks and greatest admiration to the children who have taught me most of what I know about translating theory to practice. Some offered lessons that were easy for me to figure out and master. Others had to be patient and persistent as I tried to make them fit into preconceived molds. Eventually, however, each of them was able to teach me something, and expand my horizons.

Further thanks must be offered to the birth, foster, and adoptive families who have shared with me their wealth of experiences. Finally, plaudits to the many dedicated child welfare professionals whom I have met while conducting training workshops throughout the country. Most particularly, however, I want to thank those within the areas of the country where I have spent most of my professional life—Colorado and Washington. They have allowed me to share in their work on behalf of children.

This book is filled with many case examples. Many are composites of several cases. All reflect real children, real families, real problems, and real solutions. Although names and details have been changed in each case, some readers may think that they recognize themselves, their children, or cases they have told me about. If so, thank you for your input.

It is my hope that each child within the system will have at least one adult who will become his advocate, insuring that he receives the thoughtful and timely decision making that he deserves. It does not matter who this person is—a parent, a caseworker, a supervisor, an administrator, a consultant, a CASA volunteer, a therapist, a teacher, a physician, a lawyer, or a judge. I know of cases in which people in each of these positions have been the child's primary spokesperson.

Without a strong advocate the child's road through the system is likely to be one of roadblocks, potholes, and detours. I would wish for each child as smooth a journey as is possible, with good companions along the way, and a loving destination.

Vera Fahlberg, M.D.
Issaquah, Washington
1991

Face red with anger, tears rolling down cheeks, mouth downturned, twenty-month-old Ardith lashes out, pulling a handful of hair from the head of her four-year-old brother, Prentice. He sits quietly withdrawn, little emotion showing on his face, strapped in a seat belt next to Ardith's car seat in the back of a car. Ardith and Prentice do not know where their parents are. They do not know the person transporting them. They do not know where they are going.

Unaware of the true significance of this trip, they are joining 360,000* other American children, each on his on her unique journey through the child welfare system.

*This figure is taken from a survey by the American Enterprise Institute and the American Public Welfare Association.

Introduction

Although much is available in the child welfare literature about families and casework process and procedures, there is little that has the child as the primary focus of attention. This book is an attempt to fill that gap. It is written especially for child welfare workers. However, I expect that parents (especially foster and adoptive), child welfare advocates, educators, and mental health professionals will also find information that will help them understand and become more effective in their relationships with children. This work includes much of the material previously published in the series *Putting The Pieces Together*. Although the philosophy and style of the previous publications have been maintained in this volume, the information has been updated, revised, and substantially added to. Theoretical considerations are combined with the practical aspects of working with children in the child welfare system.

The goal of all social work intervention is to help child and parent grow and change in ways that facilitate both the development of self and of healthy interpersonal relationships. As professionals, we cannot accomplish this goal without extensive contact with all family members, always modeling and encouraging the development of attachments. When we model avoidance, lack of caring, and emotional distancing, that is the pattern that children and families will learn or maintain. If we model caring, concern, and emotional nurturance, we increase the likelihood that positive changes will occur.

This book focuses on the child, his feelings, needs, and behaviors, once the decision has been made that he needs to be placed in foster care. Although I am a strong advocate of family preservation services, neither this topic nor the initial child protection assessment are included here.

Throughout the book, there is much discussion about the relationships between children and their parents. The word *parents* is used to mean primary caregivers, who may be birth parents, foster parents, adoptive parents, or other relatives. Research reflects cultural biases, such as mother being the primary attachment object. This will be apparent, particularly in the early chapters of this book, as most child development research done to date is based on mother as primary caregiver. I am pleased to see a growing number of fathers sharing this role, believing that this bodes well for fathers, mothers, and children. However, with the aim of clarity, and wanting to avoid having to use plurals or he/she consistently, I have arbitrarily chosen to use the feminine pronoun to refer to the adult and the masculine to refer to the child in the body of the text. I hope that no one will be offended by this choice. Attempting to balance this, I have tried to provide numerous examples using each sex as child, parent, and caseworker.

Extensive experience in presenting this material to child welfare staff has taught me that it is easy for adults to feel overwhelmed by the content and immobilized with guilt about past decisions. It is my hope, however, that readers will use this information to stretch their thinking, and consider new ways of working with the children they are currently responsible for, rather than focusing on the past. I realize that in many instances I am identifying what optimally needs to be done to meet the needs of the child while, simultaneously, causing the least amount of subsequent trauma. Sometimes it will be impossible to achieve the optimum. However, we will never achieve any goal unless we first identify what we are striving toward. Once a child has been removed from his birth family, it is the responsibility of the child welfare system to insure that his needs are better met than they were when living with his family of origin. This contract on the child's behalf must always be taken seriously.

I intend to challenge the status quo of the child welfare system. It is important that each of us who have chosen to make a commitment to the children who have become part of this system continually question our own practices and beliefs about the importance of each child and his paramount need to be part of a larger unit, the family, if he is to reach his fullest potential as a member of society. If "the system" makes it difficult for us to meet the child's needs, then we must change the system rather than asking the child to forego his basic requirements.

This is not a cookbook with recipes for ways to manage a case from intake to discharge. Instead, it is a compilation of the background knowledge and skills necessary for understanding, working with, and planning for children and their families. In one case, a social worker may want to start by using an assessment skill outlined in the middle of the book. In another situation it is the knowledge of the impact of separation or loss and ways to minimize its trauma that will take precedence. In a third situation someone working with a high risk family soon after the birth of a new baby is likely to focus on the information on developing attachments, and so on. The subject covered in each of the chapters has literally had volumes written about it. My objective is to provide enough information to lead the reader toward making informed decisions, without competing with the experts in each of these subjects.

Several themes will be evident throughout the book. Resurfacing from chapter to chapter are the significance of interpersonal relationships, the necessity of building alliances with children and adults by enhancing communication skills, increasing the individual's knowledge of self, and the importance of developing a plan for continuity of relationships throughout a lifetime.

The book starts by looking in detail at the functions of close interpersonal connections and how attachments between children and their families develop. It then proceeds to a discussion of normal child development. All adults who come in contact with youngsters in the child welfare system need to know what is normal for age and what is not. Separation and loss are the subject of the third chapter. Descriptions of the normal grief process and the factors that influence it are described. Transitions, unfortunately, are the norm within the child welfare system. Caseworkers and caregivers alike need to be knowledgeable as to ways to minimize the trauma of moves when they must occur. These are the areas covered in Chapter Four.

Chapter Five looks at assessment and case planning skills, without which successful resolution of any case is unlikely. Children in care have developed a variety of survival skills for coping with their personal vulnerabilities and the traumas of their lives. These coping mechanisms are frequently perceived by adults as problem behaviors. Chapter Six is devoted to the treatment of common behavioral problems of the child in placement, addressing both immediate interventions and the underlying needs.

Although grown-ups are responsible for making the major life decisions on behalf of children, it is difficult to make the best determinations unless the child's perceptions of the situation are taken into consideration. In general, children use non-verbal communications more extensively than speech. Adults need to learn to listen to children's behaviors and to enhance their own skills in communicating with children. These topics will be addressed in Chapter Seven. Because children in care have frequently experienced disruptions in continuity, within this chapter there is a section on the Life-Book, a tool which encourages communication and clarifies for the child, and meaningful adults in his life, his history through time.

Upon a first reading ideally the reader will identify new techniques or ideas to use with a child or family with whom you are currently working. In addition, there is a hope that the book will stand as a reference to which you can return when faced with questions or problems.

There is no such thing as "a typical case" in the child welfare system. Each child and his family are unique. Therefore, numerous case examples, as well as exercises, have been interspersed throughout the text to help the reader start to apply the material to practice. However, in addition, in the next few pages you will learn more about Ardith and her brother Prentice, as well as several other children, with whom you will be reconnecting from chapter to chapter as each completes his or her *Journey Through Placement*.

Ardith
Prentice

Ardith's mother, Rose, was known to CPS prior to her daughter's birth. Her older son, Prentice, had been in care on two previous occasions. The first occurred when Rose left him, at age eighteen months, alone all night while she was out drinking and using cocaine. His second placement had occurred after his stepfather broke Prentice's arm shortly before Ardith's birth.

At the time of her daughter's birth, Rose appeared to be drug and alcohol free. She stated that she had not been using "since I found out I was pregnant." Hospital notes indicate that Rose asked for rooming in, that she breast fed, and that she seemed to enjoy holding, touching, and soothing Ardith.

Ardith's father was prosecuted for child abuse. While he was in prison, Rose divorced him. However, on several occasions during the first year of Ardith's life, police were called to her home because of neighbors' complaints about drug dealing in front of the home and the sounds of physical fighting. Rose's caregiving was inconsistent. On occasion she demonstrated many positive interactions with Ardith. Other times, according to the home-based worker, she seemed unresponsive.

When Ardith was fifteen months old, therapeutic day care services were initiated for both her and her brother Prentice. Frequently the children arrived at the daycare setting dirty and unkempt. Sometimes Ardith was aggressive. Other times both children were clingy with personnel. When Ardith was twenty months old, on two consecutive days Rose seemed to be under the influence of drugs when the daycare van returned the children home. Both children were placed in a receiving home. Prentice's paternal aunt, who had frequently cared for him, came forward and asked that he be placed with her. Rose did not follow through on the initially scheduled visits and a month later Ardith was moved to a longer term foster home, while Prentice was moved to his aunt and uncle's home.

Martin

Martin is sixteen months old. His eighteen-year-old mother received no prenatal care. In the hospital following his birth, his mother, Sylvia, avoided touching him. She avoided face contact with him. Sylvia herself had a history of multiple foster care placements. The hospital notified Child Protective Services of their concerns. A public health nurse provided in-home monitoring throughout the first month of Martin's life.

The first of Martin's multiple moves occurred when he was one month old. Because of physical and emotional neglect and a lack of weight gain, he was placed in fostercare at that time. Sylvia indicated a willingness to work with a parent aide, and the baby returned to his mother's home after two months. However, once again it was noted that mother-child contact seemed infrequent and uncomfortable. Martin was losing weight. At age four-and-a-half months he was again placed in fostercare. After six weeks, he was moved from the receiving home placement to a longer-term foster home.

At age eleven months, with reservations on the part of the caseworker, Martin was returned to birth mother's care. On numerous occasions during the past five months Martin has been left with mother's friends for a day or two. Sylvia and Martin have been living a transient life-style. During the five months, Sylvia has had at least two different live in partners. Alcohol and drugs have been part of her life. Although Sylvia acknowledges that she is having difficulty managing him and feeling emotionally close to him, she is unwilling to make an adoption plan for her son.

Judy

Judy, a twelve year old of Korean heritage, joined her adoptive family as the youngest child in the family when she was four. She had been abandoned at a train station. She lived for a year in a Korean orphanage, where she was described as "a helpful engaging child who loves everyone." Judy made the trip to the United States with an escort. Her adoptive parents, the Hasletts, have three other children —two sons and a daughter— by birth.

Two years ago the Hasletts approached the local social service department asking that Judy be placed in foster care. They indicated that there had been problems from the time of her arrival in their home, but that they had thought things would gradually improve. Her parents indicated that Judy was a stubborn, manipulative child who had become the source of numerous family problems. She would take food from the cupboards, but would complain about whatever was served at the table. She stole from her brothers and sister, usually taking their prize possessions. Although she was somewhat affectionate with her father, an easy going man, she actively avoided contact with her mother.

Peer problems were evident at school. Teachers had indicated that her academic achievement was at grade level. When in the third grade, she had had some behavior problems. Her teacher that year was not very structured and Judy was one to always push the limits. Other teachers had indicated that school behaviors were within the normal range.

Judy and her family were in therapy for two years prior to the Hasletts approaching the social services department. In-home services were offered to the family. They reluctantly complied with this plan. The in-home therapist noted that everyone in the family seemed fixed in their interactions. When any one person changed slightly, the others reacted in a way that insured that the change was short-lived. By the time this intervention was initiated, the family seemed to be invested in proving that Judy needed out-of-home placement, rather than in solving the problems.

Following her placement in foster care, Judy's parents refused to follow through on any treatment plan, and Judy demonstrated little if any interest in returning to live with them. Subsequently, the Hasletts were allowed to relinquish their parental rights. In the Caldwell foster home, Judy demonstrated a variety of behavior problems, including not following through on reasonable requests, poor physical hygiene and lying. However, the food problems were not evident here and she did not steal. About a year after she entered care the agency started making an adoption plan for Judy. Shortly after her eleventh birthday preplacement visits were initiated with the McConnell family, who had one older son by birth and a seven-year-old Korean daughter who had joined the family when she was eighteen months old. Within six months of the adoptive placement it was clear to everyone involved that neither the McConnells nor Judy were willing to make a long-term commitment to becoming permanent family members. Judy was placed in the Dougherty fosterhome. Her behavior problems escalated. Judy repeatedly asked to return to the Caldwell family. Ms. Silver, Judy's new caseworker, facilitated this move as soon as there was an opening in the Caldwell home.

Denise
Duke
Lily

The three Gilbert children live in two separate foster homes. Denise lives with a single parent, Shelby Stein, and the two younger children have lived in the Wentz foster home for a year and a half. They recently became legally free for adoption. Their birthmother, Anna, has a history of drug and alcohol abuse, a transient life style, and multiple boyfriends. The three children have different birth fathers.

Denise was in care for fourteen months between the ages of eighteen months and three years because of neglect and suspected abuse. The abusive boyfriend left the home and Anna seemed to stabilize her life. Denise was returned to her care several months before Duke's birth.

A year and a half ago personnel at Duke's school contacted CPS when he was noted to be very aggressive and sexually acting out with classmates in kindergarten. Staff at Lily's daycare center indicated that she was very withdrawn and would not defend herself when peers picked on her. Denise's teachers commented that she was an excellent student who seemed very adult-like. On the rare occasions that she played with classmates she was quite bossy. CPS investigation led to the younger children describing physical and sexual abuse. All three children were placed in care.

Although they were initially placed together, within a few months Denise was moved to her current placement while her brother and sister remained with the Wentz family. Denise demonstrated many parentified behaviors when living with her younger siblings. She was competitive with the foster mother and frequently told Duke and Lily, "You don't have to mind them. They're not our real parents anyway." Denise has consistently denied that there was any abuse in her original family. Anna, too, denied that there was any abuse. Anna was inconsistent about showing up for scheduled visits during the first six months that the children were in care and then totally disappeared from the scene. The younger children have developed a strong attachment to their foster family. The foster parents are older, experienced caregivers who are not interested in adopting any children, but who work well on facilitating moves to adoptive homes.

Denise's foster mother has been very ambivalent about making a long-term commitment to Denise. She and Denise, living alone, have a sister-like relationship as opposed to a more typical mother-daughter relationship. On the one hand, Shelby is concerned about this, on the other it has worked well for them. Denise wants to be placed with her younger brother and sister. When they have visited at Shelby's home, the latter sees Denise become very bossy and demanding. She knows that she could not parent the three children together.

Thirteenth century historian Sallimbeni, of Parma, Italy, reports that Emperor Fredrik II of the Holy Roman Empire conducted an experiment to find out man's original language. He gathered a number of babies and employed wet nurses to physically care for the children, but they were strictly forbidden to talk, cuddle, or sing to the babies.

By not having any human contact, these children were supposed to develop as naturally as possible. The Emperor never found out about man's original language—the children died one after another without any apparent reason.

As reported in *Dagens Nyheter*,
a Stockholm newspaper, 1990

Chapter 1 will look at those vital first connections which infants make with primary caregivers—the relationships which not only lead to language development but to the child becoming human in every sense of the word.

Attachment and Bonding

Attachment between humans is a complex process. How attachments develop and function is not yet completely understood. However, it is essential that those who participate in making major decisions about the lives of children and families have a basic understanding of attachment theory. Attachment and separation are the heart of child welfare work.

Attachment behaviors in humans, as in lower forms of animal life, serve the primary purpose of providing safety and protection for the young, the old, and others who are less capable of meeting their own needs in these areas. However, in humans they no longer are present only for meeting physical needs. In addition, these interpersonal connections provide for socialization and stimulation of intellectual development. Throughout an individual's lifetime, attachments both provide connections to others and help us develop a sense of self. Attachments help us define ourselves as humans, as sons or daughters, as mothers or fathers, as brothers or sisters, as wives or husbands, as friends. They aid us in our own quest for identity.

For most, the earliest attachments are to parents, who become sources of both safety and gratification. An understanding of how attachment normally develops between children and parents is critical to the child welfare worker's job. In this chapter we will look at the kinds of interactions that facilitate formation of these connections between parent and infant and then we will examine how these interactions gradually change as the child develops.

An understanding of how child and parent behave when there is normal attachment and bonding between them is the basis for an assessment of the strengths and weaknesses of family relationships. Social workers need to be able to facilitate the development of stronger intrafamily relationships. Sometimes this means helping to strengthen a weak or distorted parent-child attachment; sometimes it means helping a child connect emotionally to a new foster or adoptive parent. Both assessment and facilitation skills are critical in child welfare cases.

This chapter has five sections. The first defines attachment and looks at the importance of family in terms of the child's long-term development. The role of attachment in fostercare is explored in this section as well. The second section describes the usual ways that attachments between parents and children are formed. This information serves as a base for the practical material in the rest of the chapter.

Section III looks at ways to assess attachment and bonding. Section IV identifies some of the effects of lack of normal attachment, while the final section focuses on strengthening weak attachments or promoting new attachments when a child beyond infancy joins a family.

I   The Importance of Attachment

Attachment has been defined as "an affectionate bond between two individuals that endures through space and time and serves to join them emotionally" (Klaus, 1976). When children have a strong attachment to a parent, it allows them to develop both trust for others and self reliance. These earliest relationships influence both physical and intellectual development as well as forming the foundation for psychological development. The child's earliest attachments become the prototype for subsequent interpersonal relationships. Table 1-1 highlights the many positive long-range effects of a child's strong, healthy attachment to parents. Many children who enter foster care are in jeopardy of losing some or all of these strengths.

Table 1-1

Attachment Helps the Child

attain his full intellectual potential
sort out what he perceives
think logically
develop social emotions
develop a conscience
trust others
become self-reliant
better cope with stress and frustration
reduce feelings of jealousy
overcome common fears and worries
increase feelings of self-worth
reduce jealousy

A child who is well-attached to one caregiver can more easily develop attachments to others. We see this in families as the infant extends attachments to other members of the nuclear family such as the other parent and siblings. The fact that a child's strong attachment to one person eases the development of attachments to others is a crucial one for foster care. It means that children can be helped to become attached to a foster parent, and then to extend that attachment to birth family members, adoptive parents, or others. Rutter points out that if "mothering" is of high quality and provided by figures who remain the same during the child's early life then at least up to four or five multiple parenting figures need have no adverse effect (Rutter, 1981). However, young children, unlike adults, are unable to maintain strong attachments to a number of different individuals who have little connection to each other or who might be hostile to each other (Goldstein, 1973). Although attachments can be extended to include others and can even, with the cooperation of previous parenting figures, be transferred to new caregivers, interruptions in parenting caused by separation and loss universally carry a measure of harm.

Parents are responsible for creating the environment that helps children achieve their maximum potential in terms of physical, intellectual, and psychological development. The child's job is to make use of the environment. Neither can accomplish the other's work; it is only in the context of the parent-child relationship that the child is able to successfully move through the stages of child development.

Studies done of children raised in institutions have shown that adequate physical care is not enough to lead to the development of a physically and psychologically healthy child with optimum intellectual functioning. For normal development to occur, the child needs a primary attachment object. This person, who responds to the child's needs and who initiates positive activities with him, seems to be indispensable for normal development. The process of engaging in lively social interactions with a child and responding readily to his signals and approaches is called "mothering." It does not so much matter who this individual is so long as there is someone who meets these needs.

Bowlby has noted that the securely attached child with positive expectations of self and others is more likely to approach the world with confidence. When faced with potentially alarming situations, he is likely to tackle them effectively or to seek help in doing so. In contrast, those infants whose emotional needs have not been consistently met respond to the world either by shrinking from it or doing battle with it (Bowlby, 1973). Children securely attached as infants are more resilient, independent, compliant, empathic, and socially competent than others. They have greater self-esteem and express more positive affect and less negative affect than do children who were anxiously attached as infants (Stroufe, 1983).

Families As Facilitators of Attachment

The normal infant is able to form attachments with any caregiver. This person may be a birth parent, a foster or adoptive parent, or even a sibling. Neither blood ties to the child nor the sex of the primary caretaker seem to be as important as the connections this person develops with the child. A key factor seems to be the carer's sensitivity to the baby's signals. However, when the caregiver initiates a variety of interactions, as opposed to only providing routine care, the attachment becomes stronger. Mothers and fathers usually respond to infants differently. In general, fathers are more physical and stimulating while mothers are more verbal and soothing. Yogman believes that mother's and father's roles do not have to be interchangeable or identical. There are advantages to having them be reciprocal (Yogman,1982).

In most societies the infant and his primary caregiver are members of a larger unit, the family. The family's sense of entitlement and empowerment in raising the child is usually supported by society as a whole, although either internal or external factors may inhibit the sense of entitlement. For example, American culture has traditionally identified birth parents as more entitled to the child than anyone else, even if they are not themselves providing for the child. Two important aspects of adoption are the legal empowerment of the adoptive family and their developing sense of entitlement to parent their adopted child (Bourguignon, 1987).

——————— *Table* ——————— 1-2

Families Provide

a primary caregiver for the child
care by specific adults to whom the child can become attached
continuous contact with these adults on a day-to-day basis
gradually changing relationships with a small
    number of individuals over a lifetime
safety and security
stimulation and encouragement for growth
reasonable expectations
experience in identifying and expressing emotions
support in times of stress
others with whom to share successes

The family provides the environment in which attachments with the child can grow. Table 1-2 highlights the functions the family plays in relation to children. Obviously, at different times in an individual's life, the relative importance of these tasks varies.

Although a primary caregiver seems to be critical for normal development during early life, it is the continuous, but constantly changing, contact with a small number of individuals that is an especially important aspect of identity formation. Long-term relationships indicate that growth and change are possible. Relationships are not static. Normal parent-child interactions gradually change throughout their lifetime together. Even the relationship between parent and infant is different from that between adult caregiver and toddler.

As the child heads off to school at age five or six, the parent must be able to encourage the child to be less dependent and less exclusive in his relationships. When the youngster becomes a teen, and again when the adolescent leaves home, relationships change in fairly dramatic ways. In most families we do not think of contact between parent and young adult offspring ceasing when the young person leaves home. Family relationships continue to change when the now young adults become parents of the next generation. Many people upon reaching middle age find themselves meeting more and more of their parents' dependency needs. Indeed, eventually the adult "children" may become the caretakers for their own elderly parents, thus completing the cycle.

These long-term relationships identify the strongest attachments. The continually changing nature of such lifetime bonds helps individuals achieve a strong sense of identity, self-worth, and responsibility. People who lack long-term attachments may have more difficulty sorting out what to attribute to their own actions and what to ascribe to changes in the environment.

Providing physical and psychological safety and security is a basic parental task for caregivers of the young child. The importance of this gradually diminishes as the young person becomes more capable and self-reliant. As we will see in this chapter, stimulation and encouragement for change and growth are major determinants in the child's achieving his intellectual potential. The freedom to explore and try new things must constantly be balanced by the family having reasonable expectations for the child and placing limits which will protect him from serious harm while helping him learn social skills.

Although few parents would think to list helping the child identify and express emotions as a family responsibility, it is primarily within the family unit that the child learns these skills. In general, schools focus on what the child is not to do. Parents, especially through modeling, teach the child whether or not certain feelings are acceptable in this family, and how they may be expressed.

Finally, family members are the ones with whom most individuals want to share their successes. Likewise, most turn to relatives for support in times of stress.

Attachment in Foster Care

When moving to a new placement, children coming into care are faced with forming new attachments to their carers. The nature of these attachments will vary according to the purpose of the placement, the needs of the child, and the capacity of the carers (Aldgate, 1988). Given the potential long-term effects that lack of attachment can have on a child, it is crucial that the foster care system respond in ways that help the child develop attachments with their primary caregivers whomever they may be. No matter if the plan for a child in interim care is reunification—as it usually is at the outset—or a move into an adoptive home—as it sometimes becomes—the development of an attachment to foster parents should be encouraged. Children need ongoing relationships to continue their growth and change.

Traditionally, children in foster care have been provided with day-to-day care by a primary caretaker within a family context. However, there are other aspects of family care that foster children have been denied. Many children in foster care have moved from one family to another never having experienced the continuity in relationships which seems to enhance self-esteem and identity formation.

Many children in care have never learned psychologically healthy ways to connect with others. Their past relationships may not have supported growth and development. Unfortunately, few children in foster care receive adequate help in resolving the grief they experience when separated from their birth families. These unresolved separations interfere with their forming new attachments. A small number, probably only three to five percent of the children who are identified as having some form of attachment or separation problem, are truly unattached children—those who have never had the experience of being emotionally connected to an adult caregiver.* These are the children Selma Fraiberg (1977), was describing when she said, "If we take the evidence seriously we must look upon a baby deprived of human partners as a baby in deadly peril. This is a baby who is being robbed of his humanity." Although the prognosis for these children must be guarded once they are beyond the preschool years, luckily most of the children in foster care who have attachment problems or unresolved separation issues have a much better prognosis with adequate diagnosis and treatment. In the past, attachment between child and foster parent has often been discouraged. Ostensibly this was done to decrease the pain of subsequent separation and to diminish loyalty conflicts between the birth and foster families. Although interrupted relationships are traumatic—and should be avoided whenever it is possible to meet the child's needs without a move—the long-term effects of a child being without attachments for significant periods of his life are even more detrimental. Once a child has experienced a healthy attachment, it is more likely that with help, he can either extend this attachment to someone else or form additional attachments if necessary.

The foster parent role has two components. The first is to help the child develop healthy attachments, so that continued growth and development are facilitated. The second is to aid in extending the attachments and behavioral gains achieved while in interim care to subsequent caregivers who may be birth parents, adopters, or new foster parents.

Foster parents who have the ability to form normal bonds must be selected. They will need to learn how to encourage connections with children who suffer from

* *This figure is based on my own personal experiences with hundreds of children in the child welfare system and confirmed by personal communications with Kay Donley and Claudia Jewett-Jarrett.*

24

attachment or separation problems. Caseworkers must develop their abilities to assess attachment in children, to identify attachment problems, to help families develop and transfer attachments, and to facilitate the grieving process when a child moves.

Foster parents are responsible for creating an environment that allows the child to form healthy adult-child relationships. Children in care frequently need to develop both an increased trust for others and stronger self-reliance. With substitute parents, children may learn alternate ways of interacting with others and of expressing emotions. If this is to happen, however, the children must develop attachments to their foster parents.

Many times children in foster care will need help learning how to express their emotions in ways that won't get them into more trouble. Children living with abusive parents may have learned to associate the expression of feelings, thoughts, or desires with being physically hurt. Yet, the children entering foster care have many reasons to have strong feelings. Usually they have lived with birth parents who have not themselves been very successful in discharging their own emotions in non-harmful ways. When frustrated or angry, abusive and neglectful parents commonly become hurtful to their children. Physical violence may be the norm in some of these families. Others totally withdraw, sometimes by using alcohol or drugs, when under stress. In either case, their children have not been exposed to good modeling for coping with anger or frustration.

Usually families are able to provide growing children with remembrances of their past which keep memories alive. This helps the child develop a sense of self. In foster care the importance of the child's recollections is often diminished. For children in care memories are frequently fragmented rather than whole. Their current parenting figures not only will not have shared the child's past, but frequently have no avenues open for helping the child access and clarify knowledge of past events.

The child welfare system encourages an artificial termination of the foster parent-child relationship. Traditionally, foster parents have been discouraged from maintaining contact with foster children once they have left the home. It is precisely those young people whose basic needs were not uniformly met when they were very young who may most need the emotional support of a family to successfully transition from adolescence to adulthood.

The children who grow up in foster care may not, as adults, have support systems. To whom will they turn in times of pressure? Commonly, even as adults they turn to the system at times of stress. With whom will they share their successes? This poses an even bigger problem. It is a rare person who is strong enough to consistently strive for success when there is no one else to notice or care. The child's need for a permanent family to whom he can relate throughout his lifetime is a basic one.

II The Development of Attachment and Bonding between Child and Parent

Parent-child relationships are usually reciprocal. Adults certainly influence the child, yet even infants have an impact on their caregivers. Winnicott in the 1950's noted that there is no such thing as a "baby." There is only a "mother and child couple." Forming relationships, even in the earliest days of life, is cyclical—adult and infant each influencing the actions of the other. However, there are circumstances where reciprocity is not present in a particular parent-child dyad. Either parent or child may be unresponsive to the other. One member of the pair may feel connected to the other without the reverse being true. Therefore for clarity of communication, in this book, *attachment* will be used to describe the child's connection to the parent or others while the term *bonding* will be used to describe the parent's link to the child.

In general, well attached children have parents who are securely bonded to them. However, in some situations a parent may be bonded to a child who is not well attached because the child has difficulty forming normal relationships. An extreme example of this occurs in childhood autism, a condition in which the child has problems forming close interpersonal relationships with anyone. Yet the parents of the autistic child are usually initially well bonded to their child and only through time modify interactions with this baby as the child's lack of responsiveness influences the adult behaviors. In other cases we find children who are actively seeking approval and love from parents who, for a variety of reasons, are not well bonded to the them. In the child welfare system there are a significant number of cases in which bonding and attachment do not seem to go hand and hand.

Setting the Stage for Bonding

Between conception and birth the stage is set for bonding between parents and child. During this time, parents begin to develop images of what the unborn child will be like. They form expectations and hopes for their child, for themselves as parents, and for their future relationship with the child. The mother and unborn child have a unique relationship with the child being dependent upon the mother's body for all nutrients, while the mother's body undergoes many hormonal and physical changes in providing for the unborn child.

Klaus and Kennell identify two adaptive tasks for the mother during pregnancy. The first is to identify the fetus as an integral part of herself. The second is to become aware of the fetus as a separate individual. The latter is usually associated with fetal movement (Klaus, 1976). This is when parental fantasies of the child usually start. How the mother cares for herself during the prenatal period has a profound impact on the development of the unborn child.

Unfortunately, prenatal neglect and abuse are not uncommon in our society. Irrespective of whether or not the baby and birth mother have an opportunity to develop a relationship after the infant's birth, their interdependency during the pregnancy and birth processes leads to an interpersonal connection which cannot be duplicated in any other form of relationship.

Events during the prenatal period may affect the kind of relationship that will develop between parent and child. These factors include features of the pregnancy itself, such as the timing, the mother's condition during the pregnancy, and the presence or absence of prenatal complications. Both neglect—defined as not providing for the child's basic needs—and abuse—defined as providing the child with something which is harmful to development—can occur during pregnancy. The unborn child may not receive adequate nutrition, an example of prenatal neglect. He may be exposed to harmful substances, such as alcohol or drugs which cross freely from the mother's blood system to that of the child, an example of prenatal abuse.

The relationship between the child's parents during pregnancy may affect their subsequent bonding with the child. The kind of parenting that the parents themselves received strongly influences the expectations that they have for their child and for themselves as parents. Characteristics of the infant *in utero* come into play as well. Mothers sometimes note marked differences in their offspring even prior to birth. One may rarely move while another kicks and turns frequently. The characteristics of the child and the way the mother perceives them affects the developing bond.

Emily

During an assessment of the Smith family, it became apparent that in spite of all five children having significant problems, Emily, who was eleven, was the scapegoat in the family. In obtaining the family history, Mrs. Smith indicated that soon after she became pregnant with Emily, her second child, her serviceman husband was to be stationed overseas. Because of the pregnancy, she and the older son were unable to accompany him.

During the prolonged separation, not only was Mrs.Smith isolated from her primary support system, but her husband became involved with another woman and the marriage subsequently broke up. From her viewpoint, if only she had not been pregnant with Emily, her life would have been different. It was apparent how strong this feeling was when Mrs. Smith showed the evaluator a photo of Emily taken at age 21 months. Emily was sitting on the floor, huddled against the leg of a table. Her face was drawn; there were large grey circles around her lifeless eyes; her arms were drawn up to her chest. She looked like a typical failure-to-thrive child. Mrs. Smith's comment as she shared the picture—"Look what she was doing to me even then"—summarized their life-long relationship.

Bonding at Birth

Direct bonding between parents and child may begin during the very first moments of the child's life. Desmond (1966) found that during the first hour of life the normal infant is awake with eyes wide open. Subsequently the infant usually falls into a deep sleep. The newborn infant when held horizontally reflexively turns toward the person holding him. Parents are pleased when the infant looks at them. In turn they will usually gently caress the child. Most parents of newborns use their first contact with the child to explore, to count fingers and toes, to see if he is physically normal.

This initial examination is part of the claiming process. After first insuring that the baby is normal, parents switch the focus of their exploration, identifying the ways that their infant is unique yet resembles other family members. During this process the parent is consciously and unconsciously looking for ways to tell this child from all others. Studies based on video-tapes of mother and child interactions made during deliveries and post-partum hospital stays indicate that when the mother doesn't take an active part in this claiming process there is a high risk of severe mother-child difficulties in future months.* However, it is not only adults who influence the development of the parent-child relationship. The infant, himself, is a powerful factor. A child who is born with physical abnormalities will affect the parents just as surely as they will impact on him. The child who is either under-responsive or very fussy influences the parents' bonding to him. Medically fragile infants and those with physical abnormalities are at greater risk for attachment problems than other babies. This is not because of maternal inadequacy but because high risk infants' cueing and response capabilities are often unpredictable and atypical. Infants not only initiate interactions but actually shape mothering behaviors (Foley, 1980).

Attachment and Bonding in the First Six Months

The nervous system of a newborn infant is not well organized. Especially during the first month, the newborn must make adjustments to life outside the womb. Sensitivity to internal and external stimuli is usually less than it will be as he gets older. The newborn is irregular in many areas. He doesn't eat, sleep, or eliminate on schedule. The infant startles in response to a variety of stimuli. His movements seem jerky and uncoordinated.

Throughout the first year of life and thereafter, the child's nervous system will become better organized. Interactions between the newborn and his parents are a major force in this process. The influence of parent-child interactions on the child's developing nervous and hormonal systems may explain why some children who are not well attached have poor cognitive development and may be delayed in terms of physical development.

* *The film* Mother-Infant Interactions *may be obtained from the Kempe Center for Child Abuse in Denver, Colorado*

28

Interactions between parent and child involve all senses—touch, sound, sight, smell, and taste. The child has the capacity to participate in these exchanges even in the first six months of life. However, children do not initially have control over their voluntary muscles. There is a natural order in which control is gained. In general, the child acquires muscle control from the head downward and from the central part of the body outward.

Therefore, it is with his face muscles that the infant begins to actively participate in the attachment process. The infant first learns to focus on objects eight or nine inches away, the distance between his eyes and mother's face when he is nursing at the breast. From the age of four weeks, infants prefer looking at the human face to looking at other kinds of stimuli. By eight or nine weeks the infant is able to follow the movement of the human face and closely attend to it.

Face-to-face contact is important in developing connections with an infant. Spitz (1965) found that infants showed signs of pleasure even when they were presented with a mask of the human face. Covering the lower part of the mask did not change their response. However, when the upper part of the mask was covered, even just one eye of it, the infants did not respond with pleasure. He speculated that the infant's response to human eyes may be innate rather than learned.

Between six weeks and eight months, the baby's smile becomes more and more selective (Fraiberg, 1977). By the time they are three to three and one-half months old, most infants demonstrate a preference for their own mother's face. Though infants at this age continue to show pleasure in response to others, reactions are more strongly and consistently evident in response to the mother. This preference for a specific face develops a full two months before the infant shows pleasure at the sight of a bottle or other object. Simultaneously, there is differential stopping of crying and increases in smiling and vocalization in response to mother's face (Ainsworth, 1967).

From the time of birth, loud noises distress the normal infant and soft sounds quiet him. Infants respond preferentially to the higher pitched female voice. Wolff (1966) has demonstrated that infants turn towards sounds and that from the time the child is three to four weeks old he recognizes the voice of his mother. By the age of four weeks the infant gurgles and coos in response to the human voice. Vocalizations increase when they are responded to. In fact, one of the functions of babbling seems to be to keep the adult close and to promote interaction between parent and child, thus facilitating attachment and bonding. Body contact between parent and child also contributes to the attachment between them. In most societies infants are in more frequent body contact with their mothers than they are in western industrialized countries. The rhythmic movements that the child experiences as he is carried about by his mother are similar to those experienced before birth, and, as such, are likely to provide comfort and a sense of security.

Rhythmic movement encourages growth in premature infants. Cradles and rocking chairs have long been used to help soothe fussy babies. In recent years an increasing number of parents have been using sling-like supports, such as a Snugli, to permit closeness with their babies as they go about their daily housework and out on excursions. Some fussy babies respond positively to this swaddling effect.

Overall, in these early months, infants respond most to the particular sensations that promote contact with other humans. They prefer looking at the human face and listening to the human voice. They prefer the feel of soft clothes and the sense of rhythmical movements experienced as their parent carries them. They prefer the taste of their mother's milk. MacFarlane (1975) showed that by five days of age the breastfed infant could discriminate the smell of his mother's breastpad from others.

Thus, infants are especially sensitive to developing attachment behaviors during the first six months of life. However, before sixteen weeks differential responses are fewer in number and less consistent. By sixteen to twenty-six weeks the differential responses are more numerous and apparent. From six to seven months on, the preferential responses are plain for all to see in the majority of infants.

―――――― *Table* ―――――― 1-3

The Infant's Differential Responses to Primary Caregiver

3-6 weeks: more vocal in response to caregiver
9 weeks: crying stops faster when held by caregiver
10 weeks: increased smiling in response to seeing caregiver
15 weeks: increased crying when caregiver departs from sight
18 weeks: watches caregiver when held by others
21 weeks: greets caregiver more warmly than others
22 weeks: explores more when in sight of caregiver
24 weeks: tries to follow caregiver when she leaves

Attachment and Bonding from Six to Twelve Months

When he is between six and nine months old, the child learns to consistently distinguish between family members and strangers. The baby has developed an internalized beginning representation of family members. He begins to demonstrate fear or anxiety when approached by a stranger. The strength and frequency of these fear reactions increase as the child nears a year of age.

By the age of eight months, the child is playing a more active role in trying to keep adult caregivers close to him. He obviously tries to catch the parent's attention. His increasing mobility makes it easier for him to achieve this aim. Attention seeking activities on the part of the child are an important part of attachment building and should not be discouraged. By the age of nine to twelve months, child and primary caregiver will have developed a unique relationship in terms of who initiates interactions, how they are initiated, and how they are responded to. Often, one can virtually observe this delicate balance being achieved. Over the course of the first year, attachment between mother and child should increase, but dependency should decrease.

The infant's urge for closeness and attachment is so strong that if his caregiver doesn't stay close, the child tries to draw her to him. When a parent rejects the child, clinging and whiney behavior increases. In these cases, closeness to the parent is maintained with primarily negative rather than positive interactions. This has been described by Ainsworth (1952) as "anxious attachment" as opposed to the "secure attachment" which develops when the mother demonstrates that she is ready to remain close, thereby freeing the child's energies for other activities.

According to Ainsworth (1952) the anxious, insecure nine to twelve month old may falsely appear more strongly attached to his mother than the secure child who can explore in a strange situation using mother as a secure base. The securely attached child may not be as distressed by the appearance of a stranger. He will show awarenesss of his mother's absence, greet her on her return, and then resume previous activities.

In contrast, the insecure child is one who does not explore even when his mother is present. He becomes extremely alarmed by the appearance of a stranger. He seems helpless and in acute distress when mother leaves, and on her return is either disinterested or in distress, but in either case he is incapable of making an organized attempt to reach her. He clings excessively. On the other hand, the avoidant child actively ignores the parent, turning or moving away. He does not look to the parent for comfort or stimulation.

Attachment and Bonding after One Year

In general, toddlers continue to exhibit many attachment behaviors. The primary psychological tasks for this age are for the child to recognize that he and his primary caretaker are two separate individuals, and for him to develop a sense of self as being capable and effective in interacting with others. This is made easier because the toddler is increasingly mobile. He is able to process more environmental stimuli. Speech development helps increase his autonomy and awareness of his own feelings and those of others. *Me*, *mine*, *you*, and *no* are all words that help the toddler accomplish these tasks.

After the child is three, it becomes easier for him to accept mother's temporary absence. However, throughout life attachment behaviors increase during times of anxiety and stress. Observing a child when he is tired, frightened, or not feeling well is often a useful way to learn more about his attachments. The well-attached child will seek out his primary caregiver at this time and that individual will usually know how to comfort him. Even as adults, when we are sick, frightened, or vulnerable, we want to be close to the people to whom we are attached. Dependent behaviors increase at these times.

Reciprocity Between Parent and Child

The interpersonal interactions leading to attachment begin at birth but continue to evolve as the child matures. We can analyze these interactions in terms of how the connection between parent and child is built. Many are initiated by the infant fussing or crying when he is uncomfortable. The adult responds to these overtures. As the child gets older, an increasing percentage of interactions are initiated by the parent with the child responding.

It is usual for interactions between parent and child to be reciprocal. The responses of one partner encourage the other to continue the interaction. For example, a child cries when he is wet and uncomfortable. The caregiver responds by changing him while simultaneously talking and smiling. He smiles back and gurgles. The interactions are pleasurable for both and each stimulates the other to continue the interchange.

In developing attachments, it is important for the adult to be sensitive to the child's signals. Some children, even as infants, demonstrate a marked preference for one sensory modality over another. Sometimes hypersensitivity to one form of stimulus—touch for example—makes it difficult for the child to either achieve relaxation or for him to use his other senses.

In the program "Life's First Feelings" televised on the PBS Nova series in 1986 a child with such an aversion was shown. This infant actively rejected close cuddling. Body contact did not quiet him when he was fussy. In fact, it seemed to add to his discomfort. His mother was starting to question her ability to parent. During the assessment of this child it was clear that soft touch led to discomfort no matter who was holding him, indicating that the problem was in the child not the mother. However, the evaluators noted that this child was very visually responsive. When held facing the examiner, but without frontal body contact, the baby smiled, cooed, and took an active part in maintaining interactions. The parents were taught to engage him in interactions visually, then bring him in for a quick hug, followed by re-engaging visually. The goal was to use his strength (visual responsiveness) to overcome his weakness (tactile defensiveness).

Bowlby (1970) says that there are two characteristics of the interactions between mother and child that strongly affect the kind and degree of attachment that will develop. These are the speed and intensity with which the mother responds to the infant's crying and the extent to which the mother herself initiates interactions with the infant. We'll take a closer look at both interactions initiated by the child and those that the mother initiates and how each contribute to attachment.

The Arousal-Relaxation Cycle

Infants have a relatively high perceptual threshold. When, however, an infant experiences displeasure or tension, because of either internal or external stimuli, he discharges it. The infant moves his arms and legs. He becomes red in the face. He cries. He squirms. It is clear to everyone that he is uncomfortable.

1-1 *Figure*

The Arousal-Relaxation Cycle

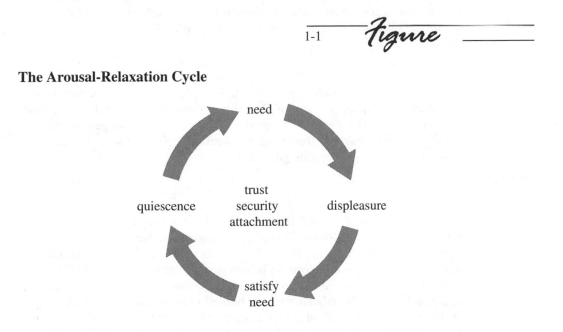

Figure 1-1 depicts a typical successful care-providing interaction between parent and child. The interaction is initiated by the child's need and consequent expression of displeasure and completed by the caregiver's response.

So long as this discomfort is present, the infant's perception of the outside world is blocked. Thus, when an infant or child continually experiences tension, his ability to perceive what is going on around him is seriously limited. As a result, intellectual development, dependent upon these perceptions, is hampered or blocked.

During the infant's first few hours and days negative excitation occurs in response to any stimulus which overcomes the newborn's relatively high perceptual threshold. It is the relief of this unpleasure which is an integral part of the attachment process (Spitz, 1965). The opposite of displeasure in an infant is not happiness or pleasure but is instead a state of quiescence or contentment. The parent's role when the infant is discharging tension is to help the child return to a quiescent state. Those infants who have abnormally high or low perceptual thresholds will be at risk for attachment problems.

This cycle, triggered by the child's need and completed by the parent responding in a way that meets the need and alleviates the physical discomfort, is called the "arousal-relaxation cycle". Repeated successful completion of this cycle helps the child is to develop trust, security and to become attached to his primary caregiver.

Scrutiny of the diagram reveals several places where completion of the arousal-relaxation cycle might be interrupted for a parent and child pair. Some parents fail to consistently respond to their child's overtures in ways that meet the infant's needs. For them the cycle is not completed.

Martin

The public health nurse noted that Martin, whom we met in the introduction, frequently cried loudly, with obvious distress. Sylvia, his birth mother, did not respond to his signals. When the nurse suggested that she respond, Sylvia would say that she didn't want to"spoil" her son. "He needs to learn that he won't get everything he wants."

This kind of parental lack of response is not the only possible cause of disruption of the arousal-relaxation cycle. If a parent consistently meets the child's needs before he is uncomfortable, or if she protects the child from any stimuli that might disturb him, the cycle will not be completed. According to Spitz (1965) it is probably as harmful to deprive an infant of the feeling of discomfort as to deprive him of quiescence. In addition, the child himself plays an active role in completion of the cycle. Although all infants have needs, if for some reason the child does not signal discomfort, the cycle will be interrupted. On the other hand, sometimes parents try to respond to their infant but find themselves unable to relieve the discomfort and help him achieve quiescence. There is increasing evidence that children who are drug exposed *in utero*, particularly those exposed to cocaine or crack, show abnormal physical responses to basic needs and environmental stimuli. Attachment problems are prominent in these children.

Premature infants also exemplify children whose behavior may not readily fit into a pattern that promotes attachment and bonding. These babies generally do not respond to environmental stimuli in the same way as other infants. They may, or may not, have decreased awareness of internal discomfort. They certainly have problems signaling their discomfort. In addition, such infants are frequently isolated from the continuous parental contact which leads both to bonding on the part of the parent and attachment on the part of the child. Delacato (1974) has speculated that many children with organic problems may have abnormal perceptual thresholds—higher than normal in some cases, lower than normal in others. This means that these children may either rarely experience discomfort or experience it very frequently. In either case, the child would not consistently experience the relief from an unpleasant state that is key to forming an attachment to a parent.

A case example of a breakdown in the formation of attachment between mother and child stemming from an abnormality in the child follows.

Tad, at age three, had delayed speech development and diminished trust for his parents. Both parents seemed to be well-adjusted adults who had had their needs met as children. The pregnancy had been desired. The parents were hoping that their first child would be a boy. The marriage appeared stable.

Tad had developed a rare type of seizure disorder on the third day of life. The parents were advised that about one-third of the children with this particular disorder die within their first year, one-third continue to have serious developmental disabilities, and the remainder enjoy normal development.

They were further advised that the prognosis could be somewhat anticipated by the effectiveness of medication in controlling the convulsions. The mother noted that the more she touched Tad the more likely he was to have a seizure. Being a "good mother" her reaction was obviously to minimize the amount she stimulated him.

Although she met his basic physical needs, she did not hold him, rock him, or play with him during the first few months of his life. Although Tad stopped having seizures by the time he was six months old, his medical problems had undermined his mother's confidence in her parenting abilities. She continued to be somewhat restrained with him, unconsciously afraid that she would reactivate the seizures.

A program that encouraged both bonding and attachment between this three-year-old child and his parents was instituted. Despite the development of a more normal parent-child relationship, some delays in the child's development remained. It will never be certain whether these delays resulted from brain damage related to the seizures or from the lack of stimulation he experienced in his first few months of life.

Tad

Fussy babies are difficult to comfort and satisfy. They may be tactually defensive as the child mentioned in the Nova series. Swaddling, using a Snugli, or a program of gradual desensitization may be helpful both in overcoming the fussiness and in promoting relaxation and attachment. Other fussy babies are overly sensitive to sounds. Loud noises, especially vibratory sounds— such as food processors, power tools or mowers, and low flying jets—are particularly troublesome. Low volume soothing background noise seems to decrease the fussiness of these babies. The baby who is overly sensitive to high-pitched noises, to light touch, or to certain holding positions are challenging to parent. Their caregivers must be willing to experiment to determine which interactions will soothe, comfort, and encourage them to relate to others(Greenspan, 1989). He goes on to note, "Sometimes children make it difficult to relate to them. The more difficult it is, the more the child needs it."

A significant proportion of infants are allergic to cow's milk. For these children providing a bottle increases rather than decreases their discomfort thereby interfering with the development of a healthy attachment. Accurately diagnosing the causes of fussiness and initiating sensitive interventions can facilitate relationship building between infant and parent.

The Positive Interaction Cycle

We've seen that the arousal-relaxation cycle is initiated by the child's needs and that successful completion of this cycle contributes to both bonding and attachment between parent and child. The primary caregiver feels effective in meeting the child's needs, enhancing the bonding, and the child learns to trust this parent figure as a source of comfort, encouraging attachment. However, the extent to which the parent initiates interactions with the infant also influences the connection between them.

Social interactions include a rich variety of stimulation involving any of the senses. Smiles, coos, soft caresses, the smells and tastes of favorite foods are all likely to lead to a positive response on the part of the infant. Toys and objects frequently accompany parental overtures once the child is several months old. From about nine months on, reciprocal social games such as peek-a-boo, clapping hands, and waving bye-bye come to the fore. Several months later, the toddler will imitate a wide variety of parental activities. As the youngster continues to mature, positive social interactions become increasingly complex. Although they are not high-intensity interactions, they are pleasurable to both child and adult.

Figure 1-2 illustrates the positive parent-child interactional cycle. As this cycle has only two parts it can be initiated by either child or adult.

There is some evidence that these sorts of social interactions between adult and child contribute more to the bonds between them than do the interactions that occur around meeting the child's physical needs. For example, Ainsworth (1952) indicated that social interactions, not routine care, are the most important part of parenting. The more social interactions an infant has with someone, the more strongly attached he becomes to that person and the more likely he is to feel lovable and worthwhile, important components of self-esteem. In addition, it is in these interactions that stimulation for growth and change occurs. Stimulation seems to have the strongest correlation with intellectual development. (Rutter, 1981)

36

The Positive Interaction Cycle

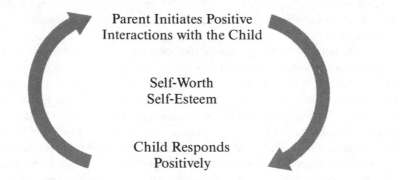

Parent Initiates Positive
Interactions with the Child

Self-Worth
Self-Esteem

Child Responds
Positively

Claiming

Claiming is a third way to build attachments and bonds. Claiming behaviors are those which separate the "we's" and "they's" of the world. Although claiming behaviors are observed in a variety of groups—professional, religious, political, ethnic, etc.—the focus here will be on claiming in families. During their first contact with the infant, parents usually start the claiming process. The child is explored for physical abnormalities. Parents want to know that their child is normal, like all others. They insure that the facial features, numbers of fingers and toes, and basic physical appearance are normal. This takes a very brief period, seconds rather than minutes. This superficial exploration is usually followed by a much more detailed examination as to ways that this infant is unique, most particularly ways that this infant reflects his genetic connections. Ears, fingers and toes are closely scrutinized to see whom this child resembles. The sense of interpersonal connections is enhanced by this claiming. When they see physical similarities, parents experience further feelings of entitlement.

Claiming behaviors can be either positive or negative. Hopefully the newborn will be positively claimed by both extended families, who will comment favorably on his similarity to other family members. However, a parent may only liken the child to a family member with whom there is a very conflicted relationship. Occasionally, disclaiming by extended family members occurs, indicated by comments such as, "No one in our family has ever had such a problem." This is most likely to occur if the child is born with obvious physical or mental handicaps or if extended family members strongly disapprove of one of the parents and the child is seen to be similar to that individual. When this occurs, hopefully someone will help both parents and extended family members grieve for the child they didn't get and come to accept, cherish, and claim this particular infant as a full family member.

Attachment in Infant Adoptions

When a newborn infant joins an adoptive family, in general the processes of attachment and bonding are similar to those which occur when a baby remains with the family to whom he was born. Obviously, adoptive parents will never experience the unique type of bonding which occurs between a birth mother and her child during pregnancy. However, the development of attachment after birth proceeds in a nearly identical manner whether the infant is genetically connected to the parents or not.

Although there may not be the same physical similarities in adopted children, identification of the child as a unique individual of particular value to the family enhances the claiming. Ideally adoptive parents would have a predictable period within which to prepare for a child, an opportunity for a psychological pregnancy. During a psychological pregnancy, the adopters would be able to prepare themselves for parenting. There would be opportunities for making physical preparations. Just as importantly, they would have time to fantasize about the child and imagine themselves acting as parents in a variety of situations. The closer the adopted child is to the fantasy the parents held prior to the adoption, the stronger the parents' sense of bonding to their child (Smith, 1983). Unfortunately, they frequently have very long waits, followed by quick placements.

Brodzinsky and others (1990) found that the quality of mother-infant attachment in middle class adoptive families with infants of the same race as the parents was similar to that found in non-adoptive families. These infants were between three days and ten months of age when they joined their families. They hypothesize that the increased number of adopted individuals within the population of mental health recipients later in life is not secondary to insecure attachments early in life, but to other factors. Brodzinsky has noted that as children of school age begin to understand the implications of adoption, including the reality of being relinquished by birth parents, they often feel confused, uncertain, and insecure regarding current adoptive family relationships. These feelings may play a role in the subsequent development of problems in children who were adopted as infants.

Adopters of infants should be aware of two factors that are, however, likely to influence the attachment process. If the infant developed an attachment within another family prior to joining the adoptive family, the grief process will affect the child's early adjustment. Ways to minimize the trauma of separation and facilitate the transition from one family to another will be looked at in detail in subsequent chapters.

Secondly, studies have indicated that there is a significantly higher percentage of adopted individuals with the diagnosis of Attention Deficit Disorder than is found in the general population (Deutsch 1982). These children, even as infants, may be more difficult to calm and may have sensory weaknesses and preferences which will influence the way they process stimuli and connect with their parent partners.

Assessing Attachment **III**

Assessing attachment and bonding are important skills for those involved in child welfare. Historical information helps us speculate as to the nature of the relationships. However, it is direct observations that either affirm or contradict these suppositions. It is difficult, if not impossible, to accurately assess relationships unless the observations are completed in a comfortable setting. Assessors need to closely observe parent-child interactions and then organize the observations so that conclusions can be reached as to the nature of current relationships and what would need to change to strengthen the connections.

Ardith

Ardith is visiting with Rose. The observer notes that when the toddler sees her mother coming down the hall, she raises her arms expectantly. Rose smiles and embraces Ardith, holding her close while giving her a kiss. The child hugs mother in return and smiles.

During the remainder of the visit it is noted that Rose both responds positively to Ardith's overtures and, using the toys available in the room, initiates a variety of interchanges with her child. Mom correctly reads Ardith's postural cue when she needs her diaper changed. Ardith imitates Rose's gestures and tries to repeat the single words her mother uses.

Ardith does not cling to Rose, but plays with the toys, frequently bringing them to her mom. When asked by the observer, "Where's Mommy?" Ardith points to Rose. She then crawls up on her mother's lap lying face down across it. Rose starts rubbing her daughter's back, commenting to the observer that this has always been a favorite activity for Ardith.

When Ardith tries to leave the room to explore beyond its boundaries, Rose tells her "no." When the toddler persists in opening the door, Rose gets up, turns the lock on the door, and then distracts Ardith with her favorite doll.

At the end of the visit, mother hugs child tightly, kissing her. With tears in her eyes, Rose says she'll see Ardith again soon. Ardith tries to cling to her mother as she leaves. After Rose leaves, Ardith, looking anguished, has tears streaming down her face. She allows the assessor to pick her up and physically comfort her.

The material already presented in this chapter can be used to develop a system for organizing the information gained by direct observations. Thinking in terms of the arousal-relaxation cycle we want to watch how the child signals needs or intense feelings. Does the parent accurately decode the child's signals? Is the parent able to adequately help the child achieve comfort and relaxation? How does the parent indicate her own intense feelings? How does the child respond?

Thinking in terms of the positive interaction cycle we want to observe the frequency with which child and parent each initiate positive interchanges and the response of the other. In a truly reciprocal relationship we would expect that the proportion of positive interactions initiated by the child and by the parent would be fairly even, not one-sided. Are most responses those that encourage another positive interaction, or are the responses "shut down" in type? For example, a five-year-old girl, with excitement, shares a drawing with her parent. The parent might respond with positive affect either verbally or behaviorally, thereby encouraging another interaction. On the other hand, the parent might respond with a critical comment. This is just as likely as a total lack of response to discourage the child from continuing the interaction. Sometimes it is a child who ignores parental overtures rather than vice versa.

Martin

His caseworker made the following observations when Martin was ten and a half months old and had been living in the Olney foster home for approximately four months. "When Mrs. Olney talks to Martin, he consistently turns his face away from her. Each time she or another family member pick him up Marty physically resists, pulling away and arching his back. Martin feeds himself using his fingers but turns away when his foster mom offers food on a spoon. When I handed him a toy, he looked at it briefly and then put it down. He rarely vocalizes except for crying and whining. I have never seen him smile. Mrs. Olney says she rarely sees smiles and has never heard him laugh."

Is the parent aware of the child as a separate individual with needs of his own or are all of the child's behaviors related to parental needs? Are the expectations for the child's behaviors and the disciplinary techniques appropriate for the child's age? Is there evidence of positive claiming? This may come verbally or behaviorally from either parent or child. For example, the child who is imitating a parent or who says "my mommy" is himself demonstrating claiming behaviors.

Providing for adequate physical safety, while simultaneously supplying sufficient stimulation for growth and change, are two major components of the job description for parents. The younger the child, the more important these two areas of parenting. It is easiest to determine their adequacy by observing the child in his home environment. Is adequate physical safety provided? Is age appropriate stimulation for continued developmental progress provided?

The four Observation Checklists that follow include some specific items to note in assessing the child's attachment level. Some of the observations reflect the attainment of normal development levels since they seem to be dependent upon the formation of attachments.

**Observation Checklist: What to Look for in Assessing
Attachment and Bonding: Birth to One Year**

Does the child . . . ?	**Does the parent . . . ?**
appear alert?	respond to the infant's vocalizations?
respond to people?	change voice tone when talking to or about the baby?
show interest in the human face?	engage in face to face contact with the infant?
track with his eyes?	
vocalize frequently?	exhibit interest in and encourage age appropriate development?
exhibit expected motor development?	
enjoy close physical contact?	respond to the child's cues?
signal discomfort?	demonstrate the ability to comfort the infant?
appear to be easily comforted?	
exhibit normal or excessive fussiness?	enjoy close physical contact with the baby?
appear outgoing or is he passive and withdrawn?	initiate positive interactions with the infant?
have good muscle tone?	identify positive qualities in the child?

_____ *Table* _____ 1-5

Observation Checklist: What to Look for in Assessing Attachment and Bonding: One to Five Years

Does the child.......?

explore his surroundings?

respond positively to parents?

keep himself occupied?

show signs of reciprocity?

seem relaxed and happy?

look at people when communicating?

show emotions in a recognizable manner?

react to pain and pleasure?

engage in age appropriate activites?

use speech appropriately?

respond to parental limit setting?

demonstrate normal fears?

react positively to physical closeness?

show a response to separation?

note the parent's return?

exhibit signs of pride and joy?

show signs of empathy?

show signs of embarrassment, shame, or guilt?

Does the parent.......?

use disciplinary measures appropriate for the child's age?

respond to the child's overtures?

initiate affection?

provide effective comforting?

initiate positive interactions with the child?

accept expressions of autonomy

see the child as positively "taking after" a family member?

seem aware of child's cues?

enjoy reciprocal interactions with the child?

respond to child's affection?

set age appropriate limits?

respond supportively when the child shows fear?

**Observation Checklist: What to Look for in Assessing
Attachment and Bonding: Grade School years**

Does the child......?

behave as though he likes
himself?

show pride in accomplishments?

share with others?

accept adult imposed limits?

verbalize likes and dislikes?

try new tasks?

acknowledge his mistakes?

express a wide range of
emotions?

establish eye contact?

exhibit confidence in his own
abilities?

appear to be developing a
conscience?

move in a relaxed way manner?

smile easily?

look comfortable when speaking
with adults?

react positively to parent
being physically close?

have positive interactions
with siblings and/or peers?

Does the parent.......?

show interest in child's
school performance?

accept expression of negative
feelings?

respond to child's overtures?

provide opportunities for child
to be with peers?

handle problems between
siblings with fairness?

initiate affectionate
overtures?

use disciplinary measures
appropriate for child's age?

assign the child age
appropriate responsibilites?

seem to enjoy this child?

know the child's likes and
dislikes?

give clear messages
about behaviours that are
approved or disapproved of?

comment on positive behaviours
as well as negative?

Table 1-7

Observation Checklist What to Look for in Assessing Attachment and Bonding: Adolescents

Is the adolescent.....?	**Does the parent.......?**
aware of personal strengths?	set appropriate limits?
aware of personal weaknesses?	encourage self-control?
comfortable with his sexuality?	trust the adolescent?
engaging in positive peer interactions?	show interest in and acceptance of adolescent's friends?
performing satisfactorily in school?	display an interest in the teen's school performance?
exhibiting signs of conscience development?	exhibit interest in teen's activities?
free from severe problems with the law?	have reasonable expectations regarding chores and household responsibilities?
aware of his parent's values?	stand by the adolescent if he gets in trouble?
keeping himself occupied in appropriate ways?	show affection?
accepting of adult imposed limits?	think this child will "turn out" okay?
involved in interests outside the home?	
developing goals for the future?	
emotionally close to parents?	

Identifying Signs of Attachment

Danny, age two and a half, the son of Carl and Tammy T. was born premature and with a Cleft palate. He had a history of failure to thrive during infancy. He was hospitalized repeatedly for this condition, and in this hospital he always gained weight. At six months he "accidentally" broke his leg while his father was overseas. At present, Danny has been in foster care for several months. Reportedly, Carl abused Danny leading to a black eye and bruises on the buttocks. It was Tammy who called the caseworker and reported the abuse, knowing her report probably would lead to foster care.

Danny

The parents have not followed through with therapy as ordered by the court. They recently separated and are planning a divorce. The father in particular has asked for Danny's custody.

In her interview, Tammy reported that Danny is in foster care "because my husband got mad and hit him." She does not see Danny as a child who easily frustrates adults although she stated that he is affectionate and "easy going now."

When the father was interviewed, he readily admitted spanking Danny excessively with a belt, but stated that the black eye occurred when Danny ran from him to avoid a spanking, slipped, and hit has eye on the corner of the bed. The discipline was taking place because Danny had repeatedly gotten out of bed when put down for a nap. Tammy was napping at the time according to Carl and did not see what happened. Carl is able to give considerable information about Danny's likes and dislikes. He, too, sees Danny as resembling himself.

Tammy initially refused to visit with Danny in the nursery at the time of the evaluation because "he is not interested in seeing me; he is more interested in the toys." Carl played with Danny in the nursery while Tammy was being interviewed. Danny did not protest when his father left the nursery to go with the interviewer. The father reassured Danny that he would be back shortly and made a point of leaving his coat in the nursery as he told Danny that he would be back.

When we tried to test Danny, he protested about the separation and asked his father to go with him. On the way to the office, Danny imitated his father's walk with his thumbs in pocket. He crawled up into his father's lap in the office, took off his dad's glasses, and put them on. His dad's comment as he took his glasses back was "Oh remember our little game." Carl was interested and pleased with Danny's performance levels during the testing. Although we had some difficulty understanding Danny's speech, Carl did not.

When Tammy came in mid-way during the testing, Danny interrupted his task and ran to her with arms up-raised. She picked him up, and her affect was appropriate. When his parents left, Danny indicated that he did not want them to go. He clung to his mother and clearly said "I want to go with you." He cried momentarily and tried to follow when they left, but he was easily distracted following their departure.

Using a chart like one below, list comments and/or observations made in the history that will aid you in assessing Danny's attachment to each of his parents.

Danny and Mother

Mother initiates-child responds
1.
2.
3.

Child initiates-mother responds
1.
2
3.

Danny and Father

Father initiates-child responds
1.
2.
3.

Child initiates-father responds
1.
2
3.

James Anthony, M.D. (1985) described a tool which is particularly useful in eliciting children's (ages four to ten) perceptions of adult-child interactions. He uses a series of cards with line drawings of family members—mother, father, grandmother, grandfather, older, younger siblings, etc—and Mr. Nobody. The latter card shows a man's back. The cards representing a specific child's family plus Mr. Nobody are spread on a table. Then the child is presented with a series of small cards, which the examiner reads, asking him to place each on the appropriate picture. One series of cards starts out with, "This is who I go to when I..." Items in this series include things such as "when I am hungry," "when I want a hug," "when I feel sick," " when I want to play a game," etc. A second series of cards, each starting out with, "This is who comes to me when they..." relate to interactions initiated by others. Examples include "want a hug," "want to yell at someone," "want to share a secret," etc. Examiners can easily make up their own cards. This exercise helps to determine whether the child perceives others as interacting with him, either positively or negatively.

On the next page you will find an example of a chart reflecting similar interactions which can be used with older children who have had a variety of placements to determine their perceptions of the nature of past relationships. (Cruger, 1988). Names of families with whom the child has lived are inserted at the top. The adult discusses with the young person his view of which family member met each of these needs.

Additional tools for assessing parent-child interactions have been developed by a variety of professionals. Several are listed at the end of this chapter for those who are particularly interested in learning more about this topic.

Interactions for Determining Children's Perceptions about Past Relationships

	Family Member	Family Member	Family Member
Food			
Shelter			
Protection			
Supervision			
Help Learn Right From Wrong			
Medical			
Do Fun Things With			
Give Affection			
Discipline			
Listen To			
Most Admire			

IV   Identifying Attachment Problems

Attachment problems may result from dysfunctional family dynamics, individual vulnerabilites on the part of the child, past traumatic events, or unresolved grief which interferes with the child's forming new relationships. The signs and symptoms of attachment problems in a particular child will be the result of the way his parents behaved toward him, his environment, and his own particular psychological traits. In general, children who have been severely neglected are the most likely to suffer from a true lack of attachment, while those who have been intermittently neglected and/or abused will more likely show abnormalities in the types of interpersonal relationships they develop. Having had some, but not all, of their needs met, they will show signs of "uneven parenting" (Clarke 1989). They are likely to exhibit a variety of behavior problems, including signs of being out of balance in terms of dependency vs. autonomy.

Bourguignon and Watson (1987) identify three forms of attachment disorders. The traumatized child, having been seriously traumatized in an earlier relationship is reluctant to trust or hope again. The inadequately attached child, having primary attachments that were interrupted, unhealthy, or intermittent in nature has difficulty re-establishing new attachments. The most severe disorder, the non-attached child, generally occurs when a child has been deprived of early opportunities to make a primary attachment. Subsequently this child may be described as having a character disorder.

Attachment difficulties may evidence themselves as psychological and behavioral problems, cognitive problems, and developmental delays.

Attachment and Its Relationship to Psychological or Behavioral Problems

Bowlby (1970) noted that children with attachment problems have difficulty relating normally with others. Their relationships with adults frequently seem superficial and their expressions of affection may not seem genuine. Commonly, parents describe these children as manipulative. Comments such as, "I give and give to this child and it doesn't seem to matter," are frequent.

How do these symptoms relate to attachment? Remember that the child's first relationship with a primary caregiver sets the stage for future relationships. In these first relationships the child learns what he can and cannot expect from others. Young children assume that whatever they have experienced is normal and usual. Children who experience adults as being unreliable in terms of their availability and affection may have subsequent difficulty developing new interpersonal relationships.

It is most difficult for children with attachment problems to grow socially. They have great difficulty learning to build and maintain relationships of any sort. They have trouble showing concern for others.

Having never received unconditional love, they have difficulty showing affection. They frequently continue in their immature ways, acting self-centered and impulsive.They may have difficulty internalizing expectations, rules or laws. Their first concern is, "What's in it for me?" They may never have acquired the social emotions which usually develop during the toddler years. These are the "connector" emotions which are related to conscience development.The development of these emotions and the stages of conscience development will be explored more fully in the next chapter.

Because children with attachment problems do not trust others, many of the behaviors they exhibit are aimed at keeping people at an emotional distance. Closeness in the past has led to either physical or emotional pain. Gratification has been absent or inconsistent. Adult behaviors may have led to the child being traumatized. Separation from previous caregivers, if there was any attachment, even if it was not a healthy one, is likely to have led to the pain of loss. It should be no wonder that the child in placement is likely to perceive adults as the source of pain rather than comfort.

Specific behavioral or emotional symptoms such as poor eye contact, withdrawal, aggression, indiscriminate affection, over competency, lack of self-awareness, constant control issues and delayed conscience development are frequently seen in children with attachment problems. Their treatment will be discussed in Chapter 7.

Attachment and Its Relationship to Cognitive Problems

Numerous researchers have described cognitive delays or problems in those children who did not have an attachment to a primary caregiver early in life. Animal studies indicate that sensory stimulation influences neural growth while deprivation leads to atrophy and decreased growth of neurons. Given that post-natal brain growth is most rapid within the first two years of life, it makes sense that children would be most susceptible to damage during this time. Studies have indicated that stimulation which is initially provided by primary caregivers is most important to cognitive growth (Rutter, 1981). When the attachment process is disturbed, the child is at risk of reduced learning since during the early years it is in the course of parenting that the world is brought to the child (Mosey, 1980).

Anna Freud (1951) noted that children raised without a specific caregiver suffered from language delays and problems with abstract concepts. Others have observed that these children demonstrate increased impulsivity and a lowered frustration tolerance (Fraiberg, 1977). Goldfarb (1954) compared a group of children who spent their first three to four years of life in institutions with a control group who spent their entire lives in foster care. He found that, comparatively, the institutionalized children were retarded intellectually, had distinctly impaired conceptual ability which was most evident in terms of time sense, were impulsive, and many had problems attending to tasks. In addition to the signs of impaired cognitive functioning, the institutionalized group were noted to be demanding of affection but had no genuine attachments. They showed signs of delayed or absent conscience development and an impairment in social maturity. This study went on to demonstrate that the intellectual impairment was marked and persistent when children were not transferred to an enriched environment prior to age four. Goldfarb attributed these problems to the institutionalized children being deprived of primary caregivers.

Tizard (1986) writes that those children who were reared in institutions prior to joining adoptive families at age four usually developed deep attachments for their new parents but that they continued throughout their growing up years to show the same social and learning problems as those not placed for adoption.

Many of the symptoms described in these varying studies are similar to those exhibited by children with Attention Deficit Disorder. In children in out-of-home placement there is a significantly higher proportion of children with these symptoms than in the population as a whole. One can speculate about which of these children were born with organic problems and which have symptoms caused by relationship problems between child and parent.

There is evidence of a strong genetic component in Attention Deficit Disorder. It is certainly possible that the parents of children in care may themselves have similar problems. Studies have indicated that, although hyperactivity per se usually diminishes during adolescence, most individuals with ADD continue to have a variety of difficulties in adult years. As adults, these individuals may continue to be rigid in their thinking and expectations. Low frustration tolerance, problems thinking ahead, and impulsivity in parents obviously would put a child in their care at increased risk for abuse or neglect. Simultaneously, children with these symptoms are more challenging to parent.

Other factors, in addition to the genetic ones, influence the child's intellectual development. Rutter (1981) comments that prematurity, prenatal damage, postnatal malnutrition, and social privation can all lead to intellectual retardation. In any one case it is not usually possible to determine the relative influence of each of these factors. Prenatal neglect or abuse, such as drug or alcohol use, may lead to abnormal development of the nervous system. Prenatal and/or early life malnutrition have a long lasting negative impact on intellectual development (Rutter, 1981).

During the latter months of pregnancy and on into infancy and early childhood, a major task is organization of the nervous system so that it develops regulated patterns of responsiveness. According to Gesell (1946), during the first year of life the infant must learn how to learn. Although individuals continue to learn throughout their lives, patterns of learning are set down during the early years. As the child matures, his perceptions become more discerning and he is aware of things he didn't previously note. He incorporates the new perceptions into his basic fund of knowledge.

It is through the relationship with a primary caregiver in the first year of life that the child learns how to learn. Reciprocity in this relationship helps the child sort out his perceptions of the world and teaches him what varying perceptions mean. At birth, the infant does not recognize objects in his environment or specific internal states of distress. He does not, for example, know that the discomfort that we call "hunger" is relieved by the intake of food. However, if a parent consistently feeds the child when he is hungry, he will learn to associate alleviation of that form of internal discomfort with food. Through a series of interchanges with his primary caregiver the child first learns sequencing, the precursor of basic cause and effect, and thus learns to learn. The primary caregiver entering the room becomes associated with comfort. The discomfort of an empty stomach becomes associated with the relief provided by food. By seven to eight months the child has learned enough about the sequence of events that he demonstrates anticipatory excitement when he hears a car at the usual time of day and disappointment or confusion if the sound is not followed by the appearance of the expected person.

When the infant is in a state of high arousal, he is unable to attend to his environment. His energies are used to cope with the increased body tension and little is available for processing his environment. As a result, intellectual development, dependent on perceptions, is inhibited or blocked when the child's needs are not met so that he can become relaxed but attentive.

Thus we can speculate that the cognitive problems may come about in differing ways. They may occur for genetic or prenatally determined structural or biochemical reasons. These particular problems would not necessarily be affected by the quality of mothering the child receives after birth. However, similar symptoms might be seen in the child who has not experienced the mothering necessary to organize the nervous system and help the child learn how to learn.

Practically speaking, by the time the child is old enough for the nature of his problems to be identified, determining the underlying cause does not matter much. The important task then is helping the child learn to compensate for his problems.

Attachment and Its Relationship to Developmental Delays

There is ample evidence that some children do not physically thrive because of problems in parent-child interactions. Growth delays may range from Failure To Thrive on a non-organic basis to Deprivational Dwarfism. Maternal deprivation may lead to deficiencies in the hormones which stimulate physical growth (Rutter, 1981). Studies have indicated that touching and rocking premature infants leads to decreased breathing problems and increased weight gain. When adults don't respond to an infant's overtures, the baby disengages and his body shows signs of physical irregularities such as drooling and hiccuping (Nova, 1986).

For preschoolers entering the foster care system, significant delays in language development are the most common developmental problem (Elmer, 1977). A second, but less common, area of delay is in gross motor development. Slow development in this area commonly accompanies Failure to Thrive. However, other children whose physical growth is normal may also show some mild delays in this area without any physical abnormalities. These delays may reflect either the lack of a well organized nervous system and/or lack of adequate stimulation. Gross motor problems secondary to stiffness and problems flexing muscles are evident in many drug-affected babies and a significant percentage of them suffer delays in motor development (Schneider, 1987).

Fine motor delays may reflect problems that accompany various forms of nervous system problems and are seen with some frequency in children with Attention Deficit Disorder. Other children have delays in only certain areas of fine motor functioning due to lack of experience. For example, some may be behind in pencil and paper related skills, cutting or puzzles, yet in other tests of fine motor development that depend less on specific exposure they will function at age level. Obviously, there are many other possible causes of delays due to a wide variety of medical conditions.

Inconsistent performance in the various sub-areas of developmental functioning—physical, gross motor, fine motor, language, and social—emotional—is the common, rather than unusual, occurrence in children with attachment problems.

A summary of the symptoms that are frequently seen in those with attachment problems is provided in Table 1-9 which follows. Although any of the problems listed on the chart may have a variety of causes, children with attachment problems usually have clusters of problems in each of the areas of development.

Symptoms That Are Commonly Seen in Children with Attachment Problems

Psychological or Behavioral Problems

Conscience development
1.   May not show normal anxiety following aggressive or cruel behavior.
2.   May not show guilt on breaking laws or rules.
3.   May project blame on others.

Impulse control
1.   Exhibits poor control; depends upon others to provide.
2.   Exhibits lack of foresight.
3.   Has a poor attention span.

Self-esteem
1.   Is unable to get satisfaction from tasks well done.
2.   Sees self as undeserving.
3.   Sees self as incapable of change.
4.   Has difficulty having fun.

Interpersonal interactions
1.   Lacks trust in others.
2.   Demands affection but lacks depth in relationships.
3.   Exhibits hostile dependency.
4.   Needs to be in control of all situations.
5.   Has impaired social maturity.

Emotions
1.   Has trouble recognizing own feelings.
2.   Has difficulty expressing feelings appropriately; especially anger, sadness, and frustration.
3.   Has difficulty recognizing feelings in others.

Cognitive Problems
1.   Has trouble with basic cause and effect.
2.   Experiences problems with logical thinking.
3.   Appears to have confused thought processes.
4.   Has difficulty thinking ahead.
5.   May have an impaired sense
6.   Has difficulties with abstract thinking.

Developmental Problems
1.   May have difficulty with auditory processing.
2.   May have difficulty expressing self well verbally.
3.   May have gross motor problems.
4.   May experience delays in fine-motor adaptive skills.
5.   May experience delays in personal-social development.
6.   May have inconsistent levels of skills in all of the above areas.

V Promoting New Attachments for Children in Care

How can children beyond infancy be helped to develop close interpersonal ties when they have never previously experienced healthy attachments? When a toddler has never developed an attachment to a caregiver, time is of the essence. Fraiberg (1977) notes that "the unattached child, even at age three to four, cannot easily attach himself even when he is provided with the most favorable conditions for the formation of a human bond." Once again we find it useful to refer to the three ways that attachments develop—the arousal-relaxation cycle, the positive interaction cycle and positive claiming. All three can be used to facilitate relationship building between adults and children beyond infancy. Indeed, they work in enhancing adult-adult or child-child relationships as well.

Martin

Let us look at how the development of attachment was facilitated in Martin's case. Following a case planning conference, Martin was moved to Bert and Donna LaBelle's foster home. The LaBelles have three birth children. Two are emancipated, but live in the area. Their youngest daughter, Danita, a senior in high school, lives at home. Currently there are two other foster children—Dwight, eleven, and Charita, four—living in the family.

Mr. Sawyer, Martin's caseworker, arranged for Jane Paulson, a psychiatric nurse with training in infant mental health, to work with Martin and the LaBelle family. Jane recommended that during Martin's first week in the home his behaviors should be closely observed. Special attention was to be paid to times that Martin signaled discomfort as well as note made of his reactions to various sensory experiences. How did he respond to sights, sounds, and touches? Were there times when he tried to engage others in interactions? What play skills did he have? She asked the LaBelles to record several short segments of videotape of Martin in a variety of situations to use as an aid to treatment planning and to be kept as a baseline for comparison in the future.

The LaBelles noted that the only time of day when Martin cried and fussed was when he was put in his crib or when he was held close. He tolerated touch and being held better when it was not accompanied by face-to-face contact. Although he rarely reacted to people talking to him, he would sway rhythmically when Danita was listening to music.

Jane Paulsen helped the LaBelles devise a plan for responding to Martin's discomfort. When Marty cried after being put to bed, either Donna or Bert would pick him up, cradling him tightly in their arms. He would usually struggle and increase his crying. They would persist, sometimes making comments such as, "I know it's hard." Other times, they would converse quietly with each other while one of them was holding Marty. Still other times, they would put some classical music on the stereo before going in to pick him up. They noted that although it frequently took an hour to calm him, once Martin stopped crying his body was totally relaxed and he would seem more alert, paying closer attention to their faces for a brief period before closing his eyes and falling asleep.

Jane and Donna decided that additional attempts at relationship building would focus on expanding the areas of interaction that Martin best tolerated. Donna carried him in a backpack several hours a day as she worked around the house. When Danita came home from school, she would dance to her music with Martin on her back in the carrier.

As Martin became increasingly comfortable with these interactions, Jane advised that they expand the contact to include some of the interactions usually enjoyed by younger children and their parents. Donna bathed Martin in the mid-morning when she had more time. She would then rub lotion on him. She noted that he responded by becoming more engaged and alert when she rubbed vigorously with textured towels than when she used light touch. Playing background music, Donna started blowing raspberries on his stomach as she dried him. Initially he was unresponsive. Gradually he looked more startled. Within several weeks be was showing little signs of anticipatory excitement after his baths.

Jane suggested that they then encourage more face-to-face contact. After his bath, when he seemed relaxed, Donna would hold him in her arms, as she would have a newborn, and give him a bottle filled with his favorite juice. Initally, Marty looked away and would forcibly eject the nipple from his mouth. Donna continued to hold him, rocking rhythmically while singing. He responded more positively to songs with a faster rhythm than to soothing lullabies. After ten days of offering the bottle, Martin took three to four ounces before he swatted the bottle away. Donna continued to hold him and sing for another ten minutes. Subsequently, each day he drank a little more from the bottle.

Most children who have had interruptions in parenting during what seem to be the most critical ages, from six months to four years, do not have the severity of problems seen in Martin. If the individuals who are taking on the parenting of these children are patient but persistent in forming emotional connections with the child, usually new attachments will form. As we will see in a later chapter careful attention to transitions is especially important for children of these ages.

But what about the school aged child who joins a new family? Can he, too, be helped to build strong new attachments, or will he be left to struggle through life without the benefit of healthy interpersonal ties.

Richard, a particularly sensitive and perceptive nine year old had spent much of his life in foster care. Problem behaviors included lying, stealing, not completing school work, and not getting along well with peers.

Richard

55

During an evaluation he asked, off-handedly, "By the way, do you know what happens to kids who don't get enough loving when they are little?" The examiner responded, "Well, I think I know. But I'd sure like to hear what you think."

"If kids don't get enough loving when they are three, four, or five they become uncontrollable later," Richard replied. "Some foster kids who are eight, nine, and ten can't be controlled by their foster parents."

The examiner asked, "What do you think can be done about that?"

"I don't know," Richard replied, "but I know what you think. You think if they get extra loving later on it will make up for it."

Most older children can be helped to form attachments to new caregivers who can, in turn, bond to youngsters living in their homes. Once again the arousal-relaxation and positive interaction cycles plus claiming behaviors will be used.

In older children the needs which initiate the arousal-relaxation cycle may be either physical or psychological. The critical factor is discomfort that leads to high arousal. The intense emotions may be either negative—such as anxiety, fear, anger, rage, or sadness—or positive—such as extreme joy or excitement. In either situation the feelings are strong enough to lead to changes in the autonomic nervous system. Pupils get larger or smaller, mouths are drier or wetter, there is increased muscle tension. In these situations the parental role is not so much to meet a physical need or take away an emotion, but to be supportive and empathic during the expression of emotion until the body tension that accompanies the intense feelings subsides. At the point of relaxation the child is most open to attachment.

Charles

Because of his uncontrollable behaviors, Charles, age thirteen, was to be admitted to a residential treatment facility where the core treatment task was seen as developing strong healthy attachments between residents and center staff. Charles' father was accused of murdering his wife. The trial date had been set. Charles was certain to have many strong feelings during the court proceedings. Therefore, it was decided that it would be therapeutically advantageous for Charles to be admitted immediately prior to the trial.

John, a staff member, talked daily with a court observer who relayed information as to the progress of the trial. John would then share the information with Charles. During the early weeks of his placement, Charles was frequently experiencing extreme tension. Sometimes he would become enraged by the shared information. At these times his behavior would exceed his abilities for self-control and he would have to be physically held by the treatment staff. Other times, he would fall into the depths of despair, sobbing uncontrollably. On rare occasions he would deny having any feelings. No matter what the news or his

56

behavioral responses, Charles was given emotional support in coping with his strong feelings about the testimony and about the subsequent conviction of his father. The emotional support he received from staff members facilitated the attachment process. He learned to trust that adults would be available to him, that they were not frightened or overcome by his strong feelings. With the basic trust established he was able to make more rapid progress in other areas of psychological and behavioral functioning. (Fahlberg, 1990)

At the end of temper tantrums, children relax. The barriers to attachment are lowered and a child is, for a brief period, open to developing trust for the available adult. When a child is ill and faces a trip to the doctor, with the accompanying fear of the unknown, he is likely to be highly aroused. The parent who is emotionally available to the child throughout painful procedures, allowing expression of feelings and providing physical comfort after the event, encourages attachment.

Children in interim care usually experience intense emotions at the time of moves. Caseworkers and parental figures who allow and encourage the child to express feelings are simultaneously encouraging attachment building. Many times adults try to avoid situations in which the child will have strong feelings or try to minimize emotional outbursts. Or, they may believe that if they provide physical comfort along with psychological support for children after an outburst, they are rewarding the child or reinforcing negative behaviors. Actually, when children feel overcome by emotion they need and deserve to have immediate adult physical and psychological support. This is how trusting relationships develop. As the old adage says, "The time when each of us most needs love is when we least deserve it."

The positive interaction cycle works as well for children who are beyond infancy as it does for babies. Parents initiate positive interchanges with the child, who responds positively, and both parties are likely to continue the interchanges with a positive focus. These are usually low key, less emotionally charged interactions. They include comments such as, "Good morning," "How was your day?" or activities such as playing a game, helping with a chore, reading a story, or giving a hug. It is easiest for parents to begin initiating the positive interactions when a child first moves in. The parent is proactive rather than just reactive to the child. This is particularly important when working with a child who exhibits many negative behaviors.

It is this "bank account" of positive interactions and feelings for each other that most families count on when a crisis occurs. Families who have experienced many positive interchanges, who have been effective in solving problems in the past, and who are emotionally close to each other, focus on getting through the crisis and getting back to normal. Families with no "bank account" of positive interactions are likely to view the crisis as the straw that breaks the camel's back and, indeed, the family ties may break with someone leaving as a result of the crisis. Although a crisis is frequently the precursor for a disruption of family ties, it is rarely the real cause of the breakup.

A third way to facilitate attachment and bonding is by encouraging claiming. How do we recognize who are family members and who are not? Most families have a variety of rules and expectations which may never have been clearly identified or verbalized but which differentiate family members from friends or acquaintances. For example, casual acquaintances are not expected to take food from the refrigerator, without asking, during a visit. Yet, we might expect that family members will feel free to do so. On the other hand, we are more likely to tolerate a visiting child's misbehaviors without comment than if our own child were acting the same way.

Children from the age of four usually understand the concept of "practicing." They can be encouraged to "practice" getting close to new parents. For example, when a child moves to an adoptive family and a permanent parent-child relationship is being created the child might be asked to practice calling his new parents "Mom" and "Dad" right away; to practice giving hugs and kisses at bedtime; or to practice sitting on Mom's or Dad's lap every day for ten minutes. During that time they can be read to, sing songs, talk quietly, or whatever. It is to be a time when they can practice learning to be comfortable being physically close.

When the child is too old to sit on his parents' laps, he can practice having fun with them by playing games or sitting close while reading a story etc. Parents are given similar instructions so that the child understands that learning to be close involves both children and adults working at it.

Sharing histories is another way to facilitate attachment. Not only is the child asked to share his past with new parents, but other family members need to share their past history with the child. The game Reunion* provides one avenue for doing this. Sharing family photo albums provides another. Having other relatives—grandparents, aunts, uncles, etc—share the "family stories" about the parents when they were young, helps the child see his new parents as real people with a past history. The more that the new family member can see others in the family as individuals, as opposed to people playing the roles of Mother, Father, etc., the greater the likelihood that he will form a unique relationship with each.

Usually it is knowing the more intimate details of each person's personality and of life within a particular family that helps someone joining the family feel like an insider, as opposed to being an outsider. Many times children who have recently joined a family have problems discriminating between times that Dad is teasing and when he might be serious. Those already living with him most likely have learned the subtle cues that differentiate Dad's behaviors. The "new" child will need the assistance of other family members in gaining this skill. On the other hand, it is common for children who have recently joined a family to have trouble differentiating between when Mom is serious vs. when she is furious. Again other family members are more likely than Mom herself to be able to identify the cues.

*Reunion is a board game available from the Ungame Company. (See resource list at end of Chapter 7)

The Andersons were preparing an album to be shared with children who would be joining their family by adoption. They included pictures of the house, family members, and pets and discussed the interests of various family members. In addition, they added a section on how different members of their family showed anger. There was a space for each parent and child. However, it was not filled in by the person whose name appeared at the top of the space. It was filled in by the other family members. What did they see or hear when Mom was angry? When Dad was upset? When teen-aged son was frustrated? To the new children, it wouldn't matter what family members thought they were doing when they were angry. New family members needed information to help them decode how others were feeling. What would they see and hear? The parents also asked the other children in the family to identify, "To whom do you go for what?" The teenager already in the family laughed and said, "Thats easy--for permission to do things, go to Mom. But go to Dad for money, Mom's tight." The parents had never really thought about or discussed this before, but they laughed, recognizing it as the truth and not seeing it as manipulative or harmful. Sharing this information ahead of time not only helped the Andersons become more aware of their own interactions but it helped the children joining their family to more quickly behave like other family members.

Andersons

Claiming can be done both in terms of physical and psychological characteristics, in terms of shared knowledge, and in terms of shared experiences. In claiming, the focus is on similarities rather than differences. Through claiming the parents come to accept the child as their own and as accepted family members (Bourguignon, 1987).

To encourage attachment we want to involve the child in family events and let him know about family rituals. Although rituals in the animal kingdom developed initially to inhibit aggression, through time they acquired a secondary function of shared communication, which in turn increased feelings of connectedness. Ceremonies have a triple function: to suppress overt aggressive behavior, to hold the group together, and to set the group off as an independent unit (Lorenz, 1966). Rituals and traditions add to family stability and a sense of belonging while simultaneously meeting an individual's need for intimacy (McNamara, 1991).

Because the development of close interpersonal relationships is so critical to the child's continued development and sense of well being, attachments should be encouraged between adult caregiver and child no matter where the child is living. However, there is a difference between the child being a permanent legal member of a family either by birth or adoption, and the child being an important, but temporary, member as occurs in foster or group care. Foster parents do not have the same legal entitlement to parent the child as birth or adoptive parents have. Although these caregivers may make use of the arousal-relaxation and positive interactions cycles in the same ways for all family members, varying degrees of claiming can help differentiate between those who are permanent legal members of the family and those who are not. For example, foster children do not usually take the foster family's surname, but adopted children do. Adoptive families frequently have a formal portrait of the entire family done soon after a child joins the family by adoption while it is much more common for foster parents to display in their homes a variety of snapshots or individual pictures of the children who are in interim care.

Child welfare workers can help individual foster families develop strategies for utilizing varying degrees of claiming to differentiate between children in the family who are permanent legal members of it and those who are not. This can be individualized based on family composition, the foster child's relationship and contact with his birth family, the long term plans for the foster child, etc. Exercise 1-2 will help you focus on this task.

Table 1-10 suggests ways for families to encourage attachment using all three modes of relationship building. Some of the suggestions under claiming would only be appropriate in adoption. Finally, Exercise 1-3 looks at encouraging attachment in an adoptive family.

For the reader who is particularly interested in this area, at the end of this chapter is an annotated listing of resources that describe additional ideas or techniques that can be used to promote attachments in older children.

------- *Exercise* 1-2

Differentiating between Levels of Claiming in Interim Care Versus in a Permanent Family

Parents and children need to understand who are permanent legal members of the family and who are not. Many mixed messages are given in the interim care system. Foster parents may be told to treat the foster children "just like your own" while simultaneously saying, "but don't get too attached, as they will be moving back to their birth parents." This exercise is meant to help you to focus on ways that agencies and families differentiate between children who are permanent legal members of the family and those who are not.

Make a list of agency rules, regulations, or policies that lead to foster families behaving differently toward birth or adopted children and foster children. Assess both the positive and negative impact on the relationships.

Regulation	Impact
1.	1.
2.	2.
3.	3.

Make a list of ways that you have seen foster families treat foster children differently from birth or adopted children (not because of agency rules). Assess both the positive and negative impact.

Observation   **Impact**

1.   1.
2.   2.
3.   3.

_____ *Table* _____ 1-10

Ways to Encourage Attachment

Responding to the Arousal/Relaxation Cycle

Using the child's tantrums to encourage attachment

Responding to the child when he is physically ill.

Accompanying the child to doctor and dentist appointments.

Helping the child express and cope with feelings of anger and frustration.

Sharing the child's extreme excitement over his achievements.

Helping the child cope with feelings about moving.

Helping the child cope with ambivalent feelings about his birth family.

Responding to a child who is hurt or injured.

Educating the child about sexual issues.

Initiating Positive Interactions

Making affectionate overtures: hugs, kisses, physical closeness.

Reading to the child.

Playing games.

Going shopping together for clothes/toys for child.

Going on special outings: circus, plays, or the like.

Supporting the child's outside activities by providing transportation or being a group leader.

Helping the child with homework when he or she needs it.

Teaching the child to cook or bake.

Saying "I love you".

Teaching the child about extended family members through pictures and talk.

Helping the child meet understand the family "jokes" or sayings.

Teaching the child to participate in family activites such as bowling, camping, or skiing.

Helping the child meet expectations of the other parent

Claiming Behaviors

Encouraging the child to practice calling parents "mom" & "dad".

Adding a middle name to incorporate a name of family significance.

Hanging pictures of child on the wall.

Involving the child in family reunions and similar activities.

Involving the child in grandparent visits.

Including the child in family rituals.

Holding religious ceremonies or other ceremonies that incorporate the child into the family.

Buying new clothes for the child as a way of becoming acquainted with child's size; color preferences; style preferences, and the like.

Making statements such as "In our family do it this way" in supportive fashion.

Sending out announcements of adoption.

Encouraging Attachment

Sharon

Sharon, age eight, will be moving from her fosterhome to an adoptive family within the next few weeks. She will be the youngest in a two parent family with three sons ranging in age from twelve to seventeen. Father is a clergyman; mother is a teacher. Sharon's past history reveals considerable emotional and physical deprivation, rejection, and physical abuse. She has been in and out of foster care since she was four years old. Sharon has had seven moves including two returns to her birth parents' care.

Behavioral problems noted in her current foster home include enuresis both at night and during the day. A medical workup was negative. Sharon has many fears, including fear of the dark, sirens, and new situations. She is prone to nightmares. Sharon becomes very upset when family members tease each other or rough house. She is described as a demanding and manipulative child.

Although there is no known history of sexual abuse, Sharon demonstrates sexually provocative behaviors. She raises her dress in front of men and boys and asks them openly if they want to go to bed with her. Sharon has difficulty telling the truth. Sometimes she lies about her misbehaviors. Other times she tells meaningless lies, such as saying that peas are her favorite vegetable when, in fact, she does not like them at all. She frequently brings home small objects (i.e. pencils, hair clips, etc.) from school saying either that she "found"them or that, "a friend gave them to me."

Although academically Sharon is at grade level, she has many gaps in her basic fund of knowledge. She exhibits problems with logical thinking and basic cause and effect. She does not always complete her school work and may "forget" to turn in work she has completed. She is reading above grade level but has difficulty in math. Play skills are poor and she has difficulty keeping friends.

Sharon is physically attractive and demonstrate excellent self-care skills. She shows appropriate affect for the most part and is outgoing and affectionate. Sometimes she is inappropriately affectionate with relative strangers. However, she is able to talk openly about feelings and tells of many ways that she and her present foster parents have fun together.

In this exercise we are asking that you only focus on building attachments. Later in the book we will return to Sharon and her family so that you may help devise additional strategies for addressing her behavioral problems. Using three columns—one for the arousal/relaxation cycle; one for the positive interaction cycle and one for claiming behaviors—list as many ways as you can think of that Sharon's adoptive family might help her to develop attachments to them.

Additional Tools for Assessing Parent-Child Interactions

Additional tools for helping practitioners learn more about the nature of parent-child relationships during infancy and the toddler years have been developed by a variety of professionals. Some rely on information gained primarily from adults. Others are based on information gathered during contacts with the child.

The Marschak Interaction Scales are available for assessing parent-child relationships at a number of different age levels, including prenatal, infant, toddler, preschooler, school age, and adolescent. They are available from the Theraplay Institute in Chicago, Illinois.

Massie and Campbell (1982): *Scale of Mother-Infant Attachment Indicators During Stress*, designed to be used with infants from birth to eighteen months of age. It grades the intensity with which a mother and infant respond to each other during periods of mild to moderate stress.

Mosey, Foley et al (1980): *Attachment, Separation, Individuation Scale.* This scale organizes observational data in a systematized way. It can be used for diagnosing problems and prescribing interventions in infants and toddlers. Department of Education and Berks Intermediate Unit #14, in Reading, PA holds the copyright.

Norman Polansky et al (1981): *A Childhood Level of Living Scale* with one section on physical care and one on emotional/cognitive care. It is used in combination with their *Maternal Characteristics Scale* to assess mother-child relationships.

University of Washington in Seattle: *Nursing Child Assessment Satellite Training Project (NCAST)*, an assessment tool which has six subscales which include: 1. the parent's sensitivity to the child's cues, 2. the parental response to the child in distress, 3. the parents' capacity to encourage the child's social and emotional development, 4. parental capacity to foster the child's cognitive development, 5. the child's clarity of cues, and 6. the child's responsiveness to the parent. It may be ordered from NCAST Training Project; University of Washington, WJ-10, Seattle, WA 98195. Telephone number, 206-543-8528.Waters and Deane(1985): *Attachment Q-set* for assessing secure attachment in toddlers. They describe this tool plus the Strange Situation Procedure described initially by Ainsworth in assessing toddlers in a monograph in the Bretherton and Waters publication of 1985 listed in the bibliography.

Resources for Building Attachments

The following are readings that provide ideas as to additional ways to enhance attachments. They cover a broad spectrum from those described by Greenspan, that might be used with any child, to the very intrusive Rage-Reduction Holding

Therapy, which is used only with very disturbed children. In reviewing these tools, several common denominators are noted. Each involves repeated episodes of highly focused attention between adult and child. In each, there is physical contact between adult and child. Finally, in all, adults are involved in trying to decode the child's behaviors, identifying his needs and underlying emotions.

Allan, John: This psychologist has described a variety of holding techniques which include holding for pleasure and holding for relaxation, as well as holding for control. Two of his articles are "Identification and Treatment of Difficult Babies." *Canadian Nurse*. Vol 72 (12) pp 11-16, 1976. and "The Body in Child Psychotherapy" in Schwartz-Salant, N. and Stein, M. (Eds) *The Body in Analysis*, pp 145-166. Wilmette, IL: Chiron Publ, 1986. In the latter, John talks about the dangers, as well as the benefits, of holding therapies.

Anderson, Josephine: This MSW prescribes therapeutic holding by parents. As an experienced therapeutic foster care provider she has had extensive experience using these techniques. They are described in "Holding Therapy: A Way of Helping Unattached Children." This article appears in *Adoption Resources for Mental Health Professionals*, edited by P. Grabe, Transaction Publishers, 1990.

Cline, Foster: This psychiatrist describes Rage Reduction Holding Therapy in his article "Understanding and Treating the Severely Disturbed Child" which is also included in *Adoption Resources for Mental Health Professionals*.

Greenspan, S. and Greenspan, N.T.: Stanley Greenspan is a psychiatrist who has been at the forefront of the infant mental health movement. In *The Essential Partnership*, Viking Publishing, 1989, he and his wife describe how *Floor Time* can be used to enhance relationships and emotional development in the child under four. This book provides many wonderful examples of ways that parents—birth, foster, or adoptive—can facilitate their children's growth and development.

Jernberg, Ann M.: In "Attachment Enhancing for Adopted Children," another of the articles in *Adoption Resources for Mental Health Professionals*, Ms. Jernberg briefly describes Theraplay, a technique which focuses on meeting the child's earlier unmet dependency needs. This technique is described in much more detail in her book entitled *Theraplay* published by Jossey-Bass in 1979.

White, Michael: This family therapist has written a paper on the *Ritual of Inclusion: An Approach to Extreme Uncontrolled Behavior in Children and Young Adolescents*. In it he describes a time-in form of holding. He may be contacted at Dulwich Centre, 345 Carrington Street, Adelaide, 5000 Australia.

Throughout Spring we see sprouts emerging from the ground. Stalks spring up, they leaf, they bud and finally they blossom. Some show themselves earlier and grow faster than others. Some lag behind the crowd. But no matter the timing, the progression from stalk, to leaf, to bud to blossom is the same. Careful inspection of the blossoms reveals that although they are more similar than different, each is unique.

Likewise in the development of children, we see variations in timing and final form, but a consistent pattern of growth and overall configuration.

This chapter is about the Springtime of Life, the period we call Childhood and its usual patterns of development.

CHAPTER 2

Child Development

An individual child's developmental progress is a result of his unique intermix of genetic endowment, temperament, and life experiences. Although not all children demonstrate the same behaviors or reactions to developmental challenges, there are some universal underlying themes evident as the child progresses up the developmental ladder. Since the child consistently builds on the foundations of previously acquired skills, the sequencing of developmental milestones is much more consistent than is the actual age at which they are attained.

Specific developmental stages are identifiable by the physical, psychological, and emotional characteristics which are distinctive for each period. At each of these levels, the child faces specific developmental tasks. Parents are responsible for creating an environment that encourages the child to achieve his full potential in terms of physical, intellectual, and psychological growth. The child's job is to make use of the opportunities provided by the family. Children cannot accomplish the tasks of child development on their own. On the other hand, adults cannot accomplish the tasks for the child. Successful mastery is completed only within the context of relationships.

Because the physical, emotional, and psychological aspects of a child's development are so interrelated, delays in one area often affect subsequent development in other areas as well. In general, the earlier environmental deprivation or other abnormalities have occurred, the more severe the long term effects.

Although all children must accomplish the same developmental tasks, each individual youngster approaches them in a way that reflects his unique predispositions and experiences. The child's personality, physical abilities, and other individual attributes will certainly affect the way in which he demonstrates the traits associated with a particular developmental stage. Nevertheless, significant commonalties exist.

Ideally, families help children accomplish their developmental tasks. Within the family children learn to trust others and to value themselves. They learn about their emotions and those of others. They learn to talk and how to think.

Knowledge of the tasks and characteristics associated with each stage of development is key to helping a child grow. Parents who understand developmental issues are less likely to be as upset by normal behaviors and more likely to support the child in his struggle with the basic challenges of each stage. They are more readily able to perceive what a child needs in order to grow, and to create a helpful environment. They are more likely to meet the child's needs so that undesirable, but normal, behaviors will be unlikely to persist into later stages of development.

Perceptions, abilities, and behavior of all children change as they mature. As children face opportunities and difficulties presented by each stage of development, most exhibit some behaviors that are not seen as particularly desirable by their parents. The fact that an undesirable behavior reflects normal development does not mean that it should be ignored. On the other hand, it should not be treated as a major problem.

In fact, knowledgeable adults view the child's behaviors, that others may see as objectionable, as signals of progress. They view the toddler's struggle with toilet training as an opening for teaching the child self-awareness and the positive emotions that come with mastery of a new skill. The preschooler's curiosity about sex is not viewed as something bad, but rather as an occasion for helping him feel good about his own body while simultaneously learning society's expectations as to when and how to satisfy his needs. They view the grade-school-aged child's tendency to go from one activity to another, without sticking to any, as an opportunity to help him learn to assess his strengths and weaknesses, his likes and dislikes. They view the adolescent's rebellion as a sign of his personal declaration of independence and they help him learn negotiation skills rather than engaging in all out war.

Families provide safety and security, stimulation and encouragement, and reasonable expectations and limits. Children need both emotional support and structure as they meet each developmental challenge and cope with inevitable frustration in the process. Children who do not receive support become bewildered, insecure, and lacking in self-esteem.

Normal fears and worries accompany each developmental stage. The parents' job is to help children cope with and overcome these fears. Making children feel inadequate because of their fears is counterproductive. It cannot possibly help them learn to feel brave and capable. Neither should parents reassure children excessively nor try to remove all possibilities for fear. Not only would this be an unrealistic goal, but if accomplished it would deprive the child of the joy of mastery.

Caseworkers need to be able to distinguish between normal behaviors for varying ages and those behaviors that indicate unmet developmental needs. Knowledge in this area prepares social workers to do a better job of child and family assessment and case planning. Caseworkers must be able to help parents meet the responsibilities accompanying normal development. They need to be able to identify children "stuck" at earlier developmental stages. They need to understand the steps in cognitive development so that, through time, they can help the child understand his life history and reprocess the meaning of early life events.

In this chapter we present material on child development in a manner that we hope will be helpful to child welfare caseworkers and the caregivers who are responsible for children in placement. As each stage of development is discussed, the major developmental tasks are outlined and the changes in perceptions, abilities, and behavior that children experience are highlighted as well as the normal fears and worries which accompany each stage. For each stage there will be information as to how parents can help their child accomplish the tasks at hand. Information which may help identify parents who, because of their own needs, may have difficulty with their children during a particular stage will be shared.

This chapter has six major sections. The first five sections describe normal development in the infant, toddler, preschooler, grade school child, and the adolescent. In each of these sections, the primary tasks to be accomplished during that stage of development are outlined first, followed by a more complete discussion of normal developmental progress with attention to special issues of concern for the child in placement. At the end of the section on preschool development there is a listing of the usual sequence for attaining developmental milestones in the subareas of development: personal-social, fine motor, gross motor, and language. The final section of this chapter summarizes two special developmental issues: conscience development and normal sexual development.

This material can be used not only to understand normal child development but also to help formulate treatment plans that are responsive to the child's needs. It can be used to predict the possible effects of parent separation or loss at differing ages in the child's life. Sometimes parents, although present, do not create the environment necessary for facilitating completion of developmental tasks. Combining a review of family social history and knowledge of child development may lead to identification of possible delays in children's skill levels and ideas as to ways to close these gaps. Finally, knowledge of normal child development can be used to help identify the times when providing opportunities and the knowledge necessary for reintegration of early life events makes sense.

The First Year of Life   I

During the first year of life, the primary developmental task is building feelings of safety, security, and trust in other human beings. When parents meet the child's dependency needs they are facilitating this. During the first year when a parent wonders, "What should I do when...?" the guideline for deciding should be, "What will help my child learn to trust me?" (Hymes, 1969) Infants develop security and trust as a result of day-to-day experiences, not from occasional special or traumatic events. It is the quality of the daily interactions between parent and child that helps children develop physically and mentally. These interchanges aid in organizing the child's nervous system and in setting the stage for learning how to learn, a primary task of the first year of life (Gesell, 1940).

Even during the first year it is not possible to separate a child's innate characteristics and behavior from the effects of nurturing. Infants deprived of mothering will appear grossly retarded within the first year of life. They may not be able to sit, stand, or walk. Vocalizations and social interactions will be limited. They may have "failure to thrive" syndrome and be of low weight. If needs for security and affection are not met, these individuals may not be able to give love or incorporate social values as they mature.

As already mentioned, the primary psychological task to be accomplished during the first year of life is for a child to develop trust in others. The accomplishment of this task, like all other psychological tasks, is primarily a reflection of day-to-day living rather than occasional isolated experiences.

The infant's dependency needs usually "hook" an adult caregiver into interactions. The baby signals discomfort, the adult responds to the need, while simultaneously initiating a series of pleasurable interactions. Needs become associated with emotionally nurturing and gratifying responses. The infant learns that adults are available and that he is worthy of their attention and caregiving. Repeated successful completion of the arousal-relaxation cycle, (fig1-1 on page 33) is critical if children are to develop a sense of trust and security, becoming attached to parents.

At birth, infants do not discriminate between various states of discomfort. They experience and react in a similar way when afraid, hungry, or in pain. Gradually, as the cycle is successfully completed on different occasions, they start to differentiate states of discomfort and associate them with specific forms of relief. The foundation for learning basic cause and effect is laid. When a parent consistently identifies when a child is hungry and feeds him, she is teaching the baby to associate that internal sensation with food. Gradually he learns that the cause of the discomfort is an empty stomach.

This cycle helps us understand why so many children who come from abusive and neglectful homes have not only problems with lack of trust but also with identifying the source of their own body discomforts. For many, completion of the cycle has been infrequent or inconsistent. It is not uncommon to see five- or six-year-old children who were abused or neglected during the first year of life have difficulty distinguishing when they are hungry from when they need attention, or even problems differentiating the discomfort of an empty stomach from that of a full bladder.

During the first year of life children make tremendous gains in physical development. The rate of growth and development is so great that caregivers see changes on nearly a daily basis. At no other time in an individual's life will developmental changes from month to month be so consistently noticeable.

The child's nervous system becomes organized during the first year of life. The rate and level of this organization seems to be at least partially related to the quality of the relationships that infants have with their primary caregivers while learning to recognize and understand many stimuli.

In general, children gain control over their bodies in progression from head to foot and from the central part to the extremities. Thus, infants first gain voluntary control over the eye muscles and are first able to focus on objects eight to nine inches away. From birth, infants are interested in looking at the face of a human partner. Within the first month most infants learn to follow objects to the midline, and within two months three quarters of them are following beyond the midline (Moss, 1968).

The muscles of the lower part of the face are the next to come under voluntary control. Infants smile responsively prior to three months. Next comes control over the neck muscles, allowing the infant to lift his head and neck when lying on his stomach and gain control over the head when held upright. Large muscle control of the upper extremities is acquired next. Between three and four months most can put their hands together and use their arms for support to raise their chests up when lying on their stomachs. In fact, near this age children learn to roll over, first from stomach to back and later from back to stomach. Shortly thereafter the head does not lag when the child is moved from lying on his back to sitting upright.

Between three and four months children develop enough control over their hand muscles to be able to grasp a rattle for a short period of time. By five months most infants will reach for an object, and by six months most will transfer objects from one hand to the other, frequently putting the object in the mouth in the process. Near this same age they learn to pick up small objects by using a raking motion. Most children can use a thumb and finger grasp by the age of nine months.

By this same time children are gaining control over the large muscles in their lower extremities. They can pull themselves to a standing position and can stand if there is something to hold onto. Within the next month and a half, most will learn to walk holding onto furniture and will learn to stand momentarily by themselves. Babies learn to stoop and recover at about the same time as they learn to walk alone, usually at about one year of age.

Also by a year of age most have learned to pick up small objects with a neat, pincer-type grasp. The combination of this grasp and their new mobility leads to a frustrating period for parents. Children see and pick up every tiny thing on the floor and put everything they have picked up into their mouths.

Language begins to emerge during the first year of life. Children *in utero* can hear. Newborns respond with distress to sharp sounds and prefer soft sounds. By three or four weeks infants turn toward sounds and respond most prominently to the voice of the primary caretaker (Wolff, 1966). Even before they are four months old, infants make a variety of sounds. They babble, coo, chuckle, gurgle, and laugh. Infants are very responsive to the human voice. Their vocalizations increase when someone talks or plays with them.

Midway through the first year of life, infants begin to make vowel and consonant sounds and even put some sounds together into syllables. Between six and nine months children imitate parents' speech sounds in a nonspecific fashion. By this time they are gaining control over the muscles associated with lips, tongue, and mouth. This physical fact, combined with a willingness to imitate, leads to a spurt in speech development at this time.

Martin

When the caseworker's observations, completed when Martin was ten-and-a-half-months old and after he had been living in the Olney foster home for four months, are reviewed in developmental terms, it is apparent that this infant has delays in all four major areas of developmental functioning.

However, it is in the personal-social area that his most obvious delays are evident. He rarely smiles and never laughs. He is not responsive to people and shows no stranger anxiety or separation discomfort. He shows no interest when adults initiate games of peek-a-boo or pat-a-cake. With a solemn expression, he allows his hands to be passively moved in the latter activity, but makes no attempt to continue it on his own. His interest in toys is so low that he makes no attempt to attain those slightly out of reach.

He does pick up objects and transfers them from one hand to the other, but he does not bang them together or explore them with his mouth. Rather than playing with toys, he picks them up and sets them down.

Language delays are also obvious. He rarely vocalizes. He does not imitate speech sounds and does not use consonant-vowel combinations such as pa or ma. Sounds are primarily of the gurgle type.

His least significant delays are in the areas of physical and gross motor development. His height and weight are at the lower end of the normal range. He is able to sit without support and pulls himself to standing, but rarely tries to walk while holding onto furniture.

During the first year of life there normally are fluctuations in children's emotional responses. During the first month of life infants are becoming accustomed to life outside the uterus and are often quite disorganized. The first challenge of the parent-infant dyad is for the child to feel regulated and calm so that he can use all of his senses to start processing his environment (Greenspan, 1985). Between four and six weeks they become more stable and tend to settle into a more scheduled pattern. Still, periods of emotional disequilibrium and increased fussiness usually re-emerge for short periods at two months and again between four and five months of age. During these periods children often fuss for no apparent reason, and little seems to work in comforting them.

Between six and nine months, children consistently distinguish between family members and strangers. By this age, infants are beginning to demonstrate fear or anxiety when approached by a stranger. The strength and frequency of these fear reactions increases as children near one year of age. This makes it increasingly difficult for children to develop an attachment to a stranger during this period.

Throughout the first year of life, children gradually become more perceptive, take a more active part in their relationship with others, and become less dependent. Anticipatory and imitative responses of sounds and actions reveal the beginnings of memory (Pulaski, 1978). Awareness of cause and effect, or at least of sequencing, gradually develops. By eight to nine months fear and sadness have joined the facial expressions indicative of pleasure, distress, disgust, joy, and anger which were evident even earlier (Greenspan, 1985). The child is increasingly reaching out to his world in a purposeful manner. He is learning that the world is a more reliable place. He smiles, parents smile back. He is sad, parents comfort.

Fears and Worries During Infancy

During the first year babies usually startle in response to fear-producing stimuli. Loud or unexpected noises may be frightening to the infant as are sudden movements. Threats of falling or being dropped and threats of bodily harm or pain lead to fear responses.

The Parents' Role

The primary tasks for the parents during the child's first year of life are to meet the child's basic needs "on demand" and to provide stimulation which will encourage the child to use all of his senses and enhance motor development. Parents need to be consistently available and responsive in a way that helps the child learn to trust them. When children feel secure they are better able to attend to their environment and begin to learn what different sights, sounds, smells, tastes, and touches all mean.

By providing caregiving in a rhythmical, consistent manner, the parent helps the child organize his nervous system. The foundation for cause and effect is laid down. Providing visual, auditory, and tactile stimulation that fit with the child's perceptive and motor skills stimulates development.

Parent Issues

The infant's dependency may evoke memories of unmet nurturance on the part of adults who themselves had inadequate parenting. These parents may be looking to the child to meet their needs rather than vice versa. They and their babies are at high risk for potential problems with serious long-term consequences. Mothers who do not acknowledge their pregnancies, or who do not begin to perceive their unborn child as a separate person, are at high risk for bonding problems. If parents and children were apart during the early weeks of the child's life, for any reason, they are at greater risk for the development of parent-child difficulties.

II The Toddler Years

Emotionally, the primary tasks to be accomplished between twelve and thirty-six months are for the toddler to psychologically separate from his primary caregiver and to begin to develop a sense of self. When parents are faced with a "What should I do when . . .?" question about toddlers, the standard for deciding is, "What will make my child feel more capable?" (Hymes, 1969) Identity formation accompanies the increasing autonomy. Although language starts before the toddler years and certainly continues long after, it is during this stage that it first becomes functional. Finally, the social, or connecting, emotions emerge during the toddler years, setting the stage for interpersonal relationships and conscience development.

At about twelve months, when children stand and walk, their perspective of the world literally and figuratively changes. Simultaneously they develop the capacity to pick up very small objects. As a result of these two developmental achievements they are eminently capable of "getting into things" as they exploit their two newly acquired skills. During the early part of the second year, the child begins to figure out ways to achieve his objectives. For example, he may climb up on a chair to reach a desired object. He finds new uses for familiar objects. The toy that was previously passed from hand to hand or banged against another is now stacked one on another. He sees something he wants inside a container and he dumps it out. He learns to follow simple directions.

As noted earlier, by age one children are capable of showing a variety of emotions — frustration, anger, sadness, fear, and affection. Using intentional non-verbal gestures, the child demonstrates his emotions. Facial expressions, sounds, posture, movements of extremities all become part of the gestural system (Greenspan, 1989). According to Greenspan this gestural capacity, which usually develops during the first half of the second year, is the foundation for language, reasoning, and the use of ideas in relationships.

By age one most children are using "Mama" and "Dada" and have two or three other words in their vocabularies. They jabber a lot. They respond to their own names, to "No, no" and to "Give it to me." By eighteen months most children have a vocabulary of about ten words (Gesell et al. 1940). They can say *no* and may use the pronouns *me* and *mine*. They are using words to replace or accompany gestures.

74

Language development is essential because it makes possible the higher mental processes that allow humans to attain self-control and to delay gratification. It gives children a way to express emotions other than by acting them out. It makes memory more accessible. Children's memories of the months before they acquire language are scanty and are usually stored either as visual images or as emotions which may subsequently be resurfaced by sights, sounds, smells, touches, or pain.

Typically, children at twelve months are very social. In a secure setting, they may even seem to be somewhat indiscriminate in giving affection as they smile and talk with everyone, so long as a parent is close by. However, between twelve and eighteen months, they become apprehensive about being physically separated from their primary caregivers. Normal toddlers are frequently underfoot. Since the developmental task for toddlers is psychological separation and individuation, when mother is physically absent, toddlers feel out-of-control of the situation and become more anxious and apprehensive. As toddlers lose sight of mother and then find her again, they are learning about themselves as individuals. They use the parent as a safe haven from which to explore the world. It isn't until between eighteen and twenty-four months that the toddler learns to carry an image of his loved ones within his mind's eye. From that time on, parents no longer have to be in the room for the child to know that they exist.

Prominent words in the vocabulary of eighteen month olds are *me*, *mine*, and *no*. These words support their emerging autonomy. Children begin to distinguish between *you* and *me*. They begin to separate their own identity from their mother's, learning that there are two individuals. Games such as "Point to your nose. Point to my nose" help them make this differentiation.

The eighteen to thirty month old is going through a normal oppositional, stubborn, egocentric stage which is necessary to the development of his identity. His defiance and resistance during this period is not so much aggressive as self-protective. The toddler is trying to establish himself in the world. Although the child's behaviors may be frustrating to adults, if the youngster does not gain this sense of self as worthwhile and capable there will be serious long-term consequences. Those children who do not exhibit the normal oppositional stage are more likely to be dependent later on in life.

A child's identity is comprised of several parts. From infancy on, adults talk to and handle males and females differently. Gender is an important aspect of identity. Position in the family is another component. Much has been written about the importance of birth order on development. Birth order combined with the sex of the child in some families has a particularly powerful impact on identity formation. Expectations for oldest daughter versus oldest son may be very different. However, the child's psychological position in the family may relate to other factors as well. A child may have been identified as "my active child" even before birth. Timing of a particular child's birth in relationship to other family events may be important. For example, a male child born soon after the death of a paternal grandfather and named after him may have different expectations placed upon him than he would have had if born at a different time. Indeed, an individual's given name is an important aspect of identity. As a toddler, the child learns that a "No" or that praise is directed to him when accompanied by his name.

As toddlers reach their second birthday, their abilities to perceive things and to imitate behavior have become more developed. By now they have learned that objects have functions. They love to mimic parents and to "help" with household tasks. They remember past events and imitate them later.

During the second year the toddler shows signs of pride, pity, sympathy, modesty, and shame, which are some of the social emotions. These emotions connect the individual to himself and to others. Sympathy and empathy are frequently seen when a toddler tries to comfort an upset parent with, "Po' Mommy."

The pure joy that lights up the face of the toddler who has just learned to "do it myself" is indication of another of the social emotions, pride. Usually twos are aware of praise and smile when they hear it. Yet, some children in interim care seem never to have learned to experience joy and accomplishment from a job well done.

During the second half of the second year, as the child learns to recognize himself in a mirror and in pictures, he also develops the capacity to be aware of when something is different about him. He demonstrates signs of embarrassment. This seems to be a precursor for shame and guilt. We can see toddlers begin to internalize the attitudes of others during this period. As they approach an object they are not to touch, the parent says "No" in a firm voice, sometimes accompanied by a tap on the offending hand. Later, as the child approaches this object he himself is likely to say, "No, no." Not yet quite able to stop himself from touching, he continues to need a parent's reinforcing, "That's right. That is a no-no." As he withdraws his own hand he might give himself a tap on the offending fingers. This is the beginning step in acknowledging right vs wrong and is, as such, a precursor to conscience development.

Two year olds still do not fully accept their mothers as separate individuals. They alternate between being dependent and being self-contained. The resurgence of fear toward strangers that occurred at eighteen months subsides. However between eighteen months and three years the child is learning to form a mental image of objects so that he can hold them in his memory even though they are not within sight. This will help him tolerate separation from primary caregivers. He can create them in his mind's eye so that he need not feel abandoned by them when they disappear from view.

Children of this age will play alone or play in parallel with other children. However, they are still self-centered and not yet ready to share. Between twenty-four and thirty-six months, they go through a period where extremes are the norm. They are either very dependent or very independent. Moods change from hour to hour. They are extremely aggressive or extremely passive, very helpful or very stubborn.

Toilet training becomes feasible, and for most children daytime training is completed by the third birthday. True toilet training cannot occur until children become aware of the sensations of a full bladder and a full bowel. However, many mothers learn to identify the signals of an impending bowel movement and place the infant or toddler on the toilet even though the child has not himself yet become aware of the discomfort of a full bowel.

Commonly, toddlers first become aware of wet or full pants right after the fact rather than before, or they "go" right after they get off the potty chair rather than while they are on it. Although this is frustrating to parents, it indicates that the child is beginning to relate the potty chair to voiding or defecating. However, the child has not mastered the proper sequence yet. For most, these are necessary steps in toilet training, for until children become aware of the discomfort after it occurs, they cannot become aware of the full sensation prior to urinating or defecating. Children who have a low sensitivity to skin sensations may be delayed in terms of toilet training. Others who have experienced considerable pain in the genital region may have learned to mute sensations from that part of their body.

Since children at this age tend to be obstinate and messy, parents often attribute difficulties in toilet training to their stubbornness. With most children this is not initially true. However, if parents make a control issue out of toilet training or use harsh disciplinary techniques, then the stubborness of this age may extend to toilet training as well. This is not likely to happen if parents are relaxed but helpful about teaching toileting skills.

Toddlers have difficulty moving toward a moving object. Until about age three they have problems following the parent who is walking. Usually until age three, parents must transport their toddlers by stroller, grocery cart, or in their arms. When parent and toddler are out for a pleasure walk, it is common to see the adult walk a short distance, remain stationary until her child catches up with her, and then repeat this sequence. A coiled cord with a velcro closed wrist band, used as a tether between parent and child, allowing the child to have his hands free and more freedom to move while still keeping him physically close in public places meets the needs of both child and parent better than many alternatives.

From age two to three-and-a-half children develop a higher level of understanding of self and others. Organized pretending emerges. The stage is set for the child to learn to think ahead. The toddler's vocabulary grows by leaps and bounds. Between the ages of two and three, children begin to add "s" to words to make plurals. They learn to use the words acquired earlier in sentences. They use nouns, pronouns, verbs, and some adjectives.They begin to understand prepositions, although they don't yet use them. Their vocabulary increases to over one thousand words (Gesell et al. 1940). They use words to resist and to ask questions.

At two, most children combine words into phrases or short sentences. Their jargon has about disappeared. They use nouns more than other parts of speech. The vocabulary of the average two-year-old is around three hundred words (Gesell et al. 1940). Most can name some animals, objects, and parts of the body. They will usually try to imitate single words said to them. Pronouns come into use during the period between eighteen and thirty months, usually emerging in this order: *mine, me, you,* and *I*. At two most children are still prone to calling themselves by their given names, i.e. "Billy want a cookie." The rhythm of typical two-year-olds' voices are singsong, and they often echo what others say.

As toddlers gain independence, their anger is aroused chiefly by interference with their physical activity. When eighteen-months-olds are angry, they are apt to tantrum, crying intensely and throwing themselves on the floor. They may also hit, kick, and struggle if an adult tries to control them. The one-and-a-half-year-old may be rough with animals and younger children. They are apt to pull hair and to hug too tightly. By twenty-one months, frustration may also stem from their inadequate abilities to express their wants and needs.

Typically, twos are not as aggressive as the eighteen month old. However, they may hit, poke, or bite other children. Ownership is important to them and they will frequently engage in a tug of war over toys and other objects. Although they may be messy, generally they are not destructive.

By thirty months, toddlers have become more destructive and are more aggressive both with other children and with adults. They may attack other children with the intent to hurt, usually in disputes over toys. Without warning they may even walk up and hit a stranger. They may, again, have kicking, hitting, and head-banging tantrums.

The Fears and Worries During the Toddler Years

During this period, the child "catches fears" from parents. Biological mechanisms are strongly influenced by the emotional messages of caregivers. Responding to the caregiver's affect, the toddler will learn to avoid some dangers, such as steps. During the first half of the second year, children become afraid of separations from their parent and may cry vigorously when they see a parent leave. The sounds of mechanical gadgets, particularly those that move, such as vacuum cleaners and certain mechanical toys, may provoke fear during this period.

Twos are afraid of noises such as trains, thunder, animal sounds, or the flushing of toilets. Seeing something that parents seem to value as much as a stool go down the drain may lead to the fear that they too will go down the drain. Separation from mother, particularly at bedtime, is still frightening.

During the second half of the third year children are prone to spatial fears. They may fear being moved rapidly themselves, and may react to having objects in their environment moved from their usual places. They notice and object to being taken to a known place by a different car route. They are especially fearful of large objects approaching them.

The Parents' Role

What kind of environment helps children accomplish the psychological tasks at hand for the child one to three? During this stage children need parents who can give encouragement, without pressure, for the development of new skills, parents who help them feel "big" and capable. Toddlers need to be provided with the environmental tools necessary for success in feeling capable. For example, a small stool placed at a sink so the child can get a drink or wash his own hands increases self-esteem.

It is the parents' responsibility to insure the child's safety and well-being. Changes in the environment, such as using gates to block off steps and placing cleaning materials, medicines, and poisons in inaccessible places, can do much to prevent accidents. It is dangerous for a child this age to be left unsupervised, even momentarily, in a bathtub or children's wading pool. In fact, even the water in a toilet may be a hazard to the unsupervised toddler. Keeping the toilet lid down or the bathroom door closed is prudent. Late during this period children learn to turn door knobs. Until then keeping certain rooms of the house closed off is a serviceable safety technique.

The toddler's short attention span and distractibility are parents' principal allies during this period. Substituting a safe toy for a forbidden one usually works. Reasoning is not yet effective. However, even during the second year, the adult can start to use effective discipline by physically getting down to the child's level, establishing eye contact and saying "No" in a firm voice. Initially the toddler may smile and once again reach for the forbidden object. Again, the parent needs to move the child's hand away from the object and firmly say "No" before switching gears and using distraction to involve the youngster in an alternate activity. Although many parents use a quick tap on an offending hand or a single swat on the bottom to interrupt a behavior by getting the child's attention, alternate methods are preferable even with a child this age. Certainly, harsh physical punishment does not help psychological development.

Children of this age are creatures of routine. Changes in routine or abrupt transitions usually result in children who are more easily frustrated and upset than normal. Most parents who have disrupted their toddler's usual nap routine to take them for an afternoon appointment have learned that they "pay" for this change in routine for the remainder of the day. Stop/start games facilitate the emerging sense of self. Toddlers enjoy being in charge of games such as being lifted high. They will squeal saying, "Stop," but as soon as the parent puts them down they will say, "Do it again." Gentle tickling games in which the child is in charge of starting and stopping the activity are another example of this type of activity.

Parent Issues

If parents perceive the normal negativism of the toddler age as a personal attack and get into repeated win-lose battles, they may well set the stage for future difficulties with the child. Through such conflicts children learn to behave as though their integrity as a person is in danger if they submit to even the smallest demands of another. Resistance and conflict, rather than mutuality, may then become the primary mode of interaction. Parents need to maintain expectations and consistency while avoiding control battles.

Rigid, inflexible, controlling adults or those with unresolved issues around aggression are at high risk for problems in parenting the toddler. Mothers who themselves have unresolved separation anxiety may be threatened by the increasing autonomy of the child. Since toddlers are inherently messy, parents who are rigidly compulsive about cleanliness and neatness are at high risk to abuse even the normal toddler.

III The Preschool Years

During the years from three to five-and-a-half or six, when there is once again a major change in the child's perception of the world, the focus is on the youngster becoming efficient and proficient within a small group setting such as the family. Play is the work of the preschooler. It is used to facilitate their continuing individuation and independence. Magical and egocentric thinking characterize the thought processes of the child this age. The former leads to their believing that wishes make things come true, the latter to their thinking that they are responsible for everything that happens to themselves and to others who are important in their lives. It does not allow for coincidences.

Play is used to solve two internal psychological conflicts. Three, four, and five-year-olds use intellectual powers and imaginative skills as they play. We see two recurring themes in their play (Hymes 1969), big vs. little and good vs. bad. Through play they continue to work on the balance between dependence and autonomy. On the one hand, preschoolers love to play at being baby. When taking on this helpless, infantile role, they may want to rock, suck from a bottle, or get into a crib. They are likely to want to play under tables or to construct a cozy corner or tent for this type of play. Or, the dependent role may be the sick person while playing doctor, or the pupil while playing school.

This is contrasted with sometimes wanting to be big, strong, and in charge. When the preschoolers take on this role, they want to be the mother or father, the doctor or nurse, or the teacher. In acting out these roles, they are likely to be very bossy, even tyrannical. This play reflects feelings and thoughts, not necessarily experiences. Psychologically healthy children sometimes take the dependent role and other times the independent one. If a child insists on taking only one or the other of these roles, he is signaling a problem in the resolution of this struggle.

A second theme of the preschooler's play is aimed at integrating the "good" and the "bad" aspects of self. Because of the power of the spoken word, they now know that sometimes they are good, while other times adults may tell them they are bad. In integrating these two, hopefully, they determine that they are good people who sometimes do not-good things. This helps them learn that they are capable of change, becoming able to forgive themselves for their mistakes. Children this age are frequently involved in "good guys" vs "bad guys" play. Once again, the psychologically healthy child sometimes assumes one role and other times the opposite. Because this play usually has an aggressive aspect to it, adults sometimes discourage it. However, it is necessary to healthy psychological development.

During the preschool years, children frequently create imaginary friends, who may be blamed for anything the child does wrong. Or sometimes the imaginary friend becomes the personalization of the scared, dependent, little aspect of the child. Thus a preschooler may say, "I'm not afraid of the dark but Sammie is. You better leave on the light or he may be scared and cry, and then I couldn't sleep."

Lily

Lily, the youngest of the Thompson children whom we met in the introduction, had few play skills when she came to the Wentz fosterhome. She showed no signs of imagination. The foster parents had had considerable experience working with children who demonstrated a variety of problems. They realized that Lily needed to learn how to play and how to imagine. They used the concept of floor time described by Greenspan (1989). Every day one or the other of the foster parents would spend about half an hour on the floor playing with Lily. Initially they introduced toys that usually were used by toddlers. As Lily learned to use these toys, the Wentz parents gradually added more age-appropriate toys.

Selecting two or three toys, they would suggest that they could play having a tea party or going to a store or to a playground. Lily had difficulty initiating pretend activities on her own. Usually she needed ideas as to the choices she might make. The adult would then pay careful attention to all of Lily's non-verbal gestures and cues helping her become a more active participant in the play, even though she wasn't initially using many words. Gradually, they supplied words to go with her actions.

Within several months, there was noticeable improvement in Lily's language skills. Her coordination in handling toys, too, had improved. Over time she developed an active imagination and was able to pretend when playing by herself. However, the foster parents understood that it was important that they continue to spend time playing with Lily each day, helping her learn to trust that adults were consistently available for her and interested in her.

From three onwards, the child's need to be physically near a parent is no longer so urgent. Threes can feel secure when with people that they got to know while in the presence of their parents. Sensitivity to this is an important consideration when moving children into foster or adoptive placements, as well as in planning babysitting, daycare or preschool experiences.

In general threes seem to be in good equilibrium. They are able to process most of what they perceive. They are usually happy and contented. They enjoy play by themselves. They seem to have achieved some measure of emotional and physical self-control. Usually they are friendly and helpful. They have learned to help dress and undress themselves, and although they may have occasional accidents, they usually do not need diapers in the daytime. They enjoy both gross and fine motor activities. Three-year-olds begin to take turns, a precursor to true sharing.

Three's readiness to conform to the spoken word is an outstanding characteristic. It is possible to bargain with a three. "You do this and I'll do that for you." They realize that they are separate persons from others. While bargaining works, reasoning does not. Reasoning requires more conceptual skills than three-year-olds usually have. Distraction is still a useful disciplinary technique.

In general threes are less rebellious than they were at two. They exhibit increased self-control and are less aggressive than earlier. When they resist, they usually use language rather than biting, scratching, or kicking. Children this age commonly use verbal threats to assert themselves and express anger. Increased use of language allows them to express wants and desires so that they are not so easily frustrated, and vocalization may be used to express anger and frustration when it occurs. Anger is now aroused less by interference with physical activity and more by interference with possessions or plans.

Threes frequently ask questions to which they know the answers. This behavior is, in part, an effort to find out which information is consistent and which is inconsistent. From the child's point of view, the world is a very confusing place. Some perceptions seem constant, others do not. What is acceptable behavior at one time may not be acceptable at a different time or in another setting. For example, although hitting may always be interrupted, loud boisterous play may be all right at certain times of day but not when parents are trying to sleep or when a baby is napping.

Threes are capable of prolonged anxiety and jealousy. Their greatest fear is that of parental abandonment. As children turn four, some of the stubbornness that was seen at two resurfaces. However it is usually less intense and frequently has a playful quality about it. Four-year-olds enjoy silly talk, silly names, silly rhyming, silly showing off. They love dramatic, imaginative play.

Fours are talkative and give long explanations in answer to parental questions. When they misbehave, they are prone to blame others or deny their involvement. They may behave badly on purpose in order to get a reaction. They are able to focus on similarities and differences. At four children use questions to order their experiences and to begin to conceptualize and group things. *Why* and *how* frequently introduce their questions. They can count by rote. The names of colors have been learned. They learn to use prepositions. As adverbs become evident in their language, all parts of speech have been mastered.

Typical fours are likely to return to some physical aggression while continuing to be verbally aggressive. Biting, hitting, kicking, and throwing things are not uncommon at this age. Verbal aggression with name calling, bragging, and boasting is present as well. Fours tend to be rough and careless with toys and may aggressively exclude others from the group.

Although able to dress and undress themselves with little assistance, fours frequently enjoy help as a form of nurturing. They begin to have a sense of past and sense of future. When told "in a little while" or " in a half an hour," they want to know how long that is.

Between the ages of four and six children go through the Oedipal stage, in which they compete with the parent of the same sex for the attention of the parent of the opposite sex. This is an important aspect of the continuing development of sexual identity and will be addressed in detail in the section on sexual development later in this chapter.

Children at five again are in a state of equilibrium. Once more, their perceptions and abilities seem to mesh. Five is an age of self-containment and independence. In general fives are more serious and realistic than they were earlier or will become later. They are oriented to the here and now. When children of five paint or draw, the idea precedes the production, rather than the reverse, as occurred at age four. Drawing and dramatic play are more realistic.

Because five is an age of stability, they are less frustrated and less aggressive. When angry, fives may stomp their feet or slam the door. "I hate you," or, "I wish you were dead," are common verbal expressions of anger for both four and five-year-olds.

By age five, children's language is essentially complete in structure and form. They lose infant articulation. They sound grown up now. Usually by five the melody and rhythm of speech are smooth. The most common articulation errors at this age are substituting an *f* or *d* for *th*, softening *r* until it sounds like *w*, and substituting *w* for *l*.

Fives have acquired an ear for detail. They are able to ask the meaning of single words, rather than asking what an entire sentence means. Fives ask fewer questions and the ones they do ask are more relevant to what is going on. They ask for information rather than to maintain social interactions. Because they have difficulty suppressing their own view even temporarily, a genuine interchange of ideas remains limited. They have trouble suppressing themselves even momentarily and will frequently interrupt. In show and tell activities, they are interested in doing the showing and telling rather than the listening.

Five-year-olds enjoy brief separations from their homes and parents. Most are friendly and talkative with strangers. This is not to be confused with indiscriminate affection, which involves more than talk. A vein of politeness and tact is emerging. They become increasingly aware of the differences between the two sexes and of how individuals vary from one another. They compare and contrast themselves with others. There is an emerging sense of shame and a sense of status.

Bargaining continues to work as a disciplinary technique because activity levels usually increase under stress, some form of time-out may help them regain their self-control. Distraction does not work as well as at earlier ages.

Fears and Worries During the Preschool Years

Visual fears are the predominant ones for the three-year-old. Masks, costumes, strange appearing objects, the dark, and animals may all provoke fear reactions. The greatest normal fear of a three is that parents will not be available when needed. For this reason the fear of being left alone at night is still present and threes may continue to react adversely to separation from parents at bedtime while accepting daytime leave-takings gracefully.

Since the child's imagination emerges between the ages of three-and-a half and four, he becomes vulnerable to fearful thoughts and dreams at that age. Overall, preschoolers' fears seem unreasonable to the adults in their lives. Fours are afraid of a wide variety of stimuli. Frequently they are afraid of the dark. Sirens and other loud, sharp noises provoke fear. It is not uncommon for fours to be puzzled by or frightened of people who look or act "different." Many fours are afraid of dogs.

Fear of the dark, however, is the single most common fear for fours. They may want a night light or ask a parent to accompany them into a dark room. If parents agree to such simple measures, it will help the child learn to trust his own ideas about ways to overcome fears. With an adult close by, the child may want to look under a bed or in a closet to insure that there is no one hiding. However, if the parent joins in the search for hidden persons it gives the message that they, too, are fearful.

Children of this age use the words "afraid" and "scared" and may even enjoy being mildly frightened by an adult in play, if, in general, the adult has been trustworthy. However, as with the start and stop games of the toddler years, the four needs to have some measure of control over this activity. Threats of a bogeyman or monster coming to get them are not helpful to the four.

In general, five is not a particularly fearful age until the child reaches the disequilibrium that occurs between five-and-a-half and six. Most of the fears of early fives are concrete, down to earth fears, such as the fear of bodily harm, fear of falling, or fear of being bitten by a dog. Thunder or sirens at night might arouse fears. The fear that parents will not be available when needed is still present and demonstrates itself especially in terms of fears that something will happen to the parent while the child is at school. Indeed, for a child with school phobia, it is usually separation anxiety that underlies his fear.

The Parents' Role

Parents need to help children differentiate between fantasy and reality. This does not mean that they have to interrupt imaginary activities, just identify them as such. Although magical and egocentric thinking are normal during this stage of development, adults need to make certain that they do not reinforce the negative aspects by implying that children are the cause of adult problems or behaviors or by inferring that strong emotions, such as anger or hate, lead to physical harm *per se*. In the following example we meet a mother whose reaction to her young daughter's anger and jealousy negatively reinforced the child's magical egocentric thinking.

Monica, age four, is quite jealous of her little sister, Tasha, who is two. Monica has always been an active, assertive, sometimes aggressive, child. Tasha, on the other hand is quieter and more easy going, rarely given to outbursts. Their mother becomes easily frustrated by Monica, who reminds her of her own older sister who would frequently tease her when she was a child.

Monica

One day, Mother overheard Monica screaming at Tasha, "I hate you. You are the dumbest sister ever. I wish you'd never been born." Tasha had accidently broken Monica's favorite doll. Mother entered the room, swept Tasha up cuddling her, while telling Monica, "You should never say you hate your sister. You know you don't really mean it. How would you feel if something bad really did happen to her? Then you would be sorry."

At this point, Monica switched the focus of her anger to Mom, screaming at her, "And I hate you too. I wish you were dead." Mother burst into tears, commenting under her breath, "This child will be the death of me yet."

Because play is used to address the psychological tasks of this age, children need to be provided with adequate opportunities for both individual, and peer group play.

Parents can be helpful in the resolution of the Oedipal conflict by acknowledging the normalcy of the feelings, while gently expressing reality and facilitating identification with the parent of the same sex.

Parent Issues

Because preschoolers are quite open about their sexual curiousity, those parents who do not feel comfortable acknowledging and accepting their own and others' sexuality will have difficulty helping their children feel comfortable with their own bodies, accepting the normalcy of tactile pleasure in the genital areas. Parents with their own unresolved Oedipal conflicts may have difficulties parenting a child of the same sex.

Some rigid adults use religion as an excuse for harsh physical discipline of children these ages, particularly in response to sexualized behaviors.

Parents who themselves have difficulty differentiating fantasy from reality, such as those who are psychotic or who use mind altering drugs, will not be able to help their children with this differentiation.

Shauna lives with her single mom, who is schizophrenic. In spite of taking her medications on a regular basis, Mom continues to have auditory and visual hallucinations. Sometimes she carries on conversations with people who are not visible to Shauna. When the child asks her mother if she is pretending, Mom continues to behave as though her hallucinations were reality. Sometimes when

Shauna

85

Shauna is pretending that she is playing with her imaginary friends, Mom tells her that is silly, no one is there. Other times, Mom ignores her and still other times she incorporates Shauna and her imaginary friends into her own hallucinatory schema.

In Exercise 2-1 we will explore ways to meet a child's unmet dependency needs when they evidence themselves several years later. A series of Developmental Charts follows the Exercise.

Exercise 2-1

Identifying Unmet Dependency Needs and Dealing with Behavioral Regression.

Travis

Travis is five. He has been in and out of foster care since he was two because of repeated episodes of neglect by his mother and physical abuse by several of her boyfriends. In the foster home where Travis lives, there is an infant and two toddlers. Occasionally, the foster mom finds Travis sitting under the desk, rocking and sucking on a baby bottle he has taken from a younger child.

He continually grabs the toddlers' toys from them. He seems to prefer playing with their toys as opposed to playing with ones used by most children of five. Sometimes he speaks very clearly; at other times he uses "baby talk." At bedtime Travis rocks himself in the bed until he falls asleep.

1. What unmet dependency needs does Travis appear to have?
2. How would you explain his problems from a developmental standpoint?
3. What suggestions do you have for Travis' foster parents for meeting his early dependency needs so that they will not persist in later years?

Development Charts

Personal-social

0-4 weeks:

Looks at a face transiently
At 3-4 weeks smiles selectively in response to mother's
voice
Increasing body tone
Growing capacity to stay awake
Gradually increasing stabilization of basic body functions
From third week on human voice leads to quieting of cries

1-3 months:

Smiles responsively to human face
Individual traits becoming more obvious
Orients more toward mother than anyone else
Increasing attention span
Uses vocalization to interact socially
Most smile spontaneously

4-6 months:

Smiles at image in mirror
Head, eyes, and hands work well together in reaching for
toys and the human face
50% like to play peek-a-boo
Smiles readily at most people
Self-contained: plays alone with contentment
Takes solid food well

6-9 months:

Onset of stranger anxiety
Most reach for familiar persons
Shows desire to be picked up and held
Feeds self finger foods
Feet to mouth
Pats mirror image
Plays peek-a-boo
Starting to drink from a cup
Chews and bites on toys at play
Rarely lies down except when asleep
Well-established routines
Beginning responsiveness to own name
Beginning responsiveness to "no, no"
Difference in interactions with various family members
May hold own bottle

9-12 months:
Repeats performances for attention
Social with family, shy with strangers
Beginning self-identity
Capable of varying emotions such as fear, anger, and
   anxiety
Beginning sense of humor
Actively tries to get attention
Becoming aware of emotions of others
Plays pat-a-cake
50% drink from a cup by themselves

12-15 months:
More demanding, assertive, and independent
Poor emotional equilibrium
Vocalizing replaces crying for attention
Sense of me and mine
60% use spoon, spilling little
50% imitate household tasks
Most drink from cup unassisted
Reacts when mother leaves

15-18 months:
More claiming of mine
Beginning distinctions of you and me
Concentrated interest, but wary of strangers
Resistant to changes in routine and/or sudden transitions
Autonomy expressed as defiance
Sharp discipline not helpful
Scolding or verbal persuasion not very useful, as words
   are not yet important techniques
Does not yet perceive other persons as individuals like self
Imitates and mimics others
Most use spoon well
50% can help in little household tasks
Most can take off pieces of clothing
Solitary or parallel play
Shows or offers toy to examiner

18-24 months:
Continued solitary or parallel play with other children
More social with mother
Follows mother
Helps dress and undress self
Can wash and dry hands
May indicate wet or soiled diapers
Most can do simple household tasks
Pulls person to show

18-24 months, Continued	Asks for food and drink
	Understands and asks for "another"
	Mimics real life situations during play
	Self-centered but does distinguish between self and others
	Conscious of family group

2-3 years:

- Can put on clothing
- Most can dress self with supervision
- About age 3 most learn to separate from mother easily
- Play interactive games
- Toilet trained
- Unzips, zips
- Unbuckles and buckles
- Unbuttons and buttons
- Identity in terms of name, sex,
    and place in family well entrenched by age 2 1/2
- Initiates own play activities
- Dawdles
- Likes praise
- Alternates between dependence and self-contained
    behavior
- Shows pity, sympathy, modesty, and shame
- Good steering on push toys
- Can carry a breakable object
- Can pour from one container to another
- Auditory fears are prominent
- Gets drink unassisted
- Learns to avoid simple hazards (careful of stairs,
    stoves, etc.)

3-4 years:

- Outstanding characteristic of 3-year-old is readiness to
    conform to the spoken word
- Can bargain with a 3-year-old
- Little errands near the house
- Capable of prolonged anxiety of fear
- Understands taking turns
- Starting to share
- Less rebellious than at 2 or 4
- Uses language to resist
- Toilet self during day
- Associative group play becoming prominent
- 50% dress without supervision by age 4, except for
    back button and tying shoes
- Visual fears become more prominent
- Fear of loss of parents

4-5 years:	Dogmatic and dramatic
	May argue about parental requests
	Control issues prominent for many children
	Begins cooperative group play
	Good imagination
	Unreasonable fears are common
	Nightmares prominent
	Alibis
	Likes silly rhymes, silly sounds, silly names, etc.
	Physically aggressive
	Most dress without assistance, except for back buttons and tying shoes
	Washes face and brushes teeth
	Self-sufficient in own home
	Likes to dress up in grown-up clothes
	Laces shoes
	Can go on errands in the neighborhood
	Calls attention to own performance
	Tends to be bossy and critical of others
	Beginning sense of time in terms of yesterday, tomorrow, sense of how long an hour is, etc.

Fine Motor Skills

0-1 month:	Follows to midline
	Mouth and eye muscles are the most active
	Sucking reflex
	Seeking movements with mouth
	Grasp reflex (but no reaching)
	Hands usually closed

2-3 months:	Grasps rattle briefly
	Follows dangling objects past midline
	Puts hands together

3-4 months:	Looks at small objects
	Many reach for objects (frequently using both hands)
	Most follow to 180°
	Sucks at hand or fingers
	Regards hands

| 4-6 months: | Reaching for objects with alternating one-handedness |
| | Many transfer objects from one hand to the other |

4-6 months, Continued	Looks for objects which leave visual field
	Rakes pellet or raisin with hand
	Inspects objects with hands, eyes, and mouth
6-9 months:	Grasps objects in each hand simultaneously
	Transfers objects
	Thumb-finger grasp (most)
	Tongue control (noted when being fed)
	Beginning sense of twoness (container and contained, i.e., puts in and takes out)
9-12 months:	Most work for toy out of reach
	Most have neat pincer grasp
	Bangs together objects held in each hand
	Momentarily brings one object over another
	Grasp release crude
12-16 months:	Visual preference for circle
	Neat pincer grasp
	Puts ball in box
	Puts pellet or raisin in bottle
	Tower of two cubes
	Most scribble spontaneously (palmar grasp of pencil or crayon)
16-18 months:	Grasp release exaggerated
	Turns pages several at a time
	Knows where things are or belong
	Starts to point
	Frequently gives evidence of knowing that something has been completed (i.e., waves good-bye, reports soiling)
	Holds spoon
	Holds cup
	Dumps pellet from bottle after demonstration
	Many copy vertical line
18-24 months:	Tower of four cubes
	Many do tower of six cubes
	Most imitate vertical line
	Dumps pellet from bottle spontaneously
	Strings beads or places rings on spindles
	Matches colors frequently

18-24 months, Continued	Folds paper once imitatively
	Turns pages singly
	Can wiggle thumb
	Can wiggle tongue
	Tries to snip with scissors
	Uses color names incorrectly
	Uses number words to accompany serial pointing (a precursor of true counting)
	Starts to imitate horizontal line
	Imitates train with blocks
24-30 months:	Tower of eight cubes
	Holds pencil by fingers (instead of palmar grasp)
	Imitates horizontal line well
	Continuous circles
	Can unzip and zip
	Unbuckles after imitation
	Adds chimney cube to train
	Completes formboard
30-36 months:	Likes crayons
	Likes puzzle type toys
	Folds paper lengthwise and crosswise but not diagonal (cannot yet imitate diagonal line with pencil either)
	Tower of nine or ten cubes
	Most can match colors, but not correctly name them
	Imitates building of three cube bridge
	Copies a circle
	Buckles after demonstration
	Points to simple geometric shapes (when named)
	Completes formboard quickly and correctly
	Learning to unbutton
36-48 months:	Copies cross
	Smooth grasp release
	Draws picture and names it after drawing
	Copies three cube bridge (no imitation)
	Understands longer vs. shorter
	Understands "give me the heavy block"
	Draws person with two parts
	Can button
	Can lace

48-60 months:	Counts five objects correctly
	Draws a person with three parts
	50% copy a square without demonstration (additional 25% copy square after demonstration)
	Draws unmistakable person, but arms and legs may still come directly from head
	Copies a triangle
	Copies linear figures (e.g., <, T, L) with rare reversals; may continue to have some problems with diagonals

Gross Motor Skills

0-1 month:	Lifts head when on abdomen
	Head averted to preferred side when on back; only momentarily to mid-line position
	Equal movements of extremities

1-3 months:	Head up to 45° when on abdomen
	Grasps rattle briefly
	Head erect when held in sitting position
	Bears fraction of weight when held in standing position

3-4 months:	Head up to 90° when on abdomen
	Head more frequently midline
	Arm and hand movements in large part correlated with position of head and eyes
	Can roll from side to back

4-6 months:	Rolls first from abdomen to back
	Rolls from back to abdomen
	Bears increasing amount of weight when held upright
	No head lag when pulled to sitting

6-9 months:	Sits without support
	Increasingly mobile
	Stands holding on
	Pushes self to sitting
	Pulls self to standing (close to 9 months)
	Leans forward and can push self back to erect position

9-12 months:	Crawls with left-right alteration
	Walks with support

9-12 months, Continued	Stands momentarily Takes a few unsteady steps
12-15 months:	Stands well alone Walks well Stoops and recovers Falls by collapse
15-18 months:	Runs stiffly Climbs up on furniture Walks backwards Walks into ball in attempt to kick
18-21 months:	Kicks ball forward after demonstration Some throw ball overhand Walks up steps holding on with one hand, marking time Down stairs on abdomen or bottom Runs fairly well Pulls toy when walking Squats in play
21-24 months:	Runs well Walks down steps holding on, marking time Kicks ball on verbal command
24-30 months:	Jumps in place with both feet Most can throw ball overhand Walks on tiptoe after demonstration (many walk on tip toe spontaneously before) Many try to pedal tricycle and some succeed Tries to stand on one foot
30-36 months:	Alternates feet going up stairs Jumps from bottom step Most can pedal tricycle Most can stand on one foot momentarily Many can do broad jump
36-48 months:	Most can stand on one foot for five seconds Many can hop on one foot Most can do broad jump
48-60 months:	Most can hop on one foot Most can skip alternating feet Most can balance on one foot for ten seconds Most can do forward heel-toe walk

94

Language

0-4 weeks:
Cries prior to sleep
Cries if uncomfortable or in state of tension; undifferentiated initially, but gradually varies with cause
Responds to bell
By 3-4 weeks, infant smiles selectively in response to mother's voice
Quieted by human voice and soft sounds

1-3 months:
Startles to loud sounds
Babbles and coos increasingly
Most laugh out loud
Most squeal and gurgle

3-6 month:
Increasing vocalizations
Crows and squeals
Spontaneously vocalizes vowels, consonants, and a few syllables
Responds to tone of voice and inflection

6-9 months:
Says *mama* and/or *dada*, nonspecific
Beginning imitation of speech sounds
Turns towards voice
Many single syllable sounds—ma, da, ba
Spontaneously blows bubbles

9-12 months:
Imitates speech sounds
Obeys "give it to me"
Says *mama* and/or *dada*, specific
Experiments with sounds

12-15 months:
Increasing use of jargon
Communicates by gesture
Vocalizes more than cries for attention
Usually has three- to five-word vocabulary
Understands word *no*
Shakes head to indicate *no*
Points to picture of dog

15-18 months:	Vocalizes *no*
	Vocabulary of about ten words
	50% will start to point to parts of body
	Uses words with gestures
	Fluent use of jargon
	Points to pictures of common objects (may name them while pointing)
18-24 months:	Uses words *me* and *mine*
	Markedly increases vocabulary
	Points consistently to body parts
	Combines two to three words
	Names pictures of common objects
	Follows simple directions
	Most discard jargon
	Understands *yours* vs. *mine*
	Starts to use *you*
	Most words are nouns
24-30 months:	Half will use plurals
	Says first name
	Most have vocabulary of three hundred words
	Prone to call self by given name
	Uses word *I* (by 30 months)
	Speaks with sing-song rhythm
	Phrases and three to four word sentences
30-36 months:	Most use plurals
	50% give first and last name
	Increasing use of verbs
	Beginning use of adjectives
	Tells own sex by 36 months
	By 36 months most have one-thousand word vocabulary
	Learns to listen and listens to learn
	Expressive
	"What's that?" is common question
36-48 months:	Uses words for ordering perceptions
	Uses questions to learn language structure
	Increasing use of words to assert autonomy
	Most give first and last name (not necessarily true for foster children, as last name is rarely stressed at this age)

36-48 months, Continued	Tells age by holding up fingers usually
	Most answer simple comprehensive questions
	Most understand prepositions and are starting to use them
	Most understand color names
	Most understand larger vs. shorter
	Counts to three
	Repeat three or four digits
	Repeats three or four nonsense syllables
	Has 50-75 percent use of consonants
	By age 4 has vocabulary of fifteen hundred words

48-60 months:	Uses color names
	First understands then uses adverbs
	Uses prepositions
	Defines words in terms of use
	Understands opposite analogies
	Uses questions to order experiences and conceptualize; lots of why and how questions
	Counts out objects correctly to five at least (many can count out eight to ten objects correctly)
	Names common coins
	Consecutive vs. comparative thinking (big, bigger, biggest instead of big vs. small)
	Loves new words, especially "funny sounding" words
	Increasing use of imagination
	Enjoys humor and self laughing
	50% can identify composition of common objects
	Follows two or three stage command
	Elaborate replies
	Vocabulary of over two thousand words
	Correct usage of all parts of speech
	By 5 years most infantile articulation disappears
	100% use of consonants
	Corrects own errors in learning to pronounce new words

IV The Ages Six through Ten

Using the family as the base from which they venture out, children between six and ten turn to mastering situations encountered outside the family unit. They devote their energies to learning in school, to developing motor skills, and to social interactions primarily with peers of the same sex. The issue of "fairness" or lack of it in life is important to children at this stage. Identifying with parents, there is further incorporation of family values, and conscience development progresses to relying on internal, as opposed to external, controls. It is a period during which children become increasingly aware of their own strengths and weaknesses.

Usually between ages five-and-a-half and six, just as at one, there is a change in the child's perspective of the world. It now widens to include a variety of situations occurring outside the home and involving non-family members . He is once again aware of more than he can comfortably manage. Because of this the child once again enters a period of disequilibrium, with increased frustration and regression to earlier levels of behavior under stress. The outstanding characteristic of the the six-year-old is his poor ability to modulate. Typical sixes are very active. They constantly wiggle, bite their nails, kick tables, or fall off their chairs. They are either dancing with delight or drooping in despair.

Sometimes as children approach age six, they again aspire to more than they can manage to accomplish easily. They become more easily frustrated. Screaming and tantrums may recur. Their insistence on having their own way is a sign that sixes feel out of control of their lives.

Sixes are good at starting things, but poor at completing them. They depend on positive direction and guidance from adults. A well-regulated schedule of consistent mealtimes, bedtimes, and other daily rituals is helpful at home. At school, first-graders need a teacher who is in charge in the classroom, but who understands the children's needs for physical activity and physical closeness.

Not infrequently, six year olds regress to behaviors normal for earlier ages. They may revert to sucking thumbs, talking baby talk, and retrieving favorite stuffed animals from the toy box. Children are usually as confused by these behaviors as their parents. Telling them that they are acting like a baby or making fun of them doesn't help. If parents comment that children this age often use baby talk, but that adults like it better when the child talks in a more grown-up way, it will often help. This gives the child a chance to express himself again and gives parents a chance to praise him for correct performance.

In general, with six-year-olds, praise works better than alternative disciplinary measures. This means that parents need to look for behaviors they can commend and avoid focusing on negative behaviors. Frequently the creative parent can find a behavior to praise that interferes with an undesirable behavior. Complimenting children for doing something correctly works better than commenting on the undesired behavior. The focus needs to be on what the parent wants the child to do rather than on what he is not to do.

Mrs. Covelli had noticed, when visiting her adopted daughter's first grade classroom, that the teacher frequently commented on how quietly the children at table number two were working, rather than reprimanding the children at a different table for being noisy. It seemed to work. She decided to try a similar approach at home in addressing April's habit of sucking her thumb when she was watching T.V. Observing April over a period of a week, Mrs. Covelli noted that if her daughter had a small toy in her hand when she was watching T.V. she did not suck her thumb but instead fingered the toy. Mom started making comments such as, "I like seeing you play quietly with toys when you are watching T.V." Subsequently, when she noted April's thumb in her mouth, Mom would not directly comment on the thumbsucking, but would hand the child a favorite small toy and make a positive comment about playing with it.

Although sixes enjoy doing tasks with someone, they do not do well when sent off to do a task for someone else. "Let's clean your room. I'll make your bed while you pick up your clothes and toys," works much better than, "Go clean your room." Repeated reminders seem to be necessary for children of this age.

Many normal six-year-olds take things that belong to others and then do not accept responsibility for their actions. It is not uncommon for first-graders to come home with small toys and pencils that they "found." Having children return them to the owner or turn them in to the lost and found is more positive than forcing them to apologize for having them.

As children enter this period of emotional disequilibrium, aggressiveness tends to return. Since they are going through an age of increasing frustration, there tends to be a recurrence of temper tantrums. This is an ideal time to teach children more appropriate ways to express frustration, since they have verbal and intellectual skills they did not previously possess. Children may destroy things if sent to their room, or they may refuse to remain in the room because of their increased aggressiveness. They are quite likely to call people names. Most commonly these names involve bathroom type words, such as, "You are a big piece of poop." Sixes are likely to make verbal threats. Overall, they tend to contradict, argue, and resist. They may hit or kick at either adults or other children. Cruelty to animals is occasionally present at this age.

As they reach seven, children usually calm down. They do not like interruptions and become very absorbed in whatever they are doing. It is not uncommon for a seven-year-old to lie on the floor watching television or playing before dinner while his mother calls several times for him to come and set the table. The child does not respond, and the mother is convinced that the child is choosing to ignore her. However, he may be concentrating. This is the age at which children normally learn to screen out distractions and focus on one thing. To check this out the parent can touch the child's shoulder lightly. If he is concentrating, he will usually startle, but then be able to "hear" the parent.

Children who don't acquire this ability to focus on one stimulus and screen out others have other, usually more severe, problems. Distractability is one of the several signs of Attention Deficit Disorder, which will be more fully discussed in a later chapter. If children seem to have difficulty concentrating, it is a good idea to check and be sure that they aren't suffering from some kind of learning disability.

Sevens, like sixes, enjoy physical closeness and occasional quick touching from the teacher. Children at seven still depend on reminders and guidance from adults. When they're upset, they are likely to become sullen and withdrawn. It's at this age that children frequently stomp off and slam doors. Seven-year-olds need reassurance from adults that it is okay to make mistakes, and they need help correcting those errors. They don't respond well to lectures or scolding.

Many children in first or second grades have high expectations of themselves. Such children may frequently be disappointed and frustrated by their own performance. They may act out or start crying, feel embarrassed, and then feel even more frustrated. If this sequence of events occurs at school, the children still have a lot of uncomfortable feelings when they return home. It is quite common in this kind of circumstance for a child to pick a fight with a parent so he can release his pent-up emotions. This doesn't mean the children plan this kind of event. It happens because they are not yet very good at handling strong feelings.

Adults often wish children would just talk about their feelings. However, children of this age still have difficulties talking instead of acting out when they feel things strongly. However, they may be able to talk about the feelings in retrospect. The goal of the supportive parent in this situation is to help children learn more appropriate ways of expressing frustration while, at the same time, not making the children feel that they are "wrong" or "bad".

Sevens have not yet learned to lose. Frequently if children this age see that they are going to lose, the game never quite gets finished. The playing board gets upset, or the child provokes the parent who may say, "If the game isn't going to be fun, just put it away." Children of this age still frequently cheat in order to win.

Sevens cannot yet laugh at their own mistakes. When humor is used with them, the children may believe that adults are making fun of them rather than minimizing the seriousness of the behavior. Sevens are becoming aware of "fairness" and "luck." Helping the child to learn to reason can be used with children who constantly bombard parents with cries of, "It's not fair!"

Max

Max, seven, frequently comments on his parents' unfairness in their treatment of him compared to his nine-year-old brother, Jess. "I never get to do anything. Jess gets to do everything he wants. It's not fair."

Dad takes Max aside saying, "Now let me get this straight, you want me to treat you the same way as your brother?" Max vehemently agrees. Dad continues the discussion. "Let me make certain that I understand. You think that every time Jess goes to a friend's home, you should go somewhere also. Is that right?" Max nods his agreement. Dad continues, "And if Jess gets a new pair of shoes you should get some also?"

"That's what's fair," is Max's rejoinder. Dad, looking perplexed comments, "Does that mean that when Jess gets in trouble and can't play Nintendo for two days, you should be restricted too? I don't think I approve of that kind of fairness. Do you?"

Dad can then move on to helping Max begin to accept that true fairness is meeting each person's individual needs, not treating everyone in an identical manner.

Of course, true fairness in dealing with children is not always equalizing everything, but rather giving to each according to his needs. Some children need more attention than others. Some need more discipline than others. In fact equalizing everything for siblings poses many more problems than it solves. It implies that the child is in no way special or unique, and that ,in and of itself, does harm to the child's self-esteem.

By age seven most have made obvious gains in their cognitive functioning. There is a significant maturing in time and space orientation. Their attention span has noticeably increased. When helped to do so, for the first time they are able to put themselves in other's shoes, consciously recognizing the impact of their own behaviors on others. They can recognize similarities in objects even though there are apparent differences as well. Most sevens can tell time and recite the months of the year although it is common that they may omit one or two months. They have an understanding of the order in which seasons occur. Their internal sense of time is developing.

Seven-year-olds are less aggressive and have fewer tantrums than they did at six. They exhibit less resistance to requests, using the "It's not fair," comment instead. If angry, sevens may stalk off to their room. In general, they prefer to withdraw from parents rather than stay and fight as they did at six.

Eight is an expansive age. Although eights may be selfish, at times demanding considerable attention, at other times they are gay and cheerful. They are impatient with themselves and with others. Eights may be snippy in talk with family members. They are curious about what others are doing so they may seem snoopy as well. Verbally, they are often out-of-bounds. They boast, exaggerate, and may share private family information with virtual strangers.

Eight-year-olds are improving their gross motor skills, but physical injuries are common as they misjudge what they can do. They are just beginning to be capable of prolonged periods of group activity and are beginning to learn to lose at games. They are sensitive to criticism, especially when it is dispensed in front of others.

Their intellectual abilities, too, expand. A sense of connection between past, present, and future is emerging. Eights are interested in their past history. They enjoy reviewing baby books and family albums and like to hear about their own escapades as younger children. In addition, they are interested in the future and what it will hold for them. They may be certain that they will become Olympic medalists or movie stars. It is best that adults treat these boasts as possible long-range goals, helping children focus on the skills they need to start developing now to facilitate their long-range goals. Time will put their true potential into perspective.

Eights express a deepening interest in life and life processes. They are better observers than they were at seven. They begin to see conclusions, contexts, and implications that they did not see before. Deductive and inductive reasoning skills begin to emerge. Eight is the age of the riddle. Nothing infuriates the child this age more than having his riddle ruined when a sibling pops up with the answer. Tactful adults pretend that they don't know the answer to the riddle. Eight-year-olds are developing a sense of humor.

When they feel attacked or criticized eights are more likely to respond with hurt feelings than with aggression. When very angry, they may become verbally aggressive with name calling prominent.

Although typically nine-year-olds experience quick extreme emotional shifts, these swings are short lived, and the children appear to be more stable. Children of this age are becoming more independent. They are more responsible, cooperative, and dependable. They are capable of concentrating for several hours. This is an optimum age for them to perfect their proficiency in basic subjects at school. In fact, if a child cannot read, use basic math concepts, and write by the end of third grade, it is unlikely that these skills will be acquired without considerable special effort on the part of both the child and the school.

Nines like to plan ahead. They may appear absent-minded, but they are usually just busy thinking. They like to classify, identify, and order information. Hobbies that involve collecting are common in this age group.

Nines are beginning to learn to function within a group and to subordinate their own interests to those of the group. In fact, in fourth grade the teacher becomes more of a facilitator, and peer pressure becomes increasingly important. Combined with the intellectual gains they made at eight the child has now made a considerable leap in cognitive skills. He is able to take information learned from a variety of sources—i.e. school, home, T.V.—and combine it to form his own unique insights. Prior to this, most learning is by rote memory, the child giving back what he has taken in with little modification.

Nines work hard and play hard. They become interested in competitive sports, and although they may not like it, they learn to lose. In fact, the nine-year-old's interest in sports is primarily related to the social aspects of the game—an attitude that frustrates more competitive parents. However, the child's outlook will gradually change to the desire to do well as he gets older.

Around age nine, most children start to internalize their guilt feelings. Rather than being fearful of external consequences for misbehaviors their anticipation of the guilt feelings which will follow misbehaviors frequently are enough to help them follow through with expectations. They carry parental expectations within themselves and are no longer so dependent upon the immediate presence of an adult.

By age nine swearing shifts from elimination related words to a vocabulary associated with sex. Fighting and "beating him up" are common talk among boys, but again the actual aggression is more likely to be verbal than physical. Nines are critical of others and may object to what others say or do.

Ten, like five, is another age when children's perceptions and abilities seem to coincide. In general, ten-year-olds seem relaxed and casual. They can participate in discussions of social and world problems. In fact, this is a good age for parents to openly share their values with their children.

Friends are coming into direct competition with family for the ten's time and interest. It is not uncommon for a ten to believe a friend over a parent. Boys may fight, wrestle, shove, and punch to show friendship, while girls hold hands, gossip, and write notes to each other. Sharing secrets and pondering mysteries with friends delight children of this age.

Ten-year-olds still enjoy family pursuits as long as they don't interfere with activities with friends. Peer influence is increasingly important. Tens do not like to be singled out in front of friends. A wise parent or teacher knows it is more effective at this age to criticize, correct, or even praise the child in private rather than in front of other family members or the class.

It is not uncommon for children of nine or ten to have one last physical tantrum when confronted by parents about something. Following such an outburst, the child is quite likely to be embarrassed by his own behavior. However, ten with its overall emotional equilibrium, is not characteristically an angry age. Instead crying is a common response to frustration.

Fears and Worries During the Grade School Years

Sixes, in general, are more fearful than they were at five. It is common for sixes to be afraid of thunder, lightning, and fire. They also have a fear of deformities and a fear that parents may die, thereby abandoning them. Sixes are very fearful of even slight injuries to themselves and respond out of proportion to the severity. It is common for the child this age to scream at the sight of his own blood. Rather than ridiculing or minimizing the child's fears, it is best to clean the wound, put on a Band-aid, give the child an extra hug, and reassure him that he will heal well because he has a strong, healthy body. This fear of bodily harm seems to be related to the youngster's emerging awareness of death combined with his lack of knowledge about the potential effects of various injuries.

Nightmares are most prominent between the ages of four and six. The child who awakens afraid needs the reassurance of a trusted adult that he is safe and secure.

Seven-year-olds fear the unknown and are quite likely to be fearful when they find themselves in a new or unfamiliar situation. However, they are beginning to learn ways to cope with their own fears, and are no longer so dependent upon adults for help. Frequently they are ashamed of fears and may be embarrassed to be seen crying.

By age eight, children's fears are decreasing, although they may worry about not being liked by peers. Eights love to frighten others with snakes, bugs, and scary stories.

Nines are more likely to worry than be afraid. They are upset by their own mistakes and worried about school failure. They enjoy frightening others and being frightened themselves. They are, in fact, proud of being "frightened to death" and living to tell about it. Usually nine-year-olds are not afraid if no one is home after school so long as they know what to expect. Ten, overall, is a less fearful age than the next two years. However, fears of being killed or kidnapped may be present.

The Parents' Role

The security of family relationships is what the child depends upon as his source of energy for coping with widening environmental challenges. Parents need to allow and encourage their grade school children to have opportunities to spend considerable time with peers and to become aware of their own likes and dislikes, as well as their strengths and weaknesses. This means that children need to be provided with opportunities to explore a variety of interests and try a range of activities, always learning more about themselves. This is a special problem for latch key children who are frequently excluded from after school peer group activities.

Parents sometimes want children to make long term decisions without the benefit of first trying an activity to see if they enjoy it. Team sports provide a variety of advantages for the child. They facilitate gains in gross motor skills. They provide opportunities for children to have time with peers in a supervised, structured, but non-academic setting. And, finally, they usually last for nearly an ideal time span, long enough for the child to get through both the initial ups and downs of a new activity and to find out what their aptitudes and interests are, yet short enough that there is a logical ending point. Similar time frames, six weeks to three months, can be set up for other activities as well. When a child is expressing an interest in playing a musical instrument, the parent might suggest that they rent the instrument and contract for a specific length of time at the end of which the child can either decide to drop the lessons or to continue.

In their interactions with the child eight and up, parents can facilitate inductive and deductive reasoning by leading children through the steps. They can help the child understand how past life events affect current and future adjustment, using themselves as examples. It is only when the child recognizes himself and others as the same people they have always been, in spite of changes in abilities or appearances, that he can really think of origins.

During this period of development there are many opportunities for parents to help children learn acceptable ways of discharging their many emotions. When they are excited and happy what can they do that won't get them into trouble? Most become more active, but the physical discharge of energy inside the house—throwing a ball or jumping on furniture—may lead to their getting into trouble. Are they allowed to cry when sad or are they admonished with statements such as, "Oh, its not really so bad. Cheer up." Even young boys are frequently told, "Big boys don't cry." How can they release the tension that comes with anger and frustration, particularly when they are angry at a parent?

Denise

We met Lily's older sister, nine-year-old Denise, in the introduction. She no longer lives with her younger siblings, but resides with a single foster parent, Shelby Stein. Although Denise never talks of being angry at her birth mother or about earlier life events, she frequently becomes angry with Shelby. When she glares at or talks back to her foster parent, the latter sends Denise to her room. En route, Denise stomps off. Shelby is quite likely to call Denise back saying, "There is no reason to stomp; go back to your room the right way." If Denise slams the door when sent to her room, she is asked to close it correctly.

Rather than helping Denise learn to express her anger and frustration in admissable ways, Shelby is teaching her that it is not acceptable at all to be angry at a parent. This will not be helpful to Denise in acknowledging earlier life events and her feelings about her birth mother.

Providing clear messages about family values facilitates conscience development. However, families should make a clear distinction between minor and major values. Family habits, such as food preferences, the frequency of changing clothes or bathing, the words permitted to be used in anger are all minor values. For any child, but most particularly for a child joining a new family, they can be explained with, "This is how we do it in our family," as opposed to focusing on an absolute right or wrong. Major values on the other hand reflect basic attitudes about the rights, boundaries, and worth of both the individual and the group.

Duke

In addition to having Lily in their home, Mr. and Mrs. Wentz are also foster parents for her brother Duke. In confronting Duke's aggressive behaviors, they differentiate between major and minor values. Early in his placement, Duke would physically lash out at Lily whenever he was angry, frustrated, or was feeling out of control. Both foster parents consistently interrupted his physical outbursts, giving calm but firm messages that it was not acceptable for anyone, child or adult, to physically hurt someone else even when he was angry.

On the other hand, when Duke would start to masturbate in the living room, their message was quite different. They would comment, "We know that touching your penis feels good. It is okay to touch yourself. But, we have a rule in this house about where you may do this. In our family, when children want to touch their private parts, they need to have privacy. You may touch your penis when you are alone in your bedroom."

It is important for children during the grade school years to learn more about themselves as babies and preschoolers and to incorporate this knowledge into their continually evolving sense of identity. This is a time for integration of the past with the present and future. Children in the foster care system who do not have access to information about their early years and about their birth parents are likely to have difficulty with this.

Parents who adopt children at younger ages will need to share additional information with their children as they reach these years. This need in no way reflects upon the children's feelings toward the adoptive family, but rather relates to a healthy desire to increase knowledge of themselves and integrate it into their knowledge of self. Between ages nine and ten is a good time to review the child's Lifebook.

Parent Issues

Parents who are themselves very controlling or self-centered may be threatened by the relationships that their children develop outside the family. They are likely not to allow the child adequate opportunities for interacting with adults and peers away from home.

Children with behavioral or academic problems may be abused or emotionally rejected particularly by parents who themselves had similar problems when they were children. The child's behaviors trigger old feelings to resurface in the adults. As these feelings resurface the parent may lash out at the child.

As at earlier ages, parents who are rigid in terms of their beliefs about right and wrong may resort to exceedingly harsh physical punishment, rejection, or negative labelling when the child is demonstrating normal-for-age behaviors that the parents condemn. Adults who have not themselves developed adequate outlets for their own strong feelings may feel threatened by their child's emotional outbursts.

Adolescence   V

Adolescence is the period of transitioning from childhood to adulthood. Teens continually remind parents that they are no longer children. Although this is true, grownups must also remember that the adolescent does not yet have the skills necessary to be an adult in our complex society. An adolescent is neither child nor adult. Adolescence is accompanied by physical, intellectual, and psychological maturation. Ideally during this transition the young person will gain the skills necessary for becoming a successful adult.

Although much of the focus of this section will be on the psychological tasks, it is the intellectual gains which can help the young person and adult together work to accomplish these undertakings. It is during adolescence that the individual takes the final steps to adult thought processes. The adolescent becomes able to reason logically about things he has never himself directly experienced. "How might it have felt to have been born to a different family? To have had different life experiences?" He is able to hypothesize. He no longer needs an adult to help lead him through the stages of complex inductive and deductive reasoning. He can do it on his own. That is not to say, however, especially in emotionally charged situations, that adult guidance and collaboration in reasoning is not useful. It is.

The primary psychological tasks of adolescence echo the tasks of years one to five. The young person must once again psychologically separate, this time from the family, finding his place in society as a whole, rather than solely as a member of a family. He is cutting emotional ties instead of seeking gratification within the family (Viorst, 1986). A surge in identity formation once again accompanies the separation process. Blos (1962) comments that the adolescent separation process occurs at two levels. Externally, he withdraws some of his emotional energy from the parents and reinvests it in peer relationships. Internally, too, he disengages from his early childhood identification with the parents and internalizes new models provided by a more diverse group, such as teachers, peers, and heroes. Without this disengagement, he points out that identity formation cannot progress.

Simultaneously the adolescent is expected to move from depending upon external controls supplied by adults and toward relying on using internalized controls, thereby exhibiting both independence and self-control. The complexity of these tasks is compounded by the sexualization that accompanies the rapid hormonal changes of adolescence.

In our culture, in children we value dependence, obedience, and lack of sexual interactions with others. However, we expect adults to be independent, responsible for their own actions, and able to form a meaningful sexual relationship with another adult (Jewett, 1980). Adolescence is the process of changing from one set of expectations to the other. It does not happen overnight. It does not happen smoothly. Not only the young person, but also adults living with him, find themselves caught up in this period of rapid change with its accompanying stress.

Adolescents are moody. Normally they alternate between sometimes being unreliable and other times being dependable and responsible. They have both abundant sexual and aggressive impulses. Adults need to help them separate the two and learn to cope with each in socially acceptable ways. As they psychologically separate from the family, they are likely to oppose family rules, values, and expectations. While they are rebellious with adults, they seem to be overcompliant with peers. At the same time they have a strong need to belong in a family and to be taken seriously. Without this, it is difficult for them to successfully accomplish the tasks that face them during these turbulent years.

Although many people equate adolescence with the teen years, the physical and emotional changes that mark this stage of development usually start during the preteen years. This is especially true for girls, who, on the whole, physically mature two years ahead of boys. The sequencing of the physical changes is discussed as part of sexual development later in this chapter. Not only does adolescence start before the teen years, but if we define adulthood as being emotionally and financially independent, this stage now extends well into the twenties. Preoccupation with body changes precedes the identity struggles (Viorst, 1986).

In early adolescence, until about age fifteen-and-a-half, the focus is on becoming comfortable with body changes, psychological separation, gaining self-control, and beginning to sort out the identity issues. During the latter part of adolescence, skill acquisition, continued identity formation, and preparing for emancipation, while remaining emotionally connected to family, takes precedence. During this phase there is increased value clarification and commitment to ideals.

The adolescent is trying to answer four questions about himself: 1) Who am I? 2) Where do I belong? 3) What can I do, or be? and 4) What do I believe in? (Jewett, 1980). Adolescents, like preschoolers, are prone to ego-centric, magical thinking. A major goal for all adults working with teens is to help them expand their thinking by becoming aware of the many choices between the extremes of either/or thinking. There are two periods during adolescence when identity formation is a central issue. The first is in early adolescence as the young person, in the process of psychologically separating from parents and identifying more with the peer group, is addressing the questions, "Who am I?" and, "Where do I belong?" The second occurs very late in adolescence, usually after emancipation. During this latter period much of the emphasis centers on "What kind of a person am I?" and "What do I believe in?" This relates to long term goals, to decisions around employment goals, interpersonal adult-adult relationships, and continued value clarification. All of these are involved in the once again emerging sense of self as a whole, separate from family, that determines the end of adolescence and the beginning of adulthood. It is difficult for the young person to attain this more advanced aspect of identity without some physical distance from parents. On the other hand, one component of identity considers the question, "How do I relate to my parents and siblings now that I don't live with them?"

Control issues are a necessary accompaniment of spurts in identity development. *Me*, *mine*, and *no* once again are evident behaviorally, if not verbally. Teens are egocentric, seeing their own needs as paramount, and other family members' needs as secondary. When a young child exhibits control issues, parents usually have the physical and psychological power to take charge of the situation. However, with adolescents the adults' power base is strongly diminished. Their primary power with teens resides in the strength of their relationships, rather than in physical power. Adolescents may demonstrate a series of provocative behaviors that encourage adults to respond by setting up control issues. Rather than focusing on taking responsibility for his own behaviors, the young person then puts all of his energy into resisting adults, trying to prove that they have little control over him. Adults, especially parents, need to facilitate the development of further self-control and responsibility on the part of the youngster.

Many teens in placement need a level of supervision that is no longer routinely supplied for adolescents. Although the young person may not need physical control, he may still need an adult presence to insure that he does not get into trouble and that he is interacting with others, not isolating. For families with all adults working outside the home this is difficult. Rarely is before, or after, school day care available for this age. Some families whose youngsters have previously been attending a day care center have been able to continue sending their adolescents there. Some teen girls have become "helpers" for the regular daycare personnel working with younger children. This may even help the older girl both fill in some of her earlier play and social skills while allowing her to observe alternate disciplinary techniques without having her be in charge of other children.

Gradually, adolescents shift their dependency needs from family to peer group. The adolescent who doesn't know how to be rebellious is likely to select friends who are. Unfortunately, victims and victimizers tend to be drawn to each other. With the onset of dating, dependency needs shift to members of the opposite sex.

Especially in early adolescence, it is important for adults to insure that youth have adequate opportunities to spend time with peers. However, since many demonstrate poor self-control, they may need to be involved in some form of adult supervised, semi-structured activity, such as a team sport, a club, or an adolescent church group. Adolescents need to learn which activities provide them with pleasure without putting themselves at risk for getting in trouble. Entertainment provides opportunities to increase feelings of self-worth, to develop interpersonal connections, and to relieve stress and frustration.

In general during adolescence, young people experience a year of expanding horizons with new challenges followed by a year of consolidation of gains. Both parents and teens can expect a year of turmoil to be followed by a year with some measure of reprieve in which to renew and once again strengthen relationships before moving into another year of rapid change.

Typical elevens show some similarities both to the early toddler stage and to children of five-and-a-half to six. They can fly into rage on short notice and burst out laughing with little provocation. They are once again emotionally unstable and always in motion. They are assertive, curious, investigative, talkative, and sociable. Elevens have a vast appetite both for food and for experience. They tire easily. Yet they commonly dislike going to bed at night and don't want to get up in the morning. They are in such a state of disequilibrium that even their temperature control is uneven. They always seem to be either too hot or too cold. Foods that previously tasted good may now be identified as too salty or not spicy enough, etc. Although they are beginning to take an interest in clothes, they usually don't take good care of them.

Elevens are beginning to see parents as individuals, not just as Mom and Dad, and are becoming critical of them. They dislike work and commonly spend more energy avoiding tasks than it would take to accomplish them. This is, the poorest age for getting along well with brothers and sisters. In general elevens best behaviors are away from home. Frequently adjustment at school is smoother than at home. Elevens like school more for friends than for learning. They compete for grades and in athletics.

Children at eleven become angry more often than they did at ten. It is common for them to yell, hit, and slam doors. Violent verbal retorts are frequent. Typical twelve-year-olds are less insistent, more reasonable, and more companiable than elevens. They try to win the approval of others. Although their peer group is increasingly important to them, they are less competitive within it than they were at eleven. They are able to do more independent work at school, and in general need less supervision. In fact at this age school is a source of great satisfaction for most children because of their capacity for prolonged periods of factual learning and because of their increase in conceptual ability. If they have problems in school, then a major source of positive feedback is eliminated. It is a parent's responsibility to insure that the school is responsive to the needs of their preteen. Twelves enjoy discussions and debates, but they are calmer in their arguments than they were at eleven or will be at thirteen.

This is normally a period that favors integration of the personality. Parents often describe the their twelve as likeable. Children this age have great enthusiasm for things they like and hatred for things they dislike. They are able to deal with others and can themselves be dealt with through humor. A wide range of difference is noted in the rate of physical growth among "twelves." Both boys and girls show an increasing interest in the opposite sex.

Twelves often assert themselves by talking back to parents. However, they may still strike out physically or throw things when they are angry. As the young person gets older, verbal responses become more and more frequent. Compared to age twelve, thirteens are less outgoing and inquisitive. Indeed they may sometimes seem isolated and moody. They use withdrawal from the family as an opportunity to mull over and incorporate experiences. This is not an indication of retreat from reality but rather of becoming introspective. In addition to mental reflection, thirteens spend a lot of time in front of the mirror reflecting on changes in their physical appearance. With the many changes in their bodies, the young person is having to integrate the new person as represented by the body changes with the old perceptions of self. The mirror fosters self-discovery and self-assurance.

In spite of the fact that thirteens are themselves very sensitive to criticism, they are frequently critical of parents. Commonly their censure reflects concerns or problems that they are trying to resolve in themselves. Although those in early adolescence don't yet have a clear picture of who they are, they know who they are not—"I'm not you Mom/Dad" is a frequent verbal and behavioral statement. Because of the thirteen's sensitivity to criticism, this is a good age for parents to be more verbally supportive than judgmental..

Many thirteens will argue about everything—is the sky blue or is it gray? is it hot or not today? is it fair for them to have to do chores? and on and on and on. Since by definition it takes at least two people to continue an argument, parents are provided with ample opportunities to model ways to stop arguments. As Claudia Jewett (1980) pointed out, wise parents frequently respond with the comment, "We have a difference of opinion." By doing this adults model that family members do not have to agree on everything, but can be respectful of differing views. Simultaneously parents save their energy for the conflicts that are important.

Once again, for good students school is a source of gratification. Thirteens are even better able to organize their time than previously. Their concentration is more sustained and their self-control is more evident. They become selective about what they choose to compete in, usually selecting those activities at which they excel.

Thirteens are more likely to be annoyed or irritated than to have outbursts of anger. They are not demonstrative. At the same time they are more aware of their own feelings. When they do become angry their most usual response is to leave the room. Sulking is common and they may get tears in response to anger. This in turn leads to embarrassment on the part of the young person. After physically withdrawing when angry, they need some time to regain self-control and get a handle on their feelings before an adult tries to resolve an argument, discussion, or disagreement.

At fourteen, youth typically become expansive and outgoing again. They are less withdrawn and appear happier, seeming to enjoy life. They are friendly both at home and away from it. Although they may be highly embarrassed by parental conduct, relationships within the family are usually less tense than at thirteen. Fourteen-year-olds and their families in general have more respect for, and confidence in, each other. Fourteens become increasingly objective and capable of self appraisal. With help they are capable of looking at both sides of an issue.

Girls at fourteen usually have the bodies of young women, while many boys have not yet matured physically. This is an age when further sex education is both needed and eagerly received. It is a peak age for telephone calls. The telephone not only allows adolescents to spend more time with peers without leaving the house, but it also allows them to talk about sex and relate to members of the opposite sex without risk of it leading to immediate sexual encounters.

Physical responses to anger and crying are less common at fourteen than they were previously. Swearing, name calling, and sarcasm are sometimes used. However, even these responses are frequently thought, said in private, or conveyed to a peer or sibling, rather than spoken directly to an adult. Leaving the room remains common at this age. When the young person is frustrated and is heading out of a room mumbling under his breath, the cautious parent does not ask him to speak up. Because of the adolescent's spurt in physical development, with its simultaneous increase in aggressive impulses, parents and teens may become locked into patterns of family violence if the parents themselves have problems with aggression.

Fifteen-year-olds frequently seem to be lazy or indifferent. They don't appear to expend much energy. In reality, their energies are focused inward rather than outward. Although most are not as intensely moody as at thirteen, there is a similarity in terms of withdrawal from the family. As at thirteen, this is related to preoccupation with feelings and thoughts.

Fifteens are experiencing a growing self-awareness and perceptiveness although they tend to cover up their emotions in front of others. They are trying to sort out their own potentials and limitations. "What can I do or what can I become?" begins to join the questions, "Who am I?" and "Where do I belong?" that were of prominent concern in the first part of adolescence. As a means of asserting independence, fifteens seem to resist even reasonable restrictions imposed by others.

Sixteens are usually more self-assured and self-reliant. By now both adolescents and their parents take this increased independence for granted. In general, there are fewer arguments between parents and adolescents. Sixteens have their emotions pretty well in hand and seem to be not so touchy or moody. In most states sixteen is the age of the one adolescent ritual of our culture—getting a driver's license. The driver's license is more than its name implies. This piece of paper signifies that society accepts that the adolescent has earned some independence. This poses a special problem for adolescents in foster care. Many are not able to get driver's licenses because of rules and regulations around insurance coverage. This reinforces their perceptions that they are different from others their age and that society as a whole views them as less adequate and capable than their peers.

As young people move into later adolescence, starting at about fifteen-and-a-half, their opposition usually becomes less pronounced. They no longer have to be so compliant with peers. It is okay for them to be different. They are more able to see advantages and disadvantages to situations. In general they demonstrate an increased tolerance both for peers and for adults. They are now starting to look toward emancipation and need to focus on acquiring the necessary skills.

By the time they become adults, youth need to have learned how to take care of themselves physically and psychologically. Physical self-care skills include personal hygiene, grooming, care and selection of personal property including clothing, shopping for food, cooking, managing a personal budget, etc. Psychological self-care skills include learning ways to take care of one's self emotionally. By adult years, an individual needs to be able to accurately determine when he needs help, to access the help that is indicated, and to assess its usefulness. They perceive seeking help when appropriate as a sign of good self-esteem rather than an indicator of incompetence. An inability to ask for help can become a major inhibiting factor in the development of autonomy and a sense of self-worth.

The person who does not have the social skills necessary to interact with others in an acceptable way is immediately marked as a "loser" even if he is highly successful in other ways. Such skills range from small interactions, such as answering the telephone, asking directions, and purchasing groceries, to much more complex interactions such as asking someone for a date, interacting with a potential employer, or being a good sport in a competitive situation. In addition, there are a whole separate set of skills that are particularly important to the development of meaningful interpersonal relationships. These include communication skills, sensitivity to others' needs and feelings, recognition of realistic expectations of others, etc. Many youth in care have problems making and keeping friends and need active teaching to learn the necessary skills. These skills seem to be easiest to acquire in group settings in which an adult leader facilitates acquiring and practicing them.

Everyone has to contend with emotions such as anger, sadness, joy, excitement, fear, etc. Adolescents experience emotions in a particularly intense manner. Many unacceptable behaviors reflect inappropriate expressions of underlying emotional states. Adolescents need adults to validate their feelings while, at the same time, they help the young person explore which of the acceptable behavioral expressions of the emotions work best for this teen. Having the skills to express these emotions appropriately and to manage them in a constructive way is essential for harmonious family life as an adult.

Most abused and neglected youth come from families where adults have had problems coping with their own emotional states. Anger and frustruation on the part of adults may have led to children being abused or ignored. The adolescent in placement will need help in learning how to manage these emotions in productive ways. Which behavioral expressions of emotion will lead to adequate relief without getting the young person into trouble with adults? Which may lead to an escalation of the underlying feelings?

Interpersonal conflict is an inevitable and potentially growth enhancing part of everyone's life. One of the most needed, yet underemphasized, skills is conflict resolution. The importance of reciprocal, rather than power-based, relationships becomes most evident here. Many youth have learned to make their only interpersonal connections through conflict. They may indeed think that "normal" families are conflict free. Services set up to serve adolescents need to themselves model conflict resolution skills rather than engaging in power-based interactions.

Jill

Jill, fifteen, has lived with the Kline foster family for two years. The plan is for her to continue to be a member of their family for the remainder of her adolescent years and, hopefully, beyond.

Her therapist, Mr. Ranier, and the Klines have a serious difference of opinion as to whether or not Jill should have contact with her birth parents. Their parental rights were terminated two years ago, but Jill has had very infrequent contact with them for five years. Mr. Ranier thinks that contact would help Jill in her struggle to clarify her own identity, and that it might even enhance her commitment to the Kline family. The foster parents, based on previous experience with a different child, think that contact at this time will pose more problems than it will solve.

Ms. Waters, the caseworker, knows that it is important to empower Jill's long-term caregivers, the Klines. However, she also respects the therapist's opinion. As the representative of the agency who is the legal parent in this case, the final decision rests with her. After a conference with her supervisor, it is decided that rather than using an authoritarian approach to the problem, they will use their consultant, who is well respected in the area, as a mediator in the case.

Initially, Dr. Norris, the consultant, meets with Ms Waters, Mr. and Mrs. Kline, and Mr. Ranier. Dr. Norris asks all of them to list their own primary goals for their relationships with Jill. Dr. Norris then moves on to have them describe their fears or worries about the alternate option.

During this process, it is determined that family, caseworker, and therapist all have similar long-range goals. The differences lie in their perceptions of which implementation will be most helpful and least harmful. Since they have an agreement on overall goals, Dr. Norris suggests that Jill at fifteen should have considerable input into the conflict resolution process. She is invited to the next mediation session which proceeds along the lines of restating the agreed-upon goals and then assessing the various options for attaining them. Jill's own fears and worries, as well as her hopes and dreams, become part of the assessment process. Everyone is involved in helping evaluate the pros and cons of each of the choices. As all involved add their input, the most helpful path toward attaining the goals becomes clearer to everyone.

In addition to these interpersonal and psychologically based skills, youth need to have basic academic and vocational skills to function in community schools or jobs. This is essential to a successful adjustment in our society. Without school and work skills, the odds for successful emancipation are greatly reduced.

According to Viorst (1986) "growing up means narrowing the distance between our dreams and our possibilities." Either/or thinking is especially prominent in its influence on setting goals for the future. Adolescents are prone to overestimating or underestimating their own abilities. They believe reality is reversible and there is a lack of sense of permanency about any decision. Problems delaying gratification may influence choices.

Young people repeatedly question their own ideals and those of others. They may try to live in a variety of value systems at the same time. Discussions about the importance of values and how each adult member of the family developed his own standards can help the adolescent intellectually explore alternatives without necessarily actively trying out each of the options.

Idealism is a common characteristic of late adolescence. Commitment to an ideal helps fill the void caused by increasing independence from family. The idealism of some adolescents may center on "rescuing" birth family members. The danger of all idealism is that the young person may set unrealistic goals and then perceive himself as a failure when he is unable to achieve these expectations. The adolescent may need assistance in learning to assess others' readiness to change. They may need aid in determining how to help others change without either rescuing or controlling them.

Marilyn is nineteen. In spite of some tumultuous times in early adolescence, currently she is making good choices in her life. She has been talking with her adoptive parents about her concerns for her twenty-five-year-old biological brother who is always in trouble with the law. Currently he is in jail. Marilyn wonders what she can do to help Cliff.

Marilyn

Her parents are concerned that if she becomes involved with Cliff she will be vulnerable to psychological, and possibly even physical, harm when he gets out of jail. They want to protect her from that. On the other hand, they remind each other that it was their own dual beliefs that those who are blessed with more have a responsibility to share with others, and that when given help and support, people can change that led them to adoption. They had adopted Marilyn when she was seven. Certainly some of their own magical thinking about love conquering all has been modified during the past twelve years. However, they also realize that their commitment to Marilyn has forced them to really change and grow in positive ways, just as much as it has seemed to help her.

They decide to talk to Marilyn about both their pleasure that she has chosen many of their values and their current concerns. They are open about the difficulties that parents of adolescents have in allowing their young people to take risks. Recognizing that the change process throughout the years has been a mutual one for themselves and their daughter, they enter into a dialogue with her about ways that each of them, in the past, tried to change other family members. When were they successful? When were they not? How had they themselves known when they were ready for change? Were there times when they felt that someone was trying to *rescue* rather than *help* them? How had they reacted to those situations?

In the course of this discussion, Marilyn was able to realistically look at how much help and support she was prepared to give to Cliff. How would she recognize if he was ready to make changes? How would she recognize if he was using her? Not only did Marilyn's parents feel more trusting of their daughter's ability to handle the situation, but everyone in the family learned more about his or her impact on other family members. Their already strong connections to each other were enhanced even more.

Fears and Worries During Adolescence

Earlier fears seem to resurface during ages eleven and twelve. Wild animals, snakes, and being alone in the dark are common fears at these ages. Shadows on the walls or unexplained sounds at night lead to fears of intruders. Other sharp abrupt sounds and sights, such as thunder and lightning, precipitate anxiety. Worries about war or the future of mankind are not uncommon among teens. The idealism of late adolescence may in fact increase these fears and worries.

In general, however, during the teen years fears become less prominent while worries increase. Worries usually center on school and social concerns. Worries about personal appearance, social acceptance, popularity, grades, performing in public, and applying for a job surface.

Fears and worries about physical symptoms are also common in adolescence, both early and late. Frequently youth in early adolescence are acutely aware of their bodies. When his heart beats faster after exercise or when he is anxious, the adolescent may worry about the possibility of having a heart attack. Any small lump or nodule may be misinterpreted as a symptom of cancer. In late adolescence as young people take on increasing responsibility for their own health care they may again worry about the significance of symptoms. They worry that they are not seeking medical advice when they should. They worry that they might seek advice over nothing and feel foolish. They are uncertain as to which type of doctor to consult. As they approach adulthood, the older adolescent may feel so overwhelmed about major life decisions such as long-term work or educational goals that they have difficulty making any decisions.

The Parents Role

Young people cannot accomplish the tasks of adolescence without parenting figures playing a helpful supportive role. The lack of positive family role models for identification leaves the adolescent vulnerable (Erikson, 1963). Adolescents need parents to model how responsible adults get their own needs met. To individuate, they must have parent figures to oppose, to separate from. It is primarily within the family, that the young person begins to sort out how he is like and how he is different from others.

A primary goal of the adult-adolescent relationship during this developmental stage is to create an environment in which the young person is forced to take more control, and thus more responsibility, for his own behaviors. The confusion of the young person over self-responsibility and projection of responsibilities onto the parents is duplicated in the confusion of the parents, who are torn between protecting and controlling the adolescent and permitting him to experiment in ways that are alien or repugnant to them (Scherz 1971). This does not mean that adults should not have reasonable expectations for the youth's behaviors. It does mean that these need to be presented not as control issues to prove that the adult is in charge but as logical expectations which are for the teen's benefit. Again, a major goal is to help the adolescent get out of either/or thinking and to help him explore a variety of choices.

We met Judy, twelve, in the introduction to this book. With her recent move back to fostercare after a disrupted adoptive placement, Judy regressed in terms of her school performance. Her foster parents realized that they could not be in charge of Judy's homework. They refused to check on her assignments. On the other hand, they were willing to assume responsibility for insuring that she had opportunities to complete her work. They set up a ninety minute study time for her each weekday evening. They suggested that if her grades indicated that this was not adequate preparation time for her, they would increase it. On the other hand, if her grades improved they would be willing to cut back some on the study hall time to see if she could complete the work more quickly. They identified it as her job to complete the school work while they would help her determine how much time she realistically needed to spend on studying.

Judy

Since oppositional behaviors are a necessary part of adolescent development, adults need to insure that the young person has some areas in which rebellious behavior does not have to lead to serious acting out. The concept of "healthy hassling" is a useful one. Parents select several issues on which they will make their views well known without drawing an absolute, "You will not————" line. Examples might include the volume and type of music teens listen to, the

117

condition of their bedrooms, or the type of clothing they wear. The adolescent knows that the parent does not approve, but sometimes tolerates, opposition in these spheres. Resistance in these areas meets the adolescent's need for individuation without him having to resort to drugs, alcohol abuse, or sex as ways of demonstrating behaviorally that adults cannot control all areas of his development.

Adults living or working with teens need to be comfortable setting limits in a non-punitive manner. They must recognize the difference between tolerating behaviors and approving of them. Parents of teens need to develop a tolerance for mood swings and be able to live with fads. A sense of humor and the ability to see themselves as capable of continued change and growth are two traits critical for adults living or working with adolescents.

Parents of teens, especially foster or adoptive, need to be cognizant of adolescent sexual issues. Adolescents are very sexualized beings. Adults must be supportive in helping the young person cope with their sexuality while at the same time they, as parent figures, continue to form non-sexual relationships with them. Unresolved sexual issues that adults may have are likely to resurface.

Parents need to insure that suitable academic and vocational programs are available to meet their adolescent's needs. Likewise, adult caregivers are responsible for insuring that adolescents are supplied with health care services, including therapy when it is indicated. They act as advocates for the adolescent, helping him clarify his needs and access appropriate services. Sometimes they themselves will confront systems on behalf of their young person; other times they will support the adolescent in asserting himself with service providers.

Facilitating skill development in a variety of areas is another of the roles of the parent of an adolescent. As we saw earlier, these include not only in academic and vocational areas, but also the arenas of social and interpersonal communication, emotional management, physical and psychological self-care, conflict resolution, and entertainment skills.

All adults working with adolescents need to help them expand their thinking from the usual constricted either/or mode that is so prevalent during the teen years. Adults can help them explore the wide variety of alternatives available between the extremes that adolescents commonly initially focus on.

Greg

Seventeen-year-old Greg has always aspired to be a foreign correspondent. However, the results of recent aptitude tests indicate that written communication is a weak area for him. Although he can articulate his thoughts well, his basic writing skills are weak. A second area of strength that he enjoys is in the area of math and science. In spite of being exceptionally gifted in these areas, they are of lower interest to him. It seems to his parents that because these skills come to him easily, he does not value them. He places the highest value on the vocational areas associated with his academic weaknesses. On receiving the results of the aptitude tests, Greg's immediate response is, "If I can't get into a good school of Journalism, there's no use in my attending university at all. I think that I'll just get a job at the local factory, earn some money, and bum around Europe.

Although his parents see the latter option as a reasonable short-term goal, they encourage him to explore a variety of alternatives. Might he consider broadcast journalism? Are there ways he can combine his math or science strengths with his desire for foreign travel? Would he consider attending summer school classes in English attempting to strengthen this weaker area?

Parent Issues

Parents who themselves need adolescents to be either very dependent upon them or independent of them may have difficulty helping the teen successfully renegotiate this delicate balance during adolescence. The parent needs to be able to accept the adolescent's vacillation between dependence and independence with equanimity. Adults who are rigid and controlling are likely to become locked into nearly constant conflict with their young person who, even when normal, will be provocative. On the other hand, a parent who has to always be liked and appreciated will have difficulty setting reasonable limits for their young person.

Fourteen year old Samantha and her mom have a pretty normal relationship. Occasionally, when Sam's mom has been very supportive of her daughter's feelings, the teen comments, "You are the best mom in the world. You understand everything." Mom replies, "I'm glad I'm doing a good job. Mom's of fourteens are supposed to be understanding."

Samantha

However, just as frequently when Mom sets limits that her daughter does not like, Sam will scream, "You don't understand anything." Calmly Mom responds, "I'm glad I'm doing a good job. Mothers of fourteens aren't supposed to understand *everything*."

Adolescent sexuality forces adult caregivers to reassess their own sexuality. Parents who are sexually repressed and those who were very sexually active during their own adolescence are both likely to have increased problems with their teen's emerging sexuality. According to Green (1980), the mother who herself became pregnant as a teen is at particular risk for not coping well with an adolescent daughter's sexuality.

Parents who have difficulty managing their own anger and aggression are at high risk for becoming involved in physically violent interchanges with teenagers who themselves have difficulty controlling their own anger impulses.

119

It is not uncommon for parents to be jealous of their young person, who may have many more educational and vocational opportunities for the future than the parent did at the same age. Young people usually enjoy good health. In late adolescence, if not before, they will most likely surpass their parents in terms of current athletic prowess. Older adolescents are enjoying good health, good looks, and looking forward to being sexually active at about the same time as many of their parents are starting to become aware of their own physical vulnerabilities. It may be the parents' turn now to feel that "Life's not fair."

VI   Special Developmental Issues

In this section two developmental issues that frequently are of concern to adults who live with or work with children in placement will be discussed in detail. The first is the development of conscience and the incorporation of family values. Many children and youth in care have delays in conscience development. A few have no conscience. It is important that adults understand the stages of conscience development, and, no matter what the age of the young person, try to identify ways to facilitate further growth in this area. The second issue to be addressed in this section is normal sexual development from infancy to the onset of adulthood. Because of the high incidence of sexual abuse, estimated to be 60-70% of the children in the child welfare system by the time they exit from it, adults need to know what is normal and what is abnormal. They need to be in a knowledgeable position to facilitate healthy growth in this area.

Conscience Development and Values Incorporation

What is conscience? According to Selma Fraiberg, "Conscience consists of a set of standards and prohibitions which have been taken over by the personality and which govern behavior from within" (1959). Judith Viorst (1986) points out that conscience not only limits and restrains us but also contains values and ideals. She goes on to say that it encourages us and praises us for doing well. It speaks to our thoughts instead of our don'ts. Our parents are in our mind, even after their death. Viorst goes on to identify three types of conscience problems. Some individuals cannot acknowledge guilt because they don't believe they could experience it and survive. Others have guilt which is able to punish after the fact but never warns ahead. Finally, there is the psychopathic individual who displays a true lack of guilt with neither restraint or remorse. Within the child welfare system there are a small number of children who fall in this third category, some

120

who fall in the first, and many who can feel remorse after the fact but whose conscience does not provide an adequate early warning system for them.

The social emotions which develop as a response to attachment are a precursor to conscience. Children, fearing the loss of love of their attachment objects, try to please them and gradually internalize their values, standards, and constraints. This does not mean that adults need to threaten children with loss of love. That fear is present in all children with healthy attachments. Indeed, parental threats overwhelm the child, undermining his sense of trust. Threats of abandonment are particularly harmful.

Conscience development evolves over a number of years. It does not develop in a matter of days, weeks, or months. Although children at about age five develop an internal critical voice, most are nine or ten before their sense of right and wrong is strong enough to prevent them from misbehaviors even when they are unlikely to be detected by adults. This is because true guilt requires that the individual be able to mentally reverse an act and consider alternative possibilites, a cognitive skill usually not acquired until age nine or ten (Viorst, 1985). Until then, children are most secure if they are receiving adequate supervision from adults so that they don't have to struggle to maintain a level of self-control that is beyond their abilities. Conscience development, however, continues long beyond the initial internalization of guilt, as values continue to be modified and clarified throughout an individual's lifetime.

Too much or too little guilt both are problematic. Excessive guilt or shame inhibits personal growth and may lead to marked internal discomfort. Although those with too little conscience may not feel personal suffering, their behaviors frequently lead to considerable pain for others as they steal, assault, and murder without guilt. Once again, the goal is to achieve a balance. A healthy conscience produces guilt feelings proportionate to the act. Healthy guilt leads to remorse, not self-hate (Fraiberg, 1959).

The foundations for conscience development are laid in the toddler years. Toddlers start to understand and incorporate parental messages about acceptable and unacceptable behaviors. They develop the social emotions which allow for sympathy and empathy to develop, for a sense of pride and self-worth to emerge, and for an awareness of embarrassment to precede the development of shame.

Perceiving parental disapproval visually, auditorily, or sometimes by touch via a tap on the hand, they learn to stop themselves from touching desirable but forbidden objects. It is important that parents give clear messages, without accompanying threats or harsh physical discipline, about which behaviors they approve and which they disapprove. Short messages are more effective than lengthy ones. Initially the disapproval might be expressed by the single word, "No," said in a firm tone.

Approval might be conveyed by, "Good," spoken in a soft tone, possibly accompanied by a physical caress. When children are speaking in short sentences, around age three, then parents need to use short sentences for their messages of approval and disapproval. "I really like it when you . . ." or "I don't like that at all." As children approach school age, simple explanations of the reasons behind the disapproval help them understand and clarify parental values so that they, too, can be incorporated. Messages starting with the word *I* are more helpful that those starting with *you* as the latter often become a form of name calling or passing judgement on others.

Taylor, age four, is teasing his two-year-old sister by holding out her favorite toy and then snatching it back just as she reaches for it. His mother might say, "You are a naughty boy, teasing your sister that way. Stop it." This "you" message labels him, and unfortunately he may come to truly believe that he is naughty and fulfill his mother's prophecy.

On the other hand she might say, "Taylor, I don't like it when you tease your sister. In this family, we think being kind to people is important." Here the mother gives a non-judgmental message which is clear about the family values that they expect Taylor to internalize.

Taylor

Four and five are at the same time the most truthful and untruthful of all ages. Basically children these ages are very honest, often to the embarrassment of their parents because they lack tact. At the same time, not wanting to displease parents or incur their anger, they certainly are not above projecting blame onto others, even an imaginary friend. Adults frequently demand that their children always tell the truth. However, in reality this is not what they usually want.

When children say something bluntly truthful, either about an adult or another child, parents frequently say, "You don't really mean that." This is especially common when fours or fives honestly express their emotions of the minute about a sibling with a comment such as, "I hate you." Parents in fact, consistently try to talk children out of being honest. The brutally truthful way that children of this age express strong feelings may make adults uncomfortable. Gradually many children learn not to share their strong feelings. They sometimes even say, "Adults don't want to know." Adults seem to forget the transitory nature of feelings, implying that if a child "hates" someone at the moment it means he will never again love that person.

Parents are forced to reassess their own values when they are living with a preschooler. Frequently parents hold two values that are incompatible. Take for example "honesty" and "respect for your elders." When these two values conflict, which is the child to select? Parents need to clarify and even rank their own values if they are to transmit them successfully to their children.

Usually adults want children to be honest about their own behaviors. Hopefully, adults can accept the child's honesty about his own strong feelings.

When it comes to comments about others, most parents want children to be honest so long as they have something positive to say, but otherwise to keep quiet! Children learn this as they acquire the ability to think ahead about the impact of their words upon others.

The years between four and six are crucial for conscience development. During this period most children do a number of things of which their parents disapprove. However, most of the time children these ages are under the supervision of adults so that messages both of approval and disapproval can be consistently provided. This is an important requisite for conscience development.

It is rarely necessary, and usually unwise, to begin an interchange with a preschooler with a phrase such as, "Who took the cookies?" The response is likely to be, "Not me," despite obvious evidence to the contrary such as crumbs on the face and hands. If the parent then moves to, "Don't lie to me, I know you did it," the child feels deceived. The implied message in, "Who took the cookies?" is that the adult does not know the answer. The parent who understands conscience development and wants to facilitate it will say something along the lines of, "I see you took some cookies. You know the rule is that you must ask first. You can sit right here until you are ready to talk about it." The underlying message is, "I already know what is going on so there is no advantage in lying. In fact, the advantage lies totally in talking about the truth."

When parents are trying to encourage honesty about misbehaviors, then they need to focus on truth telling rather than the rule infraction per se. When a child is honest adults need to either forgo or lessen the consequences of the misbehaviors. If consequences are equally severe when the child tells the truth as when he lies, he may interpret the message as, "You get into just as much trouble when you tell the truth. Become a better liar." When a child breaks a rule that requires more direct discipline it is not the time to work on honesty, but to take the approach, "I know that you did thus and so, and this is the consequence."

The most useful adjuncts to the development of conscience during the preschool years are the parents' "big eyes and ears" that keep track of the child's activities. Children, with their magical thinking, frequently believe that parents know everything. Many times they think that parents have eyes in the back of their head. The parent may choose not to correct these misperceptions as they facilitate, rather than hinder, conscience development. However, the parents' big eyes and big ears should not be limited to catching the child doing something wrong. Parents need to make positive comments such as, "It sure sounded like you were having fun playing with your trucks in your room." The important thing is for the child to believe that parents already know what is going on with them and that therefore they might as well be truthful.

Many of the children in the child welfare system spent their preschool years in homes where parents did not provide adequate supervision and in which clear messages of approval and disapproval were rarely provided. Therefore, the frequency of delayed conscience development among those in care should not be surprising. However, since this period of close supervision is such a necessary stage of normal conscience development, it becomes apparent why it is difficult to remediate conscience delays once the child is old enough to be away from parental supervision most of the time.

The next step in conscience development is positively reinforcing the child when he catches himself misbehaving.

Phillip

Eight-year-old Phillip was moved several times before joining his adoptive family at age seven. He has little reason to trust adults. His dishonesty is of great concern to his parents. They have taken the time to learn more about the steps in conscience development and are working toward helping Phillip progress in this area and incorporate their values.

One day when his mom happens to glance out of an upstairs window, she sees her son start to misbehave. Phillip looks toward the kitchen window, and in spite of not seeing his mother there, he stops himself. Later Phillip's mom comments to him, "I noticed that you stopped yourself from teasing the dog today. That's really great." The message to Phillip is twofold. First, "I know what you are doing and I would have stopped you if you hadn't stopped yourself." Second, "I like it when you can control yourself and I don't have to."

By the time children are six, parents can usually learn to recognize how their child expresses anxiety when being untruthful. For one it may be avoiding eye contact; for another, it may be frequent licking of the lips, gulping, or rapid clenching and releasing of the fists. Once parents have learned to identify these give aways with certainty they should share their knowledge with the child. For example, a parent might say, "Your mouth is telling me one thing, but your eyes are telling me something else. I have learned that you have very truthful eyes."

Many parents are reluctant to do this. However, a guilty conscience by definition is when an individual feels uncomfortable internally when doing something wrong, even when they do not fear being caught and punished by another. This internalized guilty feeling is accompanied by anxiety. Helping children recognize these feelings and their own behavioral clues demonstrates to them that they are capable of telling the truth themselves. Parents can say, "Pay attention to your eyes. What are they telling you?" This starts to help the mouth give a message that is congruent with the eyes. It helps the child to recognize his own discomfort and correct his own behavior. However, usually the child is age nine or ten before he has sufficiently internalized adult standards and expectations so that he can behave well even when an adult is not present to monitor him.

Between the years of six and ten children commonly confront their parents about discrepancies between parental actions and words. Children might ask, "How come you say, 'always be honest,' but you lied to that salesman on the telephone last night?"

Ten-year-olds are particularly open to talking about parental views of the world as a whole and major values. They are interested in their parents' ideas about the environment, the likelihood of war, and other topics they hear about on the news. Low pressure times may be used with children this age to share information. Conversations over meals or making use of travel time in the car can be used for discussing values. Tens are old enough to understand parental standards, yet young enough to accept them more readily than they will during the teen years.

In the past children were not exposed to as many different value systems as most now confront. Communities and neighborhoods were more homogeneous. Children's friends, neighbors, teachers, and schoolmates were more likely to hold values not too different from those the child learned at home. In more recent years neighborhoods have come to be comprised of families with differing expectations, standards, and prohibitions. Children, even in their early school years, may be exposed to values in sharp contrast to those held by their parents. Additionally, television and movies sharply impact on the development of values.

Wise parents will make certain that their children have contact with some families who have similar values. This becomes even more important during adolescent years than it was previously. At this time the young person is more open to learning about values outside the home environment. It is usual for adolescents to confide in an adult other than their own parents. This confidante may be the parent of a friend, a teacher, or a young adult. Parents should try to insure that their teen has opportunities to share with adults who hold values similar to their own.

With older grade schoolers and adolescents, parents need to talk about value-laden topics at times when there is not tension between themselves and their young person. When teens do not feel that the message is aimed at changing them, but more at talking about ideas and perceptions, they are more likely to hear and accept adult values. Many parents postpone talking about important values such as attitudes about drugs, alcohol, and sex until the adolescent years. Parents need to think well in advance about these values and be modeling responsible behaviors themselves. Then during the teen years they can, while continuing to model, provide more verbal or written information. Written information needs to be accurate, but balanced if there are differing viewpoints.

Some adolescents have to first reject parental values before they can accept them as their own. Otherwise they may see themselves as giving in and being just like their parents, a fate worse than death in the eyes of most teens. This represents one aspect of psychological separation from the family. Parents need to be able to assert that their values have worked well for themselves without getting into control battles over them. Parents who achieve this are quite likely to find that eventually their young people choose to accept and incorporate most of the parental values. However, this acceptance comes from active choice rather than because of bending to pressure.

Unfortunately some parents try to make control issues out of values. This is rarely successful. The statement, "You may not ever smoke pot," is impossible to enforce unless adults keep the adolescent under direct supervision all of the time. "We don't allow anyone to smoke pot in our house," is certainly easier to enforce. Clear statements of approval or disapproval do not have to lead to control issues about a particular value. Again, taking care to start declarations with, "I think . . .," or, "I believe . . .," rather than, "You must . . .," or even, "You should . . .," provides more positive modeling about tolerance combined with strong personal beliefs and leads in general to less resistance.

Many parents believe that tolerating behaviors is the same as approving of them. In adult-adult relationships behaviors that are not approved of are tolerated in friends or relatives. For example, relatives may curse in spite of others' disapproval. However, because of other positive attributes, family members do not cut off contact with them, nor do they necessarily expect them to change their behaviors to gain the approval of relatives. In helping adolescents become young adults, parents have to develop a similar attitude. Parents need to ask themselves, "Is this behavior or value so important to me that it is worth risking my relationship with my child?" Occasionally the answer will be yes. Usually it will be no.

In Exercise 2-2 we will return to Sharon, whom we met in Exercise 1-3 on Encouraging Attachment in Chapter 1, pg. 63. However, this time we will be focusing on ways to overcome her delays in conscience development.

Exercise 2-2

Overcoming Delays in Conscience Development

Sharon

Sharon, age eight, will be moving from her fosterhome to an adoptive family within the next few weeks. She will be the youngest in a two parent family with three sons ranging in age from twelve to seventeen. Father is a clergyman; mother is a teacher. Sharon's past history reveals considerable emotional and physical deprivation, rejection, and physical abuse. She has been in and out of foster care since she was four years old. Sharon has had seven moves including two returns to her birth parents' care.

Behavioral problems noted in her current foster home include enuresis both at night and during the day. A medical workup was negative. Sharon has many fears including fear of the dark, sirens, and new situations. She is prone to nightmares. Sharon becomes very upset when family members tease each other or rough house. Sheis described as a demanding and manipulative child.

Although there is no known history of sexual abuse, Sharon demonstrates sexually provocative behaviors. She raises her dress in front of men and boys and asks them openly if they want to go to bed with her. Sharon has difficulty telling the truth. Sometimes she lies about her misbehaviors. Other times she tells meaningless lies, such as saying that peas are her favorite vegetable when, in fact, she does not like them at all. She frequently brings home small objects (i.e. pencils, hair clips, etc.) from school saying either that she "found"them or that, "a friend gave them to me."

Although academically Sharon is at grade level, she has many gaps in her basic fund of knowledge. She exhibits problems with logical thinking and basic cause and effect. She does not always complete her school work and may "forget" to turn in work she has completed. Sheis reading above grade level but has difficulty in math. Play skills are poor and she has difficulty keeping friends.

Sharon is physically attractive and demonstrates excellent self-care skills. She shows appropriate affect for the most part and is outgoing and affectionate. Sometimes she is inappropriately affectionate with relative strangers. However, she is able to talk openly about feelings and tells of many ways that she and her present foster parents have fun together.

1.	At what age level does Sharon seem to functioning in terms of conscience development?
2.	What specific advice would you give to the adoptive parents about dealing with Sharon's various types of Lying?
3.	What would be your advice about the found objects?
4.	You may also choose to give suggestions about her fears and her preference to "pretend" that she is an adolescent.?

Sexual Development

"Is it a boy or a girl?" Even if they have no real preference, parents want to know the sex of their newborn immediately. This is not surprising since Sigmund Freud pointed out that, "When you meet a human being the first distinction you make is 'male or female'" (Viorst, 1986). From birth on, adults interact differently with male and female children. Discussion proceeds and research continues, with the aim of clarifying how many of the differences noted between the sexes are innate versus environmentally or socially determined. No matter how the differences come about, hopefully within the family setting both sexes are equally valued in spite of being perceived as different and unique. At any rate, long before children enter school their gender identity and feelings about sexuality have been shaped by their early experiences with family members (Bernstein, 1978).

There are several different facets to sexual development. The first relates to physical development. Through time the child develops an increasing awareness of, and interest, in his genitals. Adults need to know which sexual behaviors fall within the normal range at varying ages. Cognitively, as he matures, the child learns to differentiate between the two sexes and the expectations for each. He gradually acquires knowledge about the workings of male and female bodies and the birth process. Finally, there is the relationship to psychological development. This area includes intrapsychic struggles, such as the Oedipal Complex, identification with the parent of the same sex, developing sexual relationships with non-family members, and the clarification of adolescent and adult sexual values.

But, back to the beginning. Ultrasound pictures have indicated that male fetuses have reflex erections several weeks before birth. (Hagens,1988). From birth on, penile and clitoral erections are normal. They commonly accompany other physically satisfying interactions such as nursing, touching, and handling. Female infants are known to have spontaneous vaginal lubrication. The initial sexual arousal reactions are probably reflex and the infant is most likely unaware of them. However, teaching about sexuality begins at birth. Through early interactions the infant learns if physical contact with others yields pleasure or discomfort, reassurance or rejection (Bernstein, 1978). Although the adult goal as caregivers provide the touching and caressing so necessary to life is not sexual arousal, these stimuli through time become associated with body awareness in general, and sexual reactions in particular.

From a very early age children's pleasurable self-stimulation in a variety of areas is inhibited by parents. For instance, the mouth, which is a source of pleasure for babies, may become off limits for anything except food. Even fingers and thumbs are frequently prohibited. The genital area, too, with its abundant nerve endings, is a source of pleasurable touch throughout life. Orgasms have been observed in children of both sexes prior to a year of age and it is apparent that the child can initiate sexual stimulation that can lead to orgasm even during late infancy (Hagens, 1988). Yet, once again, adults tend to interrupt the child's attempts at self-stimulation.

During the toddler years there is an increasing body awareness, especially in the genital area as children attain sphincter control of the bladder and anus. However, children learn that they are not to touch these parts of their bodies. The confusing thing is that these are precisely the areas of the body that are the most pleasant to touch because of the increased number of nerve endings responsive to soft touch. Children who discover that the areas that give them the most pleasure cause disgust in their parents will often come to feel that their genitals are bad, their feelings are wrong and that they are unworthy as people (Fraiberg, 1959).

To feel positive about one's own gender an individual must feel good about one's genitals. Toddlers learn to recognize boys vs. girls, men vs. women.

They demonstrate an awareness of differences in behaviors and attitudes as well as differences in body parts and appearances. In learning about sex differences children learn both facts and values (Bernstein, 1978). Although the toddler may experiment with opposites, males indicate a preference for behaviors and attitudes that are more masculine while girls become more feminine.

Parents themselves tend to increase their differential reactions to male and female children during the toddler years. Young children get good feelings about themselves if they perceive that their sex, being a male or female, is appreciated by both parents. If either parent does not value the child's sex, then youngsters are likely to develop problems with self-esteem and have difficulty feeling comfortable with their own gender identity. This is a time when it is especially important for a baby to have a close relationship with both parents. The child's emerging sense of sexual identity serves to strengthen his hold on reality and his ability to build positive self-esteem (Greenspan, 1989).

By the completion of the toddler years, the child has developed his or her core gender identity, which is the sense each of us have about our own sex. According to Stoller (1976) it is a result of five factors: the physical effect of sex hormones on the fetus; sex assignment at birth; parental attitudes about the child as a male or female; effects of patterns of handling, conditioning, imprinting; and finally the child's bodily sensations, especially from the genitals. Gender identification as a whole, inclusive of sex related roles and relationships, will continue to develop throughout the years.

As the child progresses into the preschool years, he becomes increasingly interested in his own and others' bodies. During these years, children want to compare and explore. They will look, touch, and sometimes attempt to insert objects into their body openings (Hagens, 1988). If they have seen sexual intercourse they may imitate it. They are interested in making certain that the difference between the two sexes is consistent. Do all boys have a penis? Does no girl have one? Girls in general are curious about the penis since they do not have one. Boys are fearful that they may lose theirs. They place a value on their penis. It feels good, it looks good, and some people don't have one (Viorst, 1986). This leads to castration fears. Adults should never use threats of bodily harm upon finding a preschool age child involved in masturbatory activities or sex play with other children. However, just as parents help them learn in other arenas of daily life, they can also help the young child learn to limit this behavior to appropriate time and place. For example, most preschoolers gradually learn that while they cannot touch their sexual organs in public, they may do so in private.

The preschooler has developed a sense of self as a sexual being—"I am a boy with a penis (or a girl with a vagina) and I am curious." (Greenspan, 1989). Part of the adult's job is to help the child retain positive feelings about the sexual organs while teaching him to limit his behaviors to those that are accepted within our society.

Duke

Mrs. Wentz has just entered Duke's bedroom where he is playing with a neighbor boy of the same age. She finds that the two have their pants off and are masturbating each other. Being experienced in working with young children with sexual behaviors, she is prepared for this occurrence. She comments, "I know that children your age are curious about bodies. Touching that part of your body feels good. That's the way bodies are made. However, in this family we expect children to keep their clothes on when they are playing. Even though we know it feels good, we have a rule in this family that no child is to touch another child's private parts. I want you boys to put your clothes on now and then you may choose either to come have a snack or to play a game out in the family room, where I am working."

At the same time children learn that although they may touch many parts of parents' bodies, other parts are off limits. They become curious about sex and reproduction. The preschooler's interest in his own body is coupled with an increasing curiosity about how and why Mom and Dad are physically different from each other, what happens in their bedroom, and where babies come from. The preschooler is interested in seeing how adult bodies compare with children's bodies. Most see a parent undressed occasionally and are likely to ask questions such as, "How come you have those (pointing to mother's breasts) and I don't?" A response might be, "When girls start to become women they get breasts. All women have them. When a lady has a baby her breasts make milk for the baby."

A girl may point to Dad's penis and ask why she doesn't have one. An appropriate response would be, "Every boy and man has a penis. That's where their urine comes out. Girls have a special opening for urine, but they don't have a penis." Boys may wonder why their father has a large penis with hair around it while theirs is small and lacking hair. Again, reassurance about the normal body changes that will occur in adolescence should be given.

Although preschoolers are interested in knowing more about where babies come from, they are not yet very good at understanding knowledge shared with them. Because of their concrete thinking they easily misinterpret information shared. If they are told that babies grow in Mummy's tummy, they will of course think that they get in there via the mouth and exit via the anus. If they are told about eggs or seeds they relate the information to their knowledge base of chickens and gardening. Children of these ages, prone to, magical thinking, come up with wonderfully creative connections for the information provided by word of mouth and books. For example, a little girl asked her first grade teacher, "How does the doctor make my mommy pregnant?" The teacher asked what made her think that the doctor made mommy pregnant. The child replied that the previous evening Mother had announced, "I went to the doctor today and I am pregnant."

It becomes clear that adults need to be careful to present information in ways that minimize the likelihood of the child misconnecting, rather than correctly connecting, information. During this stage children have some very basic questions. "Where was I before I was born?" or, "Where do babies come from?" is the first. Once they get the answer to that question their next two are, "How do babies get in there?" and, "How do they get out?" Remembering their propensity for concrete thinking and their inability to perceive that at one time they did not exist at all, adults can be led to formulate helpful answers. "Before you were born you were inside Mommy, in a special growing place called a uterus (or womb)." Or, if talking to a child who was not born to the adults in this particular family, an appropriate response might be, "All babies grow inside a woman's body in a special growing place called a uterus." Using correct terminology is important to diminish the likelihood of the child confusing ingestion of food and elimination of body wastes with the processes of conception and birth. When a child asks how he got into the uterus, the parent might respond along the following lines, " It's a wonderful thing. A special part of mommy's body makes ova (don't worry about using strange words, children are constantly exposed to new words as they develop their vocabulary and they may as well learn the correct ones). When an ova is joined in the uterus by a sperm which comes from the daddy's body, a baby starts to grow." The response to the third question, "How do babies get out?" again should be anatomically correct. "Babies come out through the only opening that the uterus has. They come out through the vagina." It's important to let the child know that there is only one entrance to the female uterus, the vagina. Nothing that goes into the body via the mouth is able to get into the uterus and nothing in the uterus leaves it other than through the vagina. Unless children are provided with accurate information they are likely to be confused about how many openings a woman has "down there." They need to be told that women have three openings—one for urine, the opening to the vagina which goes to the uterus, and the anus for bowel movements. These three openings do not connect to each other. If the child asks how the sperm get from the daddy's body into the uterus, he can be told, "Sperm come out daddy's penis and go through the vagina into mommy's uterus."

In general at this stage of development, answers to questions about sex need to be accurate, use correct terminology, and be short. The preschooler does not have a long attention span for verbally shared information. Short answers, which may need to be repeated, can gradually be elaborated on through time.

During these same years, the child's psychological development also includes an aspect related to sexuality. The Oedipal stage, characterized by the child competing with the parent of the same sex for the attention of the parent of the opposite sex, usually occurs between the ages of four and six. A preschool age boy may say, "When I grow up I am going to marry Mommy," or a girl of the same age will make similar declarations with regard to her dad.

During this stage children may start to become sexually reactive to being physically near the parent of the opposite sex when that adult is nude. Nudity may now be overstimulating for the child. Seductive behaviors on the part of parents can excite, baffle, and frighten young children (Viorst 1986). Overstimulation is as harmful as pulling away from touch. At this stage movies, videos, and television programs showing adult sexual interactions are confusing and not helpful to the child's development. During the Oedipal stage it is probably wise to limit the child's opportunities to see the parent of the opposite sex nude. It is time to start teaching privacy and to model modesty. This does not, however, mean that adults need be embarrassed or themselves over-react if the child accidently sees them undressed. It does mean that the parent makes attempts to limit the opportunities.

In coping with the feelings elicited by the Oedipal conflict, children soon realize that to get the exclusive attention of the parent of the opposite sex something must first happen to the parent of the same sex. Preschoolers are faced with a dilemma. The parent they want to "get rid of" is also an important love object. To win means to lose as well. Guilt is associated with these thoughts of getting rid of the parent of the same sex.

In addition, the magical thinking that is so prominent at this age increases a child's fears that something may happen to the parent of the same sex because the child has wished to eliminate that parent. The child may act out in order to be punished. If the punishment occurs at the hands of the parent of the same sex and is extreme, the child's fears of retaliation for the "bad" thoughts are reinforced. If the discipline is appropriate and fair, then the child's fears will more likely subside. It is best if the parent of the same sex takes an active role in handling any overt demonstrations of the Oedipal conflict in the child. Parents can reassure children that they too had these same feelings when they were children, that the youngsters are normal, and that the parents understand the feelings and are not upset by them. The usual mode of resolution of the Oedipal conflict is through identification with the parent of the same sex.

If, because of death or interim care placement, children lose their parent of the same sex, they become increasingly frightened by the apparent power of their own wishes. Children may even view loss of the parent of the opposite sex as punishment for "bad" thoughts. They may think that the parent of the same sex was losing the battle and decided, "If I can't have him/her then no one can." At any rate loss of, or separations from, parents, either one or both, during this critical stage in development may lead to long lasting difficulties with sexual identification or to the persistence of the magical thinking into later years.

Sometimes parents who do not have a satisfying marital relationship behave in ways that escalate the Oedipal conflict. For example, a father who is not receiving much attention from his wife may become overly involved with his young daughter and focus all of his attention on her. Or, a mother who is lonely may take her son to bed with her whenever Dad is out of town or working nights. Such behaviors on the part of parents may increase children's fears of retaliation from the other parent.

During grade school years children usually spend more time with friends of the same sex. Although sexual curiosity continues, children this age tend to express it less openly than when they were younger. By this age, children are

132

more likely to masturbate in private. Mutual masturbation, although not necessarily desirable, continues to be common, especially among boys. However, they are more likely to take care that they are not found out. Although they may not always abide by them, they have become aware of the social rules.

2-2 *Table*

Normal Childhood Exploration*

is of limited duration
involves children of similar ages
involves visual and tactile exploration
involves curiosity, not coercion
is voluntary on the part of each child involved
children silly and giggly while involved
children embarrassed if an adult walks in
diminishes when children are told to stop

Cognitive growth in understanding information about sex is evident and grade schoolers need to be provided with additional information. If facts are not offered by parents, children will look to peers for answers to their questions. Unfortunately, what they learn from the latter is frequently misinformation. Parents may want to ask a librarian to help them select age relevant books that provide information about sex. Reading with a child not only provides information but provides opportunities for mutual discussion.

Although during the early grades the child may be adamant about there having to be a man and a woman to make a baby, they are not yet really clear about the man's contribution. Gradually they become more aware of the father's role in the creation of life. Until they intellectually can realize that prior to conception they did not exist in any form, biological paternity has little meaning. Fatherhood, to the child under eight or nine, consists of living with and caring for children (Bernstein, 1978). Those children in placement who have no memories of living with their birth father now start to ask questions about him. They understand that a man was involved in their creation and contributed to their identity. Most want to learn more about him. If the nine or ten-year- old has not yet asked about the birth father, an adult should introduce the subject since children frequently think that they are not not to bring up subjects not already mentioned by adults.

During these same years the psychological aspect of sexual development is facilitated by the child increasingly identifying with the parent of the same sex.

* *information taken from Johnson (1990) and Hagens (1988) references*

133

If that person is not available, children need to have contact with other adults of their same sex. In general boys are more likely to want to be involved in active endeavors with an adult male. These may be pleasure or work oriented. They may do chores with Dad and help him work in the yard or on the car. Girls are more likely to work alongside Mother. Studies have shown that in widely divergent cultures there are consistent differences shown between children of the two sexes. Girls help adults and other children more commonly than boys. They offer psychological support more frequently. In contrast, boys more often seek attention from adults and attempt to dominate other children (Whiting, 1975).

As the youngster enters adolescence, the physical changes that accompany the transition from childhood to adulthood proceed in a recognized, usually consistent, order as outlined in Table 2-3.

Table 2-3

Sequence of Physical Changes

Female	Male
breast enlargement	growth in size of testes
straight pubic hair	straight pubic hair
maximum growth spurt	increase in size of penis
kinky thickened pubic hair	start voice change
onset of menstruation	first ejaculation
axillary hair	axillary hair
voice gets deeper	maximum growth spurt
growth slows	pubic hair thickens
	marked voice change
	growth slows down
	beard development

In general, the younger the child when physical maturation begins, the shorter the time from beginning to completion of the body changes. In contrast, those whose body changes are particularly late in starting will most commonly have a prolonged period of physical maturation which may even extend into the early twenties.

Junior high students desperately want, and need, sex education. This needs to start with information about their own bodies and how they are changing. However, they also want, and need, knowledge of the changes occurring in their peers of the opposite sex. Both sexes need to know about the onset of menustration

Sources include: Calderone and Group for Advancement of Psychiatry references listed in Bibliograpy.

134

in females and about ejaculation in males. Adolescent males who do not masturbate will ejaculate more frequently during sleep (wet dreams) and may feel very guilty about it.

After knowledge about physical and physiological changes have been shared it is time for adults to move into providing information about decision making and values as they relate to sexuality. Included in a bibliography at the end of this chapter are some suggestions as to books which might be used in educating children and youth of various ages about sex. However, new sources are constantly being developed and readers might want to check with librarians or teachers who are responsible for family life or sex education classes in their local area. Without accurate and complete knowledge, adolescents will have difficulty making positive life decisions in terms of sexual behaviors.

With the onset of adolescence, as hormonal production increases, there is usually also an increase in genital reactivity. Adolescents may become physically aroused by demonstrations of affection from the parent of the opposite sex. This body reaction does not necessarily reflect conscious desire. It is usual for adolescents to be embarrassed or worried by this arousal. Although they can usually accept quick physical expressions of affection such as a short hug about the shoulders or a kiss on the cheek, they may be uncomfortable with frontal hugs or kisses on the mouth. Physical roughhousing sometimes leads to strong sexual feelings in adolescents.

It is helpful to adolescents if there are common sense rules about privacy and some measure of modesty around the house. This protects them from feeling sexually aroused around parents or siblings. Again, most teens feel guilty when sexually aroused by a family member, yet during early adolescence sexual arousal occurs with minimal stimulation. Parents need to respect the privacy of their teenagers as much as they expect the young people to respect their privacy.

Adults also need to recognize that with the increase in hormonal production there is likely to be an increase in sexual activity on the part of the adolescent. This may include same-sex contacts as well as an increase in masturbation. Many times the significance of same-sex contacts in adolescence is exaggerated by adults and young people alike. According to the publication on normal adolescence by the Group for the Advancement of Psychiatry, mutual masturbation and group masturbation are quite common among adolescent males, and episodes of anal intercouse and oral-genital contact are not rare. Girls may engage in breast fondling and mutual masturbation. The authors caution that such behavior at this age does not necessarily indicate homosexuality. Lewis (1983) points out that adolescent males are more likely to feel self-hatred over same-sex activities as, in general, males are less tolerant of homosexual behavior than females. The same source goes on to point out that adolescents may be reassured to know that in a typical middle-class high school, about as many boys have experienced homosexual behaviors as heterosexual intercourse.

Strong emotional reactions, of any type, are frequently accompanied by penile erection in early adolescent males. Again, this is confusing to the young person. Without information about the normalcy of this reaction, anger and sex may become interrelated in an unhealthy way in his mind.

Adolescents use the parent of the same sex as a role model. They choose to be like this parent in some ways and different in others. At the same time, adolescents use their parent, or other adults of the opposite sex for affirmation and approval of their own emerging sexuality. Older adolescents seek confirmation and approval of their sexuality from peers and intense romantic attachments become the norm during these years.

Whether they are sexually active or not, adolescents need knowledge about sexually transmitted diseases and birth control methods. Again it is the parents' responsibility to insure that their young people receive accurate and complete information. Pamphlets providing accurate information in a concise, non-judgmental format about these subjects are available from various public health agencies or from private physicians.

Many sex education books used by the schools carefully avoid supporting any particular value system, fearful of offending some parents. Unfortunately some do not even discuss the value of values. This is especially harmful to the growth of the adolescent. It is important that young people be encouraged to discuss and verbally explore values about sexuality as well as other standards. During these discussions emphasis can be placed on ways to positively assert oneself and the importance of listening to the views of a partner. Mutuality, consideration, respect for partner, and intimacy are all important variables as older adolescents switch their dependency needs from parents to peer partners.

As in so many other arenas of parenting, in addressing adolescent sexuality the adult's task is to avoid overreacting, to gather and share accurate information about sex and sexuality, and to model decision making skills in approaching sexual values.

Exercise 2-3 which follows provides an example of the problems commonly seen in the adolescent who has been sexually abused and will provide an opportunity to identify the developmental needs in an adolescent who has been sexually abused and to develop a plan to meet those needs.

Exercise 2-3

Identifying the the Developmental Needs of a Sexually Abused Adolescent

Debbie

Debbie is fourteen. Her mother physically abused her, and her stepfather started sexually abusing her when she was eleven. Debbie reported the abuse to a school counselor. When the police became involved because of the sexual abuse, Debbie's mother and stepfather left the state, leaving Debbie with a neighbor.

Subsequently, the mother's parental rights were terminated. Debbie's birth father, who lives in another state, was contacted about having Debbie come to live with him. He expressed some interest but didn't follow through. So his parental rights, as well, were terminated.

Debbie has had three foster care placements since she was eleven and a half. All of her foster parents have described her as a sexually provocative child. She is seen as willful and disobedient with foster mothers, although she usually obeys the foster fathers. She is also viewed as a manipulator.

During the past two years, her grades have dropped from primarily A's and B's to primarily C's and D's. She has peer problems; most of her friends are boys and girls who also have many problems. Most of them have been in trouble with the law.

Debbie says repeatedly that everything would be fine if she could live with her dad, whom she hasn't seen in five years. She blames the judge and caseworker for keeping them apart. She does call her father, and he always accepts her collect calls. She tends to see her birth father as "super," while she sees her birth mother as a "rotten no-good whore."

Recently she ran away from her foster home after being grounded for not coming home on time. The foster family has requested that she be moved. A maternal aunt who lives about a hundred miles away has expressed an interest in Debbie. There is also a local family who has expressed an interest in adopting an adolescent like Debbie.

_____

1.   What are the indications of separation-individuation problems? Develop a plan for helping to resolve these problems.
2.   What are the indications of control issue problems? What advice would you give?
3.   What are the indications of problems in the sexual areas? Outline a plan for meeting Debbie's' developmental needs in this area.

_____

Bibliography: Sex Education

Bernstein, A. *The Flight of the Stork.* New York: Delacorte Press., 1978. A wonderful book for parents and other adults which explains how children understand, and misunderstand, information at various ages dependent upon their cognitive abilities.

Calderone, M.S. and Ramey, J. *Talking With Your Child About Sex: Questions and Answers for Children from Birth to Puberty.* New York: Random House, 1982. This book was written to help parents talk about sex with their children from infancy up until puberty. Contains a wealth of information on what is normal and ideas as to how adults can encourage healthy sexuality in their children.

Gordon, Sol. *Facts About Sex: A Basic Guide.* New York: John Day Company, 1969. A very short book which discusses the basic body changes of adolescence. It is written for the pre-adolescent and adolescent.

Gordon, Sol and Gordon, Judith. *Raising a Child Conservatively in a Sexually Permissive World.* New York: Simon and Schuster, 1983. A book for parents who want to be sex educators for their children while getting across their own values. They differentiate well between sexuality and sexual behaviors. Covers preschool years through adolescence.

Koch, J. *Our Baby: A Birth and Adoption Story.* Indianapolis: Perspectives Press, 1985. Written for the very young child (ages two to seven) in an adoption-built family. Combines sex education and adoption in a positive manner. Large print, simple illustrations and small amount of material per page lend to its use with the young child.

Lewis, H.R. and Lewis, M.E. *Sex Education Begins at Home.* Norwalk, Connecticut: Appleton-Century-Crofts, 1983. A book primarily for parents of teenagers. It does, however, discuss some of the research on early sexuality. Discusses normal sexual interactions that occur at various ages. It then proceeds to explore in detail information about adolescence in general, with an emphasis on sexuality.

Madaras, Lynda. *The What's Happening to My Body? Book for Girls* and *The What's Happening to My Body? Book for Boys*. New York: Newmarket Press, 1983. Provides information on body changes during adolescence in a detailed, but very readable manner. Written for the eight to fifteen year olds, their parents, and other concerned adults. Each book contains a chapter on the changes in the opposite sex as well.

Mayle, Peter. *What's Happening to Me?* New Jersey: Lyle Stuart, Inc. 1973. Written for the pre-adolescent describing body changes in adolescence. Pictures are exaggerated, nearly cartoon, in type.

Sheffield, Margaret. *Where Do Babies Come From?* New York: Alfred A. Knopf, 1975. A short book, with very nice illustrations, which describes conception, pre-natal development and the birth process. Written for the child of grade school years.Madaras, Lynda. New York: Newmarket Press

Imagine yourself in a situation like this:

You are at home at night. Your three children are asleep and you have just gone to bed yourself. Your spouse is out for the evening and won't be home until later. Everything is quiet, and you are settling down to sleep......

Suddenly there is a knock on the door, quickly followed by heavy footsteps. Someone in uniform enters your bedroom and announces, "You're coming with me." He takes you and your children outside. You all get into a car. You drive into a strange neighborhood, far from your home. The car stops in front of a house. You are left in the car as one of your children is taken to the door of the house. The man in uniform knocks, someone answers the door, and your child is handed over to this person. The uniformed man returns to the car. You drive further. The man takes your second child and leaves him at another strange house.

He drives further. He stops. You and your third child are taken to the door of a house. He knocks and when a person answers, the uniformed man says, "Here they are." You are handed over to the person in this house and left there.

How did you feel when the person came into the house?
How did you feel when you left your neighborhood?
How did you feel as you were separated from your children?
How did you feel as you were handed over to a stranger?
What would you want to do?

This is a fantasy about being separated from people to whom you are attached. Many foster children have lived through separation experiences like these. Chapter 3 will deal with separation and loss.

CHAPTER 3

Separation and Loss

Children entering, moving through, and exiting from the interim care system are faced with repeated separations and losses. They frequently are separated from their primary attachment objects. In addition, separations from siblings, extended family members, friends, and neighbors are common. "Of course, the pain of separation from those we love is for all of us a devastating experience, but for the dependent child the whole of his or her world collapses and everything loses meaning. The worst thing that can happen is that the trauma can be so great and the child feels so helpless in the face of it, that all feelings are clamped down on, leading to deadness and depression" (Winnicott, 1986). One of the most serious challenges of child welfare work is helping children cope with these traumatic separations.

Before proceeding further, however, it is probably helpful to clarify some terms. Rutter (1981) iterates that the term separation is used to refer to the physical loss of a particular mother figure, but not necessarily the simultaneous loss of mothering, which may be supplied by someone else. In contrast, deprivation refers to the loss of maternal care, but not necessarily to the loss of the person identified as the child's mother. Bourguignon and Watson (1987) clarify that loss is the affectual state that an individual experiences when something of significance is unexpectedly withdrawn. Separation, whether temporary or permanent, from meaningful relationships precipitates an acute sense of loss. Grief is the process through which one passes in order to recover from a loss. Aldgate (1988) points out the importance of adults involved with children in the child welfare system recognizing that separation involves fear, which needs to be mastered, and that loss involves grief which needs to be expressed.

Simultaneously with the child's grief, the persons from whom he is separated will be coping with their emotions and will need support as well. When a child leaves, the other birth or foster family members face many of the same grief issues as the children do. In this chapter the factors that influence an individual's reaction to separation will be discussed first. In Section II there is a description of the stages of the grief process as identified by both Bowlby and Kubler-Ross. There is also an exploration of the common but unhelpful strategies that individuals frequently use in coping with painful feelings, particularly at the times of loss. Although ways to minimize the trauma of the separation and loss will be explored in a separate chapter, the final section of this chapter examines the ways that unresolved grief interferes with forming new attachments, thereby inhibiting continued positive growth and change.

A major problem within the foster care system is that when a child enters care, rarely do the professionals know if the goal is to help the child cope with parent separation, or if this move will lead to parent loss. At any rate, from a child's view parent separation feels like loss when regular parent-child contact is not maintained.

I   Factors Influencing the Reaction to Separation

Children respond to being separated from their parents in many different ways. Responses vary from severe depression in children who are well attached to their caregivers and then abruptly separated from them to almost no reactions in children who have been emotionally neglected and have little connection to their parents. The reactions of most children entering the child welfare system fall between those two extremes. The two primary factors that influence an individual's reaction to loss are the strength of the relationship being broken and the abruptness of the separation.

Table 3-1

Factors influencing the Child's Reaction to Parent Separation or Loss

the child's age and stage of development
the child's attachment to the parent
the parent's bonding to the child
past experiences with separation
the child's perceptions of the reasons for the separation
the child's preparation for the move
the "parting message" the child receives
the "welcoming message" he receives
the post-separation environment
the child's temperament
the environment from which he is being moved

The child's reaction to separation from his caregiver can provide the worker with valuable information about the attachment between them. Table 3-1 lists the important influences on the child's reaction to separation.

In general, the stronger the relationship, the more traumatic the loss. In the absence of love there is no pain in loss. Commonly, the more abrupt the loss, the more difficult it will be to complete the grieving process.

Gilbert

When the Gilbert children were placed in the Wentz foster home a year and a half ago, each showed a different initial reaction to the placement.

Denise, seven-and-a-half at the time, behaved very grown up. She took charge of her siblings, sometimes comforting them but more commonly chastizing them. She talked positively of her birth mother and frequently told her brother and sister that they would all soon be going home.

Duke, barely five at the time, was indiscriminant in his interactions with adults, teens, and children alike. As soon as he met someone new, he was hanging onto them or crawling on their laps.

Lily, three, clung to Denise most of the time. However, when the latter was at school Lily would follow Lucy Wentz about the house.

The Child's Age as a Factor

Parent separation or loss has a profound impact no matter when in a lifetime it occurs. According to Wallerstein and Kelly (1980), boys, overall, appear to be more vulnerable than girls to the effects of separation. This should not be surprising given the fact that in a variety of other ways, including responses to physical illnesses, male children are more vulnerable. For both sexes, the specific effects of loss depend upon the nature of the relationship being interrupted. How was the relationship affecting current development? What function was it serving in facilitating growth and change? The effects on the child of parent separation or loss are not necessarily greater or lesser at one stage or another, they are simply different. Further, the effects are reliant upon the availability of adults, while accepting the child's grief reaction, to persist in forming a new relationship so that they can continue to progress up the developmental ladder. Fraiberg (1977) points out that in the early years the child's personality is essentially an "interpersonality," the self evolving in relation to human partners. "Therefore, when that bond is broken, the very structure of the personality is endangered and the mending of the personality will be an arduous task for the new partners."

Parent loss at any age leads to regression in terms of the skills most recently acquired. However, in the past, professionals have tended to minimize the impact of separation or loss when it occurs during infancy. Babies entering the child welfare system during this developmental period frequently have not had their needs adequately met and indeed they may improve when placed in a more responsive environment. However, it is not uncommon for children with normal attachments developed in interim care to be moved during infancy, either back to their birth families or to an adoptive home. These infants are at risk.

Even before children reach the age at which they are obviously anxious around strangers, they are affected by moves from one family to another. They no doubt are aware of changes in rhythm and routine that occur with a move. They react to the differences in temperature, noise, smell, touch, and visual stimulation that vary from household to household. Interruptions in parenting may hinder the child's progress in sorting out his perceptions of the world. Since precursors to logical thinking and basic cause-and-effect begin even at this young age, disturbances in this area may result. Children who have been abruptly exposed to different routines and environments during infancy may have their sense of security upset enough that they may become less flexible in the future.

Rutter (1981) indicates that the emotional distress of parental separation is most obvious between the ages of about six months and four years. "Probably, very young infants are 'protected' because they have yet to develop the capacities for selective attachments; conversely, older children are 'protected' because they have the cognitive skills needed to appreciate that it is possible to maintain attachment relationships over a period of absence." During the latter half of the first year the psychological tasks are to increase recognition and awareness, to differentiate primary caretakers from strangers, and to increase reciprocity and mutuality in terms of interpersonal relationships. Loss of parental figures during this stage of development is likely to lead to diminished trust for caregivers and difficulties in interacting with others.

During the toddler years, separation interferes with the development of a healthy balance between dependency and autonomy. If they do not trust that adults will be there when they need them, some of these children will insist on constantly keeping adults in sight by demanding or clinging. They may be afraid to show age-appropriate autonomy. Other children who have experienced loss of primary caregivers at this age go to the opposite extreme and become too autonomous. These children may parent themselves. They may withhold affection and may seem stubborn and resistant.

Developmental reactions to separations and losses are not necessarily of short duration, particularly when the child has not been given the emotional support necessary for completion of the grief process. The reactions may persist for years. It is not uncommon to see nine, ten, and eleven year old children in foster care who are still constantly clinging in spite of numerous attempts to interrupt this behavior. Other children show the effects of excessive autonomy through the grade school years and adolescence, perceiving parental behaviors as limiting rather than nurturing and protective.

Underlying both reactions is a lack of trust for others. In the first instance the child seems to be saying, "I can't count on you wanting to stay close so I will have to keep an eye on you." The second behavior seems to say, "I can't count on you being close when I need you, so I will have to count on myself." Since these problems are frequent for children in care, caseworkers, foster parents and adopters need to recognize that when there have been interruptions in children's caretaking during the toddler years, later experiences must emphasize opportunities for increasing both trust for others and age-appropriate autonomy. Permanent disruptions in the balance between dependence and independence are likely to lead to the young person growing up to be either a ready "victim" or "victimizer."

Identity formation is likely to be affected by a move to a new family during the toddler years. Sometimes there is a conscious effort to change the child's identified role in a family, such as in the case of a scapegoated child. Commonly with moves the child may change age position, moving from oldest to middle or any of the other possibilities. However, it is the adult's responsibility to understand and help facilitate healthy identity formation. Changes in the child's first name during this period may carry an even higher risk than at other developmental stages. Those with a permanent disruption in ego development are particularly prone to develop Borderline Personality in adolescence and early adulthood.

Johnnie is a four-year-old who was moved to an adoptive home when he was nearly three. In spite of strong recommendations to the contrary, his adoptive parents changed his name from Gerald to Johnnie. In the six months he was in adoptive placement, Johnnie developed a series of behavior problems. He did not measure up to the adoptive parents' expectations. Each time he referred to himself as Gerald, he was reprimanded.

Johnnie

The adoption disrupted, and Johnnie was again placed in interim care. Although Johnnie had been his name for only a short period, he was upset when his foster parents called him Gerald. He was adamant that his name was Johnnie. In foster care Johnnie was "too good." He seemed apprehensive about making any mistakes, any messes, or about asserting his autonomy in any way.

In an attempt to determine the nature of his conflict about the name, Johnnie's caseworker compiled a Life Story Book. She showed him pictures of himself as an infant and identified those pictures as Gerald. When she got to the part about the adoptive placement, she talked of the name change to Johnnie. She then talked about Johnnie's experience in the adoptive home and his return to foster care. She explained that Gerald and Johnnie are really one person. At this point Johnnie became agitated and repeatedly said, "Gerry is a bad boy. He's naughty. I'm Johnnie."

It was clear that Johnnie was going through the normal "good boy" versus "bad boy" conflict that each preschooler has to resolve. However, for Johnnie the name change which had occurred during the toddler years became associated with the split between good and bad. To this little boy, "Gerry" signified the "bad child" who had to move from a foster home, where he had been loved, to an adoptive home where he did not measure up. Johnnie was the "good child." However, he had not done a good enough job of being Johnnie in the adoptive home and thus had to leave. Back in foster care he was doing his best to be the "good" Johnnie so he would not have to move again.

As at other ages, there will be a regression in terms of recently acquired skills. For the toddler, most commonly these relate to eating, sleeping, and eliminating behaviors. Most toddlers depend on a family member to be their "interpreter" as they acquire language. If they are separated from that person, regression in language development will be more striking than if their interpreter, frequently a sibling, moves with them.

Children with multiple moves during the first three years of life are particularly vulnerable to severe problems in the development of social emotions, carrying with it long term implications for interpersonal relationships, conscience development and self-esteem.

For the preschooler it is their magical and egocentric thinking that most affects the reaction to parent loss. These children think they caused the loss, that it came about because of their wishes, thoughts, or behaviors. Their propensity for magical thinking is usually reinforced by a loss and is therefore likely to persist long beyond the age at which it commonly subsides.

Adults hold the responsibility for trying to identify the specific magical thinking of the child they are working with or parenting. What does the child think he did that caused the move? Or what could he have done to prevent it? What does he think he can do to have the outcome be what he desires? These are the questions the adult, not the child, must answer. Children of this age rarely openly share their magical thinking. However, by using some of the communication techniques—such as through play with puppets, stuffed animals, or joint story telling—which are discussed in the chapter on Direct Work With Children the adult may learn the answers to these questions.

Sometimes the magical thinking takes place on an unconscious basis, particularly when it reflects the "good versus bad" or the "big versus little" struggles so commonly associated with this developmental stage. Behaviors may provide clues as to the child's misperceptions. Caregivers, both before and after the move, should listen for comments that seem to make no sense, noting any odd or peculiar statements or behaviors. If carefully examined, these frequently give clues as to this child's perceptions and magical thinking. Although it is impossible to convince a child of these tender years that their thinking is flawed, when they get older the effects can be overcome if adults know the child's earlier thoughts. Corrine's case demonstrates how the "good versus bad" struggle can become entrenched in the child's personality and behaviors.

Corrine was four years old when her birth mother became terminally ill. Her father had abandoned the family earlier. Her mother had a prolonged and very painful illness. During much of this time the mother was at home but unable to meet her daughter's needs. Following her mother's death, Corrine was placed in interim care. She had many behavioral problems and her foster parents never felt close to her. Corrine joined her adoptive family when she was six.

Her adoptive parents sought help when Corrine was eight. Corrine did not mind well; she was prone to temper tantrums. She was frequently bossy with her adoptive mother. Although she had many problem behaviors, her mother identified the most distressing as The Look that Corrine gave in response to a demand being placed upon her. Mother described this look as a piercing gaze that was most commonly given just before Corrine left for school. It was a virtual guarantee that the school day would not go well and that problems would continue when she returned from school.

During the course of a therapy session, Corrine became very angry with her therapist and gave her The Look. The therapist asked Corrine what she thought she was. At this point, Corrine, extremely upset, was not monitoring her own answers. She quickly blurted out, "A wi----." The therapist supportively asked her to complete the word and Corrine said, "A witch," and then relaxed. The therapist had correctly interpreted The Look as a hex but had not been certain which word Corrine used in her own head to define her behavior.

During the discussion that followed it was learned that sometimes when her birth mother had been so ill, Corrine had wished she would die. Because Corrine was at an age when magical thinking is so prominent, when her mother did pass away Corrine came to believe that her wishes had caused her mother's death. As she became older, she felt increasingly guilty. When she was particularly angry with her adoptive mother, Corrine would place a hex on her by giving her The Look. No wonder her day at school would then go poorly. She was uncertain of her powers. Since Corrine's guilt and belief in her own power as a "witch" were primarily on an unconscious level, she was usually unable to explain her actions. When the intense anger was recreated in a therapy session the unconscious feelings rose to the surface and could be recognized for what they were, magical thinking. The adoptive mother no longer feared The Look and could assure Corrine that she would still be there both to love her and to hassle her about her chores if necessary after school.

Children who lose one parent, through either death or divorce, while retaining the other during the preschool years seem to be more prone to difficulties in resolving the Oedipal conflict than those who move away from a family.

The reader may remember that during the grade school years, the child uses his family as a base of psychological strength that he calls upon for solving out-of-home challenges. If children, during this stage, are spending their energies coping with feelings about separations and losses, it may interfere with their ability to accomplish the primary developmental tasks of this age, which include learning in school, developing friendships, and internalizing values and conscience. Separations and losses during these years are likely to cause a temporary regression to more concrete thinking and less mature behaviors. Regression in school performance is common after a move. Since families have differing values, the grade school child may become confused about "right" vs. "wrong."

Planned-for partings or losses during these years are less likely to be contaminated by magical thinking or misperceptions than were separations at earlier ages. The child's ability to understand time is important in terms of adjustment to shorter separations. However, fear of the unknown means that adults must be as honest as possible about what is happening now, what we think will happen in the future, when events will occur, and how decisions are made.

Even with their increased abilities to understand and conceptualize, these children cannot handle separations or losses without supportive help. During this period, however, they learn that they can continue to have strong feelings, either positive or negative, about people to whom they have a strong emotional connection but whom they rarely currently see. Attachments can be maintained even without frequent contact. Adults frequently forget this and think that because the child has been moved, or legal ties have been severed, the child is no longer influenced by the connection to past caregivers.

Helping children recognize the normalcy of ambivalence is useful. People commonly have a variety of emotions, sometimes contradictory ones such as sadness and happiness, simultaneously. For example, children of this age may identify, "Part of me feels sad and part of me feels mad." However, because of the emphasis on fairness at this age, they may get caught spending all of their energy on, "Why me?" or, "It's not fair," and not move further in terms of resolution of the loss. They may wonder, "Why didn't I get born into a family that could and would take care of me? Why me?"

It is during early adolescence, that parental loss is most highly associated with depression (Hill, 1972). Additionally, parent separation or loss during the teen years may accentuate the emotional instability and impulsivity that is so prominent during this developmental stage. This is most likely to happen if the teen did not desire the separation.

Frequently, however, separations at this age come about at the adolescent's instigation. In these cases the young person may see himself as the one in control of the situation. His energy may center on getting out of situations rather than learning to solve problems and remain within a family setting. If he keeps leaving families and is not able to meet his own needs, he may find himself in a difficult situation that is beyond his capacity to manage.

If the adolescent believes that he has lost all control over his life, he is likely either to become suicidal or to act out in a variety of antisocial ways. If the family does not meet his needs, he will become totally dependent on peers to meet all of his desires for approval. Frequently this adolescent, who is likely to have poor social skills, will join a group that is involved in a variety of antisocial activities.

When one parent leaves the home, there is a tendency for adolescent youth of the same sex to try to fill the role of the parent who left. Many adults, either overtly or covertly, support this adjustment by making comments such as, "You must be the 'man of the house' now that your father is gone." If adolescents are separated from the parent of the same sex they lose a primary source of identification. On the other hand, if a parent of the same sex is available up until the teen years, memories of that parent can be used to facilitate the psychological separation and identification process.

Those who have experienced parental separations or losses are less likely to be secure in their current sense of belonging. For those adolescents who have been separated from either or both birthparents, the issues around, "Where do I belong?" are likely to center around questioning where they should live and whether they belong in a family different than the one with whom they are currently living. Conflicted loyalties are once again prominent.

The Relationship with Caregivers as a Factor

In many situations the child's attachment to his parents and the latters' bonding to him go hand in hand, with each process reflecting itself in the other. However, in some circumstances there is an obvious splitting of the two. In these situations the feelings and reactions to the loss will be very different in the child and in the parent. These situations seem to be more common in the child welfare system than in the population as a whole.

A child may be well attached to a parent who is not very bonded to him. The most common circumstance, although not the only one, seems to be with a single mom who is chronically depressed and because of this is not emotionally available to her child. Currently, she is not strongly bonded to the child. The child, on the other hand, may be very attached to Mother. In fact, the child may be parenting the parent. Because the parent is not meeting the child's current needs, placement of the child is frequently considered in these situations. However, unless the child can be helped to relinquish his sense of responsibility for the parent's well being and complete the grieving process, there will be little accomplished by the placement. Although those working within the child welfare and legal systems may be able to mandate a physical separation, they are never able to impose psychological separation. Unless the child is able to form new attachments to the substitute caregivers, the desired goals of the placement will not be achieved. This possibility must always be considered.

On the other hand, there are sometimes situations in which parents are quite bonded to a child who is not very attached to them. As mentioned earlier, the most extreme, but luckily quite infrequent, example is in childhood autism. Autistic children have problems forming close interpersonal connections with anyone. However, their parents are usually bonded to them. More commonly seen are children who have lesser degrees of organic dysfunction which interfere with the way they form relationships. Although the parents may care deeply for their children, they may have difficulty decoding the child's cues and be ineffective in meeting their child's needs. Because they are not successful in this, the child does not form as close a reciprocal relationship with the parent as occurs when parents are able to easily understand their child's signals and respond appropriately. These children are just as likely to have problems relating to other adults. There is, however, the possibility that caregivers who are experienced in working with organically impaired children may have developed skills which enhance their abilities to correctly interpret the child's signals and form close relationships with them.

Past Experiences with Separation as a Factor

Those who have experienced multiple moves are less likely to show a marked reaction to a current separation. However, their prognosis for subsequently forming close attachments must be guarded. Individuals who have experienced separations develop defenses against the pain. The most common is a hesitation to subsequently become emotionally close to others, thereby protecting oneself from a repeat of the psychological pain of separation. Unfortunately, the lack of subsequent attachments is likely to lead to another move, and the child's perception of the lack of stability in adult child relationships is further reinforced. In general, the easier it is to get a child out of a family—meaning that neither child nor parent protests much—the more difficult it will be either to return the child to that home or to help him develop close trusting relationships with adults elsewhere.

Martin showed no evidence of distress or grief when he moved to the LaBelle foster home. According to Donna LaBelle, "He just walked in as though he had always been there."

The Child's Perceptions as a Factor

The child's perceptions of the reasons for a separation play an important part in influencing the reaction to a move. Does he view the separation as his fault? Most do. Egocentric, magical thinking is prominent at the time of loss. It is only human to want some measure of control over one's own destiny. Individuals tend to hold themselves responsible when things don't turn out the way they want them to. They are prone to magical thinking then.

Nathan

When Nathan lost his stepdad at age four, he believed it was because he was "too big." Now Nathan is twelve. In his adoptive home he constantly demands close physical supervision by demonstrating out-of-control behaviors. Play skills are immature. Good guys versus bad guys are prominent themes in his play. Although superficially he takes charge of many interactions with adults and

150

peers alike, there is a very immature quality about Nathan as well. Every time his parents try to treat him like a twelve-year-old, giving him more freedom and responsibility, he "blows" it and adults have to revert to closer supervision.

When Nathan was a year old his previously single birth mother married. A year later she gave birth to a second son, Billy. Mother had always been cool and aloof with Nathan, who had been a difficult child to parent. Mother became neglectful of both boys and started to abuse Nathan physically. Her husband, a kind, loving man, provided the emotional nurturing for both boys. He and Nathan had a close mutually rewarding relationship. When Nathan was four and Billy was two, because of his wife's abusive and neglectful behaviors the father left the family. He was awarded custody of his son, Billy, but Nathan remained with his mother. Subsequently Nathan had contact with neither his stepfather nor with his half brother, Billy. Within months Nathan was placed in foster care because of physical abuse. He had three subsequent foster care disruptions and one adoptive disruption before being placed with his current adoptive family eighteen months ago.

From Nathan's viewpoint, being younger, like Billy, meant having one's needs met. His desire to remain young, to be nurtured, and to be cared for had moved from the conscious to the unconscious but was firmly entrenched in his personality and behaviors by the time he was twelve. Yet, he saw himself as undeserving of having his needs met, and when attempts were made to provide emotional closeness and nurture he resisted them vigorously. His only avenue for connecting with others was to be physically out of control.

Many times adults tell children that a move is not their fault. Although this may be a true statement, it is not necessarily a particularly helpful one. By using the word *fault* there is an implication that assignment of blame is primary and easy. In general, it is more effective to start talking about needs and relationships. What were the child's needs? The parental needs? How were family members trying to meet these needs? Were things working out well for all family members or not? The focus is on reciprocity in relationships. This may help the child gain further understanding while acknowledging his control and power over his own behaviors without holding him responsible for the behaviors of adults. Discussing *responsibility* rather than *fault* places the emphasis on the more positive quality. The child can be helped to understand that each individual, adult or youngster, is responsible for his own behaviors and feelings, but is not responsible for another's actions.

Merideth currently lives in the Faraday foster home. She lived with the Faradays from age ten months until three years. At that time Merideth was placed with the Norman family, the plan being adoption. However, after six

Merideth

151

weeks in the Norman home, the parents asked that she be removed because they could not cope with her severe behavior problems. She was returned to the Faraday foster home.

An adoption specialist was asked to complete an assessment prior to another adoptive family being selected for Merideth. The specialist was told that the child knews that the move from the Norman home was not her fault. In talking to Merideth, Ms. Shilling, the specialist, asked, "Can you tell me about a time when you were sad?" Merideth quickly said, "When I had to leave mama Julie (Mrs. Faraday) I was so-o-o sad, but I didn't cry." Ms. Shilling proceeded to ask Merideth to tell her about leaving the Norman home. The child responded, "She was mean. She used to hit me." Ms. Shilling commented, "I wonder why a mother would do that." The child's response, with a gleam in her eye, " Because I was such a naughty little girl."

Merideth may have been told that the disruption was not her fault. However, she knew she had played a part in it, and rightly so. In the Norman home, this previously toilet trained child would pull down her panties and have a bowel movement on the carpet. She flushed her toys down the toilet, necessitating a call to a plumber. She scratched the neighbor's new car with a rock. And she clobbered the six year old already in the family with a toy, leading to an injury that required stitches.

Ms. Shilling proceeded to ask Merideth how she had felt on return to the Faraday home. With a sparkle in her eye and a huge grin, the child's reply was, "Just right!" Ms. Shilling knew that it would not be easy to help Merideth be successful in joining an adoptive family. Her previous wish to return to the Faraday home had been gratified. She had no desire to leave again.When moved to an adoptive family she would undoubtedly try her best to be ejected, believing that she would then once again return to the Faradays.

A major part of helping facilitate the grief process is identifying the child's magical thinking both about what may have led to a placement and about what behaviors on his part might lead to the outcome he desires. Finding out the answers to the, "If only I hadn't....I would never have had to move" and the "If only I now do....everything will be fine" can help us at least through time overcome the child's magical thinking and replace it with better reasoning skills.

Preparation for the Move as a Factor

As mentioned earlier, preparation for any move is important. In general, those experiencing abrupt losses are more likely to become "stuck" in the grief process than those experiencing planned separations. At the time of the move other factors to be considered are the attitudes of the people the child is leaving as well as those to whom he is moving and his ability to express emotions and have them accepted. Claudia Jewett-Jarrett (1988) talks of the importance of identifying the emotional tone of the parting message as a child leaves a family. Is this message a blessing? Is it a curse? Or, is it so noncommittal that the implication is that the child was unimportant to the caregiver?

Upon leaving a home, the child may perceive himself as receiving a blessing ("More than anything in the world, I hope that things go well for you in the future.") or he may perceive himself as receiving a curse ("You just wouldn't believe how difficult he has been," said to the adult moving the child in the latter's presence.) Actually, in Merideth's case she had been given a disguised curse when she left the Faraday home the first time. Numerous adults had implied by their behavior that she should be happy to be moving to an adoptive family. She thought they meant she shouldn't be sad about leaving the only family she knew—the Faradays—so she didn't cry. Unfortunately, for some children they leave without others saying so much as a good-bye.

How is the child welcomed into the new home? This, too, according to Jewett-Jarrett (1988) is important. Are family members prepared for his arrival or do the foster dad and/or other children in the family come home to an unexpected addition to the family? Is the child treated in a matter of fact manner or with a more cordial welcome? Does he become one of a number, or is he seen as an unique individual? Some children are greeted with fear, apprehension, or distrust.

The environment in which the child lives following a loss has a tremendous impact on the child's resolution of the grief process. According to Brier (1988) it is the quality of home life subsequent to early parental loss that is critically related to the development of adult psychopathology. Parental separations which are followed by placement into an adverse environment lead to more damage than when placement is in a supportive, helpful environment (Aldgate, 1988). This may occur in a variety of circumstances, for example when a child is placed with a family that is unable to meet his needs. Or it may occur following the transfer of a child from a foster home that is meeting his needs to the home of birth parents who are not supportive in helping the child grieve.

The Child's Temperament as a Factor

Some individuals at times of stress withdraw. This may be either physical withdrawal as exemplified by isolation in a bedroom or running away, or it may be psychological withdrawal wherein the person is unresponsive to others. However, other individuals become more active with stress. Their emotions are very evident. They act out. Neither "flight" nor "fight" is in and of itself preferable. Either can be done in ways that promote adaptation or in ways that prevent individuals from coping with the grief process. It is unlikely that we will be able to change a child's basic temperament. Indeed, why would we want to? However, we can help him utilize his temperament so that it works for him rather than against him.

Judy

When Judy left the Haslett family, moving to the Caldwell foster home, her primary feeling seemed to be one of relief, as though a weight had been lifted from her shoulders. You may remember from the introduction that Judy and the Hasletts had been experiencing considerable strain in their relationships for a long period of time. Separation provided relief for both parents and child as well as other family members.

Mrs. Caldwell, an exceptionally experienced and sensitive foster parent, noted that periodically Judy would look sad and be withdrawn for several hours. Occasionally the depressive symptoms might last one or two days. However, Marie Caldwell observed that most of the time Judy kept herself exceedingly busy as though she were trying to avoid thinking about the past.

The Environment the Child is Leaving as a Factor

Despite shortcomings that others may see in the child's environment, from his viewpoint the known is nearly always preferable to the unknown. His fear of the unknown is able, in his own mind, to overcome many deficiencies.

Ardith
Prentice

When placed in the receiving home, Ardith and Prentice showed quite different reactions. For the first two to three days Ardith cried much of the time according to the foster mother. The toddler was aggressive toward all of the other children but Prentice was the most frequent target of her hitting and biting. The aggression was unprovoked by others and seemed "to come out of nowhere." After several days Ardith cried less, hit less, and became increasingly withdrawn.

Prentice, on the other hand, seemed very tentative in all of his behaviors. He never lashed back at his sister and sometimes did not even attempt to avoid her physical abuse. The foster parents described him as usually being on the fringe of activities, carefully observing, but rarely participating. He tried to keep in close physical proximity to the foster mom, following her from room to room as though he were afraid to lose sight of her. If a child is actually fearful of his living environment, he may not react as adversely to the separation. Indeed, relief is occasionally observed. An adoption worker was working with six-year-old Asher on his Life Story Book. They were talking about the permanent separation from his abusive birth mom. The caseworker indicated that she realized that Asher might well be angry about the separation. Asher's response was, "I am angry at you. I'm angry that you left me with her so long. You know it was dangerous. I could have been seriously hurt."

The Relationship Between Fear and Attachment

It is important to understand the relationship between fear and attachment. The primary function of attachment behavior in the animal kingdom as a whole is protection. In human families, too, attachment behaviors are heightened when a family member is threatened. The function of both fear and attachment is protection. The common reaction is characterized by withdrawal from the feared object and movement toward a trusted person. The caseworker who is considering removing a child from a family embodies a threat. In such a situation, the child may cling to the parent and exhibit hostility or fear of the worker.

It is possible to have a conflict between the two aspects of the fear/attachment reaction. Figures 3-1A and 3-1B illustrate such fear/attachment reactions. Both diagrams portray a child, a dog, and a parent. In both cases the child wants to get away from the dog and get close to the parent.

3-1 *Figure*

$\triangleright \triangleright \triangleright$ = fear response
$\blacktriangleright \blacktriangleright \blacktriangleright$ = attachment response

A

B

In Figure 3-1A, by moving in one direction the child can both get away from the dog and get closer to his parent. In Figure 3-1B, however, the child faces a dilemma. If he moves away from the object he fears, he also moves even further from the person to whom he is attached. Most-well attached children, up to an age where they have good abstract thinking skills, when faced with such a dilemma will choose moving closer to the attachment object over withdrawing from the feared object. When children have healthy parental attachments, the effects of separation may be more severe than the trauma associated with dangerous situations. This was noted during World War II when children who remained with their parents in London were noted to be less disturbed by the bombing than those who were evacuated to the country as a protection against it (Freud, A., (1943).

155

Thus we can understand why an abused child may cling to his abusive parent when the caseworker enters the home. Though the child may fear the parent, he may also be attached to her. He both fears the caseworker, a stranger, and has no attachment to her. He chooses the parent.

The most frightening thing for a child is to be simultaneously afraid and separated from his attachment object. This is why moves are so frightening. All humans' fears are more easily heightened when they are away from those to whom they are attached.

Giving Children Permission to Have Feelings

All involved in the process of moving children need to give them permission to have their feelings. Sometimes this can most easily be done by talking about other children. "Some children who have moved have said they were mostly sad, others said mostly scared, and still others said mostly angry. Do you agree or disagree with them? How is it for you?" Some children may need to be taught more about identifying feelings. "When I get nervous, my stomach feels like something is jumping around in it. Some people say they have butterflies in their stomach. Have you ever felt that way?"

Caseworkers, birth parents, foster parents, and adoptive parents all need to learn to let children express emotions. Even when adults verbally say they want children to express their feelings, what they often mean is that they want them to talk calmly about them. When children have strong feelings they cry, scream, or act out their anger. Adults frequently tell them to stop their behaviors. Children may think this means, "Don't have the feeling." Bowlby (1980) noted that when a caregiver is afraid of feelings, children learn to hide their own emotions. When a parent prefers silence the children sooner or later stop sharing feelings or asking questions about past caregivers.

When children use unacceptable behaviors to show strong feelings, adults can accept the emotions at the same time as they confront the behaviors. They can teach the child new and more acceptable ways to express emotions. For example, if a child is angry and hits a sibling, the adult might say, "I know that you are really mad and that is okay, but it is not all right to hurt others when you are angry. When you are mad and feel like hitting, you can punch a pillow."

Soon after a move, adults should avoid isolating the child to discipline him. Sending the child to his room may send the message, "When you are naughty I don't want to be around you." Although this is a helpful message, and not too threatening, for the child who is well attached to his current parents, it may be counter-productive with the newly placed child. This child may interpret being sent to his room as, "This time you are being sent away only as far as your room, but if you continue to misbehave you may be sent away from this home." Figure 3-2 illustrates a negative cycle that might be established when misbehaviors are followed by a disciplinary response of isolation.

156

Such a negative cycle might be lessened by having the child take a chair in the same room as the adult until the child has calmed down. This action gives the message, "I will be close by until you are back in control of yourself. When you have strong feelings, you need to be close to people, not separated from them." Simultaneously, it gives the message that the adult is not afraid of the child's anger.

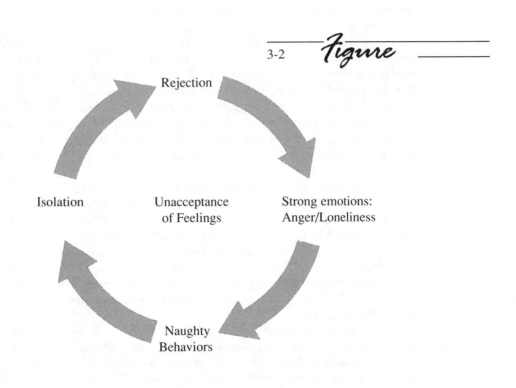

Rejection

Isolation   Unacceptance   Strong emotions:
                   of Feelings   Anger/Loneliness

Naughty
Behaviors

Explaining to Children What is Happening

Many children are given little information when they are moved. The foster care system may seem familiar and logical to caseworkers and foster parents but it frequently makes no sense to children. They need to know that foster families are families that take care of children when their birth parents cannot. They take care of children until a decision is made about where the child will grow up. Foster parents will be responsible for meeting the child's day to day needs, but will not be in charge of making the major decisions in his life. Although foster parents may have some input, these decisions will be shared by the birth parents and the caseworker. If disagreements between birth parents and caseworkers cannot be settled, then the judge may have to make the decision.

Figure 3-3 (adapted from work of Spencer) has been designed to help children understand the various roles that parents have. It provides a format for explaining who is responsible for what. It can be used both to explain a child's current situation or to help prepare him for an upcoming move.

Everyone has birth parents, a birth mother and a birth father. These will be the same two people for all of a person's lifetime. No one can change this. Children in our society also have legal parents. Legal parents make the major decisions in a child's life. "Parenting parents" meet the child's daily needs for nurture and discipline.

For many children the birth parents are also the legal parents and the parenting parents. However, in foster care and adoption the different aspects of parenting are split. The child in interim care still has the same set of birth parents as he had prior to placement. In some cases where an agency has temporary custody of the child, the legal parenting role is shared by the birth parent and the agency or court. For example, a birth parent may be required to pay support while the agency may have the right to select the foster home in which the child lives. In the case of voluntary foster care, the legal parent may still be the birth parent.

When a child is returned to the birth home, but the agency continues to monitor the placement, Figure 3-3 can be used to help explain different people's responsibilities. The birth parent has again become the parenting parent but those aspects of the legal parent role related to safety and security are retained by the agency or court.

Aspects Of Parenting

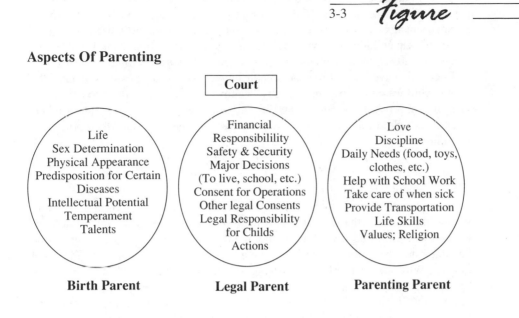

Court

| Birth Parent | Legal Parent | Parenting Parent |

Life
Sex Determination
Physical Appearance
Predisposition for Certain Diseases
Intellectual Potential
Temperament
Talents

Financial Responsibility
Safety & Security
Major Decisions (To live, school, etc.)
Consent for Operations
Other legal Consents
Legal Responsibility for Childs Actions

Love
Discipline
Daily Needs (food, toys, clothes, etc.)
Help with School Work
Take care of when sick
Provide Transportation
Life Skills
Values; Religion

Birth Parent   **Legal Parent**   **Parenting Parent**

If parental rights are terminated or when birth parents sign a voluntary release of parental rights, the agency or court now has all of the responsibilities of the legal parent. However the child continues to have the same birth parents although these adults no longer have any legal rights or responsibilities. The foster parents continue to be the parenting parents. In explaining adoption to a child, he can be told that termination of parental rights means that no one set of parents will again fill all three parenting roles. However, adoption is the combining of two aspects of the parenting—the legal parent and the parenting parent roles. Adoption means that the parenting parents now have all of the legal rights and responsibilities but they are not the birth parents. This fits as well for infant adoption as for stepparent adoption or older child adoption. After a child is adopted, the parents with whom he lives, rather than caseworkers or judges, will be in charge of the major decisions in the child's life.

The court is involved in two different ways. When there are disagreements about who should be either the child's legal or parenting parent, the court will decide. It may even be asked to participate in determining a birth parent's identity if there are disagreements. In addition, in most states the designation of who is a legal parent can only be changed with the court's approval. Older children who are joining adoptive families need to know that this is just as true when the adopting parents are being given the legal parent role as it was when that role was relinquished or removed from the birth parent.

In all cases this method of explanation validates the importance of birth parents whether or not the child is currently or ever will again live with them. Such acceptance of birth parents and what they mean to a child's life is critical if we are to help children deal with their feelings about separation from these parents and if we are to help them develop a strong sense of personal identity. For children who have at one time had an attachment to their birth parents, even if the relationship was not a psychologically healthy one, mourning their loss is a life task. It is most easily accomplished when his current family is accepting of his trauma. The child can only really say good-bye after he has established other safe relationships.

The Caseworker's Feelings

A caseworker may be faced with the task of helping a child and family with a separation in the face of her own strong feelings about the move. Perhaps the caseworker has been working with a family to prevent a move. If a separation becomes necessary the worker may have a variety of emotions. She may feel guilty, "Why wasn't I able to do enough to prevent placement?" Or frustrated, "Why isn't the system providing the alternative service that might prevent placement?" Or anger, "Why didn't the parent take my advice and follow through to prevent placement?" or sad about what the child and family will face.

Other moves may involve other feelings. Workers may feel apprehensive or excited and happy for the child. The professional may feel a sense of loss when the move means that the child will get a new caseworker. She may feel competitive with the new worker, thinking, "I know this child and his background better than anyone." On the other hand a worker may experience a sense of relief when a child moves from her caseload.

Moving a child may tap into unresolved separations or losses in the worker's past. It is important that caseworkers be aware of how their own feelings may either make a move more difficult or easier.

Troy

Troy, age six, was moving from a foster home to an adoptive home. Troy's caseworker, Mrs. Green, had developed a strong positive relationship with him. She had helped him with his Lifebook and had helped him cope with his feelings when his birth parents decided that an adoption plan would be in his best interests. She saw Troy as a very likeable child. She looked forward to making an adoption plan for him. Mrs. Green had hoped that Troy would continue to live in the same community so that she could have continued contact with him since she knew him and his past so well. However, because so many people in the community knew Troy and his birth family, it was decided that he should be placed out of the area.

160

Troy's case history was sent to the regional adoption exchange. Initially, when studies of prospective families were sent to Mrs. Green, she seemed to find some flaw in each study and indicated that she wasn't certain that the families would "really understand" Troy and all that had happened to him. Mrs. Green's supervisor confronted her about the possibility that her own feelings for Troy might be preventing her from being objective.

Subsequently, an "ideal" family was identified and selected. Mrs. Green had close contact with the family, the foster family, and Troy during the pre-placement period. The adoptive parents and the foster parents felt that Troy was ready to move after about two-and-a-half weeks of preplacement visits. However, Mrs. Green began to wonder if this was the "right" family for Troy since he was acting out some during and after the visits. He was no longer relating to Mrs. Green in the same way. He seemed to be emotionally distancing himself from her.

Again, her supervisor pointed out that Mrs. Green's own emotions might be coloring case decisions. Mrs. Green recognized this. However, she also recognized that her empathy for Troy had been important in their developing the type of relationship that had been helpful and supportive to him during his interim care placement. She was confused about what to do with all of her own feelings. She recognized that at the time of the final move she would probably be quite upset. Interestingly, on the day of the move, Mrs. Green was ill, and her supervisor completed the transition process.

It is important that caseworkers insure that children and parents are both given permission to have feelings, are provided with modeling of appropriate expression of feelings, are given support for each member's unique emotions, and are encouraged to acknowledge feelings that may be initially denied. Exercise 3-1 that follows is intended to help you examine times when your own feelings have either helped or hindered your work with families. It may be easily modified for use by foster parents by having them think of two children who have previously left their homes. New caseworkers, as well as prospective foster or adoptive parents might think about past separations from siblings, parents, or friends.

Caseworker Feelings at the Times of Moves

Purpose:
1. To identify caseworker feelings at the time of moves.
2. To demonstrate how these emotions can be either helpful or harmful in facilitating the moving process.

How to:
1. Identify two cases from your own caseload that involved moves of any type (into foster care; from one foster home to another; return to a birth home; or a move to an adoptive home.)
    You may include examples of cases that did not involve a physical move of the child but involved a transfer into or out of your caseload.
2. Close your eyes and remember where you were when the move took place. See the child. Who else was there? How were each of you dressed? What was the expression on your face? On the child's face? On he faces of other adults? What were you feeling? How did you express these feelings? To whom did you express them? How did your own feelings interfere with or help you in recognizing the feelings of the child and other family members? Who was the identified client in this case? Did your feelings at the time of the move make you feel emotionally closer to or further away from the client? How did your feelings at the time of the move affect your subsequent relationship with the client?

People involved in the child's life may have differing emotions at the time of separations. Many times the child's feelings and the emotions of the child's primary attachment object are very similar. However, this is not always true. Brothers and sisters—birth, foster, or adoptive—may have strong reactions to a child's moving away from the family. Frequently these are not recognized, expressed, or supported, particularly if they are different from those of the primary caretaker in the family.

II The Grief Process

Bowlby (1980) describes three stages that well-attached children go through when they are separated from caregivers to whom they are attached. These are most evident in the child from ages six months to four years. The child:
1. initially protests vigorously and makes attempts to recover his attachment object, such as going to the door and trying to find her.

2.   despairs of recovering caregiver, but continues to be watchful. He appears to be preoccupied and depressed. When a car drives up or when there is a noise at the door, he becomes alert, hoping it is the caregiver returning.

3.   becomes emotionally detached and appears to lose interest in caregivers in general.

Sean recently turned four. He has been in foster care for about three months. Initially he was fussy and cried constantly. Within a few weeks he became less fussy and more withdrawn. He played for hours by himself, using baby talk and making peculiar sounds. At times he ignored all adults. Other times he had good eye contact but seemed indiscriminately affectionate, responding equally warmly to all adults. He was at his age level on developmental tests.

The history revealed that Sean's mother had died when he was eighteen months old. His father became his primary caregiver. When Sean was three, the father planned a major move across the country. While Dad was moving and getting settled, he left his son with an aunt with whom Sean had had no previous contact.

When his Dad left Sean became very fussy. He regressed in toileting and smeared feces. He alternated between being depressed and having temper tantrums. The aunt requested interim care placement because of Sean's behaviors.

After Sean had been in interim care for three months his father came for his first visit with the child. Sean's face lit up when he first saw his father. He then looked apprehensive and seemed ambivalent about getting close to Dad. His father initiated many positive interactions with Sean. Eventually, Sean started clinging, saying, "Don't ever leave me again, Daddy."

Sean

When a young child is very withdrawn and emotionally detached, even professionals without the benefit of a full and accurate history may perceive the child as severely disturbed rather than grieving. The same reaction may occur in children who are abruptly moved from interim care to either birth family members or to an adoptive placement. Adults must remember that once new attachments are formed, separation from these substitute parents is no less painful and no less damaging to the child than separation from birth or adoptive parents (Goldstein, 1973).

It is crucial that when a child emotionally withdraws from new parent figures, they do not, in turn, react by withdrawing from him. Unfortunately adults sometimes withdraw to protect themselves from the emotional pain of feeling ineffective when giving to an unresponsive child. This is less likely to occur when caregivers understand the grief process and perceive past attachments as important and useful in terms of long-term adjustment. The new caregivers need to use gentle persistence to build a relationship with the child. Strategies, for building new attachments, such as those outlined for the LaBelles and Martin in the first chapter, need to be implemented. Current caregivers deserve to have both knowledge and emotional support, enabling them to help the child through the grief process while simultaneously building healthy new relationships. Without this, the likelihood of long, term attachment problems occurring is great.

Normal toddlers after only several days of separation from their parents usually show marked distress if they are not in the presence of other familiar family members. When parents return after a several day absence the toddler tends to behave in one of two ways. He either becomes quite clingy to the parent, as though fearful of a repeat separation, or he behaves in an aloof manner at the time of reunification. In the latter case it is as though the youngster is demonstrating that the parent abandoned him when he wanted her and that he will now psychologically abandon the parent when she initiates contact. Usually, in this situation, if the parent starts to leave again, the child will once again show agitation and may start clinging. In either case, the child's reaction is an attempt to get the parent re-engaged. However, the behavior sometimes puts a strain on the adult who then may in turn emotionally withdraw from the child. Bowlby (1980) states that emotional detachment may be seen as early as a week after the separation.

From about age four-and-a-half on we have found that the stages of grieving, Table 3-2, as described by Elisabeth Kubler-Ross (1975) help us understand the mourning process in both children and their parents. The shock and denial stages will be most prominent when the separation has been abrupt. The body's initial reaction to an overwhelming psychological insult, such as loss of a close family member, is to shut down. The child may show little emotion, will seem numb, and appear to be mechanical. The same outward signs may be seen in cases of severe neglect. An important differentiation for a caseworker to make when a child has had an abrupt move without a full pre-transition assessment of the child and family is clarification as to whether the symptoms are secondary to chronic emotional neglect or the trauma of parental separation. Suggestions about ways to determine which is the primary problem are included in the chapter on minimizing the trauma of moves.

───────── *Table* ───── 3-2

Stages of Grieving

>Shock
>Denial
>Anger
>Bargaining
>Sadness/Despair
>Resolution

164

During the denial phase of the grief process an individual is prone to appetite and sleep disturbances as well as having problems paying attention. He may either overeat or have little appetite. He may sleep excessively or have trouble getting to sleep at all. Nightmares are frequent during this stage. Forgetfulness is common. The child is not being resistant or manipulative when he has problems with memory and paying attention. These problems are beyond the individual's conscious control. Energies are diverted to coping with the pain of separation and loss and little energy is available to put into processing what is going on in the here and now.

The next three stages—anger, bargaining, sadness—may occur in any order and indeed may recycle. Anger is commonly displaced onto others, such as foster parents, peers, or caseworkers. Minor stimuli are apt to lead to angry outbursts. In trying to regain some sense of control over one's one destiny, the grieving individual is likely to escalate ordinary requests into control issues.

Bargaining reflects the magical egocentric thinking which accompanies most losses, but is especially prominent during the years three to five and in adolescence. It frequently takes the form of promises. "If only....then I promise I will...." During sadness and despair tears come easily. The individual looks sad and withdrawn. Clinging and increased dependence may emerge.

Resolution for children in the fostercare system is acceptance of having two sets of parents. The acceptance is on an emotional rather than intellectual basis. Once the separation or loss has been accepted, the grieving individual once again has energy for continued growth and change. During the grief process a tremendous amount of psychological, and sometimes physical, energy is diverted into coping with strong emotions. Less energy is available for day-to-day relationships and the tasks associated with normal childhood development. Without help in completing the grief process delays in emotional development become common. Again, resolution means acceptance; it does not mean that the child has to like what has happened to him. He never has to like it, but until he accepts it, he will be limited in the progress he is able to make in other areas of his life. Clare Winnicott (1986) goes so far as to assert that if we would respond effectively with children at the point of crisis when they enter care, and at the subsequent crisis points which are a part of growth, we might prevent many of them from becoming clients in one capacity or another for the rest of their lives.

Cultural factors may facilitate or inhibit movement through the stages of the grief process. In general, American culture reinforces the "stiff upper lip" mode of coping and gives little permission for full expression of tumultuous emotions, either in children or in adults. In addition, there are cultural expectations which encourage members of each sex to become stuck in different stages of the grief process.

For example, boys from a very young age are frequently given the message, "Big boys don't cry." Rarely are adults thinking of grieving when the message is given. They are usually talking about tears accompanying minor physical pain. Nonetheless the message goes in loud and strong. The frequency with which males become stuck in the anger phase of the grief process and have difficulty moving into and through the sadness/despair phase should not be surprising. Although the anger starts out as a legitimate part of the grieving, through time it becomes a defense against acknowledging and expressing sad feelings. Resolution cannot be achieved until this defense is overcome and the individual moves through sadness/despair. Anger management, although useful in and of itself, will not be enough to facilitate resolution of the grief process.

On the other hand, females in our society from a very young age are given messages that simultaneously inhibit their directing anger outwardly and reinforce their being open about sadness. Therefore, it is more likely for female children and women to bypass the anger phase and move directly to sadness and despair. However, once again, to achieve resolution the anger must be accepted and discharged. It is quite common for females to turn all of their anger inwards, becoming depressed and exhibiting a variety of symptoms which are self-abusive at some level.

Males stuck in the anger phase have related that they were afraid they would "drown in the sadness" if they ever let it come to the surface. Females stuck in sadness are frequently afraid that they will lose all self-control if they ever let loose of their anger. However, once the resistance to moving into the next phase of the grief process has been overcome the individual who was previously stuck is usually able to move through this new phase quite rapidly. Usually it takes a combination of repeatedly helping the grieving individual overcome his magical thinking by helping him face reality again and again, plus considerable supportive confrontation to overcome the resistance to coping with pain, to get him to be able to continue his progress through the grief cycle to resolution.

How Children Perceive Separations and Losses

One key to humanizing the process of moving a child from one family to another is to become sensitive to the ways that children perceive parental separations. Many children perceive moves into or out of interim care as being taken away from parents. They see both themselves and their parents as having no control over the situation. These children may feel as if they have been kidnapped or snatched. Their perception of parents as trustworthy, powerful individuals is diminished. People outside the family seem to have more power than family members. Indeed, every time there is a power-based move, at some level the importance of any and all family ties is diminished.

Children who perceive the separation as being taken away, especially if there has been no preparation, are prone to chronic fears and anxiety. Some may cope with their sense of lack of control over their own lives by withdrawing, rarely asserting themselves, and always trying to please others. Others do just the opposite, constantly asserting themselves, trying to be in control of everything. For both, an imbalance between age-appropriate dependency vs. autonomy is created or enhanced. In both types of reactions there is a diminished trust for adults and self.

In other circumstances children may perceive a move as being given away at the time of a separation or loss. These youngsters tend to feel that they have not measured up in some way. They are likely to hold themselves responsible for the events leading to the move, developing chronic guilt. They may have concomitant sadness and depression. If the child worked hard to change his behavior and measure up in a birth, foster, or adoptive home but still faces a move, he will probably be angry as well.

In general, it is more dangerous if the child perceives a move as someone coming and taking him than if he perceives it as being given to someone else after much preparation and many interactions between the two sets of parents. If a child perceives a move as being taken away by strangers, he must live in a perpetual state of anxiety, fearing every knock at the door or every visit by acquaintances.

A third reaction is for the child to feel neither given nor taken away but to think instead that he is in charge of the move. Such children believe that they chose to move and consciously did something that led to the move. This can come about either via actual events, for example a child reporting sexual abuse to a school teacher, or via magical thinking such as we saw in Corrine's case earlier in this chapter.

Although younger children often believe they have caused moves when they have not, older children may well have started the investigation or moving process with their allegations or by verbally expressing their desires. Although these may be psychologically healthy responses to an abusive situation, the fact that the youngsters were in charge of the separation may subsequently lead them to believe that they are responsible for all subsequent events and should also be in charge of all future decisions.

The least harmful perception of how a separation comes about is for the young person to see decision making as a shared responsibility. It is best if the child feels that he, along with others, has input but not full responsibility for the plan. Although Viorst (1986) describes all normal development as being accompanied by simultaneous losses, the same concept can be used to explain why moves may sometimes be unpreventable. The parent separation or loss is occurring because it is necessary for the child's continued growth and development.

Simultaneously the decision making can be expanded to include a variety of individuals rather than only one. For example, if a child is abruptly removed from birth parents because of physical abuse, the caseworker might include the parents in the decision making process (as follows) in a manner such as the one used in Lee's case.

Gilbert

Lee, age eight, has recently been placed in interim care because of bruising following severe physical discipline. He is a withdrawn, hypervigilant child who holds himself responsible for the separation because of the misbehavior that led to the discipline. Lee's parents see the caseworker as interfering in their family and were unwilling to help with the moving process.

In discussing what has happened with Lee, Mr. Thomas, the caseworker, tells him that there are laws that say it is not okay for parents to bruise children when they are disciplining them. He understands that sometimes Lee's parents become very angry and frustrated and that they have trouble discharging these feelings without hurting children. They do not seem to be able to ask for help for this problem with their mouths. They only seem to be able to ask for help with their behaviors.

Mr. Thomas then can help Lee identify other people he knows, including children in his foster home or in his classroom, who have problems handling anger and frustration or who have problems verbally asking for help. Simultanouesly he is helping Lee focus on some things he himself might need to learn to do while identifying what the parents need to learn in order to be able to have Lee return to their care. Mr. Thomas indicates that the parents, by their behaviors if not by their mouths, were involved in the decision making process that led to Lee's placement.

When parents ask for the child to be removed from their home, a caseworker might reframe the giving away by talking of how the adults involved, including parents, recognize that what the child needs to continue to grow and change is not being provided in the current living situation. Even though the move is painful, the child deserves to have his needs better met.

If the child reports abuse or neglect which leads to a separation, he needs recognition that indeed he is part of the process by bringing the situation to the attention of others. However, it is a shared decision. After investigation, child welfare personnel agree that a move is necessary. If they do not think it is indicated, the allegations alone will not lead to a separation.

Non-Helpful Ways of Coping with Painful Emotions

Understandably, people do not like pain, either physical or emotional. Children and adults alike use a variety of psychological defenses to cope with emotional pain. Although initially these defenses may be protective, through time they themselves become inhibiting and not helpful. A major thrust in therapy is identifying and overcoming the defenses which are interfering with the individual's continued growth. Professionals need to be aware of them not only in the children they are working with but also in themselves, the birth parents, foster parents, and others. The pain a child or birth parent is experiencing may tap into unresolved separation or loss experiences of an adult working with the case. If the adult tries to avoid facing her own pain, she may stop being effective to children and parents she is trying to help.

During the early phases of the grief process in particular, it is common for the grieving individual to try to numb the pain. This may be done by sleeping constantly, or keeping so busy that there is no time to think. Adults and adolescents—and sometimes even younger children—may turn to drugs or alcohol to diminish the pain.

Denial, avoidance, and minimization are all common defenses. Both adults and children may need help facing the reality of their situation. That means helping professionals must not align with the grieving individual in avoiding the pain but must provide the emotional support necessary to face and overcome it. For example, when visits are avoided because adults do not want to see a child's pain, it is not helpful to resolution of the grief process.

Displacement of feelings or projecting blame onto others are also common defenses used to cope with painful emotions. As every experienced foster parent knows, the child's angry feelings are frequently displaced onto members of the foster family. Birth parents may project blame onto caseworkers or sometimes onto the child himself, saying something such as, "He was asking for it." It is important for all adults to remember that children are <u>never</u> responsible for adult actions. No matter how a child behaves or misbehaves, adults must learn to always take full responsibility for their own actions and reactions. Although support for their feelings may be provided, the adult's abusive or neglectful behaviors must be realistically confronted.

Feelings of loss of control over one's life frequently accompanies the grief process. When faced with these feelings, individuals may try to regain control in every area they can. Again, caseworkers should not be surprised or angry when either children or adults try to reassert some semblance of control in their lives. The job of helping adults is to support children and their birth parents in regaining a healthy sense of autonomy and control. Time and again they may need help in examining how their own controlling behaviors are either working for or against them. Although others can help them identify their options, only they can make the final choice.

Physical complaints are common during the grief process. The human mind and body are not separate. When one is psychologically at risk, he is more likely to become physically ill. When an individual is physically ill, he is more prone to over- or under-react to psychological stress. Some individuals seem to transfer all of their psychological pain into physical distress. Actually physical symptoms may provide increased opportunities for emotional and physical nurturing to be provided by those who care about helping the grieving individual.

III How Unresolved Separations May Interfere with New Attachments

Children in the fostercare system cannot make optimum use of their placements until they have resolved their grief and formed new attachments. Unresolved separations may interfere with the development of new attachments. New attachments are not meant to replace old ones. They are meant to stand side by side with existing relationships. Bowlby (1980) points out that the success of a new relationship isn't dependent upon the memory of an earlier one fading; rather the new one is likely to prosper when the two relationships are kept clear and distinct. Interference with the development of new attachments may occur when the child's focus is on the past rather than the present.

Ardith

Ardith was also observed in the same playroom setting with her foster mom, Linda. The toddler's behaviors were very similar with Linda as they had been with Rose, the birth mother. Ardith's reaction when Linda left the room was the same as had been observed when Rose left her. Ardith calls each "Mama" but never addresses other adult women using this term.

Although transition times are difficult for Ardith, she seems comfortable with each of her mothers. Rose, however, says that it is still too difficult for her to see Ardith with Linda. She wonders if caseworkers think Linda is a better mother than she is. So long as she doesn't see her daughter with her foster mother, Rose is able to just enjoy her time with Ardith. When separated from her daughter, Rose worries about Ardith's relationship with Linda.

By four months after placement Ardith is demonstrating attachments to both her birth and foster mother. Although she seems accepting of having two mothers, symptoms resurface after visits. Sometimes Ardith returns to her foster home withdrawn and nearly dazed. Occasionally she is physically aggressive for the remainder of the day. Usually her appetite for dinner on the days of visits is less than normal and she frequently cries out during the night following the visit. Initially, Linda tried bringing out a picture of Rose when Ardith was upset. This did not calm her. She seemed more agitated. Linda now leaves the picture of Rose on the dresser in Ardith's room, but when the child is fussy at night foster mom just holds her close, rocking her, saying little.

We can best help free children up from the past by facilitating the grieving process rather than by trying to avoid facing the pain. Conflicted loyalties may interfere with both old and new attachments. Finally, fear of future pain and avoidance of that possibility may inhibit the development of new close interpersonal relationships. In focusing on facilitating the grief process we help counteract the factors that work against developing new attachments. Simultaneously, when adults are supportive of the child's emotions as he copes with his grief, they are making use of the arousal-relaxation cycle to facilitate the development of new attachments. They are saying to the child, "You can trust me not to be afraid of your strong feelings."

Loyalty conflicts are prominent for the child in placement. As mentioned earlier, resolution of the grief process for children separated from birth parents means acceptance of having two sets of parents. Many times it is adults who have the greatest difficulty accepting that the child has two mothers or two fathers. The attitudes of parents who are threatened by the importance of other caregivers in their child's life may pose the biggest obstacle for him. Although most parents readily accept the fact that they can love more than one child, many have difficulty accepting that children can love more than one mother or father. The child may love each in different ways, but it does not have to be one over the other.

Decreasing loyalty conflicts is an important task for all adults involved in the child's life. Foster parents can help the child by accepting his feelings about birth parents, both positive and negative, and by being supportive of contacts with the birth family even if they are painful. When foster parents behave as though it is acceptable for the child to love two sets of parents it becomes easier for both the child and his birth parents to accept the current situation. Encouraging the child to have pictures of the birth family, and not discouraging him from talking of them, are ways to allow the birth family into the foster family without necessarily having them physically present.

Likewise, when a child joins an adoptive family subsequent to having developed ties to other families, birth or foster, it is helpful to the child in integrating his overall identity to have pictures of, and information about, previous families. Indeed, in most cases some form of openness is preferable to totally cutting the child off from past connections.

Young children usually perceive the terms *Mommy* and *Daddy* as synonymous with the caregiving role. They are incapable of understanding the relationship of these terms to the birth process. Prior to school age, most children in interim care call their foster parents by whatever names others in the family call them. If the foster parents have school-aged or younger birth children in the home, the foster child will probably soon refer to the foster parents as Mommy and Daddy. Some older foster parents have children in their care refer to them as Grandma and Grandpa. Young children rarely are confused by having more than one set of parents so long as they are not caught in the middle of adult rivalries and so long as each parent demonstrates caring and concern for the child.

Irene

During a training session Irene, a caseworker, commented that her four year old son calls the daycare provider whom he has had since infancy, "Mommy" while he is at her house. At home he calls Irene "Mommy." This child is never confused. If anyone asks him what his mom's name is, he replies "Irene." He is very clear in his mind about their respective roles in his life. He is comfortable calling each of them Mommy. Irene says she has always been pleased that he feels this comfortable with his daycare provider. Neither she nor her husband have any negative feelings about his calling both mothering people in his life Mommy.

When the goal is reunification it is important that foster parents refer to the birth parents using a term that includes some variation of the words mother and father. Examples would include, "your mommy Nancy," "your birthdad," "your other mommy," or "your apartment Daddy." The foster mother might be called "Mom" while the birth mother is referred to as "Mommy." By use of names the foster parents are modeling their acceptance that the child has two sets of parents.

Children of school age are likely to feel uncomfortable calling strangers "Mom" and "Dad" from the outset. They should be provided with alternatives that are acceptable to the foster parents. Otherwise, it is quite likely that the children will fall into the pattern of not verbally identifying them at all. This makes for a very uncomfortable, emotionally distancing, situation. Through time many foster children gradually start thinking of interim care parents as Mom and Dad and start verbally identifying them by these terms. Foster parents might periodically check with the child as to whether or not he continues to feel comfortable with his original choice.

Mother's Day may lead to an escalation in loyalty conflicts especially for the child whose class his making Mother's Day presents. Should he give the gift to his current mother or to his birth mother? Mothers themselves may view this, consciously or unconsciously, as an opportunity to find out whom the child perceives as the "real mother." Mothers may use this as a love tester. Children, however, sometimes make the decision based on their perception of who needs the gift most, or who will be least upset if she doesn't receive the present, rather than based on their love for individuals. No matter how the decision is made it is unfair for the child to be put in this dilemma. Because of the frequency of divorces and remarriages in our society, some teachers now routinely ask students how many in the class need to make more than one Mother's Day gift. The sensitive foster parent will suggest this option to the teacher. At any rate it is better to discuss the difficulties associated with mixed loyalties in an open manner rather than letting them gain unspoken power.

The situation when a child is placed in an adoptive home is different. In this circumstance the goal from the outset is to create a permanent parent-child relationship and the child should be encouraged to identify the adults as "Mom" and "Dad." This does not mean that they have to simultaneously stop identifying past parent figures, whether they be birth parents or foster parents, as "Mom" and "Dad". Some agreed upon way to clarify about whom they are speaking needs to be decided upon, but the less pressure there is about choosing one over another, the better the long-term prognosis for healthy attachments to develop.

As in all grief work, the helping person's role is primarily to be supportive of the grieving individual's feelings. It is not helpful if adults become defensive or if they try to talk children out of their feelings. Adults need to be supportive as the child talks, cries, rants and raves, or just sits. It is the adult presence combined with emotional acceptance of the child's pain that is much more important than actual words.

Grieving is painful. The job of caring adults is to help children and their parents cope with pain and loss, not to protect them from the reality of life. "When a person is unable to complete a mourning task in childhood he either has to surrender his emotions in order that they do not suddenly overwhelm him or else he may be haunted constantly throughout his life with a sadness for which he can never find an appropriate explanation (Schoenberg (1970).

Imagine that you are one of the children in the fantasy exercise:

It's morning. As you awaken, you look around you. It is an unfamiliar room. You slept little last night. You've always been warned about strangers and here you are, with no one else you know, in the midst of them.

You hear people up and about. What are you supposed to do? Lie in bed until someone comes and tells you to get up? Get up, get dressed, and go downstairs on your own? Did anyone tell you last night what was expected? Your memory is fuzzy.

Where are your parents? When will you see them? Do they know where you are? One question after another engulfs you. Pulling the covers over your head, you try to block them out.

What could be done to make this transition easier?
Would you be less frightened if the adults were known to you?
Would it be easier if one of your brothers or sisters were at the same house?
Would even having your own teddy bear to hug be of any comfort?

We learned in the last chapter that abrupt losses are harmful. This chapter is about ways to minimize the trauma of separation and loss when children must move.

CHAPTER 4

Minimizing the Trauma of Moves

The previous chapters, and most particularly the research material on parent separation and loss, underscore the harm caused by interruption of parent- child relationships. However, it is possible to lessen some of the trauma that accompanies moves into, through, and out of the foster care system. To accomplish this, the two factors that we have learned have the strongest influence on an individual's reaction to separation must be addressed in the transition process.

Abrupt moves are more injurious than planned transitions. The physical or psychological danger to the child of remaining in his current environment for a few more days, so that a planned move can be effected, must be balanced against the known harm of an abrupt loss. As we have seen, the stronger the relationship, the more painful the loss. It is less damaging to err on the side of assuming that there may be a strong attachment than the reverse.

The trauma of parental separations or losses may be lessened if the child is prepared for the transition, if all participants in the moving process are, in a sensitive manner, open and honest with the child, and if careful attention is given to the child's reactions to the separation. Two major themes will run throughout all of the suggestions offered in this chapter: support for the emotions of everyone involved in the transition, and explaining what is happening to children when they are moved.

In the first section overall strategies for minimizing the trauma of moves will be explored. Preplacement preparation and postplacement contacts are both important. The developmental stage of the child at the time of the transition will help determine which aspects of pre and postplacement planning are of highest priority in a specific case. Section II looks at the specifics of transitioning children into the interim care system and involving their birth parents while their children are in care. Section III explores the foster family's role when a child leaves the care. The last three sections explore details of minimizing the trauma of transtions out of the system. Section IV looks at moves that involve reunification with the birth family. Section V outlines plans for moving children to adoptive families and the final section looks at leaving the system by emancipation.

I Overall Strategies for Minimizing the Trauma of Moves

Entrance into the foster care system is often sudden and without preparation. Once in the child welfare system, the child's traumatic separation from his birth family is frequently allowed to drift into permanent estrangement. Worse yet, the maintenance of a bond between the child in interim care and his biological family is sometimes actively discouraged. The child's feelings of loss are frequently ignored or glossed over. Contacts between parents and child may be limited or prevented. Children's emotional reactions to visits with their birth families may be misunderstood and misinterpreted. Foster parents may not receive the help they need in dealing with the increased behavioral problems precipitated by the visits. However, the truth is that minimizing the trauma of separations and losses and working to facilitate the development of new attachments are complementary, rather than competitive, tasks.

If the child cannot be maintained in his biological family and must come into interim care, part of the foster parents' role is to help him maintain his attachments to his biological family. Simultaneously, the foster parents must help the child develop healthy and strong new attachments to themselves. When the child leaves their home, foster parents must be willing to actively transfer these attachments to the succeeding permanent primary caretakers, whether those be birth family members, an adoptive family, or a new foster family. Moves from foster home to foster home should be limited to all but the most unavoidable situations. Every loss adds psychological trauma and interrupts the tasks of child development.

Foster parents need to be supportive to the grieving child when he enters their home. Unfortunately, they frequently have received little training in ways to accomplish this task. "Only People Cry," a story by Alice Winter (1963) telling of the trauma of moves from a child's perspective, is a helpful article for sensitizing foster parents to the internal struggles the child faces while accommodating to a new living situation.

Children face another move when they exit the foster care system whether they return to their birth family, join an adoptive family, or emancipate as a young adult. Once again, foster parents play a major role, this time in the preparation process. They may need help and support in this process, which is painful for them as well as for the child.

Ernest and Edna Godwin are a couple in their mid-fifties. They have been foster parents for seventeen years. Frequently, one or the other of them are co-leaders, along with a social worker, for the preparation sessions for new foster parents. They believe that they have much to offer, especially in helping new foster parents learn to cope with separation and loss both when children enter care and when they leave.

They talk about some of the things they've learned about helping children cope with separation and loss. Edna comments that she can usually tell within a day or so whether a new foster child is one who needs lots of touch or one who needs more space to cope with stress. On her first shopping trip with a new child, together they select a special frame for the picture of the birth parents that she makes certain each child has.

On a hall wall, the Godwins have a large bulletin board with snapshots of children they have parented, both past and present. Most children new to their home soon ask about the pictures. If a child asks "Grandma Edna" about the pictures, after basically answering his question, she will suggest that he ask "Grandpa" to tell him some stories about the children. For each child who has lived in their home, Ernie has several stories to share. They are usually about a special interest or skill of the child. Sometimes they focus on a positive change that the child made while in care. Children newly placed in the Godwin home rapidly learn that no child who has passed through this home has been forgotten.

As the time approaches for a child to leave the Godwin home, he and Grandma and Grandpa look through the snapshots that have been taken throughout his placement. The child selects several to take with him and the Godwins select several to keep on the bulletin board. Duplicates are made if necessary. A day or two before the child leaves, the Godwins have a going away party for the youngster. Usually the parents the child will be joining—birth, foster, or adoptive-are invited to the party. Grandpa tells the stories about this child that he will be sharing with others in the future. The child is given a small framed picture of himself with Grandma and Grandpa as a parting gift.

Minimizing the Trauma by Preplacement Preparation

Planned transitions are less harmful to children than abrupt moves. Preplacement visits can be used to minimize the trauma of separation and loss. Whenever it is impossible to accomplish one or more of the goals of the preplacement visits, this aspect will have to be addressed after the move. In general, it takes more time to correct the harm done by inadequate preplacement work than to do the work in the first place. Table 4-1 outlines the specific goals to be accomplished during preplacement visits. When we understand these tasks, it becomes easier to tailor a preplacement plan to fit a particular situation.

_____ *Table* _____ 4-1

Preplacement Visits

> Diminish fears and worries of the unknown
> Can be used to transfer attachments
> Initiate the grieving process
> Empower new caregivers
> Encourage making commitments for the future

During preplacement contacts there are opportunities to begin to address the fears and worries of all involved the child, the parents from whom the child is separating, and the family to whom the child is going. Preplacement contacts are used to transform the unknown into the known. The Parenting Parent circle of the Aspects of Parenting on page 159 can be used with the child and/or his parents to identify some of their concerns and answer their questions.

The stronger the attachment between child and previous caregiver, the more important the process of transferring attachment will be. Although we have found that sometimes verbal or written communications, without accompanying direct contact between the parenting adults, may be successful in aiding the transfer of attachment in children of school age, it is not enough for the infant, toddler, or preschooler. The younger the child, the more important it is that there be direct contact between past and future caregivers. We noted in the last chapter that after only several days of separation from parents, toddlers show marked distress.

For long-term resolution of the grief process, it is best if children are not moved while still in shock and denial. Preplacement visits encourage the surfacing of the painful emotions associated with grieving. Although the behaviors stimulated by these feelings may lead adults to want to hurry the move, this should be discouraged. If the child physically moves while still in shock or denial, when the anger and sadness finally emerge, they are more likely to be displaced onto the new family. If the child is in the "sad" or "mad" stages of the grief process when he moves, it is easier for both child and new caregivers to acknowledge the pain of loss and make use of the strong feelings to build new attachments by completing the arousal-relaxation cycle described earlier. Obviously, if a child has been in a placement for only a very short period of time or has little attachment to the current caregivers, there may be little grief associated with the separation.

It is important that new parent figures be empowered to behave like parents both in terms of emotional nurturing and in terms of providing structure and discipline. If the parent figures the child has just left have had input into the decision making and have been active in transfering attachment, it is more likely that they can aid in this empowerment rather than undermine it.

Finally, we would like to involve everyone in making commitments as to how they are going to work together on the child's behalf after the move. This includes both previous and new parenting figures, the child himself, and the caseworker. It may also include significant others such as siblings, extended family members, or a therapist. The less committed any one party is to making the placement work, the more committed the others must be if it is to be successful.

Rodney, age seven, is legally free for adoption. His single mom was chronically depressed, and rather than caring adequately for Rodney, looked to him to meet her needs. In spite of the termination of parental rights, Rodney continues to talk of wanting to return to Mom's care and of not wanting to have an adoptive family. Since Rodney still seems to have magical thinking about returning to his mother's care and is not currently willing to work toward becoming a member of an adoptive family, it will be necessary to select an adoptive family with an extraordinary level of commitment to the plan. It is quite likely that Rodney will actively reject them, particularly once he starts feeling any emotional closeness, which will increase the loyalty conflicts for him. While being committed to the adoption plan, the new parents will have to be simultaneously supportive of Rodney's feelings and not be threatened by his apparent lack of commitment to them.

Rodney

Minimizing the Trauma by Postplacement Contacts

Even when everything possible has been done to prepare the child and both families for the move, it will be important to continue to work toward minimizing the trauma of interrupted parenting after the separation. Table 4-2 lists the possible reasons for contact with previous caregivers after the separation. Although, in general, it is preferable for these contacts to be face to face, especially initially, it is possible to accomplish some of the work indirectly through telephone calls, letters, video or audio tapes, or via an intermediary.

———— *Table* ———— 4-2

Postplacement Contacts are Used to

Prevent denial/avoidance
Resurface emotions about separation at manageable levels
Provide opportunities for support of feelings
Provide opportunites to review reasons for the separation
Decrease magical thinking
Decrease loyalty issues
Continue transference of attachment/ empowerment of new caregivers
Enhance identity formation

Postplacement contacts decrease the child's feelings of diminished self worth. Children who have little or no contact with birthparents wonder what is wrong that the parents do not want to see them. Regular visits and mutual sharing of information between all adults involved are the two most potent tools for aiding in resolution of separation issues (Horejsi 1981).

Without contact, the child expends energy worrying, wondering, and fantasizing about birthparents. This energy is not then available for use in the newly forming relationships in the foster family or in addressing the current developmental tasks of the child. Although he is provided with an environment that is better able to meet his needs, the grieving child may not be able to psychologically access it. Children may, correctly or incorrectly, perceive foster parents and social workers as conspiring to keep them from birth parents. Direct contact between the birth and foster parents can help decrease loyalty conflicts for the child.

When the goal is return to previous caregivers, there are additional reasons for the postplacement contacts. The visits may be part of the assessment process and treatment plan for facilitating change in the family relationships. However, the Table 4-2 list is important even when there is no plan for return. The primary purposes of the postplacement contacts will vary from case to case. However, once the reasons for the contacts are identified, it is possible to measure success in achieving them. For example, if the plan does not include returning the child to the previous home, and if the primary purposes of contact are to decrease loyalty issues, to continue to transfer attachment, and to empower the new parents, and yet every contact leads to undermining messages being given by the previous parenting figures, it might become necessary to interrupt the contacts.

Kristina

Kristina, eleven, had lived with the Johnson foster family for three years, during which time numerous attempts at reunification were made. Eventually the agency and court decided on legal guardianship with a maternal relative. The Johnsons were not supportive of the plan. They had seen Kristina struggle with a variety of conflicting feelings during the reunification attempts and believed that the optimal plan for her would be adoption by their family.

Because of Kristina's strong attachment to the Johnsons, it was decided that she needed to have contact with them after her move to the relatives. However, with each contact Mrs. Johnson would start crying while talking about how much she missed Kristina. She then would ask a variety of questions, all of which implied that she was questioning the relatives' parenting abilities. The final comment was always, "If you have any problems or if things aren't going well for you, you can always call us. You know that you are always welcome to come back home to live with us."

Clearly, Kristina's contacts with the foster mom were not supportive of the current placement and were increasing, rather than decreasing, the loyalty conflicts and the separation trauma. Unless Mrs. Johnson could be helped to behave in an empowering manner, we might recommend that the contacts be discontinued. However, it would be important to actively involve Kristina in the decision making and planning, helping her see the concern about the double bind the visits were creating for her and listening to her input as to ways to solve the problems.

Developmental Considerations in Minimizing the Trauma of Moves

We can translate the developmental information provided in an earlier chapter into specific recommendations about ways to decrease the trauma of moves at different ages. These suggestions can be used for moves into the system, transitions through the system, or when the child exits the system.

From at least four months on, and probably even earlier, when there is a healthy attachment to the caregivers the child is leaving, it is important that careful attention be paid to moving a child. For the infant, the emphasis during preplacement contacts is on transferring attachment and caregiving routines. As many routines as possible should be maintained in the new setting. Following a consistent routine and being available on demand for these infants are especially important after the move.

It is imperative that toddlers be prepared for moves by adequate preplacement preparation if at all possible. When a move gives the toddler the message, "Strangers may come and take you away from your parents anytime without parental permission," long term chronic worries and fears are likely, as well as diminished trust in the ability of parental figures to keep children safe and secure.

The Robertsons, in their now considered classic studies of the impact of separation on well attached toddlers, paid close attention to two tactics that seemed to have the most positive effect in decreasing the trauma of separation at this age (Bowlby, 1973). They provided the children with familiar companions and possessions, and they provided active mothering by a substitute mother during the separation. Prior to the separations, the Robertsons started meeting with the children in their homes and became familiar with their routines. The children and their parents also visited the Robertson's home to become familiar with it before the transition. These contacts took place over approximately a one month time span.

When the separation did occur, many of the children's belongings including their beds, blankets, and toys accompanied them to the Robertsons' home. Mrs. Robertson took care to try to follow routines that the children had been familiar with in their own homes and to talk with the children daily about their absent mother, using a photograph of her as she talked.

During the toddler years, the primary aim during the moving process is to transfer attachment from previous caregivers to the new parenting persons as much as possible. The two sets of parents must have contact and the parents the child is leaving need to actively transfer the day-to-day caretaking tasks and routines to the new parents.

If regression to earlier levels of functioning is allowed following a move, the toddler will usually reacquire the lost skills within a few months time. If undue pressure is put on the child to continue to function at what are considered to be age appropriate levels, long-range problems are more likely.

Because memories of this age are later triggered by similar emotions, sensory input, or by events similar to those occurring near the time of a move, adults must be alert to noting the events surrounding the move on a permanent record which will accompany the child. These records can be invaluable in helping both the child and subsequent parents understand the youngster's reaction in future situations.

Peter

Eight-year-old Peter had difficulty on trips to the grocery store with his adoptive mother. He seemed to "fuzz out" at these times and to be unaware of his surroundings. He would wander off in the store as though he were in a daze. Such behaviors were not evident in other situations. The adoptive parents were very confused by Peter's behavior and were beginning to think that they shouldn't take him to the store. They mentioned their concerns to their caseworker.

She reviewed the circumstances of Peter's entering care when he was two years old. His family had been known to the police and child welfare staff because of frequent bouts of family violence. Following one such episode when the police and caseworker went to the house, a relative threatened to harm them both. Peter's mother told the officials that if they left she would immediately turn her child over to them at the nearby parking lot of a large grocery store.

Subsequent trips with his adoptive parents to a different store of the same chain resurfaced unconscious memories and the feelings of loss and confusion that accompanied his initial separation from his birth family. Once Peter and his adoptive parents understood the reasons for his behavior at the grocery store, the

182

solution became obvious. More, rather than fewer, trips to the store were indicated. The parents and Peter talked openly about his feelings and underlying fears. Emotional support was provided.

Postplacement contacts with previous caretakers are important to toddlers. If they do not occur it is common that when children they reach age four or five, they will think that the previous parental figures are dead. Pictures of previous families make it possible to verbally and cognitively deal with these feelings. When children move during the toddler years, it is nearly certain that as they mature they will need information and help in understanding the reasons for these moves.

During the preschool years, explaining in clear, understandable language what is happening and why is the most important tool in minimizing the trauma of moves. Preschoolers literally believe what they are told. Adults need to listen to themselves with this in mind making certain that they do not inadvertently give an explanation that feeds into the child's egocentric magical thinking. Not only will the purpose of preplacement visits be to transfer attachments at this stage of development, but additionally, attention needs to be paid to initiating the grief process. It is best if the child does not move while still in the denial stage.

Sasha

Sasha, a bright precocious four-year-old, had became a valued member of her foster family. Soon after her fourth birthday, an adoptive family who lived several hours' driving distance from the foster home was selected for Sasha. There were several pre placement visits. The adoptive parents saw the strong attachments between Sasha and her foster family as a negative. Although they followed through with the preplacement visiting plan, they tried to convince the worker that the move should occur faster. "It is too difficult for her to go back and forth." As Sasha was leaving her foster home on the day of the move to the adoptive home, her final comment to the foster mom was, "I'll be back."

Following the move, Sasha had eating and sleeping problems. Sometimes she would gorge food, other times she refused to eat for several days at a time. Even now, eight months after placement, she frequently awakens at night crying. Although her eyes are open and she talks to her parents during these episodes, she has no memories of them in the morning. There is frequent enuresis both during the day and night.

Identifying, clarifying, and correcting the child's magical and/or egocentric thinking is the most important aspect of preventing negative long-term effects at this age. Keeping in mind the psychological struggles that center around integrating big vs. little and good vs. bad, adults need to be watchful for behaviors indicative of problems in these areas. Once the child is capable of inductive and deductive reasoning, usually around age eight or nine, adults need to review the past with the child who left parents during the preschool years. The child may need to be reassured that his earlier thought processes were normal for his age, but that now he is old enough to really understand what happened. If this is not done, problems may become entrenched and long standing.

Attention to the details of the moving situation and the circumstances in the family from which the child moved may provide the information, as it did in Nathan's case which was described in the chapter on Separation and Loss on page 150.

Children of grade-school-age usually have good verbal skills and have developed some internalized sense of time. This makes the preparation process easier. However, adults still need to be listening for signs of magical thinking or misperceptions. Even when preplacement preparation is impossible in an emergency move, because of their increased cognitive skills there are more avenues open to helping this older child understand what has happened.

A major focus in helping children who are moving is to help them identify and express their emotions. A second strategy is to include them as active participants in the moving process. Although the children need reassurance that adults are ultimately responsible for the decision making about a move, the grade school-aged child needs to know that we can only do our job well if they share with us their feelings, worries, concerns, hopes, and dreams about the move.

After the move, parents can help a child by providing opportunities for talking about and working with the grief related emotions so that at other times he can focus on his academic and peer skills.

Because individuation is the developmental challenge of early adolescence, moves undertaken between the ages of twelve and fourteen seem to face more difficulties than those undertaken later in adolescence. It is difficult to encourage attachment and bonding between parent and young person when the current primary developmental task is to psychologically separate from the family. Placements during this period work best if the adolescent makes a firm commitment to the new relationship and if the parents understand the difficulties they face in building bonds with the early teen. Parents must be firmly committed to helping the adolescent achieve a balance between dependence and independence in forming new attachments. In later adolescence, youth not only are less oppositional in general but frequently also recognize their need for a family beyond emancipation.

Adolescents desire, and need, to have increasing control over their own lives. They need to have considerable input into decision making about their future. Except in extreme situations, they need to at least have veto power over decisions about where they will live. Contracting and getting firm verbal and/or written commitments from teens about how they are willing to work at making a placement succeed increase the likelihood of successful placements. Moves during adolescence provide opportunities to review circumstances, feelings, and outcomes of previous parental separations and losses. As such, they provide opportunities for healing if adults are willing to take the time and effort necessary. If a current move does not become part of the healing process, it will become another unresolved trauma.

When Children Enter Interim Care   II

Whenever interim care placement is being considered, either on an emergency basis or with preplacement planning, the deficiences of the current situation must be balanced against a realistic picture of what foster care can offer. Ideally, children will be prepared for the move from the birth to foster family. This should be possible in voluntary placements and may sometimes be feasible when the agency, rather than the birth parent, has instituted the placement plan. The caseworker will then discuss placement procedures and goals with both parents and child. She might use the Aspects of Parenting Chart on page 159, focusing on the Parenting Parent role or the Child's EcoMap on page 343 as part of preparation process with the child. If the child is of school age, clear information on goals to be achieved for return to the birth parents' care should be given. While he is in care, the child needs to be advised of progress that is being made toward achieving these goals. He may need some help in recognizing the goals others have for his behavior in the foster home, such as learning to mind adults or to have fun with a mother. The child should also be advised of the goals for his parents while he is out of the home. The roles of the caseworker and foster parents in facilitating change need to be identified also. This emphasizes that for a successful outcome everyone needs to work together.

Photo albums may be used first to introduce the child to the prospective foster family. There might be a couple of visits between the child and foster family prior to the placement. Once such visits have occurred, the worker is in a better position to help the child identify the emotions he is experiencing and express them in appropriate ways.

Prior to the placement, a schedule and arrangement for postplacement contacts between the child and birth parents should be set up. Definite times, such as one month or three months, should be set for reevaluation of the treatment plan and the progress toward goal achievement. These reevaluations should include input from the foster parents as well as from the birth parents. The child may have direct input into or be part of providing feedback in the treatment planning process himself if he is about age seven or older.

Children placed on a voluntary basis will have strong feelings about the placement even if they understand and agree with the necessity for it. They, like all other children in placement, need permission to have and express their emotions. Pictures of the birth family should accompany the child. On the day of the move the facts about the placement and the feelings of everyone involved might be reviewed. Loyalty conflicts and empowerment of the new caregivers can be addressed at that time.

Unfortunately, most children who enter interim care do so in an emergency situation. Usually the child has little advance warning and is not prepared to be separated from his family. After experiencing such a move, the child is prone to suffering underlying anxiety about the unknown in the future.

However, even when the entry move is precipitous, there are ways to minimize the trauma. Allowing the child to take a favorite stuffed animal or blanket to serve as a transitional attachment object can be helpful. Just as police are giving teddy bears to children in traumatic situations such as accidents, some caseworkers are using stuffed animals provided by volunteer groups to help the child facing an emergency move. Again, pictures of foster family members or both places home might be utilized. Attention to detail is always important at the time of moves, but the more precipitous the move the more important each detail becomes.

Even though trash bags are very functional for packing a child's possessions, they should not be used. The child may perceive not only his possessions but himself as rubbish. If suitcases or boxes are not available, it is preferrable to use grocery bags as opposed to trash bags. Try to involve parents in helping to pack the child's belongings for the move. At some level this gives the child permission to go. Pay attention to the child's cues as to which sensory modality is primary.

Janet

Janet, age eight, was entering interim care on an emergency basis. Her mother had been jailed and her step-father refused to care for her. He was unwilling to take part in any pre-placement planning. When Mrs. Washington was talking to Janet about the move, she noted that the child was tenaciously clinging to the stair railing. Rather than trying to talk her out of this or cajole her into leaving, she commented, "When I'm scared I always want to cling to something too. How about clinging to me while we are packing up your things and putting them into the car."

Mrs. Washington used the child's automatic behavior as a transferring behavior. On arrival at the foster home, she commented to the foster mother that Janet needed to cling to something or someone when she was scared. With Janet present, the foster parent and caseworker talked about which people and which objects Janet could cling to in this new setting. Mrs. Washington then actively transferred Janet's hands from her arm to that of the foster mom.

186

The Caseworker's Role

Most children's immediate reaction to an abrupt separation from their parents, or to abandonment by them, is intense anxiety. A comment such as, "Most kids are really scared when they move into a new home," may open the door for the child to talk about feelings.

Caseworkers must be willing to deal with what happens when that door opens. The child needs both permission to express his feelings and acceptance of those feelings, no matter what they are. Caseworkers must avoid the tendency to minimize the child's feelings. Simply saying, "Don't be sad" or, "It's not your fault!" is not helpful. The child's pain does not go away because the adults around him ignore it or are uncomfortable with it.

It is important to be honest with children who are being placed. Don't gloss over the situation by telling the child that everything is going to be "fine." The worker may have to admit not knowing the answers to some questions that the child asks. When the child wants to know how long he will be in the care, the worker needs to say that it will depend upon a court hearing the next day, or upon when the parents can be located, or whatever the truth is in each case. The child needs reassurance that he will have frequent contact with the caseworker early in the placement and will be informed about the plans being made for his future.

Unless he is in shock or denial, at the time of a move the child most likely will have very intense emotions and will be in a state of high arousal. It is a time when the people who are supportive of his feelings can start to demonstrate their ability to be trustworthy adults.

Lindsay, who is four, was entering foster care. Her mother shot her father several days ago. No one knew exactly what the little girl observed. Child Protection staff arranged for Lindsay to stay with her usual daycare provider for several days so that the transition to a foster home could be done in a planful manner.

Lindsay

Her caseworker was talking with her about the move. Suddenly, Lindsay started chattering nonstop about the murder. She described where everyone in the family was and gave a detailed account of the argument that her parents were having. She described where the gun was and how her mother threatened Dad and shot him. Ms. Kinsey, the caseworker, wasn't quite certain how she should react to this disclosure. As the child rattled on she realized that she should not interrupt her. Placing her arm around Lindsay's shoulders, she said little other than occasional short comments such as "That must have been really scary." Lindsay continued, seeming to pay little attention to Ms. Kinsey's comments. After about ten minutes, the child seemed to wind down and become physically relaxed snuggling up close to Ms. Kinsey.

As she cuddled, she began to play with a ring on the caseworker's little finger. Gradually, still playing with the ring, she started to ask questions about the foster family. She asked if Ms. Kinsey would promise to visit her there. The latter reassured her. However, Lindsay asked the question repeatedly. Finally, Ms. Kinsey said, "I know what. How about our using this ring (taking the ring from her pinky finger) as a promise ring. Slipping it on the child's middle finger she said, every time you wonder if I am coming back, you can touch this ring and remember my promise. This seemed to be reassure the child.

During the first few days that Lindsay was in her foster home, Ms. Kinsey stopped by for brief visits on a daily basis. One day she told Lindsay that she had called the jail. The people there had told her that Lindsay's mom was fine, but was worried about her daughter. Lindsay started crying. Ms. Kinsey held her a few minutes. At the end of each visit, Lindsay asked if she could keep the promise ring until the next visit. The caseworker agreed.

A month later, it was decided that Lindsay would be going to live with her maternal grandparents, whom she knew well, even though they did not live close by. Upon the grandparents arrival, Ms. Kinsey met with them and Lindsay. As she said her final good-bye to the child, Lindsay took the promise ring off her finger, handing it to her caseworker. Ms. Kinsey suggested that Lindsay might want to keep it. The child looked quite surprised and said, "No, I don't need it any more."

The positive use of a painful or frightening situation for the child can occur only if the adults involved are willing to accept the responsibility for helping the child deal with his feelings. Many children who enter the foster care system have already learned that it is not safe to let adults know how they feel. There is a danger that this learning will be reinforced as the child moves into interim care. Short term, the child who doesn't express strong feelings may be easier to deal with, but in the long run he is likely to fare poorly. Expression of feelings can have therapeutic consequences for the child and can lead to psychological growth. Lack of such expression can lead to the child becoming "stuck" in terms of continued psychological growth.

Letting the Child Know about the Foster Family

Most individuals are afraid of the unknown. If preplacement visits are not possible, then giving the child specific information about the family may still help alleviate fears and worries.

It is difficult for caseworkers to share any information when they know little or nothing about the family to whom the child is going. Some agencies have asked foster parents to prepare an album with pictures of their home, family, and pets, as well as some descriptive material about their family. These albums are kept at the agency. Even in emergency placements, the worker can take the album and share it with the child en route to the foster home. In this way the child has both a visual image of where he is going and some information about the home and family before arrival.

One caseworker told us that she uses a mini preplacement visit in some cases, particularly with school-aged children. En route to a foster home she and the child formulate questions they have such as who else lives in the family? Are there pets? Where do the children go to school, etc? On arrival this caseworker accompanies the child on a tour of the home and helps him to ask the questions. The caseworker and child then go out for a soft drink and discuss what they learned during this mini visit.

Children who enter care on an emergency basis need to see their birth parents sooner than those who move in a planned manner. Many children who have been placed in interim care on an emergency basis have the fantasy that someone has harmed their parents, or that their parents do not know where they are and, therefore, that they can never be reunited. Such thinking is especially prominent in younger children. A rule of thumb is, "The younger the child and the more precipitous the move, the earlier the first postplacement contact must be."

Early contacts should be observed, not only for safety reasons, but also because the parent-child interactions during the visit will help us understand their relationship and the impact of the separation. Prompt visiting between child and birth family is essential in assessing family relationships and facilitating early reunification. The child's needs for contact with the parent, in terms of frequency and type of contact, should take precedence over adult needs. Using contact with the child as a threat or reward, contingent on the parent doing something else, such as attending therapy or classes, should only be done when we expect something in that particular session to make a significant difference in how the parent interacts with the child during the visit. An example of a reasonable contingency might be that the parent maintains involvement in drug treatment when the parent's behavior on drugs makes it unsafe, either physically or psychologically, for the child to visit.

A child's perception of time is quite different from that of an adult. Although the very young child might not understand a comment such as, "You will see your mom in a week," if the visits are on a regular basis, such as once or twice a week, he will pick up the rhythmicity and be reassured by it. Because older children understand time, they may be able to tolerate a longer period between removal and first contact if given information about the plans.

Occasionally with teens it is desirable to have a "cooling off" period prior to the initial contact. However, even then it must be realized that prolonged lack of contact never helps clarify or remedy family circumstances.

Children in interim care should have pictures of their birth parents with them in the foster home. Pictures give the message that foster parents view birth parents as important people. Denial as a defense against the pain of grieving is less likely when pictures are readily available. Foster parents who feel threatened by photographs of the birth parents will probably not be able to help the child

189

cope with his feelings of conflicted loyalties. On the other hand, if caseworkers and foster parents use the pictures of the family as they discuss the child's feelings, they offer the message that it is okay for the child to think about and miss birth parents. If no pictures of the birth parents are available, two pictures—one for the child and one for the parent—should be taken at the time of the first visit.

When children move into, through, or out of the child welfare system, caseworkers must always be aware of the child's relationships with other family members. The child may have strong attachments to siblings—birth, foster or adoptive—and these relationships, may need to be supported and protected through time.

Involving Birth Parents when Children Move into Foster Care

Because interim care basically provides for co-parenting, birth parent involvement is beneficial to everyone involved-child, parents, foster parents, and caseworker. Although it is not always possible, we must realize that it is best for both child and parent if they each have some input into the decison making process about placement. This decreases control issues and focuses on reciprocity and conflict resolution. For this reason it is helpful whenever possible to involve the parent in voluntarily agreeing to and facilitating the placement.

In voluntary placements where preplacement planning is possible, important considerations are discussed and the parents' viewpoint is sought. Is having the child placed near their home most important? having siblings together? having the child in a home of the same religion? Caseworker, parents, and possibly the school-aged child might together prioritize a list of considerations. Even though we recognize that actual choices may be limited, we want to convey to the family that their concerns are of import. If we cannot fullfill their desires, it is still valuable to know what they think is important and to support their feelings about not having things be the way they would like. In this way, positive parenting is modelled once more.

Simultaneously, the primary goals of placement are clarified, and consideration is given to realistic options. Parents see that others, too, have to struggle with decision making and priority setting. Their self-esteem may be raised by seeing that even professionals do not have magical solutions to the problems at hand.

The fact that we acknowledge that they are entitled to opinions, and that those views are important to us may make a difference in the parent being able to be supportive of the child's feelings at the time of placement. If at all possible, even in emergency moves into the system, parents should be encouraged to give the child permission to make positive use of out-of-home placement. Optimally, we would like them to participate in a separation interview, during which we will review the facts, the feelings, and the loyalty issues.

The facts relate to how the decision was made for placement, the purpose of placement, what each individual (parent, child, caseworker) is responsible for, and information about how and when decisions regarding return home will be made.

190

The feelings of various family members are validated during the separation interview. The strengths and weaknesses of various family members in terms of acknowledging and appropriately expressing emotions is clarified. Addressing loyalty issues stresses the importance of children developing close, caring interpersonal relationships with adults in their out-of-home placement. Frequently, parents must be helped to give their child permission to emotionally connect with substitute caregivers. That help is most easily accepted if it comes in the form of support for feelings combined with gentle but persistent confrontation about the facts.

Mr. Roberts, the caseworker for Jake and Jane, has decided that their son, Matt, will need to be placed in interim care. Attempts to prevent placement have not been successful. The relationship between Mr. Roberts and the parents has become increasingly strained.

Matt

In explaining the placement planning Mr. Roberts might say, "Jake, I know it is very difficult for you that we have not been able to work together to prevent Matt's coming into care. We've had a lot of differences of opinion. In spite of our disagreements, I believe that you truly want what is best for him. Even though he is being placed, you will continue to be a very important person in his life. Right now what we have to consider is whether you are so angry at the judge and myself that you cannot help Jake by giving him permission to do well, or if you can put aside your anger at us long enough to help your child even though you don't agree with the plan for placement." When it is not possible to gain the parents' cooperation in the placement process, reframing might be used to imply that behaviorally, even though not verbally, they are agreeing to the placement. In using this tactic, a negative behavior is redefined as having a positive motive. Reframing might be used with either parent or child.

"Jane, we know that some people have difficulty asking for help. Sometimes they tell others what they need with their behaviors rather than with their mouths. I think you care about your child and were trying to ask for help when you left Matt alone. Both your needs and Matt's needs are important to us."

OR

"Matt, your parents and I both want what is best for you. However, we have a disagreement about how we can best help you. When adults cannot come to an agreement, they sometimes ask a judge to determine what should be done. The judge has decided that right now you need to be in a foster home. Your parents still do not agree with this plan. Right now your dad is too angry at the judge and me to be able to help you with the move. Managing his anger in ways that don't lead to others in the family being hurt is one of the problems that he needs to work on while you are in placement. He and I even have a difference of opinion now about whether or not it is important for you to get close to your new foster parents and learn to trust them. That's going to make it harder for you than if we could at least agree on this. I know that. However, I do trust that through time you will make the decision that you think is best for you."

Helping to Minimize the Trauma of Separation for the Birth Parents

Birth parents, as well as children, grieve when their child enters care. The same factors which influence a child's reaction to separation, listed on page 142, will influence the parents' reponse as well. As mentioned earlier, current separations and losses resurface the feelings associated with past losses, particularly those that were never resolved. Many birth parents of children who enter the child welfare system have themselves experienced a series of interrupted relationships. Many have never received support or help in coping with their overwhelming emotions. Visits with their child may retrigger these painful emotions. Their feelings may be expressed inappropriately, leading us to think that they are uncaring. Parents may resort to drinking or drug use to dull their senses and decrease pain. During the stages of shock and denial, forgetfulness is common. The parent may forget to show up for visits or for other appointments. When parents are self-blaming they may believe that they have nothing to offer the child and may tell him to "just forget me" or may not show up for visits. Other times, avoiding visits is an attempt to evade the pain. Parental feelings of anger may be displaced onto agency personnel, foster parents, or the child himself.

When parental behaviors seem unhelpful, we must determine whether these behaviors are part of a long-term pattern of dysfunction or if they are primarily a response to the separation. If caseworkers model help and support for the difficult feelings associated with loss, at best they will help facilitate resolution of the grief process freeing the parent to put energy into the real change process. At worst, they will clarify that the parental behaviors are not a reaction to the grief process but rather are an indication of severe underlying problems. Either way, there will be clarification of realistic goals for case planning.

The Foster Parents' Role when the Child Enters Care

Foster parents should understand the types of emotions children have when they enter the interim care system on an emergency basis and learn ways to supportively respond to these feelings. When a child is removed from his birth family, the most appropriate thing the foster family can do is to offer physical comfort to the child, talk little, and accept the feelings that the child may have. Foster parents can use the child's strong feelings as a basis on which they start to form a relationship with the child. If they help the child discharge his feelings, they alleviate some of his discomfort, and simultaneously increase his attachment to them. Some children will withdraw and won't want to talk. In this situation, foster parents can be physically close without insisting on talking. When a child is angry, foster parents can accept the emotion. Foster parent observations during the first few weeks after placement help caseworkers to assess the child's attachment to his parents and to understand his interpretation of the reasons for placement.

Fears, anxieties, nightmares, and night terrors are commonly seen in children who are separated from their parents. Some sleep excessively to avoid pain. Others have difficulty sleeping at all. Some children overeat when they are placed as though they are trying to fill a void in their lives. Others are too depressed or anxious to eat at all. Avoid making a major issue about behaviors immediately following moves. Instead, identify behaviors as communicating emotions.

Children need to know that it is acceptable for them to miss the family they just left. When not given this kind of permission, some children may misbehave so they will be disciplined. They can then cry for the family they have left. It helps, too, if the child knows that his former family wishes that he do well in his new home and hears that they are pleased when he does. Children in placement need pictures of both parents and siblings.

As mentioned before, visits soon after placement are necessary to reassure the child that his parents are still alive and continue to care about him. This is different from the traditional stance that the child needs an "adjustment period." Postplacement visits are likely to further tap into both the child's and parents' strong feelings about separation. Although it is often much easier for caseworkers and foster parents when there are fewer contacts between parent and child, or if the child doesn't react to the visits that do occur, the task at hand is to facilitate the grief process. This only occurs when the pain of loss is expressed. The long term prognosis for reunification is worse for children who have few contacts or minimal reaction to these contacts with their parents.

Exercise 4-1, which follows, will provide the reader with an opportunity to plan a transition into care for a toddler.

4-1 *Exercise* _____

Planning for a Toddler to Enter Interim Care on a Non-Emergency Basis

Amber has lived with her birth mother all of her life. Child Protective Services has been involved with the family since Amber was fifteen months, because of moderate neglect. Amber has been attending a special daycare program for abused and neglected children for the past nine months. In this program she is noted to be somewhat aloof from both adults and peers. She usually sits quietly playing with one or two toys. On rare occasions she is aggressive with peers. Surprisingly, her verbal skills are close to age level.

Amber

Mother, who is unmarried, gave birth to a son six weeks ago. Neither his father nor Amber's have been involved with the children. Since Colin's birth, mother is overwhelmed. The provider of the home based services notes that while Amber is in daycare Mom is moderately responsive to Colin's needs. She does not, however, provide much stimulation for him. The home based provider has observed that when Amber is home, she is much more active than she is reported to be in daycare. When Amber is there, Mother looks totally overwhelmed and emotionally withdraws from both children.

At an agency staffing it is decided that when Amber is at home both children are at risk, not only of not having their emotional needs met, but also of inadequate attention to their physical needs. It appears that Amber is at greater physical risk because of her age and ability to get herself into dangerous situations when not adequately supervised. The team struggles in the decision making process weighing the pros and cons of placing both children in interim care together, versus placing only Amber in care.

Recognizing the importance of early attachments, it is finally decided that further attempts will be made to maintain Colin in the birth home with Amber being placed in a foster home.

1. Devise a worksheet which divides a page horizontally. The top half has two columns.
2. In the column on the left identify the underlying messages you want to convey to Amber about the separation from her mother, keeping in mind that she is entering care soon after the birth of a baby brother.
3. In the column on the right, outline strategies for coveying these messages, keeping in mind that Amber is two years old.
4. In the lower half of the worksheet describe specific steps you would take during the preplacement and postplacement period to implement your goals.

Involving Birth Parents while Children Are in Foster Care

When children are in any form of out-of-home care, it is important that parents continue to be involved both in terms of direct contact with, and treatment planning for, their child (Table 4-3). Usually, the more involved the parents, the shorter the stay. Ongoing contact between parents and child is important whether the placement decision was mutually agreed upon by parents and agency or was unilateral.

Contact Is Important for

Assessment
   of parent-child attachment
   of parenting skills
   of the nature of family interactions
   of tasks necessary for family reunification
Facilitating the grieving process
Decreasing loyalty conflicts
Strengthening attachments and bonds
Facilitating changes in family relationships
Facilitating reunifaction

Parents and children must have ongoing contact if they are to work on maintaining and enhancing their connections with one another. Healthy family relationships cannot be built without consistent contact among family members. Parents need opportunities to practice newly acquired parenting skills. They should be encouraged to exercise their rights and responsibilities as the legal parents.

Regularly scheduled visits are an important aspect of minimizing the trauma of separation. The younger the child, the more important it is that the schedule be consistent. Young children have a poor sense of time but do develop a sense of rhythm for events that occur on a regular basis. Overnight visits may be confusing to the toddler, who may perceive the visit as another abrupt move. Day visits are usually not so confusing.

Parents of children in care are sometimes inconsistent in showing up for visits. However, it is important that caseworkers model good parenting by scheduling the visits to meet the young child's needs. If parents have demonstrated that they frequently do not show up for visits, then it becomes reasonable to ask them to arrive well ahead of the child. If the parent does not arrive, the child is not brought to the visiting site. Although the child may still have strong feelings about the parent not being consistent in visiting, this is less traumatic than having the child wait at the visiting site for a parent who does not show up. When siblings are in different foster homes, some caseworkers of parents who are inconsistent about showing up for visits tell the children that the visiting time is for them to get together with each other. If the parents show up that is fine. If they do not, the children still have an opportunity to visit with each other.

Regular visits help foster parents better understand the child's background and perceptions of his parents. In addition, the visits help keep to the forefront that the initial goal of placement is always assessment of what changes need to occur for the child to return home. The contacts decrease the likelihood of foster parents having rescue fantasies. Direct contact between foster and birth parents provides the foster parents with opportunites to expand their own job descripiton. By modeling healthy family relationships, ways to access help, and how to achieve a balance between independence and dependence, foster parents may become useful resources in helping birth parents change.

Even when the outcome is not reunification, permanency planning, in cases other than parental abandonment, is facilitated by consistent involvement with the birth family as it is possible to more quickly determine if interventions are going to be successful.

The two exercises which follow will provide the reader with opportunities to make plans for the moving process when children enter interim care.

Exercise 4-2

Entering Care in a Planful Manner

Judy

You will remember that Judy, now twelve, joined the Haslett adoptive family as the youngest child in the family when she was four. The Hasletts had three older children by birth. Judy had been abandoned at a train station in Korea. After living for a year in a Korean orphanage, where she was described as "a helpful engaging child who loves everyone," Judy made the trip to the United States with an escort.

When Judy was ten the Hasletts approached the local social service department asking that she be placed in foster care. The parents indicated that there had been problems from the time of placement. They perceived Judy as a stubborn, manipulative child who had become the cause of numerous family problems. She would hoard food. She stole from her siblings, usually taking their prize possessions. Although she was somewhat affectionate with her father, an easygoing man, she actively avoided, contact with her mother. Peer problems were evident at school. However, her teachers had indicated that her academic acheivement was at grade level.

Judy and her family had been in private therapy for two years prior to the Hasletts approaching the social services department. In home services were offered to the family. They reluctantly complied with this plan. The in-home therapist noted that everyone in the family seemed fixed in their interactions. When any one person changed slightly, the others reacted in a way that insured that the change was short lived. It soon became apparent that Judy would need to be placed in out-of-home care. The long-range prognosis for reunification was seen as poor.

1.   What kind of placement would you select for Judy?
2.   How should the plans for placement be shared with Judy? Should the
      parents tell her of the plans? Should the in-home therapist be involved?
      Outline your suggestions. What should she be told about long term planning?
3.   What kind of preplacement visits would you recommend in this case?
4.   What recommendations would you make for post-placement contacts
      between Judy and the Hasletts?

4-3 *Exercise*

Transitioning Young Children into Care on an Emergency Basis

Once again we return to one of our ongoing cases for this exercise. You will remember that Prentice, age four, has been in care twice before. The first time he had been left alone at night. The second placement occurred after by a non-accidental injury. Physical violence between adults and inconsistent caregiving on the part of Mom are aspects of the children's current environment. The children have been attending a therapeutic daycare program for several months. However, on two consecutive days their mother, Rose, seemed to be under the influence of drugs when the daycare van returned the children home. CPS decided that the it was not safe for the children to remain in their mother's custody.

Ardith
Prentice

1.   What attempts might be made to involve Mother in the placement planning?
      Outline a detailed plan for moving the children into care. Think of as many
      ways as possible to minimize the trauma of the move.
2.   Should Ardith and Prentice initially be placed together or in separate foster
      homes? What would be the possible advantages and disadvantages
      of each decision?
3.   Would you suggest that the children continue to attend the therapeutic
      daycare program after the transition to interim care? Are there ways that
      the staff of this program might be used to minimize the trauma of the move?
4.   How soon would you want to have the first post placement contact ?
      Outline a detailed plan for visiting.

III The Foster Family's Role When a Child Leaves their Home

The foster parent role in minimizing the trauma of moves is an important one not only when a child enters care, but also when he leaves his interim care placement. Helping children with moves is a major aspect of the job description for foster parenting. During the preparation period , the caseworker should provide emotional support to the foster parents or other member's of their family as well as for the child. Strong feelings will emerge and without adequate support will result in negative behaviors. By being emotionally supportive of foster parents, caseworkers model the type of acceptance for difficult feelings that the foster parents, in turn, need to provide for the child who is moving. In general it takes much more time to undo the harm caused by a hasty, ill planned, and inadequately supported move than to do the job well to start with. The attention paid to detail at the time of moves in the long-term is cost effective.

When children leave a foster home to return to their birth family, to move to another foster home, to be adopted, or to emancipate they are vulnerable to the same wide range of emotions that they may have experienced when they entered the system. They may be sad, angry, frightened, or anxious, as well as eager, happy, or relieved. However, when a child leaves the system, adults are more likely to focus on the pleasant aspects of the move and are less likely to acknowlege the ambivalent feelings.

The child's move to permanency is often linked to his doing well in his foster home. This may add to his confusion. The child may recognize that he should feel happy that he has done well and is gaining a more permanent placement. Yet, he is likely to feel sad about leaving the foster home and to be angry about the fact that even doing well leads to emotional pain. By acknowledging the ambivalence and allowing its expression, parents and workers can help children better cope with moves that accompany an exit from the foster care system.

The foster parents' feelings about the move often are similar to the child's. It is particularly important at the time of the move for the child to know that the foster family cared about him. Letting the child know that he was loved teaches him that relationships are important.

Conrad

Conrad is a particularly outgoing five year old. His interim care parent, who has been fostering for over twenty years, indicates that she is going to really miss Conrad. Ms. Duncan, the caseworker, asked the foster parent if she thought that she would cry when Conrad left. Foster mom said, "Heavens no! I never cry in front of the children." Later Ms. Duncan, talking to Conrad, asked, "How do you think Grandma (Conrad's term for his foster mom) will feel when you move?" His reply, "I hope she will be sad (obviously reflecting the feelings he himself would have.) I wonder if she'll go behind the door and cry like she did when Suzie left." Suzie, another foster child, had returned to her birth parents several months previously.

When Ms. Duncan told the foster mother of Conrad's comment, the latter said, "I don't know if I could possibly cry in front of him. I've never done that." Ms. Duncan reassured her, "I'll be right there and I'll try to make it real easy for you." When adults express their feelings appropriately, it gives children permission to do so as well.

When children leave a home they need to understand why they are moving. Clear explanations may diminish the child's testing behaviors in the new family.

When contact between children and previous foster families is part of the plan, it should occur when things are going well between the child and his current family. Parents are much less likely to feel threatened by contact between their child and important people from his past when things are going well than when they are having difficulties. If contacts primarily occur when there are problems, current caregivers are likely to be defensive and there is more opportunity for the youngster to "divide and conquer" adults who are important to him. In general, it is the role of the present family, not past parents, to work with the child to solve problems in their relationships. This is equally true when a child has returned to birth parents or relatives, as when he has moved on to a new foster home or adoptive setting.

Moving a Child from One Foster Home to Another

Unfortunately, many children who enter the foster care system move from one home to another several times. Yet, we know that multiple moves interfere with meeting the child's most basic need for continuity of relationships. Multiple moves in the preschool age child have a particularly detrimental effect on long-term adjustment. Each transition, even one back to the birth parents, is likely to lead to regression and developmental interruptions. Bretherton (1980) hypothesized that requiring a young child to reorganize his security regulatory system continually around new principal caregivers may finally make the child unwilling to engage in forming yet another relationship, leading to an inability to form a loving relationship with anyone. Because of the harm of multiple moves, a primary responsibility of the caseworker is to minimize the number of moves that the child faces. In addition, she is responsible for lessening the trauma of any moves that must occur.

Why do children move from one foster home to another? Oftentimes they move because of a variety of bureaucratic regulations. Although the regulations are usually designed to meet the needs of most children, in specific cases they may be counterproductive. If there is no opportunity for flexibility in the regulations, then the agency recreates the situation found in a rigid family where individual needs of children are subservient to the needs of the adults. We should always be asking ourselves if the regulations are meeting the needs of the children or the needs of adults.

When an agency uses receiving homes, an extra move will be necessary in many cases. However, there are also advantages to having receiving homes. A small number of people can be prepared for helping the child cope with the trauma of abrupt moves. Secondly, the period of time in the receiving home will allow both for adequate assessment of the child and for recruitment of an appropriate long-term placement for the child. The obvious disadvantage is that any child who will be in placement beyond a proscribed period of time will face another move. To maximize the advantages and minimize the disadvantages, receiving homes would be used only for emergency moves, not when there is time to make a preplacement plan.

Abrupt moves from one foster home to another certainly should be the exception rather than the rule. Foster parents who understand their importance in a child's life and who believe in the continuity of relationships will help children when they must move. However, frequently it is the agency itself which diminishes the importance of relationships or does not provide adequate supervision and access for foster parents, so that the latter come to believe that emergency moves are the only solution for coping with a problem child. Ideally the agreements between foster parents and agencies would state that adequate notice, for example ten days to two weeks, would have to be given by either side if there is to be a move. Exceptions would be those circumstances that would lead to emergency placements if the child were still in the care of birth parents. This would account for the exceptions necessary if a child is being abused or neglected or if there was a death or medical emergency in the foster home.

Reasonable indications for planned moves within the foster care system are:1) when the foster family is unable to meet the child's needs after receiving help and counseling on ways to meet those needs, 2) when the foster family insists on the child's removal, not just when they indicate that there are some problems, 3) when there has been abuse or neglect in the foster home but it was not severe enough to lead to an emergency move, or 4) when an older child insists on leaving the foster home. Additionally, there might be planned moves to facilitate overall treatment planning. Examples might include a child moving so that siblings could be together or so that a child could be closer to family members when the plan is reunification. However, even in these cases one must always be careful in assessing the messages to the child and the possible impact of another separation. Are children being used to meet adult needs or are the child's needs held primary?

Jerry, age two, has been living in the same fosterhome for fourteen months. For the first seven months of his life he lived with his birth mother, Sherry, although reportedly she would leave him with a variety of friends and relatives for up to two weeks at a time. It was after she left him with a friend and did not return after a week, as she had said she would do, that Jerry was placed in care. This is his second foster home. When placed in this home he was a very rejecting of parenting. His behaviors have gradually improved and he is now perceived by his foster family as a "normal toddler."

Jerry

Sherry, who is eighteen, married four months ago. She and her husband live in a town thirty miles from the foster home. The stepfather shows concern and interest in Jerry. He calls and asks for visits and Sherry shows up with him. The stepfather interacts more with Jerry during the contacts than does Sherry. In fact, the latter is quite open about the fact that if her husband was not pushing for the child to return to their care, she probably would not be seeing him. Their attorney is now suggesting that Jerry be moved to a foster home closer to Sherry so that a more frequent visiting schedule can be implemented with the goal of reunification.

Although the adults' needs undoubtedly would best be met by having Jerry be placed closer to them, the primary concern should center on the impact on Jerry of a move to another foster home.

When a child is to be moved from one foster home to another or to a different type of child care facility, an updated assessment should identify his current psychological needs and present functioning so that an appropriate placement can be selected.

Caseworkers should talk honestly with the child about the reasons for the move. The object is not to place blame on anyone, but to describe problems and unmet needs which the child or family may have, and to identify ways that these will be addressed by the plan for the a new placement. Youngsters in foster care usually understand that some children and some families have trouble getting along, but that the same child may do better in a different family setting. No matter what the reason for the move is, the child deserves to have information as to the decision making process and the goals for the new placement.

Usually foster families have strong feelings when a child needs to move from their home. Sometimes the family feels guilty about not being able to meet the needs of the child. Other times the family may be angry at the agency for not adequately preparing or supporting them in working with the child's behaviors, or they may disagree with the overall case planning. It is important that someone support the foster parents so that they can help the child move from their home in the least traumatic way possible. The foster family deserves support in identifying and expressing their feelings about the separation. Simultaneously, we model for

201

them ways they can be supportive to their foster child. If this is not done, the foster parent's feelings are likely to be expressed inappropriately and to the child's detriment.

Additionally, we must realize that different people in the foster family may have varying feelings. For the other foster children who remain in the home there may be a resurfacing of separation/loss issues. The birth children of the foster parents may have a variety of reactions.

Randy

Randy chose to drop out of high school soon after his sixteenth birthday. Although he had a job, he frequently did not show up for it. His foster parents of three-and-a-half years were unable to trust him when he was away from their home. The foster parents told Randy that to remain living with them he would have to follow two basic rules. He had to either attend school or be employed, and he had to be where he said he was going. If he believed that he would not or could not follow these rules, they would help with a move to another setting. Randy, after thinking about the decision for a couple of weeks, decided that he wanted to be placed in a group home. This was arranged.

Randy seemed relieved about the move. He felt he had been under a lot of pressure with many expectations placed on him in the foster home. His foster parents felt both relieved and guilty about the fact that the placement had not worked out as they had planned. Their goal had been to be a long-term family of resource for Randy.

The foster parents had two daughters by birth. One was six when Randy left and the other was four. Although the six year old seemed happy and more relaxed after Randy left, the four year old developed sleeping and eating problems. She looked depressed. Her parents did not initially realize the source of her problems. There was a new teacher at her preschool and initially they attributed the symptoms to her reacting to this event. However, about four weeks after Randy left the home, four-year-old Tricia blurted out, "How come I never see my brother any more?" She had no conscious memories of family life prior to Randy's joining the family. She had no understanding of "foster care." From her viewpoint, her brother, who had doted on her, had left. She didn't know if other family members would leave. She didn't know if he still loved her or if he never had. She was depressed. She needed contact with Randy and acknowledgement of her feelings.

Commonly, there is no one to work with the members of the foster family after a child leaves their home. Parents and other children in the home are left to grieve by themselves. They may not share their feelings with each other, thinking that they are protecting others from pain. The feelings may go underground and resurface years later indicating the potency of the emotions which accompany the grief process and the confused thinking that frequently follows a loss.

Sixteen-year-old Murray was in the midst of a major disagreement with his mother. Suddenly he said, "Sometimes I feel like just getting out of here. Probably you wouldn't feel any worse about my leaving than you did when Cameron left."

Murray's mom, Theresa, was speechless. The arguing stopped. Quietly she asked what Murray meant. Cameron had been one of two teens the family had fostered when Murray was in grade school. Cameron had left seven years ago. Murray replied, "I always thought you really cared about Cam, but you weren't upset at all when he left." Tears welled in Theresa's eyes. She replied, "I did care about Cam. It was really difficult for me when he left, but I thought it would be too hard on you and your sister if you saw how sad I was, so I only cried when you were at school. I think I made a serious mistake. Did you really think I didn't care?"

Murray related that he had been very confused. He had thought his mom was especially close to Cam, but when she didn't show any signs of grief he became uncertain. Now, as a teen, he himself usually felt loved. But, when he and his mom had a conflict, the confusion resurfaced and he questioned his own perceptions of her loving and caring.

Murray

Preplacement visits when a child is moving from one placement to another within the system can be used to acheive the goals listed earlier in this chapter. These visits should occur whether the child is moving to another foster home or to a different type of child care facility.

Sometimes moves within the system involve transitions from group care to family care. In these situations it is important that everyone involved understand who is going to be responsible for each aspect of preparing the child and for postplacement services and contacts. Sometimes treatment center or group care staff will be actively involved in the preplacement visiting, planning, and postplacement services, and other times they will not. Not only should the adults have a clear picture of who is responsible for what, but the youngster should be advised as to who is providing what services and who is responsible for which decisions.

Exercise 4-4 provides an opportunity to think about transitioning a child from one placement to another. In this case we will be looking at moving an injured child from a hospital to a foster home.

Planning a Move from a Hospital Setting to a Foster Home

Kenny

Kenny is three years old. He is in the hospital, following a severe head injury that resulted from abuse by his father. The head injury has left him with a partial paralysis on the right side. He also has some speech problems because of the injury. In the hospital he has become the favorite of the nurses. He is involved in both physical therapy and in speech therapy. He will soon move to a foster home.

Devise a worksheet with two columns labeled "Messages for Kenny" and "Strategies for Conveying" to help you to outline a plan for introducing the foster parents to the child and for preplacement visits.

IV   Return to the Birth Parents

In most cases when children have been placed in interim care, the plan of first preference will be to return the child to his birth family. As we will see in the next chapter, the treatment plan will identify what needs to change for the child to return to the care of his family.

However, the child's reaction to returning to his birth family is going to be strongly influenced by the length of time he has been in interim care, by the kind of experience he has had in the foster home, and the contacts with his family of origin throughout his stay in foster care. To understand the child's viewpoint, it is helpful to think in terms of what percentage of the child's life has been spent in placement.

If the child does not yet have much language, and has been separated for a significant period of time from his birth parents, particularly with minimal ongoing contact, then essentially he will be moving to strangers and the procedures such as those outlined for moving the preverbal child into adoptive placement should be used.

If regular ongoing contacts have not occurred, visits aimed at transferring parenting from the foster parents to the birth parents should be set up. If the child has had frequent visits with his birth parents while in foster care, then only the final steps, such as giving the child permission to leave and to get close to the birth parents, need to be emphasized.

If direct contact between birth parents and foster parents did not occur during the placement, it needs to occur during this transition period. Lack of contact between the two families puts the child, once again, in the untenable position of having to choose one set of parents over the other. When this occurs, everyone loses because the child feels caught in a trap, acts out, and makes the move more difficult.

If the child is verbal, a discussion aimed at the child's level of understanding should take place. This discussion should outline the gains the child has made while in foster care, as well as the changes that have taken place in the family during this period. Ideally the caseworker, the child, the birthparents, and the foster parents would all participate in this discussion.

The functions of preplacement contacts should be reviewed and once again considered as progress toward the final transfer is made. Children returning to birth parents are just as likely to have fears and worries as those entering the foster care system. These concerns may center around the question of, "What is different that makes it safe for me to live with my birth parents now when it wasn't in the past?" Or the primary question may center around new family members. The mother may have a new partner or there may be a new sibling. Commonly the living situation itself has changed. The child may be returning to the same parents but have worries about living in a new neighborhood or attending a different school.

Attachments made in foster care, as well as behavioral gains, may need to be actively transferred to the parents, particularly with the preschool aged child who has been away from the birth parents for a significant length of time. It is common for children in placement to express their loyalty conflicts by behaving one way for one set of parents and differently for the other set. This may not helpful to the child's adjustment in the long run. If the child has a discipline problem in the birth home, but not in the foster home, or if the child had behavior problems that subsided while he was in foster care, then the foster parents should be actively involved in helping with the move and transferring the behavioral gains. Table 4-4 outlines the steps involved in this transfer.

4-4 ____ *Table* ____

Steps Involved in the Transfer of Behavioral Gains

1. Birth parents observe what techniques worked in the foster home.
2. Birth parents try these techniques out in their own home.
3. Foster parents to give the child permission to do as well at home as he has done in foster care.
4. Caseworker supports both the foster and birth parents in the transfer process.
5. In some cases, having foster parent involved with the child and the birth parent after the move may be helpful.

For some older children, an open discussion with both sets of parents present may be enough. However, for other children a more lengthy process is necessary. It might begin by having birth parents come to the foster home to observe the child's behaviors there. The foster parents might then begin to involve and support the birth parents in making demands on the child and in disciplining him. A final part of the process would include having the foster parents accompany the child on a visit to the birth home. The child who usually behaves well in the foster home, but not in the birth home, is then caught in a dilemma. Should he behave in the way he usually does for the foster parent or should he behave in the way he usually does for the birth parent? The foster parent can give the child permission to do well and help the birth parent effect the desired behavior. Both sets of parents can then share their pleasure in the child's performance.

Lisa

Lisa, age five, has been in foster care for eighteen months. Prior to Lisa's entering care, her birth mother was having problems controlling her. Night roaming was common as were fears of being bathed. Both of these behaviors have diminished while she was in foster care. However, both recurred when overnight visits were instituted. Rather than stopping the visits, a plan for actively transferring one of the behavioral gains was made. The bathing routine was selected as it would be easiest to transfer. A four part plan was devised.

Initially, Renee, the birth mother, was asked to visit Lisa in the foster home and to remain until bath time. The foster mother gave Lisa her bath with Renee in the room. Obviously Lisa was faced with the choice of behaving as she usually did for her foster mom or as she usually did for Renee. As expected, she demonstrated no behavioral problems. Both the foster mother and Renee commented that they were glad she enjoyed the bath. A couple of days later Renee again visited in the foster home. This time she gave Lisa her bath with the foster mother observing. Again, Lisa did well. The third segment of the transfer involved the foster mom giving Lisa a bath at Renee's home with the latter present. The fourth had Renee in her own home bathing Lisa with the foster mom present.

In a stepwise manner a behavioral gain was actively transferred from foster to birth parent. Nonverbally the foster mother was giving Lisa permission to do as well for Renee as she usually behaved for her. Loyalty issues were diminished. Had Renee's behaviors associated with bathing regressed at any time during the process, the previous step would have been repeated as many times as necessary for a positive outcome.

If the child has developed strong attachments in foster care, then we can expect him to experience some aspects of the grief process even though he may simultaneously be more excited than apprehensive about the return home. These ambivalent feelings will need to be acknowledged and addressed, again focusing on diminishing the loyalty conflicts that are likely to surface at this point.

Finally, prior to the final return home, the caseworker will want to focus on getting commitments from the birth parents, the foster parents, and the child as to how they are going to handle problems or strong emotions after the move and as to the type of contact that the child may have with members of the foster family or friends they are leaving.

When a child returns to his birth family, he should have his Lifebook with pictures and information compiled while he was in foster care. The Lifebook will be discussed in some detail in a later chapter. Birth parents are more likely to accept the Lifebook if they were involved in putting together the preplacement information and if pictures of the birth family were obtained for the child while he was in foster care. A picture of the child and his birth parents taken on the day of the move home should be incorporated into the Lifebook immediately.

At the time of a return to the birth home, old unresolved feelings and issues are likely to emerge, both for the child and for the parents. Whenever family composition is changed by adding or subtracting a family member, the entire family system will undergo stress. Such stress should be expected when a child returns home after any appreciable time away from the birth family. It does not mean that the placement is going to fail. It does mean that increased casework services must be provided when children are returned home to help families cope with difficult emotions, clear up misperceptions, and resolve issues.

The courts must be sensitized to the needs of both families and children so that court orders allow time for preplacement visits. The balance between addressing any fears and worries the child may have and empowering the birth family is a delicate one. As in other types of situations, too rapid a transition may ignore the child's concerns about the future or the importance of his current relationships. Too prolonged a transition may infer that it is not safe for the child to move, or may make it more difficult for the child to complete the process process of mourning his current loss. The decision on timing must take into consideration the child's view and his feelings, as well as the relationship between current caregivers and birth parents.

Moving a Child to Adoption   V

Newer forms of adoption are helping to ease the transition for many children. Foster parent adoptions and relative adoptions have helped many child care and mental health professionals become stronger advocates for varying degrees of openness in other adoptive situations, even in infant placements.

Some form of openness is now more the rule than the exception in older child adoption. Increasingly, when children leave foster care to join a new family there is the option of maintaining contact with the foster family after the move. Sometimes during the child's stay in foster care, birth family members who are not able to parent the child themselves but who can be supportive of the child joining another family are identified. These relatives may play a critical role in helping the child disengage from the birth family by giving him permission to move on and become a member of another family by adoption. Sometimes it is important to the child that long-term contact with these birth family members be allowed. None of these forms of openness is co-parenting. This openness is supportive of the adoptive parents being empowered to parent their new family member and to be legally responsible for making decisions on his behalf, while still recognizing that past family relationships continue to be important to the child and, indeed, can help in his continued growth, development, and identity formation.

Foster Parent Adoption

This situation, in which the child transitions out of the foster care system without physically moving, is occurring with increased frequency. The enormous advantage for the child is that foster parent adoption protects existing attachments and precludes the necessity of another interruption in parenting while, at the same time, providing for legal permanency. The caseworker must not only assess the child's long-term needs and the family's ability to meet these needs, but also the magical thinking of each member of the immediate family. What does adoption mean to the foster parents? To the child being adopted? To other members of the foster family? How do they expect it to change their relationships? Do the parents expect the child's behaviors to change following the adoptive proceedings? Does the child expect the parents' behaviors or attitudes to change? Magical thinking about the effect of adoption is frequently prominent on the part of all involved. The Aspects of Parenting, page 159, focusing on the Legal Parent role, can be used to help identify what will change.

The primary difference, of course, will be that the foster parents will take on all of the roles associated with the Legal Parent. In addition, it is likely that there will be increased claiming on the part of parents and child for each other because of the legal protection provided for the relationship and the entitlement that it represents. The Checklist on Ways to Encourage Attachment on page 62 identifies some ideas for enhancing claiming.

The magical thinking on the part of the child might relate more to anticipated changes in the behaviors of non-parental family members. The child may think that the grandparents will now treat him the same way they treat the birth children in the foster family. This may be accurate; it may not be. The foster/adoptive parents should be able to help confirm or modify the child's expectations. The overall goal is to clarify, explore, confirm, or confront the various forms of magical thinking of each individual involved in the adoption.

Moving to an Adoptive Home

When moving a child from foster care to adoption, the relative importance of the tasks to be accomplished during preplacement visits will differ with children of varying ages because of their cognitive abilities. Therefore the specifics of the transfer process will differ depending upon developmental age. Although generalized guidelines follow, adults must view each situation as unique. They need to modify the guidelines to fit the specifics, always keeping in mind the primary reasons for the visits.

Moving the Pre-Verbal Child to Adoption

Many children join their adoptive families when they are less than three years of age. While moving these children is often viewed as an easier task than placing an older child, there are some serious concerns that must be attended to in work with the younger age group. As pointed out earlier, children ages six months to four years are especially prone to having difficulties with separation from those to whom they are attached (Rutter, 1981). If they are leaving situations where there was not a strong attachment then they are at serious risk for long-term problems secondary to not having had their developmental needs met in a timely manner.

Brenda

Brenda is six. She joined her adoptive family as a toddler after a single preplacement visit during which the foster and adoptive families did not meet. She had lived with her foster family, with whom she had had a close loving relationship, from age five weeks. Her subsequent relationship with her adoptive family was quite different. She withdrew from affection. Control issues occurred many times daily.

Her family sought therapy for these problems. One day during a family therapy session, the therapist asked Brenda where she thought people got babies. The child's response was, "Anywhere they can find them!" She was deeply afraid that someone, anyone, might come and take her away from her adoptive parents. She did not trust that the parents would be able to prevent this. After all, her previous parents had not prevented these people from coming, visiting with her, and never taking her back to her foster home. Her defense against the pain of another loss was to never again become emotionally dependent upon adults. In spite of her behaviors seeming to be willful, resistant and manipulative, this was an unconscious outcome, not a conscious, willful choice.

It is precisely because there has been an emphasis on the detrimental effects of interrupted parenting during the early years that some have advised against foster parents developing strong relationships with the very young child in their care. However, it is easier to help the child and foster parents cope with the separation problems, than to help the child's permanent family cope with the long-range effects of his not having developed a healthy attachment in the early years. On the other hand, we must recognize the difficulties posed by separating a toddler from his longtime caregivers. Everything possible must be done to to minimize the trauma and avoid multiple moves.

In moving preverbal children, there is less margin for error than when we are working with older children. Workers and parents must pay close attention to specifics, particularly nonverbal detail. While the child under three understands many more words than he can express, he is usually especially responsive to nonverbal signals. His attachment to the foster parents must be literally handed over to the adoptive parents. To do this there must be considerable contact between the two sets of parents. In addition, it means that if the foster parents strongly disagree with the adoption plan it is quite likely that the child will sense a witholding of the permission to go which is a vital part of the transfer process. In these cases work supportive of feelings, but confrontive of behaviors, must proceed with the foster parents.

Because children of these ages usually feel most secure on their home ground, initial contacts with the adoptive parents should take place in the foster home and in the presence of the foster parents. Adoptive parents need to understand that during the first contact with the child, the interactions between them and the child must occur at the child's pacing.

If a child of this age is well attached to his foster parents, he may cling or hide a little when strangers enter the home. It is unlikely that he will immediately interact with the newcomers. It often works best if prospective adoptive parents first chat with the foster parents, not centering attention on the toddler. The child will sense that his foster parents are comfortable and he most likely will then begin to initiate interactions with the visitors. It is crucial that the child be allowed to control the pacing of this encounter if he is to start to trust the prospective parents.

Adoptive parents might be asked to bring several toys to the visit. Except for one cuddly type toy that they leave with the child, they should take the remainder home with them. Then, when the child first visits the adoptive home, there will be toys that he first became acquainted with in the foster home. The nonverbal message in this is, "Things that are okay for you to play with in your foster home are okay for you to play with here."

Usually, the time from first visit to final move for the preverbal child is less than for children over three. The infant and toddler do not have a well developed sense of time. Contacts with the adopters must occur more frequently, with a shorter time span between the contacts. The focus of the preplacement contacts is primarly on transferring attachment and empowering the new caregivers, while alleviating fears of the unknown by having the adopters, who start out as strangers to the child, become known to him. The child of this age cannot initiate the grieving process until after the move. In spite of spending less overall time in the preplacement process one must be careful not to move too fast. Seven to ten days of visiting is usually about right for children of the toddler age with two to three days of contact being all that is commonly necessary for the child four months of age or younger.

During the visiting period, the objective is to arrange for the most possible contact between the child and the new parents. The adoptive parents, especially the one who will be the primary caregiver, should spend considerable time in the foster home. The contacts should occur at all times of day.

In part, this allows the adoptive parents to learn the child's routine thoroughly. Maintaining the same routine, as the Robertons learned (Bowlby, 1973) is a primary way to lessen the trauma of a move for the young child. If the child is used to eating dinner at 5:30 and going to bed at 7:30, this is the routine that should be followed initially in the adoptive home, even if it is not convenient. The younger the child, the more attention adopters should pay to the sensory experiences of the infant, trying to duplicate as many of these as is feasible. For example, using the same type of nipples for feeding an infant, would be important. The infant's sense of smell is highly developed and can be used to facilitate the transition, by having the adopters use the same baby products, soaps, detergents, and fabric softeners as were used in the foster home. As the child gets older and increasingly uses sight and sound to process his world, stimulii using these sense can be used for the transition. A familiar mobile over the crib, other familiar toys, music of the same type as played in the foster home are all possibilities.

With a newborn infant families are expected to tolerate many inconveniences in order to meet the child's needs "on demand." Even though the child joining the adoptive family may be beyond this stage of normal development he is likely to regress with the trauma of interrupted parenting and the primary goal of the adoptive parents is, just as for the parents of a newborn, to help the child learn to trust their ability to care for him. As the first few weeks pass and the child feels more secure, then changes in routine can be gradually instituted.

The recommended type of extensive contact allows the child to receive the message from the foster parents that it is okay to like, to take from, and to get close to the adoptive parents. If careful attention is not paid to giving this message, the child may subsequently have difficulty accepting both affection and external controls from new parents.

How can foster parents go about giving this message to the child? They can do it in the same way that most mothers unconsciously work at extending attachments to other family members. In the midst of feeding the young toddler, the foster mother might say, "I need to check the cake in the oven, would you finish feeding him?" while handing the spoon to the adoptive mother. The message to the child is that the foster mother trusts the adoptive mother. The foster parent literally hands over all sorts of routine tasks to the adopters during the visiting period. "Would you please change him?" "Come help me tuck him in bed." "Give your new mommy a big hug and kiss, too."

Since this type of behavior is uncommon except among family members, interchanges like this help the child realize that something unusual is going on.

The child's acceptance that things are different is essential. The child needs to know that something big and important is happening in his life.

Although it is commonly the mother who cares for a toddler most of the time, most children of this age also have close relationships with the foster father and/or others in the foster family. Positive interactions, particulary those involving ritualized play, are frequently the focal point of these relationships. These interchanges can be actively transferred to an adoptive family member, in the same way that the care giving interactions have been transferred from foster to adoptive mother. For example, foster and adoptive father might together play on the floor with the child, or take turns lifting the toddler over their heads.

After two or three visits in the foster home, a foster parent may suggest that the toddler go for an outing with the new parent—either to a park, for an ice cream, or for some other pleasurable outing. Even though this is usually arranged in advance by worker, adopters, and foster family, when it occurs it should be at the suggestion of the foster parent. This gives the child the message, "I trust these people, they will take good care of you, and they will bring you back home."

The following visit may include a trip to the new home, where the child is re-introduced to the toys bought for the initial visit in the foster home and can become acquainted with the home. Prior to this visit, the toddler-aged child usually will have seen pictures of the outside of the house, possibly a picture of his bedroom and pictures of the family pets. Showing a short video of the adoptive home to a toddler is another option. If there are other children in the adoptive family, their pictures should be presented to the child at the first or second visit in the foster home, and they should subsequently visit the child in the foster home prior to visits moving to the adoptive home. Some adopters tape small photos of the child who will be joining the family to the door of the child's room, to his bed, the toy chest, his drawers, his chair at the table, etc. Mealtime visits to the adoptive home should be included during the preplacement period. Although most toddlers will have one or two overnight visits in the adoptive home, it is difficult for children this age to go back and forth repeatedly for overnight stays.

On the day of the final move, we want the adoptive parents to come to the foster home. Both sets of parents participate in the last of the packing together. The preparation for the move and the packing should not be done secretively. The child needs to realize that something different is happening today. Although it is not helpful if anyone in the foster family is sobbing or clinging to the child, some may well look tearful and that is fine. If they are bonded to the child, foster family members will be sad, as well as happy, about the child's moving.

At the final moment of the move, both families join in loading the car while the foster parent literally hands the child over to the adoptive parent at the doorway. If, after good-bye kisses, the child cries or clings to her, the foster parent may say something like, "I'm going to miss you and you're going to miss us, but it's time to go now," and again literally hands the child over to the adoptive parent.

At the time of the move, the child should certainly take not only his clothes, but also some special toys or bedding from the foster home to the adoptive home. Such transitional attachment objects are helpful to children. Those who use them seem to be more, rather than less, attached to parent figures.

After the move, the first postplacement contact between foster parents and child should take place on the child's home ground, which is now his adoptive home. It is wise for the foster parents' other children, whether they be birth, adopted, or foster, at some point to visit the child, the child who has left their family.

Children often worry about what has happened to foster children who lived with them. These concerns easily become intertwined with guilt feelings. Most children in a foster family occasionally wish that the others weren't there. Then they feel guilty when the child moves and they get to stay. If they see that the child is happy in his new home, and that things are going well for him, it dissipates their guilt feelings. Such contact also helps alleviate the guilt feelings that many foster parents have for not adopting a particular foster child.

Jennifer

Jennifer joined her foster family as a battered child when she was seventeen months old. Although her physical wounds healed rapidly, psychological scarring was deep. She had little sense of self. During tantrums she would hold her breath until she passed out. She was very frightened of men, strange people, and any change in routine. With some professional help and a lot of patience, gradually Jennifer came to love and trust her foster family. In spite of continuing to be very fearful of change, she became a basically happy toddler.

By the time she was twenty-seven months old, Jennifer was legally free for adoption. The caseworker and foster parents had concerns that she might, following a move, regress to her earlier fears and problems. They decided on a plan of gradual transfer of the attachment and behavioral gains from foster to adoptive family.

The caseworker and foster mother met alone with the adoptive parents. Pictures of Jennifer as she had looked early in her placement and as she looked now were shared. The problems she had early in her placement and how she had been helped through them were discussed. Her daily schedule, her eating, sleeping, and play habits were outlined in detail.

Jennifer's first visit with the adoptive parents was in the foster home. Since Jennifer was still wary of strangers, the adoptive parents needed to gain her trust before making any advances toward her. Foster and adoptive parents visited together while Jennifer played. For the next week the adoptive parents made daily visits to the foster home. At first Jennifer would allow them to play with her but nothing else. She still looked to her foster mom to wipe her nose, wash her face, take her to the potty, and give her an occasional hug. As the week progressed, she gradually started orienting toward the adoptive parents. Sue Ellen and Jack, the foster parents, started calling her adoptive parents her "new mommy" and "new daddy" and talked of when she would go to live with them.

The second week the visits moved to the adopters' home. Sue Ellen and Jack took her there and stayed with her for her first visit in her new home. One day her new parents took her for an all day visit and brought her back. Foster parents took her for an overnight visit and adopters returned her the next morning. Toward the end of the second week Jennifer was happier to go with the adoptive parents than she was to return to the foster home. When the adoptive parents were present, Jennifer looked more to them for her care than she did to Sue Ellen, who was emotionally pulling back from her. She was transferring the love and trust she had in the foster parents to her new parents. She was ready to make the move.

When moving day came, both families and Jennifer helped in the packing. This was done in an exaggerated manner so she would know for certain that this was final. Jennifer left with a smile and a wave. Sue Ellen was the one with tears in her eyes.

During early visits after the move Jennifer continued to call her foster parents "Mommy and Daddy." Gradually she switched to using their first names. Following a visit about eight months after her placement, Jennifer told her adoptive mom, "Sue Ellen and Jack will always love me, but you're my mom and dad now".*

Exercise 4-5 involves planning a move to adoption for Martin, one of the children whom we have been following throughout his journey within the child welfare system.

Exercise 4-5

Preparing a Toddler for Moving from Foster Care to Adoptive Home

Martin

Since his move to the LaBelle foster family at age eighteen months, Martin has made many gains. Jane Paulson continued to be very involved with Martin and the LaBelles for the first six months of the placement. She now consults with Donna LaBelle by telephone about once a month. She is, however, willing to become more involved with Martin prior to his move to adoption, and to work with the adoptive family following the transition if Martin's careworker, Mr. Sawyer, desires that she do so.

* *Jennifer's story is an adaptation of a summary written by Maryann Kiefer, a foster parent in Colorado Springs, after her foster daughter moved from her home.*

Martin is now thirty-two months old. The LaBelles believe that his attachment to them is now strong enough that it will be possible to help him build relationships with an adoptive family. Charita, who was four when Marty was placed with the LaBelles, moved to an adoptive family four months ago. During that transition, Bert and Donna had occasionally commented that someday Marty, too, would be moving to a "growing up with" mommy and daddy. Danita continues to live at home while attending a community college and working. Dwight, now close to thirteen, continues to live with the LaBelle family. It continues to be uncertain whether or not he will eventually return to one of his birth parents or if he will remain with the LaBelle family until emancipation.

Currently when Donna leaves Marty with a sitter, a very infrequent occurrence, he cries. He usually plays in the same room that one of his foster parents is occupying. He recognizes himself in pictures and in the mirror, and is beginning to show signs of the social emotions. Touch, movement, and music continue to be the avenues most used by the foster family to engage Marty in interactions and to help soothe him when he is uncomfortable.

Bedtimes continue to be his most difficult time of day. He does now show an interest in toys. Although he has made significant progress in the area of language development, his skills are currently at an eighteen to twenty-four month level. Donna states that Marty is cooperating with toilet training, but efforts in this area have been only moderately successful.

1. What would you consider to be important factors in selecting an adoptive family for Martin? Would you be more likely to select experienced parents, or ones who had no other children and could devote all of their time and attention to Martin? Would you have strong feelings about which parent should be the primary caregiver? Would you have strong feelings about placing him in a family in which there were two working parents?

2. How would you go about explaining Martin's early life experiences to prospective adopters? Do you anticipate that problems may resurface in the future? If so, when? How would you prepare the adoptive parents for these problems?

3. Outline an overall plan for preplacement visits, including time frames from initial contact to final transition.

4. What observations during the preplacement period might encourage you to modify the plan and have a longer preplacement period than originally planned? Can you think of circumstances in which you might move forward the time of actual transition?

5. What arrangement for postplacement contacts between foster and adoptive families would you encourage?

Tasks to Be Accomplished in Moving the Verbal Child to Adoption

Introduce the idea of adoption to the child
Arrange the first meetings
Provide "homework" for child and family
Share information
Get commitment to proceed
Plan subsequent pre-placement visits
Discuss name changes
Initiate the grief process
Discuss the "worst of the worst"
Obtain permission for child to go and do well
Facilitate good-byes with foster family and other
   people important to the child
Provide ideas for welcoming ritual
Facilitate postplacement contacts
Arrange for postplacement follow-up

Moving the Child over Three to Adoption

Although the age of three is used arbitrarily, it is the child's abilities to verbalize and to separate temporarily from the adults to whom he is attached that indicate the true dividing line. Thus, with a four-year-old who is developmentally delayed, one might proceed with the move in the manner outlined for a two-year-old. However, it is important to remember that even though the older preschooler and the early grade-school child may have good verbal skills, they still do not possess the intellectual skills necessary to truly understand the legal significance of adoption, and they may have considerable problems in transitioning from one home to another.

You'll find that we make a number of very specific suggestions about how each of the tasks in Table 4-5 might be handled. Sometimes conditions may make it difficult to replicate in full the process as described. However, a firm belief in the importance of minimizing the trauma of moves, combined with creativity and flexiblity, will usually allow most of the basic tasks to be accomplished. Once again, it is important to stress that anything not addressed prior to the move will probably entail more time, money, and effort to remedy after the transition.

Introducing the Idea of Adoption to the Child

Prior to introducing the idea of adoption to a child, the caseworker needs to first spend enough time with the child that the two of them are comfortable together. Then, preferably in front of the current caregivers, the caseworker should explain the difference between foster and adoptive families in a way that the child can understand.

The Life Path, described on page 364 might be used with the child ages three to ten for explaining the goal of adoption as moving to "growing up with family." The Aspects of Parenting, page 159 can be used with children from about age seven and older. In using this tool, the social worker will be talking of the transfer of the legal parenting role. However, even more time is likely to be spent exploring the items listed in the "Parenting Parent" circle to elicit the child's fears and worries as well as his hopes and dreams. Which items seem to carry particular import for the child? Which might pose special problems within a family setting?

Usually foster families are described as providing parenting for the child until a decision has been made about where the child will live during the remainder of his growing up years. Adoptive families are "keeping or growing up with" families who plan to raise children until they grow up and who will continue to be family even when the children become adults. Children can be told that while they are in foster care many people—i.e. birth parents, caseworkers, judges, foster parents etc.—are all involved in decision making. On the other hand, although adoptive parents, like any other parent, might ask advice of others, they alone are in charge of making the decisions that most affect their children. Another change, from the child's point of view, is the last name. While in foster care, children usually continue to use the surname of their birth parent. However, when they join an adoptive family the child's last name will usually be legally changed to that of the new parents.

The caseworker needs to insure that the child understands why adoption is a plan. What is it that has occurred in this child's life that makes reunification with birth parents no longer a possibility? The caseworker can then go on to say something along the lines of, "I believe that all children deserve to have a family to be there for them during their growing up years and who will still be family to them when they are an adult. There are children like you who need a family to grow up with and there are parents who are interested in having children permanently join their families. However, as you already know, not all children and parents can successfully live together. My job is to help find a family that is right for you, a family you can join by adoption."

The child should be assured that he will have an opportunity to meet the family before a final decision about placement with them is made. After a few visits, a decision will be made as to whether the child will join this family or whether if a different family needs to be selected. Although it is the responsibility of the caseworker to make the final selection of a family, children need to know that family building is hard work. For it to succeed the child, the family, and the worker must all work together. As children become older, the concept of each person involved—parents, child, caseworker, and sometimes a therapist or someone else—having equal veto power, but no one person having sole go-ahead power can be used. In this way the young person is included in the decision making process without being responsibile for the selection. The child needs to know that his input in important. However, it is equally crucial that the child not think that he is totally responsible for choosing a family. If the child indicates, either by what he says or does, that for some reason he is totally unaccepting of a particular family, it would be unwise to proceed with the adoption.

Likewise, prospective adoptive parents need to know that if after initially meeting a child they are, for any reason, uncomfortable making a commitment to this youngster, they need to say so. In either of these situations, the worker needs to take the final responsibility. For example, when prospective parents indicate that they do not want to proceed, the worker might tell the child that she has seen some things that make her believe that this is not the right family and that she plans to continue her search for a family. The child's feelings about an interruption in the planning can be more quickly resolved when he must continue to work with the person responsible for his disappointment. Only the worker is in a position to help the child learn that she is, indeed, committed to his having a permanent family. Since the child does not have a real connection to this prospective family, there is not the same need for this family to take responsibility for making the decision or giving the child permission to move on as in cases where birth parents make an adoption plan, in an adoption disruption, or when a foster family chooses not to adopt a child already in their care but who is now legally free for adoption.

Arranging First Visits

Using pictures or albums of the prospective family to introduce them to the child prior to the first face-to-face meeting helps alleviate anxiety. Creating accurate visual images prior to the meeting seems helpful. Some agencies show videotapes of the family in their home to the child prior to the first meeting. Children may view the video as frequently as they desire during the preplacement period. This is particularly useful in long distance moves when the number of direct contacts may have to be less than if the adopters lived close by. The availability of videotaping also makes it possible for a family to observe a child prior to direct contact. This can be especially important when children have severe physical or emotional handicaps.

During the photo or video presentation of the family to the child, the worker needs to listen for fears, worries, or concerns that the child might express. In introducing a family initially, the worker might say something along the lines of, "Eddie, you know that there are children who need families to grow up with and families who want to adopt children. But, you also know that not all families and all children get along well. My job is to help find the right family for you. I have learned of a family that might be right for you. I would like you to have a couple of visits with them, so that you can get to know them and they can get to know you. Then we will all need to decide if it looks like this is a family for you to grow up with. You'll have a chance to tell me what you think, they'll have a chance to tell me what they think, and I'll have a chance to decide what I think."

During the contacts prior to a commitment being made, the child might be given "homework" to complete on the visits. Examples include: Identify three things that the dad in this family really is looking forward to doing with an eight- (or whatever age the child is) year-old boy. Find out about three things the dad really doesn't approve of eight-year-old boys doing. Similar directions about the mom are given. Two other pieces of homework frequently given relate to the child learning what types of discipline this family uses (addressing a common fear of children who are moving to a new family) and learning how the family shows affection for each other (another common concern).

Since children usually feel most secure on their home ground, many times this will be selected as the site for the initial introduction to the prospective adopters. Occasionally the initial contact might take place in an office or other site. In most cases the child should meet only the parents, not other children in the family, during the initial contact. This emphasizes that the parent-child relationships are considered to be the crucial ones in decision making. Even though the initial visit usually occurs on the child's home ground, the older child and parents might go for a brief outing during this contact. Although buying an inexpensive toy at this point would not be inappropriate, prospective parents should be advised against buying clothes or making any major purchases for the child at this stage because a placement decision has not yet been made.

If this first visit takes place in the foster home, obviously the foster and adoptive parents will have an opportunity to meet each other. There are some advantages to having the two sets of parents meet with the worker, but without the child, at some point. This type of meeting gives the foster parents an opportunity to share with the prospective adopters the little bits of knowledge that are the real key to the parenting process. In general, the younger the child, the earlier this meeting needs to take place. In some cases, with preschoolers or those with severe physical or emotional handicaps, this contact may well occur prior to introducing the child and prospective adopters to each other.

Competitiveness between foster and adoptive parents seems to be decreased, rather than increased, by real knowledge of each other. Usually foster parents are, at the time of the transition to adoption, the most important persons in the child's life. The adopters will be moving into that position. Loyalty conflicts for the child will be decreased if he can see the two sets of parents, respectful of each other's position in his life, working together to facilitate the moving process. If the foster parents are comfortable with the adoptive parents and believe that they will do a good job of parenting the child, then the move will proceed with much less turmoil and disequilibrium for everyone.

Before getting a commitment to proceed further with the adoption plan, it is important to insure that the prospective adopters have received all available information about the child's past. Full disclosure to the adoptive parents about the child's past is absolutely necessary. This cannot be stressed too much. If prospective parents cannot handle the information, they certainly will not be able to handle the product of that information, the child. Although children may be told that the parents know about their past, most don't believe it to be true. They seem to believe that if the adoptive parents knew the worst, they would not want them. As we will see, one of the most healing things that can happen at the time of adoptive placements is for children to hear that the adoptive parents, knowing "the worst of the worst," understand the behaviors and still want them to join the family.

Getting a Commitment to Proceed

Following the second or third visit, the caseworker talks separately with the prospective adoptive family, the child, and the foster family. She needs to get everyone's opinions about how things are going, so that she can decide whether to proceed with a placement plan. In talking to the child, the caseworker has an opportunity to combine the information gained in completing the "homework" during the visits with making a commitment to proceed. She might ask if the child thinks that it is going to be easy or difficult to do things with the dad? Is it going to be easy or hard to follow the rules? How does he think it is going to be receiving and giving affection in the manner the family is used to? In talking with the adopters she further clarifies their ability and willingness to make a commitment to this particular youngster.

If child, adopters, and caseworker each want to proceed then the social worker can bring the child and the adoptive parents together. Already knowing the answers, she asks each in front of the other if they want to proceed with the plan. Because most older children who are legally free for adoption have already experienced several rejections, it can be very healing for a youngster to hear from prospective adoptive parents, "We want you to be our child." Many children in foster care have not heard that kind of message before. Most adoptive families have been waiting a long time before a child is selected for them. They, too, derive great pleasure from hearing a child say, "I think these are the right parents for me." Just the act of making this type of commitment in front of the caseworker usually starts the bonding process between parents and child. It is a natural thing for them to want to hug and kiss or be physically close after such a commitment.

Setting up Additional Preplacement Visits

After getting the commitment to proceed, the plan for a further visiting schedule and the final move will be outlined. Most children over the age of three need several weeks to accomplish all of the goals of the preplacment visits. Some, particularly the child over eight or nine, may need longer. However, it is unusual for it to take more than one or two months to accomplish all of the tasks.

If the child is of preschool age, he should visit the adoptive home at various times of the day during a two to three week period. Every visit should not include treats or unusual outings. Overnight or weekend stays are also common for the preschooler. Once the child is of school age, longer preplacement visits, such as four to five days duration, are common. The child and the family need to get used to each other in a variety of ways, but most of all in the routines of daily life together. However, the child this age also needs enough time between visits to help move into the sad or mad phase of the grief process. Ryan (1985) suggests that for the four to eight-year old child a Moving Calendar, similar to an Advent calender, might be constructed. Doors on the Moving Calendar display a date. When open they reveal specific information, such as, "Adoptive parents will pick you up for a visit at 2:00 p.m." or, "Good-bye party at your foster home."

Too long a preplacement period may pose as many problems as one that is too short. Adoptive parents do not feel fully entitled to parent during the transition time. The child may infer that adults think that either the adoptive family or himself are too fragile for a move. Although it is important that the older child with strong attachments to a foster family be in the sad or mad stages of the grief process at the time of the final transition, Obviously he cannot complete the grief process prior to the move itself. It is unlikely that the child will be able to achieve much in terms of accomplishing current developmental tasks during the transition as his energies will be diverted. All of these considerations must be balanced against the overall objectives of the preplacement period.

Major drawbacks to the more prolonged preplacement period are the financial cost and logistic difficulties, particularly when long distances are involved. However, these must be balanced against the cost and availabilty of the postplacement services and contacts which would be necessary if the preplacement preparations were not adequate.

Movement into the sad or mad stages of the grief process is a major factor in determining how long the preplacement visiting period will be in older children with strong attachments to foster parents. The transition plan for the older child has to be flexible to reflect the importance of this objective.

Eight-year-old Phyllis was in the process of preplacement visits with an adoptive family. A commitment had been made by both the child and the parents. An overall plan including approximately a month of preplacement visits had been outlined. Three weeks into the preplacement period everything was going smoothly. Phyllis was showing no signs of problems either in her foster home or in the adoptive home during visits.

Phyllis

Her history indicated that she had had a very stormy relationship with her foster parents during the first nine months of her stay in their home. Temper tantrums with out-of-control behaviors had been prominent. The foster parents had worked with a therapist and learned to make use of the arousal-relaxation cycle initiated by the tantrums to develop a close relationship with Phyllis. Subsequently, Phyllis had talked frequently of wanting them to adopt her. The foster parents had several years previously made the decision that they would not be adopting any children, but readily admitted to the therapist that, although they had fostered many children, Phyllis was one of the few that they had seriously considered adopting. After careful consideration, however, they had decided to stick with their original decision to continue fostering but not to adopt. In spite of the close attachment and bonding, Phyllis had shown no signs of grieving to date during the preplacement visiting.

In reviewing the plans for the visits and move, the therapist asked, "What's happened to sad and mad?" She had talked with both Phyllis and her foster mom previously about what could be expected as Phyllis started to grieve the loss of the foster family that she had come to love so much. The therapist indicated that clearly Phyllis was not ready to move yet even though the visits *per se* were going well. Phyllis got very defensive, saying, "But you promised I would move after a month." The therapist, who had been careful not to make any promises, replied, "Most children are well into sad or mad by three weeks. I thought that was how long it would take you. However, if it takes you longer that's okay. We'll know you are ready to move when you can show your feelings about leaving the Lawsons. The foster mom called the following day to announce, "Sad and mad have arrived."

Phyllis, like most people, didn't really want to cope with the pain of loss. She was denying that it would be difficult to lose her foster family. She thought that the move would go faster if she were having no problems during the preplacement period. The therapist emphasized that readiness to move would be indicated by accepting and expressing emotions rather than by denial of the pain. In this case the therapist, who knew the foster parents well, knew that they had more difficulty showing and accepting sad feelings than angry ones and she believed it was particularly important for both Phyllis and her foster parents to acknowledge that, in spite of adoption planning respresenting the best decision in this case, there still would be a real sense of loss as Phyllis had become a loved and valued member of the foster family. Indeed, it was precisely this feeling of being loved and valued that had helped her become really ready to join an adoptive family.

Following the move, Phyllis did exceptionally well in her adoptive family. She became strongly attached to them. She maintained long-term contact with her previous foster family as well. In fact many years later when there was a death in her adoptive family, Phyllis turned to her previous foster family for support. They were able to be supportive not only to her, but also to the other members of her adoptive family.

The more that the child is aware of considerable communication between the adoptive parent, the foster parent, and the caseworker during the preplacement visits, the more secure he will be. When he knows that everyone knows everything and is comfortable with the information, it relieves him of the fear of saying or doing the wrong thing. The more that the child is able to express his mixed feelings about the upcoming move, the better. One must remember that no matter how much the child likes the prospective family, he also has other feelings—sadness at leaving the family he has learned to love and trust, fear and anxiety about the future, and anger that he has been put in the position of having such confusing emotions.

As the visits proceed and behaviors reflective of the child's grief process emerge, it is not uncommon for foster parents to question the suitability of the adopters. This happens even when they were initially quite enthusiastic about the family. In general, this should be viewed as a manifestion of the foster family's own grief process, particularly if they have a strong bond to the child. The foster family, like the child, needs empathy and emotional support for the difficult task they face in giving the child permission to go and do well, while simultaneously having to cope with their own grief reactions.

The most important message for the child to receive at the time of an adoptive placement is permission to become emotionally close to, and attached to, the new parents. The child needs permission to transfer his attachment from foster to adoptive parents, and only the foster parents can completely give this consent. Foster parents must provide more than a surface commitment to the child's transferring his attachment to the adoptive parents. When they differ, nonverbal messages are always more credible than verbal. Thus, if the foster parents say they want the child to get close to the adoptive parents but don't really mean it, the child will perceive this and be confused about which message to obey. This poses a special problem if the foster parents want the child to remain in their home on a permanent basis and the agency insists on a move. It is much less of a problem when foster parents, though not certain that the child can make an attachment to someone else, are not themselves interested in pursuing a long-term legal relationship with the child.

Most adoptive parents do not see the need for a prolonged visiting schedule and many children and foster parents want to get the whole thing over. However, it takes time to accomplish the tasks at hand. Throughout the preplacement period, the caseworker's role is that of facilitator, advisor, and coordinator. She should be available to provide emotional support and expertise to any of the members of either family. The caseworker's role is to help the other adults in completing their tasks.

Name Changes

Children need to know ahead of time about any proposed name changes. They need to be prepared for a change in last name. For a few children this can feel threatening. Usually they can be helped to understand that members of the same family commonly share the same last name. This is one of the ways that everyone knows who belongs with whom. From the child's viewpoint, the shared last name is one of the major differences between being a foster child and being adopted. Occasionally, a teen may make a strong case for not legally changing his last name at the time of adoption. However, most children desire to share the family's last name.

Early in the preplacement period the caseworker needs to extensively discuss the topic of name changes with the adoptive parents. Most likely everyone will be in agreement on having the child's last name changed to that of the adopters. However, even this may pose a challenge when the adopters have a hyphenated last name or if husband and wife use different last names.

The subject of changing first and middle names also needs to be fully addressed. Identity problems may become more severe with a change in the first name. A child's identity is usually strongly tied to his first name. Changing the first name infers that his identity is not acceptable. Although certainly not every child whose first name has been changed has developed serious difficulties, there is some risk in changing the forename once an infant recognizes his first name, usually sometime between nine and twelve months. As children become much older, eight and older, the risks can be more easily assessed, and magical thinking can be more easily confronted.

When adoptive parents insist on changing the child's first name after they have been advised of its significance to the child, the family's ability to see the child as a separate individual with needs that are apart from their own must be questioned. If the family needs to have a child who matches the fantasies they've attached to specific name, the chances of finding that child are very remote.

There are, of course, exceptions to all rules and there are some occasions when compelling reasons exist for changing a child's first name. The most common exception occurs in intercountry adoption. Although the child's original first name should become part of his new legal name, usually the child will be given an American first name as well. It is frequently difficult for Americans to correctly pronounce foreign names, particularly the Asian ones. With younger children, unable to help others correctly pronounce their name, it is probably preferable to have the child use the American first name as opposed to having his name routinely mispronounced. As they get older, these children can choose whether to revert back to their original forename or to retain use of their American name.

Occasionally the child has a first name with such negative connotations that the child would face long-term ridicule if he retained it. A child with a very peculiar sounding name may feel very "different" throughout his life. Likewise, there are cases when the first name alone poses no problems but when combined with the adoptive parents' last name it becomes a tongue twister, or the child becomes vulnerable to ridicule. In these cases, the child's name may have to be changed. Sometimes a family may already have a child with the same first name as the adopted child, and some alterations or adaptations may need to take place. However, in these cases less drastic options than changing legal names should be considered. In a stepfamily relationship more than one child may have the same first name, but it would be rare for these families to solve the problem by legally changing the first name of one of the children. Other creative solutions are usually agreed upon. The same should be advocated in situations involving adoption.

If either child or family seem to be insisting on a change of first name, or if the child is insisting on not changing his last name at the time of adoption, rather than create an adversarial relationship, it is better to encourage the child and parent to talk about what they think will, or will not, happen if they do not follow through with the name change. Not only is magical thinking highlighted if it is present, but child or parent may convince the professional that this is indeed one of the cases that are the exception to the rule.

There are some major advantages, and few disadvantages, in the child taking on an additional name or substituting a middle name that has special significance to the adoptive family. Since most children are not strongly identified with their middle name, this change does not usually carry the same potential for harm to the core identity that changing the first name may. In addition it serves as part of the "claiming process." This sort of name change implies that adoptive placement modifies, but does not deny, the child's identity at the time of adoptive placement. This is exactly what we are trying to achieve.

The Day of the Move

Work with child and family on the day of the move is very time-efficient. On this day it is easy to open both the door to the past and the door to the future, helping the child and adoptive parents see the connections. The effects of early life events, past losses, and the current separation from the foster family will impact on the child's life with the adoptive family. Reviewing the child's past and addressing the youngster's feelings about the current separation create a situation in which the new parents can be emotionally supportive to the child. The adoptive parents become the child's support system during the grief process. The painful feelings associated with loss are used to forge new bonds. The child learns that it is acceptable to share his past and his feelings with his new parents.

If the child has demonstrated any particularly bothersome behaviors while in foster care, this is a good time to encourage him to talk about them. It is important for the child to learn that his adoptive parents know the "worst of the worst" about him and still want him. If the child sees acceptance on the faces of his adoptive parents, in spite of his difficult behaviors, the child may not feel compelled to act out as much to test whether the adoptive family is going to keep him no matter what. If he already knows that they weren't turned off by the worst behavior he was able to come up with in foster care, he may be reassured that they really want him.

Steven

Steven was seven years old. He was to be adopted by the Adams family. By the time he was two and a half, his mother had perceived Steven as an "evil" child who was trying to kill her. He had incorporated that message. After several interim care placements and returns to his birth parents, Steven was placed with his current foster family when he was four. Within the first half hour of placement in the home, he had tripped the foster mother down the stairs.

225

Since Steven was at the head of the stairs laughing, she knew that the tripping had been deliberate. However, she also knew that her primary task of the moment was to help him learn to trust her. How could a four-year-old trust an adult who could be hurt by him? How could she possibly keep him safe? So she merely commented, "In this home, we don't laugh when someone is hurt."

Throughout his placement, Steven had many severe behavioral problems. He soiled and smeared feces. He set a fire in the family room. He cut an electric cord that was plugged in, shocking himself. He cut a hole in the new living room carpet. Asking for professional help to deal with Steven's behaviors, the foster parents stuck with him through all his problems. At one point Steven described himself as "Satan" because he was so bad. Gradually, Steven made many behavioral gains. The foster parents and the Adams family went to the same church. During his stay in foster care Mr. and Mrs. Adams had developed a relationship with Steven. They periodically would babysit him. They specifically applied to adopt Steven after getting to know him.

During a therapy session with Steven, the foster parents, and the adoptive parents on the day of the move, the past misbehaviors were discussed. For Steven the "worst-of-worst" was tripping his foster mother down the stairs. The foster mother had overheard Steven relating the incident to another foster child just the week before the move. With the approaching move, the old memory had resurfaced. During the session Steven was asked what he had done the first day he had come to his foster home. He looked panic-stricken. He was told it had to do with stairs. He then haltingly whispered, "I tripped Mom down the stairs." As he said the words, Steven looked at the floor.

The therapist asked, "Do you know why you did that?" Steven answered. "No." It was suggested that he ask his foster mother if she knew why he had done this. He posed the question. She replied, "Because you wanted to find out if I could take care of you!" Relief flooded his face. There was a reason for his behavior, and the reason was not that he was Satan.

Steven was then asked if he had watched his adoptive parents' faces as he had talked of tripping the foster mother down the stairs. He said he hadn't. He was asked to repeat the statement and watch their faces. They, of course, had been told of that incident as well as about his other negative behaviors before making the decision to adopt. The adoptive parents commented, "Yes, Steven,we know about that." The therapist then asked, "Knowing that, do you still want to adopt Steven?" Seeing that question mirrored in Steven's eyes, the therapist knew it was an important one to ask. The answer would be a part of the healing process for Steven. The adoptive parents answered, "Of course!"

The therapist then commented that there were certain to be times when Steven wondered if his adoptive parents were able to take care of him. "When you feel that way, do you think you will need to trip them down the stairs? Or have you learned other ways to ask for help?" After a thoughful pause Steven said, "I could ask them if they love me." There was a questioning tone in his voice as he responded. The therapist asked the adoptive parents what they thought of that idea and they quickly said they would really like that.

Interestingly, this child who had demonstrated so many very severe behavioral disturbances in foster care, did not have one serious acting-out incident during the three years that he and his parents were followed after the placement. Steven's naughty behaviors were those commonly seen in children his age and there were some disciplinary problems at school. He had problems getting along with peers, but there was no soiling, no firesetting, and no destructive behaviors.

It is common in our culture for there to be rituals signifying when an individual is leaving one way of life for another—at birth, graduation, marriage, and so on. These ceremonies encompass excitement for the future combined with some sense of loss for a past that is irretrievable. These same emotions are present on the day of the move to adoption. Adoptive parents should be encouraged to have some sort of family celebration to mark the occasion of the child's joining the family.

They may all go out to dinner. There may be cake and ice cream. Some celebration that can be repeated on the following anniversaries could begin at the time of the move. The Candle Ceremony (Jewett 1978) visually helps the child come to understand that he can take the loving and caring he has received from previous parenting figures to the new home where the flame of love can grow ever brighter. Sometimes families plan for a religious ceremony to celebrate the child's joining the family. Such ceremonies may reassure the child that he, like other children in the family, has joined it in a spiritual way.

Valerie, adopted at four, was relinquished by her adoptive parents when she was eight. Subsequently, she was adopted by the foster family with whom she had been placed upon leaving her first adoptive family. Although she had formed a strong attachment to this family, to Valerie legally finalizing the adoption had little meaning. However, a year following the consummation of the adoption she and her family, who were of the Mormon faith, made a pilgrimage to Salt Lake City, where they participated in a ceremony at the Temple. Following this, Valerie's comment was, "I know I will always be part of this family. I have been joined to them for eternity, and that's even longer than a lifetime."

Valerie

227

Postplacement Contacts

In general, if children who have been adopted are allowed contact with their previous foster parents, they often come not to need it. When such contact is prohibited, the child's need for it is more likely to intensify and become disproportionate. He may have difficulty completing the grief process. This, in turn, may interfere with his forming new attachments within the adoptive family.

As noted earlier, postplacement contacts provide a major avenue for minimizing the trauma of parent separation and facilitating the resolution of the grief process. Since in adoptions, the goal is not reunification, we need only be concerned with the items in Table 4-2 on page 180 . Although it is important to both the child and his foster family to visit each other after placement, when the transition has been a planned one, the visits can be delayed for two to three weeks. The well-prepared child will be able to use this period to focus on forming new relationships . However, a young child with a poor sense of time, and particularly one without adequate preplacement planning, may need earlier visits. Since the primary goals of the contacts are to facilitate the grieving process, decrease loyalty conflicts, and continue the empowerment of the new caregivers, these are the areas that need special attention during the contacts. If the previous foster parents are unable to support these goals for the contact, and especially if they behave in ways that increase loyalty conflicts or undermine the entitlement of the adoptive parents, then the contacts become counterproductive and may need to be stopped. However, we need to realize that in these cases there will have to be more, rather than less, work with the child to resolve these issues in other ways. The first postplacement visit, especially for younger children, should, once again, take place on the child's home ground, which is now the adoptive home. This provides the child and foster parent with an opportunity to focus more on the present than the past. Future visits can then be scheduled to meet the needs of everyone concerned.

If the families live in the same community, the child might be allowed to contact the foster family when he wishes—with one exception. When the child and his adoptive parents are having a problem, the child should be discouraged from contacting foster parents to seek solace or to ask them to take sides in the dispute. Once the parent and child work out the difficulties, then the child may call the foster parent. This encourages the child to solve problems with adoptive parents rather than to shower the intense feelings onto the foster parent. By using emotional tension to resolve conflicts, attachments and bonds are strengthened.

Many children need to have a visit back to the foster home after several months. This enables the child to reprocess old information in the new context of no longer being a member of that family. It can help children redefine their relationship to the foster family.

Commonly, when older children are placed for adoption, contact with some members of their birth family, particularly with members of the extended family, will be maintained. The reasons for this will be discussed further in the chapter on Direct Work with Children. These same general guidelines can be used when planning for the ongoing contacts with birth family members after an adoptive placement.

The exercises that follow will provide an opportunity to implement the suggestions made in this chapter in planning for the transition to permanency in two different cases.

4-6 *Exercise*

Moving the Preschooler to Permanency
Following a Previously Unsuccessful Move

Merideth

You may remember Merideth from the last chapter. She is now four and is currently living in the Faraday foster home. Merideth lived with the Faradays from age ten months until three years. At that time she was placed with the Norman family, the plan being adoption. However, after six weeks in the Norman home, the parents asked that she be removed because they could not cope with her severe behavior problems, which included defecating on the carpet, putting toys down the toilet, and hitting a sibling over the head, requiring stitches. She was returned to the Faraday foster home.

Subsequently, it became apparent that many of her problems in the adoptive home were secondary to her grieving for the foster parents. Merideth perceived herself as a "naughty little girl" and the cause of the adoptive disruption. In talking about leaving Nancy and Barry Faraday's home the first time, she told her caseworker, "I was so sad when I moved, but I didn't cry because I wanted to be happy." In the Norman home, whenever Merideth was missing the Faradays she would do something naughty, be punished, and then cry. When subsequently she was asked how she had felt on return to the Faraday home, she had responded with a sparkle in her eye, "Just right!" Her wish to return to the Faraday home had been gratified. She has no desire to leave again.

1. Merideth has reason to believe that if things don't work out in a new placement, she can always return to the Faraday home. What steps will you undertake to overcome the power of this magical thinking?
2. Outline the steps you would take for helping Merideth grieve the loss of the foster family.
3. What kind of contact between foster and adoptive families would you encourage before the move?
4. How might you arrange postplacement contact for Merideth and the Faradays in a way that would decrease rather than increase her magical egocentric thinking?

Merideth's Case Modified to Reflect Return to Birth Family

Merideth

Instead of an adoption disruption, at age three-and-a-half, Merideth experienced an unsuccessful reunification with her birth parents—demonstrating the same behaviors that were described as occurring in the previous case— and then returned to the Faradays. Throughout the current interim care placement she has continued to have weekly contact with the birth parents. Reunification has always been the plan. In transitioning Merideth back to her birth family, you will need to take care that she has opportunities to grieve the loss of her longtime caregivers. In addition, adequate support for child and parents after the return must be provided, as problem behaviors are likely to reemerge.

1.   Merideth has reason to believe that if things don't work out in a new placement she can always return to the Faraday home. What steps will you need to undertake to overcome the power of this magical thinking?

2.   Outline the steps you would take for helping Merideth grieve the loss of the foster family.

3.   What kind of contact between foster and birth families would you encourage before the move?

4.   What kind of work would you suggest be done with Merideth and her family after she returns to their care? Do you think it would be important to Merideth to have contact with the Faradays after the transition? If so, how would you arrange it so that it might decrease rather than increase her magical egocentric thinking?.

Transitioning a Sibling Group From Interim Care to an Adoptive Family

Denise
Duke
Lily

The three Gilbert children will be moving to an adoptive family. Denise, who is nine, will be moving to the Osborn adoptive family first. For a little over a year, Denise has been an only child living with Shelby, a foster mom who is single. She calls Shelby by her first name; they behave more like sisters than mother and daughter. Denise enjoys doing things with Shelby, but rejects caregiving by being very self-sufficient. Shelby has difficulty accepting any of her foster daughter's behaviors indicative of anger. Therefore, she avoids making many demands of Denise.

Denise still has not talked of the sexual abuse which occurred in the birth family. Periodically, she talks about someday returning to live with her birth mother. During visits with Duke and Lily, Denise no longer talks about them all returning to their birth mother, but her behaviors with them continue to be more like those of a parent than a sister.

Duke, six, and Lily, now four, have lived together in the Wentz home with experienced foster parents and their two teen-aged birth children. Duke continues to need close supervision to prevent him from initiating sexual interactions with peers. He continues to need reminders as to appropriate times and places for masturbation. Although he continues to be overly friendly with strangers, his interactions with them now are more likely to be verbal than physical. His low frustration tolerance is evident in many settings. With peers, he becomes physically aggressive when frustrated. When school work is difficult, he gives up easily saying, "It's stupid work."

Lily has made considerable progress while living with the Wentz family. She can now keep herself well occupied and is frequently involved in imaginative play. With peers, she continues to have some difficulty standing up for herself. She is quick to give in to the demands of others, but she does now stay engaged with them rather than isolating herself as she did in the past. Lily can tolerate routine separations, such as going to preschool, quite well. When Mrs Wentz goes to daytime meetings or appointments, Lily becomes quite fussy and appears to be anxious when she has to to go to a sitter. However, when left along with Duke in the care of her seventeen-year-old foster sister in the evening, she has fewer problems. During visits with Denise, Lily looks to her older sister for approval.

1.   How would you explain to the Gilbert children the plan for Denise to move to the Osborn adoptive family first? Would you initially talk to them about it in a group? Separately? In pairs?

2.   Make a plan for Denise's preplacement visits and for the final transition from Shelby to the Osborn family. Which aspects of the planning need detailed attention?

3.   What objectives would Denise and the Osborns need to achieve prior to having Duke and Lily join the family?

4.   Outline a plan for facilitating Duke and Lily's move to the adoptive family.

Leaving the System by Emancipation   VI

When adolescents leave foster care by emancipation, they will need help to adjust to life on their own. Sometimes a caseworker provides this help and support. Other times, a foster family serves as a base from which an adolescent goes out into the world on his own and to which he returns intermittently for advice and support. Sometimes adolescents connect with other adults for support services. Some emancipated adolescents find that once they are no longer so dependent, they can utilize relationships with their birth families for emotional support.

Few psychologically healthy young adults who grow up with their birth parents make a total break with their family at the time of emancipation. Many use their families as resource for support and consultation during their move into independent living. Long-term, most adults depend upon family members for emotional support in times of crisis and to share the joys of success. These basic needs should be taken into consideration in all cases when an adolescent will be leaving the system by emancipation. Who will be this individual's family of resource?

Because family ties are important to adults as well as to children, adoption should be considered even for the older adolescent or young adult who wants to experience being part of a family over a lifetime. In cases where the plan is not to make the adolescent a permanent member of an adoptive family, the same type of needs must be recognized and met by identifying people who can and will serve as a family of resource for the youngster who emancipates from a foster family.

Robert

Robert grew up in the foster care system. After completing high school, he was planning to attend the state university. His caseworker, along with a foster family, provided for his financial and emotional needs. The caseworker, Ms. Dodd, had known Robert for a number of years. She arranged for financial aid and made frequent contacts with him to find out how he was doing in college. She sent him birthday cards and Christmas presents. Robert spent his vacations, including summers, with the foster family. He took an active part in their family life and was an integral part of their holiday celebrations. His ties to the foster family were strengthened when he became the godfather of their youngest daughter. Both foster family and caseworker attended Robert's university graduation ceremony.

Now forty, Robert still considers himself part of his foster family. They took part in his wedding. His foster parents are identified as his son's grandparents. Robert continues to visit Ms Dodd when he is in the area where she lives. These continued contacts have been rewarding and meaningful for all involved. Ms. Dodd has had an opportunity to see how her continued advocacy on Robert's behalf from the time he was an early adolescent has paid off. She can well be proud of playing a major part in helping Robert become an independent adult who is a contributing member of society. Both she and the foster family played active roles in helping Robert break the cycle of abuse and neglect.

Steps in the move from dependency to emancipation include learning basic skills such as budgeting, shopping, meal preparation, laundry, housekeeping, becoming responsible for self-care in terms of both physical and psychological needs, and gaining financial independence.

This process commonly starts in a family setting, as this is the usual place for learning and practicing these skills. However, help in the transition can be supplied by switching from foster care funding to independent living funding while the adolescent is still in the foster home. Under this system, the young person becomes the payee and is responsible for the money and for purchasing room and board from the foster parents. As the adolescent gains skills in independence, he can be helped to physically move out of the family setting while continuing to use them for support in times of stress and to share in times of success.

Families are entitled to raise their children with a minimum of interference by others.

Family ties are important.

Continuity of caregiving is especially important with the very young child.

Parent separation or loss is traumatic for a child. Brothers and sisters should be raised together.

A child's racial, ethnic, and cultural heritages should be respected, preserved, and nurtured.

Every child deserves to have a family who is both legally and emotionally committed to him.

These are widely held beliefs shared by most Americans—yet the child welfare system is filled with the "exceptions" to these rules.

How are decisions made when these premises are not compatible one with the other, when they must be prioritized?

Case planning is the topic of this chapter.

CHAPTER 5

Case Planning

Child welfare personnel are repeatedly asked to make major life decisions on behalf of children whom they do not know well. They must achieve a delicate balance. On the one hand, they must never minimize the life-long impact of the decisions they make. On the other, they must not allow themselves to become paralyzed by fear of making a wrong decision.

Some conclusions are made as a result of well defined assessments of current conditions. Unfortunately, many decision are made by default. Some are made on the basis of the case worker's own values and biases. For example protective service guidelines may clearly indicate that a sibling group of four needs to enter interim care—a thoughtful, well substantiated decision. However, the caseworker finds that there is no single foster home with space for the four together. By default, she may have to place the children in two homes that she knows little or nothing about. The determination about how to split the siblings may take place either by default—i.e. one home might only take younger children—or on the basis of the personal bias of the social worker. Unfortunately, at the time of an unplanned move, it is unlikely that decisions as how to split siblings, when it is necessary, will be done after a careful assessment of their relationships with each other.

As we have seen in Ardith's case, while a decision to intervene in a family's life may solve one problem—i.e. physical abuse or neglect—it invariably leads to other problems—i.e. separation and loss. Foster care can solve certain problems. Others it cannot. Table 5-1 summarizes these strengths and limitations.

As in all other areas of life, a solution for one problem frequently leads to the emergence of another. The child welfare caseworker is always having to weigh the risks of one decision against the risks of another. Likewise, the positive aspects of any decision must be balanced against the positives of the alternatives.

Table 5-1

Foster Family Care

May	Does not
provide safety	solve family problems
provide shelter	provide emotional security
provide respite for families	usually provide stability
provide family while awaiting	and continuity of caregiving
legal release or termination	usually provide continuity
following abandonment	of schooling
provide an opportunity to	usually provide continuity for
assess child without the	medical care
family and vice versa	help parents deal with special
provide positive parenting	needs of the child who is not there
experience	increase attachment to birth
provide for more adequate	family or parents' bonding to
stimulation in cases of neglect	the child.

The first section of this chapter explores the importance of developing a relationship with birth parents and valuing their input in assessment and case planning. Work with birth families should, if at all possible, start before placement. When that is not feasible, it is the agency's responsibility to do everything possible to get the birth family involved immediately after the placement. Section II looks at ways to gather and organize information on the child and family. The crux of good case planning is an adequate assessment. Waiting several months or years to initiate permanency planning is universally harmful. It is essential that permanency planning be initiated immediately and be aggressively pursued so that children exit from the system in a timely manner. Treatment planning with an emphasis on identifying permanency planning alternatives is the topic of Section III.

In Section IV attention is paid to three arenas where values play a major role in decision making. These include sibling relationships, relative placements, and maintaining racial and cultural continuity in placements. Here we will see the importance of early decision making. The longer a child remains in the child welfare system, the more likely it is that system-inflicted problems will outweigh the initial good done. Delays in addressing these areas of special concern mean that frequently the criteria used for decision making must be the least detrimental, as opposed to in the best interests of the child.

236

Working with Birth Parents

In all aspects of child welfare work there should be involvement of the birth parents in the assessment and decision making. The stage is set for work with the birth family in the first interactions with them. This is true whether the initial contacts are made in the context of providing in-home services, if they revolve around removing a child, or when they occur after placement.

In all interactions with families, caseworkers, consciously or unconsciously, model parenting. If agency personnel display avoidance, lack of caring, and emotional distancing, that is what the children and families will learn. On the other hand, if caring, concern, and emotional nurturance are modeled there is an increased likelihood that positive changes will occur. Birth parents are more likely to experience positive growth and change when they themselves are reparented in the course of receiving services.

Child welfare professionals should treat families in the way that they want parents to treat their children. Birth parents who come in contact with social service agencies frequently have poorly developed interpersonal skills. Many, having themselves never experienced positive parenting, have difficulty meeting their children's needs.

John and Mary both come from emotionally deprived backgrounds. Each was in foster care during childhood. They have come to the attention of Child Protective Services because of having repeatedly left their son Paul unsupervised and because of bruising secondary to physical abuse. Mary presents as a needy, dependent individual with little enthusiasm for anything. John, on the other hand, seems to be an angry young man who is particularly resentful of any authority figure. He tends to belittle women and children.

John
Mary

Agency personnel might primarily react to the parental behaviors, possibly reinforcing maladaptive interpersonal interactions. On the other hand, social workers involved with the family may take a proactive stance and model good parenting techniques. Parents should be treated in a manner that reflects positive parenting (Table 5-2). Parents should not have to "earn" acceptance any more than their children should have to "earn" parental love. Birth parents deserve to be considered as unique individuals, products of differing backgrounds, cultures, interests, and values .Being empathic and showing caring are two ways to demonstrate positive parenting.

——————— *Table* ——————— 5-2

Positive Parenting Provides

emotional nurturing
a basic sense of acceptance
times of unconditional giving
appropriate limit setting
positive role modeling
encouragement for growth and change
teaching responsibility
teaching appropriate expression of emotions
encouragement for reciprocal interactions
a balance between dependency and independence
discipline rather than punishment
teaching life skills
teaching relationship skills

Like good parents, social workers can accept underlying feelings while still confronting negative, harmful behaviors, thereby modeling ways that helpful parents set limits. They can make use of logical consequences, identifying choices, and actively teaching new ways to handle difficult emotions. If caseworkers are to be positive role models they will avoid threats, ordering, moralizing, and judging.

As opposed to being power-based or adversarial, healthy family relationships are reciprocal in nature. It is important to model this in contacts with both parents and children. Boundaries between the social services and legal systems should be clear. The distinction between discipline and punishment should be evident here. Discipline coming from the root word for teaching, sets people up for success. Punishment, on the other hand, is essentially retribution after the fact. In general the legal system is punitive in nature while the social work system aims to be disciplinary.

Just as it is important for parents to see children as separate individuals whose needs may conflict with parental goals, it is necessary that agencies recognize that an individual family's unique needs may not be met by usual agency requirements and policies. Therefore, appropriate modeling of flexibility, as opposed to rigidity, and of conflict resolution, as opposed to using power based maneuvers, are necessary components of successful work with families.

John
Mary

Let us return to Mary and John. Both have suffered from lack of acceptance and unconditional giving. Their social worker's task is to identify the parenting skills that John and Mary each need to learn. Identification of these parenting skills will help the social worker identify the specific modeling she most needs to provide. Although sending them to parenting classes may at some point be helpful, it is unlikely that this intervention alone will meet their needs arising from lack of themselves having encountered positive parenting. Each needs to experience good parenting not just hear about it.

Mary believes that she doesn't deserve emotional nurturing. It is difficult for her to be receptive to caring or to accept that her children deserve love. She is overly dependent upon authority figures. The social worker will try to help her develop more independence. Simultaneously Mary will be provided with unconditional acceptance.

John, on the other hand, perceives every interaction as having a winner and a loser. To him being dependent is the same as being weak and helpless. From his viewpoint, when he leaves his child unattended, or when he uses harsh discipline, he is not showing lack of caring. He perceives these actions as helping to prepare Paul for an emotionally cold, rejecting world. John needs opportunites to experience dependence as nurturing and caring.

Involving Parents in the Assessment and in Treatment Planning

Unless there is no emotional connection at all, birth families have tremendous power in their relationships with their children. When there is little attachment, social workers will be working with not only the most damaged children but also the neediest parents—those who are able to exist in close physical relationships without developing emotional connections.

No matter how scanty their knowledge, at the outset of case interventions and planning the parents know more about their child than does anyone else. To adequately serve the child, if for no other reason, social workers need to work with the parents to access this knowledge. For the sake of the child and the parents both, an alliance must be built with the family.

5-3 — *Table* —

Ways to Involve Parents

Include them in information gathering
Include them in identifying problems
Include them in problem solving
Involve them in the placement process
Facilitate regular visiting
Insure that child and parent have family pictures
Participate in child's medical appointments
Participate in child's school conferences
Accessing information about community resources
Model caring and concern

When birth parents are involved in the work with children, there is an acknowledgment that they are important people in their child's life. Table 5-3 identifies many ways to involve parents in decision making as well as in direct interactions with their child whether the child is in out-of-home placement or not. (Horejsi, 1981).

Assessment tools which are visual in nature and which actively involve parents, help define the caseworker-client relationship as reciprocal rather than power-based. When using these tools, it becomes apparent that family members are experts when it comes to specific knowledge about their child and family. Social workers, on the other hand, should have expertise in child development, behavior management, family systems, the needs of children, and community services available. Working together will lead to the best plan.

During the assessment process parents are helped to more clearly identify family problems. Some can adequately express themselves verbally. Others only know how to express their perceptions and/or needs behaviorally. In the latter case the social worker may use reframing to identify negative behaviors in terms of positive strivings.

Mary
John

In talking with John about the harsh disciplinary measures he has used with his son, the social worker does not lecture, threaten, or preach. Rather she redefines dad's negative behaviors. "I think that when you spank Paul you are trying to teach him something. That is part of a parent's job. Can you tell me more about what you hope to teach him?" After John gives further information, the social worker might ask, "Can you tell me how you think that spanking may help Paul learn?" The tone of voice used in asking questions is as important as the words. We want to convey caring and concern because we want the parent to learn better ways to convey these messages to his child.

The following will have been identified during the conversation with John:

1.   He wants to help his child learn.
2.   This is an important role for a responsible parent.
3.   The social worker's role will be to help him become more
         effective in his role as a parent by providing ideas about how to
         teach Paul without using harsh physical discipline.

Meanwhile, in working with Mary, the caseworker continues to observe that she is passive, rarely initiating interactions with her child, her husband, or others. The social worker models positive parenting by using "active listening" (Gordon, 1971), expressing hope for the future and defining problem solving as a goal. "It seems like you have given up on yourself and your family. Maybe you don't think change is possible. I want you to know that I think things can be different for you. I think you deserve to have someone work with you on changing things." In this way the social worker does not fall into the same, "This family is hopeless" stance that Mary has. The social worker conveys that she believes the mother, in particular, and the family, in general, is deserving. She does not ask the mother to agree. At the same time she does not imply that she is in a position to make it all better but talks of working with.

Involving parents during all aspects of the assessment and case planning increases the likelihood of quickly identifying those families where reunification is highly likely. However, even in cases were it is unlikely that the children will be returned to the custody of the birth parents, actively involving them will facilitate permanency planning in a more timely fashion.

Assessment   II

The purpose of the comprehensive assessment is to help us understand the child's and family's situation more fully in order to provide a sound basis for decisions about future actions (Protecting Children, 1988). Not only at the time of intake is this important, but continuing reviews and updates of the assessment, so that it becomes ongoing rather than static in nature, are mandatory if children are to be well served.

For child welfare cases a complete assessment must include not only information about the parents, but also a comprehensive assessment of the child himself. Frequently this is missing in case records. It is as though the child is viewed as a passive, rather than active, participant in the family relationships and the emergence of problems. Whether problems start with parent or child, both become active in influencing the behavior of other family members. It is always important to have knowledge of both how the child impacts others and the specific effects of the family dynamics on this child.

A format for a comprehensive assessment and ideas about gathering the necessary information follows. Although initially the amount of information may seem overwhelming, it can be gathered in segments and does not have to be done all at one time. However, if it is never done, the likelihood of coming up with a case plan that focuses on the child's, rather than the parents' or system's, needs is unlikely.

A complete assessment includes information on the past history, current adjustment, direct observations, special procedures, and family history. Although these five basic components comprise a complete assessment, they do not have to be consistently completed in a single predetermined order. For example, the family history might be done first, last, or in the middle.

When completing each area of assessment there are universal underlying questions to be answered. However, the specific questions asked will depend upon the age of the child, from whom information is being obtained, and the individual examiner's style of interviewing. In general, it is best to start out with open-ended comments, i.e. "Tell me some about Johnnie as an infant, what was he like?" and then follow up with more specific questions for clarification or expansion of the information already given. Attention should be paid to the overall attitudes, non-verbal messages, and affect of those providing the verbal informationl.

Table 5-4 provides ideas about possible sources of information about the child.

Table 5-4

Sources of Information

Interviews With	Written Materials
parents	agencies' case records
relatives	case records from other agencies that
foster parents	have had contact with
previous caseworkers	child and/or family
preschool personnel	records from hospital where
day care personnel	child was born
teachers and other	records from hospitals
school personnel	where child has been treated
policemen who have had contact	well-baby clinic records
with family	public health nurse records
babysitters	school records

Rose

As Mr. Laird, the caseworker for Ardith and Prentice, talked with Rose, their mother, he noted a consistent difference in her affect dependent upon which child she was discussing. When talking of Ardith, her tone of voice softened, she looked relaxed, her eyes brightened, and there was usually a smile on her face. In contrast, when talking of Prentice, Rose's face became tense and drawn, her body appeared to be more rigid. The information on Prentice seemed less detailed. Rose was more likely to focus on the negative aspects of her son's behaviors while centering on the positive ways of her daugther.

The Past History

The past history helps identify which of the child's basic needs were probably met and which might have gone unmet at various stages of his life. It should identify what was inappropriately provided, for example harsh physical discipline or sexual abuse. Note should be made of interrupted relationships, as they tend to interfere with developmental progress. The information in the past history is used to help subsequent caregivers understand how the child is likely to view parent-child relationships. Children, particularly young children, believe that their lives are "normal." They are incapable of comparing their own situation with that of others. They incorporate their own experiences into their overall view of what family life is like and take these perceptions and their own reactions to them into any new setting.

Dawn, four, and her mother lived with the maternal grandparents. Dawn was sexually abused by her grandfather. This was done primarily with enticement rather than threats or physical force. Grandpa told her she was the most special person in his life and that they could share some wonderful secrets. The sexual contact consisted initially of Grandpa fondling Dawn's genitals. It then progressed to her fondling Grandpa's penis and finally to oral-genital contact.

When Dawn was placed in foster care she was sexually provocative with her foster father. She would crawl up on his lap and masturbate against him; she would touch him in the genital area; she would try to unzip his fly. Dawn viewed these interactions as "normal." She had not learned any other ways for forming a relationship with an adult male. She would have to be reparented, actively taught new ways to interact.

Dawn

The past history may provide clues as to possible misperceptions on the part of the child. For example, in Dawn's case, if her foster parents feel overwhelmed by her behaviors and ask that she be moved, she would most likely believe that it is because her foster father doesn't love her. Nothing will have occurred to change her perceptions of family life. She would be likely to become more, rather than less, sexually reactive.

The past history should alert us to events which usually precipitate strong feelings in a child, feelings which may never have been acknowledged or resolved. Certainly, the past history should provide clues as to how this child has coped with stress in the past. Is this a child who withdraws physically or psychologically at times of tension? Or, does this child become more aggressive or stubborn? Although the child's specific behaviors may change from one setting to another, it is likely that his basic temperament and style of coping with stress will remain the same.

In reviewing Judy's history, one might wonder if her feelings about leaving Korea have ever been addressed. The adults in her life soon after the move did not share her language and later their attention may have centered on her problem behaviors rather than the emotions accompanying her move.

Judy

At times of stress Judy hoards, probably not only food but also any good feelings she has, not sharing with others. She has difficulty feeling close to adult females. Taking others' prized possessions may reflect an unconscious belief that others are taking things (which could include love, acceptance, cultural values, her own personal history) from her. These are behaviors that one might expect to recur with stress in the future. However, as Judy is now older and is capable of abstract thinking, she can probably be helped to identify and express these underlying emotions in more acceptable ways than she has been capable of in the past.

As one is reviewing the past history, patterns may come to light. For instance, there may be a repetition of misbehaviors occurring at the same time each year, indicating a possible "anniversary reaction" to an earlier life event. Or, there might be a history of moves every two years, leading one to speculate that additional support will be needed when the child has lived in the current placement for two years.

Obviously, the past history should include information about the pregnancy, birth, and development of the child. Particular attention should be paid to eliciting information about the mother's history of drug or alcohol use during the pregnancy, as both of these factors influence the child's development. Information about the child's responsiveness as an infant, as well as his developmental progress needs to be obtained. What type of problems, if any, were evident during the first year of life? Were there problems with weaning or toilet training? The assessment should proceed with gathering information about the child's life up until the present time. Areas of special concern include developmental progress, interruptions in relationships, particularly with primary caregivers, and the child's responses to discipline. Information about school and medical history, as well as information about previous psychological or psychiatric evaluations, should be included.

Current Adjustment

The child's avenue for presenting his needs and perceptions of the world is via his current adjustment. Careful consideration of this area facilitates understanding of the impact of earlier life events on this particular child. It is the day-to-day behaviors that alert adults both to the child's current stresses, as well as to his needs.

An essential aspect of case planning is the "decoding" of current behaviors, identifying underlying needs and perceptions, so that a program for meeting needs or correcting misperceptions can be developed. The child's current adjustment helps provide a focus for developing strategies for specific interventions. Strengths, as well as problem areas, need to be identified. Just as is true with adults, a good case plan makes use of a child's strengths to address needs and overcome weaknesses.

244

Dawn's behaviors in the foster home confirmed that the sexual interactions, although certainly not appropriate nor desirable, were nonetheless not considered hurtful nor abusive by Dawn. From her viewpoint the sexual interactions provided her with positive physical touching. The fact that she likes and desires physical contact with adults is a strength. In working with Dawn it will be important to actively teach her different and healthier ways of having physical contact with an adult male as opposed to encouraging her to avoid touch. The foster father will be a central figure in the reparenting plan.

Dawn

5-5 *Table*

History of Present Functioning

Eating and table behaviors
Bedtime, sleeping, and awakening patterns
Self-care skills
Play skills and peer relationships
Response to authority
Talents
Chores
Interactions with adults
Expression of feelings
School functioning
Medical problems
Affection
Conscience development
Basic temperament
Unusual behaviors

It is quite likely that in talking with current caregivers they will spontaneously bring up areas of concern. We are more likely to have to ask questions to elicit the areas of strength. To get an overall picture of the child's functioning, it is wise to go through a behavioral review of systems, asking questions about the child in terms of a variety of day-to-day routines, as noted in Table 5-5. In addition to gathering information about the child, the caseworker is learning more about how adults perceive this child's functioning, and assessing the level of stress that the child's behaviors elicit in various family members.

Discussion of eating and table behaviors is a possible source of information not only about behavioral problems, but also about eye-hand-mouth coordination. Information about the child's general appetite can help to identify children who have a variety of eating problems including those who have never learned to differentiate various forms of internal discomfort.

Bedtime behaviors may help identify the child who needs extra emotional support before being able to go to sleep. For many children bedtime resurfaces emotions associated with parent separation or loss. For some abused children, there will be terror at the prospect of losing control over knowing what is occurring and being able to keep one's self safe. Information about bedwetting, nightmares, night terrors, sleep walking, or night wandering can provide insight into the child's levels of fears and anxieties. How the child awakens in the morning gives further information that may be helpful in creating an environment in which the child learns to trust the availability of adult caregivers.

Functioning in the self-care areas provides information about dependence vs. independence, fine-motor skills, and body awareness. This may be an area where previously unacknowledged strengths lie. Information about chores tells about the child's ability to assume age appropriate responsibilities. Responses to authority figures help identify those who are overly fearful of adults, as well as those who have problems with reciprocity and perceive all adult-child interactions as win-lose in nature.

Learning about the child's play will help us to identify strengths and weaknesses in both fine and gross motor skills, as well as the child's developmental levels in terms of play skills and peer relationships. Many times, the child who shows regression in play skills is identifying a time in life when energies were diverted to other needs such as self-protection or coping with grief. Such a child may have missed out on play opportunities and may now need help in filling in the gaps in development. Does this child exhibit any special talents?

Academic strengths and weaknesses should be noted. How does this child respond to basic classroom rules and expectations? Information about control issues at school can be compared with the child's responses to authority at home. School provides opportunites to assess peer relationships, both in the structured classroom environment and during periods, such as the lunch hour and recess, when adults are less in charge of peer interactions.

How does the child express his feelings? What does he do when he is sad? When he is frustrated? When he is angry? When he is happy? Is he basically shy or outgoing? What can we learn about his overall temperament? Although basic temperament is unlikely to change, the child can be helped to use his coping style to solve, rather than escalate, problems. For example, the child who withdraws at times of stress can be taught to utilize the withdrawal time to cool off and develop a plan for addressing the problem, whereas the child who becomes more aggressive when anxious, can be taught how to discharge that tension physically in ways that won't add to his problems. In either case, the goal is to help the child focus constructively on the problem at hand.

Information about how, and to whom, this child shows affection and how he responds to the affectionate overtures of others can help us understand how he has internalized previous life experiences. The more that the adults responsible for the child understand him, the more they can help him understand himself and work toward overcoming problem areas while furthering normal developmental progress.

Finally, it is important to know about the child's behaviors that relate to social emotions and conscience development. If he has problems telling the truth it is important to learn if he lies primarily to avoid getting in trouble, if his untruths reflect magical wishful thinking, or if he seems oblivous to what is going on around him. If he steals, from whom does he take? What types of things does he take? What does he do with the things he takes? Answers to these questions will help clarify the underlying reasons for the problem behaviors and will become useful in devising successful strategies for overcoming the problems.

Detailed information about Judy's hoarding of food—what types of food does she take? When is she most likely to take it? What does she do with it? Answers to these questions will aid adults in clarifying what need this behavior is meeting. Likewise, more information about her stealing should help clarify the underlying cause of the problem. How frequently does she steal? What is she most likely to take? How does she get access to others' belongings? Can family members predict when she might take things? Does she steal at school? From stores? Responses to all of these questions will help in determining whether this problem relates to delayed conscience development *per se*, or to Judy's trying to meet her own emotional needs when she feels particularly deprived. As we will see in the next chapter, reparenting strategies will depend upon the answers to these questions.

Judy

Family History
When obtaining the family history, the caseworker is looking for overall patterns, expectations, strengths, and weaknesses. A variety of tools for gathering and organizing the family history have been developed. Two that are particularly useful in child welfare work are the Genogram and the EcoMap (Hartman, 1979). The Genogram is a pictorial representation of the family history, including several generations. Information includes: names, birthdates, and birthplaces of family members; dates and causes of death; dates of marriages and divorces; children born of each marriage; birth parents of children born outside of marriage. Additional information may include education and occupations, medical/health history, losses, separations, and moves. The Genogram helps correlate various facets of the family history—i.e. the relationship of a birth to a death, or a remarriage to a move—and intergenerational patterns. During the development of the Genogram it is apparent that the family is the expert in terms of knowledge, while the caseworker is the expert in terms of organizing the knowledge in a useful manner. The process, once again, emphasizes the collaborative nature of the caseworker-family relationship.

In completing a Genogram with Edith, a twenty-three-year-old single mother whose second child was diagnosed as having failure to thrive at age seven months, Mr. Albion focused on the mother's own early history. Edith related that

Edith

she herself had been adopted at a year of age. She knew little about her own earlier life history. She did know that she had spent several months with her own birth mother, and then had been in interim care for several months prior to joining her adoptive family.

In addition to the new baby, Edith also has a three-year-old daughter. While completing the Genogram, Mr. Albion learned that this child, as well, had suffered from failure to thrive and had been in fostercare from ages six to twelve months. This child had done well following her return to Edith care when she was a year of age. Edith and Mr. Albion began to speculate about what might have happened to Edith herself during the second half of the first year of her life. Edith called her adoptive mother and asked for more information about herself. She learned that when she had come to her family at age twelve months, she was underweight and was not yet walking. Although initially Edith had seemed to show some developmental delays, she had rapidly gained weight and closed the gaps between her chronological age and her developmental functioning.

The combination of her own history and that of her older child led to Mr. Albion and Edith becoming optimistic about the baby's prognosis. Viewing it as a temporary problem, close contact was maintained between Emily and the infant during a short-term fostercare arrangement. The baby was successfully reunited with Edith within three months.

The EcoMap is used to organize information about the family's involvement with its environment. It assesses the nuclear family's engagement with extended family, as well as links—both supportive and stressful—with work, school, church, social services, health, recreation, social network, and neighborhood. As the information is pictorially arranged family members often come to their own conclusions and begin to understand their situation in a new way. This tool is of particular use in developing treatment plans that utilize current areas of strength and support to address areas of stress or lack of involvement. Ecomaps completed at different times—for example when a child comes into care and when return to the birth family is being considered—will identify clearly the changes in external supports that the family has made and the current areas of external stress.

Ardith
Prentice

Mr. Laird completed an EcoMap with Rose soon after visits with Ardith were taking place on a regular basis. Several months later an update was drawn. During the intervening time, Rose had completed an in-patient substance abuse treatment program. During this time, she had developed some new friendships which were supportive of the changes she was making. She viewed her therapist as being supportive of her as an individual and of her efforts to regain custody of her children. As part of her treatment she attempted to reestablish more positive

248

relationships with some of her relatives. She had also moved to an area where there was less obvious drug use in the neighborhood and had made two friends who were not substance abusers. She was involving herself in some activities which she enjoyed. Although areas of stress and weak relationships continued to exist, she was feeling better about herself because of the gains she had made.

———————

Many families have a very complex history involving several marriages and divorces, children who are half and full sibs, multiple moves, and out-of-home placements. Even after the worker obtains a full and accurate family history, it is frequently difficult to remember how old a particular child was when various major events in his life took place. Since the impact of life events such as parental separations, the birth of a new child, etc. will differ depending upon the child's age and stage of development, it is useful to have an organizational tool that helps correlate them with each child's age. The Family Life Graph, Figure 5A on the next page, was developed for this purpose. Using graph paper, a family life line— noting the year and major life events such as marriages, separations, divorces, deaths, moves, etc.—is drawn across the top of the paper. Then a bar graph, including any placement history, is constructed for each child. This graphic summary makes it possible to easily determine each child's age at the time of major family events, the number of placements a child has had, his age at the time of each placement, the placements he shared with siblings vs. separations from them, and the percentage of the child's life that he has spent with various primary caregivers.

Direct Observations

The historical information usually is the foundation for formulating ideas as to the child's reactions to earlier life events. Direct observations provide either confirmation or denial of the suspected perceptions and/or underlying needs. However, simultaneously the assessor accumulates additional information that usually is not as readily available from those with whom the child lives. Basic information to be gained by general observations without any specific "testing" includes the following: Does the child look and act his age? What is his general manner? Is he shy or friendly? Withdrawn or aggressive? Is he clumsy or graceful? Does he have to touch everything? Does he hesitate to explore anything? Does he look at the adult's face as he talks or does he avoid eye contact? Does he appear to be self-confident and assured or does he seem tentative and uncertain? Does he constantly test limits? Is he impulsive and/or easily distractible or does he stay focused on conversation or play? Although formal tests are not necessary to assess these aspects of a child's functioning, basic knowledge of the normal parameters of behavior for children of various ages is essential to a good assessment.

Figure 5-A

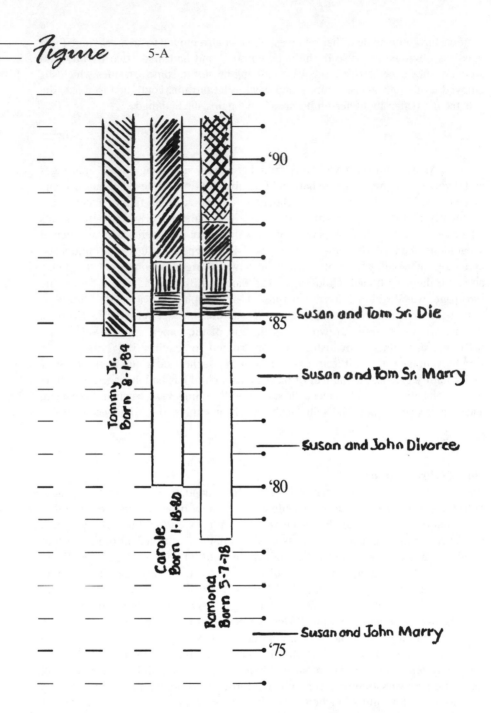

Tommy Jr. Born 8-1-84

Carole Born 1-18-80

Ramona Born 5-7-78

'90

'85 — Susan and Tom Sr. Die

— Susan and Tom Sr. Marry

— Susan and John Divorce

'80

— Susan and John Marry

'75

In addition to the general behaviors, note should be made of how this particular child connects with, or avoids relating to, others. Are there certain topics that, no matter how they are introduced, the child avoids? Most people have preferred modalities for relating to others. Some learn best, and develop stronger relationships, when visual techniques are used. For others auditory interactions are the most important. For some it is touch that is critical. Those assessing children need to utilize a variety of tasks to help determine not only which is the preferred sensory modality but also to aid in identifying any sensory weaknesses.

Judy

The caseworker assessing Judy soon after she entered care noted that when words alone were used to communicate, there was little true interchange. Ms. McGovern tried using pictures. She asked Judy to describe her perception of her connection with the Haslett adoptive family by placing a circle representing herself either into, next to, or away from a larger circle representing the family as a whole. This technique got Judy involved. The caseworker continued to use it in discussing Judy's perceptions of her connections to the Haslett's at various times in her life-- when she was five, seven, right before leaving the family, since she was in fostercare.

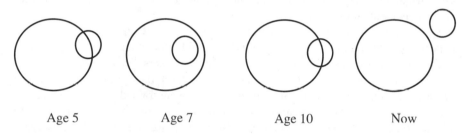

| Age 5 | Age 7 | Age 10 | Now |

The caseworker further noted that when she sat next to Judy—as opposed to across from her—and put a hand lightly on the youngster's shoulder, Judy seemed to be able to focus even better on the task at hand.

Many abused or neglected children seem to have difficulty when adults are intense or loud in their interactions. Some seem to become nearly paralyzed with anxiety while others over-react to such stimuli. These children respond best to calmer interactions. However, there are a few children who seem to process their environment, or listen, only when stimuli are intense. It is as though they have learned to tune out most of what adults say and only respond when the volume or intensity reaches a certain critical point. In interactions with children, the examiner should be using different intensities as well as varying sensory modalities to check out strengths and deficiencies.

Direct observations of preschool children will yield the most accurate information when they are done in a setting which is familiar to a child. In general, in-home observations will be more useful than those conducted in an office. Once children are of school age they usually feel comfortable with a variety of pencil and paper tasks in a one-to-one setting such as in an office. However, observing children in their homes always provides a more realistic picture of the relationships between various family members.

Because so many preschoolers in the child welfare system have some developmental delays, caseworkers should learn to administer some form of screening test such as the Denver Developmental Screening Test which requires little equipment and can be administered in virtually any setting. It includes items in the areas of personal-social, fine motor-adaptive, language and gross motor functioning. Those children with delays in any area can then be referred to a pediatrician or child development clinic for more complete testing. A series of developmental charts at the end of the preschool section of Chapter 2

When assessing the relationship between birth parents and children who are in foster care, a setting that is as normal as possible must be used. It is difficult, if not impossible, to get an accurate assessment of parent-child interactions in a small interview room with few age appropriate toys or activities present. If the child usually has visits at the birth parent's home then this is the logical place for such an assessment to occur.

Some agencies have developed creative solutions for providing for supervised visits and for assessment of parent-child interactions. One child welfare department used a large playroom staffed by homemakers. The nursery originated as a babysitting service for children whose parents were applying for financial aid or meeting with case workers. Subsequently, staff were trained to observe both the child's behaviors when separate from parents and to observe parent-child interactions. Caseworkers, or other examiners, also use this room for observing both parent-child and peer interactions. The variety of toys and other children and parents coming and going tend to put the observed adults and children more at ease. Using this type of setting, it is possible to contrast the parents' interactions with their own child with those they exhibit with other children. Likewise, it is possible to contrast the child's response to non-parental adults with his response to his own parent. This setting is particularly useful for observing interactions between parent and child when they begin a visit and when they separate at the end of it. Other agencies have small playrooms playrooms for supervised visits.

Ardith
Prentice

Observations were made during a visit between Rose and Prentice alone, followed by Ardith joining them. Prentice was tentative in his interactions at the beginning of the visit. He continually looked at his mother's face for approval. Physically he stayed close to her, sometimes literally clinging to her. Rose was impatient with him. She tried to get him involved with the toys but seemed at a loss when he didn't immediately respond. She shrunk from his touch, trying to remove his hand from her arm or avoid his sitting on her lap.

When Ardith joined her mother and brother, she quickly became the center of Rose's attention. It was as though Prentice wasn't even in the room. He stood off to the side, head down, wistfully watching his mother and sister.

Special Procedures

Although it is the caseworker's responsibility to coordinate all assessment information and to formulate a treatment plan for the child and family, frequently input from others with special expertise is needed in order to do this.

A variety of special assessment procedures might be utilized in helping to rule in or out specific conditions which would influence treatment, planning, or prognosis. The following list of special evaluative procedures is not meant to be exhaustive, but they do exemplify the types of services that are frequently indicated for children in placement. For example, if a child is falling frequently, a neurological examination would identify any physical causes such as muscle weakness or a seizure disorder. In many communities there are child development centers that provide a multidisciplinary team for undertaking complete developmental assessments. Some pediatricians and some child psychologists are trained to do thorough developmental assessments of small children. Consultation with genetic specialists is useful when there is a family history of hereditary disabilities.

Pediatric consultation can be helpful in clarifying a variety of medical problems. Since some practitioners are much more sensitive than others to the special needs of parents and children in the child welfare system, it is helpful if caseworkers develop a working relationship with one or two pediatric consultants who are interested in and knowledgeable about issues relating to child abuse and neglect. Even if these consultants do not directly see all of the children in care, they can be used as a resource for interpreting the results of medical examinations done by a variety of specialists in complex cases. With the marked increase in drug- affected infants, as well as the many children who have been impacted by their mothers' prenatal use of alcohol, specialists in diagnosing these conditions need to be identified. Likewise, with the marked increase in child sexual abuse cases it is particularly important that medical personnel who are experienced and sensitive in aiding in disclosure work and in completing the physical examinations which are an integral part of this diagnosis be identified.

Psychological evaluations usually include formal testing which provides information on the child's intellectual capacity, visual-perceptual-motor problems, and the child's underlying personality structure. Psychiatric assessments, in contrast, usually have less formal testing and more structured interviews. Psychiatrists identify thought processes, the kinds of psychological defenses the child uses to cope with his environment, and his abilities to relate to other people in a meaningful manner. Psychiatrists, as medical doctors, may prescribe medicines. Children exhibiting clusters of the signs and symptoms included in Table 5-6 on the following page need to have a full psychiatric or psychological evaluation.

A particularly useful, but frequently difficult to come by, special assessment is an educational assessment which fully identifies the child's learning strengths and weaknesses. Standardized educational tests tell us at which levels the child is able to function when materials are presented in a specific, predetermined manner. However, in many cases what is more useful is knowledge about ways to present educational material so that the child is helped to perceive, process, and retain the information. If the child is not under the pressure of a timed test does he do better? If he is given visual cues as he is presented with auditory stimuli does he retain information better than when it is presented using the auditory modality alone? Does he need feedback after doing a couple of math problems to insure that he is on the right track? This type of information is useful not only to the classroom teacher, but can also help us devise ways to assist the child in learning how to do chores and acquire new skills at home. Sometimes educational consultants or learning disability specialists will conduct this type of assessment. Other times testing done by a neuropsychologist is utilized in developing an educational and home-treatment plan for children with learning problems.

A language evaluation is indicated if the child is delayed in speech, has peculiar speech, or has many articulation errors. Any child with significantly delayed speech should also have a full hearing examination. A complete language evaluation may help pinpoint strengths and weaknesses in children who have difficulty with auditory learning. The results of such testing can aid the school in outlining an adequate plan for meeting the child's particular learning needs and help parents understand, and work more effectively with, their child. Children who learn English as a second language freqently have language problems that are not easily identified by parents or teachers.

Edith

Because of her observations, Ms. McGovern arranged for a full language assessment of Judy. This assessment showed that Judy had difficulty remembering a series of instructions presented verbally although when they were presented one at a time she could complete the tasks. In addition, she had gaps in her fund of knowledge. Judy did not really understand certain ordinary words and expressions although she parroted them. She had particular problems understanding language that involved abstract concepts with few visible cues. Telling about a happening in chronological order, and identifying cause and effect posed difficulties for her. A language therapist started working with Judy, helping her with these skills. The therapist also worked with Marie and Neal Caldwell, helping them to understand and further identify Judy's language deficits.

254

Signs and Symptoms Requiring Full Psychiatric Evaluation in Children

Extreme withdrawal from interactions; behaving as though others
    are not present.

Inappropriate affect i.e., laughing, crying, or rage for no apparent reason.

Fantasies that are so marked that they interfere with day-to-day functioning.

Total lack of interest in interacting with peers; no normal peer interactions.

Extreme lack of responsiveness to other people.

Lack of appropriate fears and/or abnormal fears that interfere with
    day-to-day functioning.

Auditory or visual hallucinations.

Failure to develop speech or disappearance of speech after it has developed.

Non-communicative speech.

Persistent abnormal rhythm to speech.

Abnormalities in reactions to stimulation; may be hypersensitive or
    hyposensitive to auditory stimuli, tactile stimuli, and the like.

Peculiar posturing or persistent walking on tiptoe.

Stereotypical finger and hand movements.

Self-mutilation.

Developmental delays combined with areas of normal or above normal
    functioning.

Marked insistence on sameness, such as routines or object placement.

Treatment Planning   III

David Jones (1987) indicates that the formation of a theraputic relationship with the abusive or neglectful family is an important ingredient of change, over and above casework and that more intensive treatment programs appear to produce better results. Both outreach and active follow-up services are necessary if children and their families are to be successfully reunited.

When parents actively participate in the assessment phase it becomes an extension of this process to involve them in the development of a treatment plan which lists problem areas, prioritizes goals, and specifies desired outcomes. The assessment should have clarified the needs, strengths, and weaknesses of both the child and the parents. Basic goal planning steps include involving the client in the process, selecting reasonable achievable goals, using identified strengths in achieving the goal, spelling out the steps necessary for success, documenting who will do what and when they will do it, and providing for review.

The initial case plan then outlines what needs to change so that there can be a meshing of the child's needs and the parents' abilities to meet those needs. Clear, relevant treatment plans identify the desired changes. As seen in Table 5-7, the treatment plan should provide a clear idea as to how an observer would know that change had occurred. An secondary goal will be to identify those situations where reunification is not going to be possible within a time frame that meets the child's needs, so that alternative long term planning can be undertaken.

Adcock (1985) notes that a treatment plan should be specific in identifying the changes that need to occur for it to be physically and psychologically safe for the child to remain in, or return to, their parents' care.

Table 5-7

Treatment Plans Should Identify

> behaviors to be increased
> behaviors to be decreased
> new skills to be acquired
> desired modification of current behaviors

How would someone recognize the difference? What would an observer see or hear that would show that there has been a change in family functioning? Changes may include acquiring new skills, increasing desireable behaviors, decreasing or eliminating undesireable behaviors, or maintaining desired behavior but with a change in rate or with a variation of a behavior. An example of the latter would be a parent who currently feeds her child appropriate amounts of food but who demonstrates change by learning to select foods with better nutritional value.

Time frames that recognize the child's developmental levels and needs should be incorporated. Long-term decision making must take into consideration the child's perception of time. If we are to meet the child's primary need for continuity in relationships, then the younger the child, the shorter the time frame for decisions about permanency. Goldstein, Solnit and Freud (1979) point out that foster care ceases to be temporary when the child's foster parents become his "longtime caretakers." They go on to describe time lines for identifying these "longtime caretakers" whose relationships with children need to be protected. They suggest a period of one year if the child is less than three years old at the time or placement or a period of two years if the child is three years or older at the time of placement.

It is important that treatment plans avoid confusing goals with implementations, which identify how the goal might be achieved. Activities such as attending classes or going to therapy are implementation strategies, not goals in and of themselves. How would one know if the classes or therapy were successful in changing parent-child interactions?

In John's and Mary's case, reasonable goals might include "John will demonstrate the ability to use discipline techniques that do not involve physical punishment and that are appropriate for Paul's age." Or, it might be stated, "John will demonstrate an ability to handle his frustration and anger in ways that do not harm his child." (Both of these include his learning new behaviours.) A goal for Mary might be to initiate playful interactions with her child three times daily. (This is an example of increasing a positive behaviour.) A possible implementation might suggest that the parents attend parenting classes to help them learn additional skills. An alternative implementation might be for John to be involved in an anger management program.

John
Mary

Parents might follow through on all implementations (i.e. attending classes or therapy) without changing their behaviors. On the other hand some individuals change behaviors without utilizing the implementation outlined in the plan. It is the ability to use the new skills, not attendance *per se*, which is important. What subsequently determines the outcome of the case is whether or not the goals necessary to insure that the child's basic needs can be met at home are achieved, not how they were implemented.

After drawing up a treatment plan, the caseworker should ask herself, "If the parent successfully completes this plan, will I feel it is safe to send this child home?" When a parent follows through on everything on the treatment plan and yet there is a reluctance to send the child home it is likely that either an important goal was omitted from the plan or that implementations were confused with goals. Children of school age should have input into, and knowledge of, their treatment plans. Birth parents sometimes treat children as objects. Unfortunately, social service and legal systems frequently do the same. The treatment plan should clearly define the responsibilities of each parent, the caseworker, the child, and sometimes others, such as foster parents or therapists. A successful outcome is only likely to be achieved by everyone working together.

Permanency planning needs to be addressed in the initial treatment plan and in every subsequent review. Permanency planning is defined as, "The systematic process of carrying out, within a brief time-limited period, a set of goal-directed activities designed to help children live in families that offer continuity of relationships with nurturing parents or caretakers and the opportunity to establish lifetime relationships" (Maluccio, 1983). What are the options? What would need to be done to implement each alternative? Since the late 1970's, permanency planning has been an integral part of the child welfare system. In permanency planning we are not only focusing on who will be raising a particular child, but, equally important, on identifying who will be this child's family when he is an adult. It is important that lifelong ties be developed and/or protected prior to the youngster's emancipation from the system. The steps in Permanency Planning are outlined in Table 5-8.

Four barriers which might prevent the return of the child to his birth family were identified by Vic Pike (1976). These include abandonment, desertion, condition, and conduct. In cases of abandonment there is a permanent absence of the parent with no intent of returning.

Table 5-8

Steps in Permanency Planning

1. Assessment of the child's psychological and developmental needs, acknowledging both his strengths and weaknesses in terms of behavioral control, as well as his physical, cognitive, and psychological development.

2. Assessment of the parents' functioning, including strengths and weaknesses.

3. Development of a plan for modifying either the child's behaviors, the parents' behaviors, or both, so that they can mesh in a healthy way and the family can remain intact or be reunited.

4. Identify those families where the interventions to facilitate change are unsuccessful in meshing the child's needs and the family's abilitites to parent.

5. Insuring that those children who cannot be reunited with their family of origin are provided with an environment which does meet their needs, including having a family of resource post-emancipation.

Denise
Duke
Lily

After Denise, Duke, and Lily were placed in foster care, their mother, Anna, abandoned them. She did not show up for visits and left the state with her new boyfriend. She neither wrote the children nor contacted social services about her whereabouts. All three children had already been abandoned by their birth fathers who had never been actively involved in their care.

In desertion there is a temporary absence of the parents who have only sporadic contact with the child. Although these separations are usually initiated by the parents, it is possible for adolescents to desert their parents.

258

Conditions carry a specific clinical diagnosis and prognosis. Conditions may be either transitory or chronic in nature. They interfere with the parents being able to meet their child's needs. The condition could be present in either the parent or the child. Examples of conditions in the parents might be mental illness, low intelligence, character disorders, or addiction to alcohol or drugs. Examples of conditions in the child might include mental illness, Fetal Alcohol Syndrome, Attention Deficit Disorder, developmental delays, or physical disabilities. If a condition is the basis for legal action, usually an expert witness is needed to identify the condition and predict the outcome.

LaTonya, age twenty-two months, has lived with her current foster-adoptive parents since she was four months of age. LaTonya was born with a series of neonatal problems as a result of her birth mother's cocaine addiction during the pregnancy. The baby remained in the hospital for two months after her birth, and then was returned to her mother's care. LaTonya alternated between periods of being extremely fussy and very lethargic. With the added stress of a difficult baby, Beth, the mother, increased the frequency with which she was using drugs. She started leaving her daughter unsupervised for up to several hours at a time.

LaTonya

LaTonya came into care at age three months. After about a month in a specialized receiving home for drug-affected infants, her condition had markedly improved. Beth had deserted her baby, visiting only one time during the month, in spite of being encouraged by her social worker and the foster parent to have regular contact. LaTonya was moved to a foster-adoptive home. Contact with Beth was sporadic. Right before court hearings, Mother would usually visit once or twice and would sign up for drug rehabilitation programs. However, after the court hearings, she would once again disappear for up to two months. A petition to terminate parental rights was filed.

In the past three months, Beth has visited regularly. She has sporadically attended an out-patient drug rehabilitation program for the past month. Beth's attorney takes the position that his client should not be punished for suffering from a medical condition, addiction. The department of social services and LaTonya's guardian *ad litem* agree that Beth suffers from a condition and take the position that she did not follow through on treatment until the petition for termination was filed. The caseworker points out that, from LaTonya's viewpoint, her parents and her family are the people she lives with, not her birth mother. The department and the guardian *ad litem* believe that timely permanency planning is an absolute need for this child and that it would be "punishing" her if she had to wait for the outcome of Beth's current drug treatment.

Our culture has a long term history of viewing children as possessions, and, in that light, of using them to reward or punish adults. It is important that the child welfare system model the inherent value of the child and the imperativeness of meeting his needs.

Conduct as a barrier again, may occur either in the parent or in the child. This term refers to an inability or refusal to behave in ways that promote relationship building and appropriate care. A conduct problem implies that change is possible, but not predictable. Examples of conduct barriers in parents might include lack of parenting skills, physical abuse, lack of housing, or lack of continuity of care. Examples of conduct in a child which might pose problems typically are those indicative of the child being beyond the parents' control, such as habitual running away, truancy, or delinquent behaviors. Even though these behaviors are frequently indicative of underlying family problems, at the time of assessment they are reflective of conduct disorders on the part of the child or youth. This framework for identifying the nature of parent-child problems is helpful both in developing a current treatment plan and in assessing long term options for permanency.

Judy

When Judy moved from the Haslett home into interim care, her parents identified the problems in terms of her conduct. From their point of view, if only she would change her conduct, then she could return home and everything would be fine. They were unwilling to provide a home for her if the behaviors continued. This became the barrier to reunification as it became increasingly clear that Judy, too, was not committed to a reunification plan. With hesitation, the agency supported the Hasletts' decision to legally relinquish their parental rights.

Whenever a child enters the foster care system, alternative long range plans should be identified (Table 5-9). From the outset these need to be evaluated in terms of the child's needs for physical safety, psychological security, continuity of relationships, including sibling relationships, developing a sense of identity, particularly as it relates to racial or cultural identity, and his special needs.

Alternative Permanency Plans

Reunification with birth parents
Placement with relatives, guardianship or adoption
Prolonged out-of-home care with ongoing contact with parents
Legal guardianship with non-relatives
Adoption planning with, or without, parental consent

In assessing the various options for permanent placement, special attention must be paid to commitment and flexibility. Commitment reflects adult interest and willingness to be available to meet the child's needs, while flexibility refers to the ability to respond to changes in the situation. Both are equally important when working with abused or neglected children. These factors need to be assessed in terms of what people say, what they do, and what they have said and done in the past.

Jones (1987) identifies an untreatable family as one in which it is unsafe to permit an abused child to live. He points out that this does not mean that the family should not receive treatment and help, but rather that the interventions should be aimed at aiding a voluntary release of parental rights rather than reunification.

Goldstein *et al* (1973) point out that attempts should be made to identify which of the presently available adults is able to make the child feel wanted, thereby becoming his psychological parent. They go on to note that it can be predicted that the adult most likely suited for this role is one with whom the child has an affectionate relationship, as opposed to one of otherwise equal potential but who does not yet have a primary relationship with the child.

Stephanie is twenty-nine months old. She has been living with the same foster family since she was three months old when her mother abandoned her. Her foster family is very bonded to her and she is well attached to them. The foster parents would like to adopt Stephanie.

Stephanie

Because of large caseloads and caseworker turnover, permanency planning was not pursued in a timely manner. Stephanie's father is serving a twelve year sentence in prison. He had seen his daughter on only two occasions prior to her entering care and not at all since her placement. The agency recently filed a petition for termination of parental rights. Father is asking that Stephanie be placed with his brother and sister-in-law. A home study reveals that, although they have never met the child, they seem to be able and willing to adequately care for the child.

261

The foster parents have hired an attorney. At the court hearing an expert witness explains the importance of attachment and the trauma of a removal from parents who already have a normal parent-child relationship with Stephanie and who are committed to being her permanent legal family. The expert refers to Goldstein, Solnit, and Freud's work citing the above recommendations as well as their two guidelines that, "If the child's placement is to be altered, the intervenor, except in custody disputes in divorce or separation, must establish both that the child is unwanted and that the child's current placement is not the least detrimental alternative".

Testimony centered on defining Stephanie's best interests, not on lack of adequacy of the relatives or lack of timely permanency planning on the part of the agency. The court agreed that the child's best interests would be served by remaining with her long-term caretakers as opposed to moving to unknown, but adequate, relatives.

Placement with relatives should be considered early in the placement, rather than after substitute caregivers have become the psychological parents. Some relatives might be an adequate short-term resource, helping to minimize the trauma of a child being placed with strangers on an emergency basis. Others might be more appropriate as a long-term resource when return to the birth parents is not possible and if they develop or maintain a relationship with the child while he is in placement.

Prentice

Observations of Prentice with his Aunt Kelly and Uncle Wayne revealed that although the child's behaviors were much the same, the adult responses were quite different than those noted between Rose and her son. Kelly and Wayne involved themselves extensively with Prentice. The more they did so, the less clinging he demonstrated. They talked positively of his resemblance to his dad, Kelly's now-deceased brother. When Prentice did not immediately respond to their affectionate overtures, they reached out more rather than less. Although still somewhat tentative in initiating affection, Prentice was gradually becoming responsive to their affectionate overtures.

Prolonged out-of-home care with continued contact with parents may become the plan of choice. Such a plan might include placement with relatives, in a specialized residential school, in an institution, in other forms of group care, or in foster care. Although long-term out-of-home placement has frequently been overused by default, there are times when it meets the young person's needs better than any other alternative.

262

Robin, sixteen, has lived in the same foster care group home for the past nine months. She gets along well with her foster parents, and the five other adolescents who live in the home. She is getting A's and B's at school and is involved in several extracurricular activities. Her boy friend is also on the honor role.

Robin

Until age twelve, Robin lived with her birth mother and younger brothers. Then she and her mom, who is an alcoholic, started having serious conflicts. Verbal hassles would frequently escalate to physical confrontations. Robin's mother became increasingly rigid in coping with her daughter's emerging adolescent behaviors. Robin rebelled by disobeying her mother's rules and sneaking out of the house. Because of the increasing physical violence between the two of them, Robin was placed in interim care for the first time shortly before her thirteenth birthday.

Her behaviors rapidly improved when she was in care. After several months, visits with her mom were going well. She returned home about a year later. However, within three months the mother-daughter relationship had deteriorated to its previous low point. Mother was drinking more. Robin was becoming more rebellious. She was once again placed in care, this time for close to a year-and-a-half. As before, Robin did well and mom's drinking subsided markedly. However, following a second return home, the old patterns reemerged. Robin and her mom returned to a destructive relationship.

The past history revealed that Robin's parents had divorced when she was seven. She has had minimal contact with her dad since she was ten. He lives out of state, is remarried, and has started a new family. Robin does not get along with his new wife and is quite clear about not wanting to live with them.

Although there are no relatives who are a resource for her to live with, she has a close relationship with a grandfather who lives in the area. In addition she occasionally sees aunts, uncles, and cousins. When not under the stress of living in the same home, Robin and her mother have some enjoyable times together. They look forward to their visits, but are concerned that if the visits continue to go well, reunification will again be attempted. Robin, her mother, and her foster parents all agree that continued placement with regular contacts with family members allows both for her needs for continuity of relationships and for the physical and psychological safety and security that are necessary to free her up to put energy into academic acheivement and peer relationships. The caseworker, too, is convinced that long term fostercare is the best plan. However, agency policy does not allow for this option for permanency.

Although it provides less legal protection than adoption, sometimes legal guardianship becomes the permanency planning option of choice. Although legal guardians fulfill some of the responsibilities listed in the Legal Parent role, usually they cannot remove a youngster from the area of the court's jurisdiction without its

263

approval (Stein, 1981). Guardians do not have the same reciprocal rights of inheritance as birth or adoptive parents. Guardianship is most commonly used when children are placed with relatives on a long-term basis. However, there are other situations in which this may be the least detrimental alternative.

Darrell

Eva Larkin has just finished her report for an upcoming court hearing on four-year-old Darrell Day. As the Court Appointed Special Advocate (CASA) volunteer responsible for focusing on Darrell's needs, she recognizes that on this occasion she disagrees with the caseworker as to the permanency plan which is best for the child. Social services staff have filed for termination of parental rights so that Darrell can be adopted by his foster parents, with whom he has lived continuously since age six weeks.

Lorna, Darrell's mother, opposes this plan. However, she is willing to agree to the foster parents, the Jeffersons, having legal guardianship of her son. Lorna recognizes that she is neither willing nor able to raise Darrell and she feels comfortable with his current placement. Lorna has a good relationship with the Jeffersons, but has always viewed social workers as adversaries.

Eva has repeatedly visited Darrell in the Jefferson home. He seems securely attached to all members of his foster family. When shown a picture of Lorna, he identifies her by saying, "That's Lorna. She's my born-to mother." When asked what that term means, he replies, "I grew in her tummy." When asked about his parents and siblings, he consistently identifies them as members of the Jefferson family. Darrell says that Lorna sometimes comes over to visit. "Lots of times she takes me out for ice cream. Sometimes we go to the zoo." Eva has asked him who gets to decide if he goes out with Lorna. Looking suprised at the question, Darrell replied, "We have to ask Mama first."

Eva has discussed both guardianship and adoption with the Jeffersons, expressing her concerns about insuring permanency. They seem to understand the legal difference between the two alternatives but believe that the best plan is to go along with Lorna's wishes. From early in the placement, Lorna has always felt comfortable dropping in on the Jeffersons. Mrs. J. says, "She acts just like my older kids. Sometimes she plops down on the couch and watches TV. She feels free to get snacks from the refrigerator. If she wants to take Darrell out, she always checks with me first. Sometimes she brings Darrell gifts. She's like a special friend to him."

Mrs. Jefferson went on to talk of her relationship with Darrell's grandmother, whom she occasionally sees at church. The grandmother buys Darrell clothes now and then. She calls frequently to ask how he is doing. Mrs. J. sums up the relationships with Darrell's birth family with the statement, "We're like family. Why would we want to take them to court?" Mr. Jefferson added, "We get along fine with Lorna and her mom, but Lorna doesn't trust social services. She trusts us, but if we agree with the social worker on taking her to court, she's going to think we're on their side. Things will change then. We don't think that'll be good. Guardianship is fine with us."

Eva asked the Jeffersons how they thought it might be when Darrell got older, especially when he reaches the teen years. The Jeffersons have two teens and two young adults in their family. Mr. Jefferson's quick reply was, "Who ever knows how it will be when kids are teenagers? I guess we'll face that when the time comes. He'll probably still be seeing Lorna then. He'll understand better who she is. Maybe we'll all decide he needs to live with her for a while. Maybe not. If Lorna and us can agree with each other now, we'll probably be able to agree then. If we get into a big court battle now, we'll probably have lots of hassels in the future."

Eva Larkin understood why the social worker thought adoption would be the best plan, but after listening to the Jeffersons, she decided that more harm than good would probably come from a contested court hearing. The relationships between Darrell, Lorna, his Grandma, and the Jeffersons seemed to have reached a balance that met all of their needs.

Having parents aid in making an adoption plan for the child should be included in the list of various long-term options for the child. Unfortunately, our society frequently views this plan as an admission of failure on the part of the parent or system rather than viewing it as one of several proactive positive options. When parents are willing to make this plan, they can be an active participant in giving the child permission to form a new relationship with adoptive parents. The following is a letter written by a birth mother who was making an adoption plan for her son who was in foster care in another state.

Dear Justin,

I'm sorry that I didn't write for so long. I know that you've been waiting for a letter from me, but there were some important things that I had to think about and some decisions I had to make. You know how long it always takes me to decide things.

I hear that you've learned how to read now and can ride a bicycle, too! Gee, you're getting to be a big kid. I hope you will be good at reading.

You know something, Justin? Everyone is good at some things, but everybody finds out that there are some things that they can't do well, no matter how hard they try. Well, I am like most people. I can do some things pretty well, like driving a car and playing the piano. But some other things I can't do. Maybe I could do some of them if I tried, but there is one thing I've tried to do for six years that I don't think I can ever do right. That's being a good mom for you, Justin. I feel bad that I can't give you the kind of love and attention you need. I've known for a long time that I wasn't able to. I know that things haven't been right between us. Even though we loved each other we weren't able to get along together. I hoped that we could, but it just didn't work out for us.

So I had to go away and decide what would be best for us. I've decided that it would be best if I let you have a chance to have a mom and dad who could give you the kind of love and attention you need. I have asked Mrs. Arnhem to find such a family.

I know that it will be hard for you to understand this. I suppose that you'll be really mad at me, but I hope that your new parents will help you learn to understand. I hope that you'll learn to love your new mom and dad and that you'll be happy with them. That's important to me. I'll never forget you.

I've given Mrs. Arnhem some pictures of you when you were little and a picture of your dad and me when we were happy together. I kept the one of you learning to ride your first tricycle and the one of you and me at the zoo so I can always remember how cute you were.

I will always love you, even though I can't be your mom anymore.

Mommy Barbara

Finally, the state taking the initiative in legally terminating parental rights needs to be viewed as an option when parents are unable to meet the child's needs and are unable themselves to work toward making an adoption plan for the child.

When selecting permanent legal families for children, social workers tend to prefer placements in families who are most similar to, or admired by, themselves. Yet it has been shown that middle class professionals do not necessarily provide the most stable or suitable placements for children in care, either on a foster care or adoptive basis (Barth 1987).

During the 1990's the expected influx of children and families affected by the HIV virus requesting services will encourage us to look at new alternatives for providing the most helpful resources.

Sabrina
Seth
Tiffany

Maureen's husband, Harry, an intravenous drug user, died of AIDS two years ago. Maureen has three children—Sabrina, eight, Seth, five, and Tiffany who was born shortly after her father's death. Although Maureen herself never used intravenous drugs, she contracted the HIV virus from Harry. Recently she has become increasingly ill. The two older children do not test HIV positive. Tiffany was born with a positive test, but she has reverted to testing HIV negative.

During her husband's prolonged illness, Maureen's support system, including her family, abandoned her. She is now quite isolated. She has no one to turn to for help when she is ill. She knows no one who is willing to care for her children.

A local agency, recognizing the need for services to families like Maureen's has begun an innovative program. One of the experienced foster families who has been trained to work with families affected by HIV is selected to work with Maureen and her children. Joan, the foster mother, will care for Tiffany while Maureen goes to her many medical appointments. In addition, Joan attends the older children's school conferences and activities when their mother is too ill to do so. When Maureen is able to participate, Joan provides transportation for her.

Joan's family will provide respite care for all three children, both when Maureen just needs a break and during her hospital stays, which undoubtedly will be increasing in frequency and duration.

Joan knows that the most difficult part of her job will be to be a friend and support to Maureen as she copes with her illness and impending death. Gradually, the foster family will have to help the children accept their mother's illness and eventually they will share the children's grief.

Joan's family is actively involved in a group set up by the agency for providing support to foster families who have chosen to become involved with children and families affected by HIV. The hardest times for Joan are when Maureen lashes out in anger at anyone available. At these times Joan reminds herself of the alternatives the children would face if she were not part of their lives and turns to the support group for help with her own feelings. *

Let's check in on the children whose journeys through the system we have been following and make certain that plans for permanency are in place for each of them.

From the time Rose came forward to visit Ardith and Prentice, her caseworker, Mr. Laird has actively involved her in the case planning. He presented various long-term options ranging from reunification with both children, to having Ardith return home but having an alternative permanent plan made for Prentice, to having Rose involved in making an adoption plan for both. Rose became actively involved in treatment for her addictions. During this time she developed a variety of positive support systems.

Ardith
Prentice

When not under the influence of drugs, Rose demonstrates a healthy relationship with Ardith. Reunification of mother and daughter should be relatively easy to accomplish if mother continues to be substance free. On the other hand, even when not using drugs, Rose's relationship with Prentice did not meet either of their needs. For Prentice to be able to successfully return to his mother's care, there would have to be dramatic changes in their relationship.

Mr. Laird helped Rose look at the alternatives afforded by long-term placement of Prentice with his paternal aunt and uncle. Kelly, the aunt, had been Rose's best friend during their teen years. She was the sister of Prentice's father who

*This case is based on infomation from a program at Lothian Regional Council, the public welfare agency in Edinburgh, Scotland. Leake and watts (463 Hawthorne Ave., Yonkers, NY, 10705) publishes a Pediatric AIDS, Foster Care Network Bulletin for providing current information on this topic.

who died from a drug overdose two years ago. Kelly and her husband, Wayne, had known Prentice all of his life. He was blossoming while in their care. Alternative plans might include either a relative adoption or guardianship. Kelly and Wayne favored the permanency of adoption. It is likely that contact between Prentice, Rose, and Ardith will continue throughout the years.

Martin

While Martin was living with his birth mother between ages twelve and sixteen months, it became increasingly clear that he would again need placement. Agency staff started permanency planning even prior to Martin's final move into the system. Sylvia, his mother, was unwilling to participate in making an adoption plan for her son.

Mr. Sawyer, the caseworker, and his supervisor weighed the alternatives. Should Martin be placed in a foster-adoptive home or in a regular interim care home while the agency filed for termination of parental rights? Although a single move was certainly preferrable to two, the supervisor was concerned about the importance and difficulty of developing an attachment between Martin and adult caregivers. It was finally decided that the risks would be less in placing Martin with an experienced interim care family that had had previous success in working with toddlers with attachment problems, than in placing him with an inexperienced family who, if successful, might be a permanent resource.

During Marty's placement with the LaBelle family, Sylvia has not maintained contact with him, nor has she followed through on other aspects of the treatment plan. Her parental rights have been legally terminated by the court. Long-term planning for Martin included a transition from the LaBelle home to an adoptive family.

Judy

Judy has had a post-adoptive relinquishment and an adoptive disruption. Ms. Silver, the current caseworker, has always believed that adoption is the best long-term plan in this case. Judy has recently moved from the Dougherty foster family, where things were not going well for her, back to the Caldwell home where she previously had done well. Judy herself is quite adamant that she is unwilling to commit herself to another placement with an unknown family. Adoption has not offered her permanency in the past. In her mind, emotional connections take precedence over legal ties. Her life experiences have taught her that the two do not necessarily go hand-in-hand.

Ms. Silver is, understandably, concerned about the lack of permanency usually afforded by the fostercare system. In her contacts with Judy she emphasizes the importance of a family, not just prior to emancipation, but as an adult. Judy is persistent in her desire to grow up in the Caldwell home. The Caldwells have a foster-group home for six children ages ten and older. Although they are committed to Judy, there are unwilling to adopt her, primarily because of how it would impact their relationship with the others in their care. However, they are willing to verbally commit themselves to Judy, both for the remainder of her growing up years and subsequently.

Maureen Caldwell, especially, has a close relationship with Judy. She and her husband have been foster parents for eight years. They are known to work well with adolescents. Although, on occasion, they have indicated that certain youth were not doing well in their home, they have never asked that a child be abruptly moved. They have always been cooperative in planning for transistions. They are supportive of adolescents maintaining contact with their birth families whenever possible. Two previous foster daughters, now in their twenties, continue to be viewed as family members. Reluctantly, Ms. Silver agrees that long-term placement with the Caldwell family will be the permanency planning option selected for Judy.

As we have already seen, the Gilbert children are legally free for adoption. An adoptive family for the sibling group of three is being recruited.

Special Issues IV

Children are probably at their point of highest risk for long-term psychological damage at the time of removal from their birth families. This does not mean that the removal is not the best plan. Rutter (1981) has noted that the critical issue is whether the children have a stable placement in families that meet their needs. These children do better than those who remain in a disturbed, or unresponsive, environment. However, the move into the system is frequently done on an emergency basis and with little attention paid to the importance of considering long-term planning immediately. When children enter the child welfare system, all too frequently little attention is paid to sibling relationships or other family connections. Many times, the importance of racial and cultural issues also takes a backseat at this point in time. However, in permanency planning all of these become critical aspects of decision making. When there is a delay in focusing on these factors, it is invariably the children who pay the price.

Most individuals in our society, including those involved in child welfare, have strong opinions on the importance of family ties, including sibling relationships, and having children grow up with others of the same race and cultural background. A variety of research projects have provided factual information. It is important that those who are responsible for the permanency planning decisions differentiate between facts and opinions. This does not mean that values are not important; indeed they are. However, they must be identified as such.

This section will provide some facts, so that educated opinions can be formulated. There are pros and cons to every option and it is wise to consider them all when making life-long decisions on a child's behalf. In some cases value conflicts become apparent. For example, there may be siblings who have always lived together but who have different fathers, and therefore different relatives and possibly different racial or ethnic heritages. Agencies must then prioritize their values if there are to be guidelines for staff and consistency in decision making. Or, better still, they may provide guidelines for assessing priorities in specific cases. The least detrimental option in one case may not be the same in a second case where the childrens' views of the situation are different, as we will see later.

Relative Placements

If, despite all efforts of the caseworker and others involved to prevent placement, it becomes necessary to remove a child from his home, placement with known adults should always be considered. In families throughout the world, children are traditionally placed with relatives or neighbors during times of crisis within families. Such placements may occur when a parent dies, is ill, needs respite, is incarcerated, or simply when a child has needs that are better met by other family members. Some agencies make it a point to try to place those who must move on an emergency basis with someone they know. Then, if placement will continue beyond the mandatory 48 (or in some states 72) hour court hearing, they can make a planned move to a longer-term placement.

Placement with relatives should always be considered whenever out-of-home placement is necessary. There are definite advantages to such placements. The child's trauma of separation is reduced when he is placed with adults known to him rather than with strangers. Placement with relatives identifies families as important resources in times of stress. Child and relatives may have already developed reslationships built on trust and love. In addition, it may be easier for the child and birth parents to have frequent contact when the child is staying with relatives. There is more likely to be ongoing contact with other relatives as well. Loyalty conflicts may be reduced.

Since relatives are usually aware of the child's history, they can help the child accept the past while embracing him as a member of the family group. If the youngster sees that other family members do not have the same problems as their parents, it may help him realize the importance of his own personal life choices in terms of long-term functioning. When placed with relatives, a child may not have to deal as much with the "good family" versus "bad family" split as in a non-relative placement.

Although relative placements should always be considered when out-of-home placement is necessary, it is important that caseworkers also be aware of some of the possible pitfalls of such placements. When relatives themselves contacted the authorities about an abusive or neglectful situation, the parents may believe that the relatives are conspiring with child welfare personnel against them. Placing with these relatives may cause further strain on family support systems that will be needed if the child is returned to the parents.

Placement with relatives may change other family relationships. For example, if grandparents provide long-term parenting for a grandchild, the child's relationship with the birth parents and with aunts and uncles will become more like a sibling relationship. Grandparents in our society have a different role than parents. The parental role includes more discipline and less indulgence in general. If grandparents serve as parents, they must be willing to parent, rather than grandparent, the child.

Sometimes relative placements are not possible or useful because there is no willing individual in the extended family with the skills necessary to provide both adequate nurture and structure. Workers need to consider whether the family dysfunction that is necessitating the placement extends to relatives who are being considered as a placement resource. In some cases relatives may be so highly critical of, or competitive with, the parent who abuses or neglects the child that they may undermine reunification plans. Extreme competitiveness is most common when the relative is a sibling of the parent. On the other hand, relatives may not be accepting of a child because they see him as "just like" the non-related parent whom they have never accepted.

5-10 ___ *Table* ___

Placement with Relatives

Advantages	Disadvantages
1. Reduces separation trauma	1. May decrease family support systems
2. Promotes sense of family responsibility	2. Parents may see relatives and agency as in collusion
3. Provides knowledge of child's past	3. Change in family relationships
4. May facilitate parental visiting	4. Overall family dysfunction may have led to parental problems
5. Decreases good/bad family split	5. May increase stress between non-relative spouse and the relative caregiver
6. Provides contact with relatives who have made positive life choices	

A relative may make a home available only out of a sense of family obligation and not from real caring, concern, or understanding of the child's needs. Occasionally, a strong sense of family loyalty may effectively hide the real issues so that they are never resolved. At other times, a family placement may be so comfortable that the birth parents may not be motivated to make the changes necessary for reunification.

In summary, children should have the assurance that if they are placed with relatives their needs will be met, and that if they are placed with strangers it is because no relatives were *both willing and able* to meet those needs. The advantages and disadvantages of relative placements are summarized in Table 5-10.

Sibling Relationships

Agencies have rarely acknowledged that sibling relationships have an intrinsic value. The bureaucracy frequently views them as just another hurdle to be overcome in providing services. Donley (1989) has pointed out that child welfare services should be encouraging sibling care settings from intake onward throughout the continuum of services provided. She goes on to encourage that assessment should always include examining sibling attachments. There should be exploration of known, remembered, and unacknowledged sibling relationships. The psychological status of sibling relationships are just as important as the legal relationships. Donley points out that to children in care, sibling relationships are the most visible part of the birth family relationship. Adults must become responsible for learning more about each child's wishes.

Sibling relationships are unique for a variety of reasons. Although much emphasis has, through the years, been placed on sibling rivalry, recently additional aspects of these same-generation realtionships have been identified. Siblings may act as comforters, caretakers, role models, spurs to achievement, faithful allies, and best friends (Viorst, 1986). In general, they are the longest relationships that an individual will have during his lifetime, longer than parent-child or spousal liasons. Throughout a lifetime siblings tend to come together to share their joys and their times of pain.

The experiences of siblings throughout their early years give them a shared past that others will never come close to. Only siblings can, through time, reminisce about the details of their life as children. Viorst points out that, "Sisters and brothers share what—no matter how close—no other contemporaries can share: the intimate, resonant details of family history." Sometimes this is true even when they did not live together as youngsters.

Meagen

Meagen, twenty-five, has recently met her ten-year-old sister, Aimee, after a nine year separation. Meagen had run away from home when she was seventeen. Her father had sexually abused her; her mother had emotionally abused her. She had always felt quilty about leaving her younger sister behind.

Aimee has been in foster care for two years. She had reported sexual abuse as soon as it occurred. She had been more adversely affected by the emotional abuse and distancing of her mother than by the sexual abuse. Although she received considerable support and therapy for the sexual abuse, others did not seem to understand the depth of her feelings about Mother, who had not physically but emotionally abused her.

Soon after she and Meagen met, they were reminiscing. Meagan asked Aimee if their mother had punished her by depriving her of meals while she, herself, sat in the rocker eating Hershey bars. Here, at last, was someone with whom Aimee could share her detailed memories—someone who would truly understand.

In general, sibling relationships are less power-based than parent-child relationships. Sibling relationships provide an arena for having to learn to cope with jealousy, aggression, and interpersonal conflicts. Aggression between siblings provides for physical touch, learning about conflict, and learning about self-protection. In most families youngsters are expected to stand up for themselves in sibling relationships, but not necessarily in adult-child conflicts. In most cases of sibling conflicts no one leaves because of the difficult emotions. Brothers and sisters usually remain in the same family and have to come to grips with these difficult but universal life tasks. Sibling relationships help enhance a sense of self and provide opportunities for learning skills such as sharing, and cooperation in completing tasks. Ineffective parents may either avoid or exaggerate sibling aggression.

According to Banks and Kahn (1982) one of the most important functions siblings serve is in the development of identity. Although not necessarily on purpose, most individuals reveal more of their core identity to siblings than to anyone else during their growing up years. Siblings compare themselves to each other, discerning similarities and differences, enhancing identity formation. Here, as in so many areas of psychological functioning, a balance is critical. It is unhealthy when siblings are viewed as "the same" not allowing them to become individuals in their own rights. On the other hand, perceiving them as so different that any sense of connection is minimized can be equally harmful. The latter seems to be a common perception within the child welfare system and, again, deemphasizes the importance of close interpersonal connections in general.

Banks and Kahn (1982) identify three factors that serve to enhance the intensity of the sibling bond. They are accessability to each other; lack of parental meeting of needs; and the need for a meaningful personal identity. They have pointed out that, in general, sibling attachments are even closer than usual when there has been inadequate parental care and attention, a condition which is certainly present in many cases when children are entering care. However, in some circumstances of parental underinvolvement there is extreme rivalry. For there to be increased loyalty between brothers and sisters, they must first have learned basic reciprocity. Banks and Kahn (1982) have noted that siblings tend to organize themselves into emotionally significant pairs which can interact with each other in either a positive or negative fashion. In sibling groups of three—or other odd numbers—there is frequently a child who is "odd man out."

There is evidence that the presence of siblings minimizes the trauma of parental separations or losses (Tizard 1986). A twelve-month-old child spends nearly as much time interacting with older siblings as with mother (Lawson 1974). Siblings may become transitional objects for one another during a placement. They are particularly important with very young children. Research has shown that in the Strange Situation setting, an older brother or sister can comfort the toddler, who uses the siblings as a secure base (Tizard 1986). The McNamaras (1990) point out that separating siblings can make it more difficult for children to deal with separation and loss, begin a healing process, make attachments, and develop a healthy self-image. For the child in care, separated from most members of his family of origin, having someone with whom he shares a history of growing up can be particularly important (Melina, 1990). Attachments are particularly strong between the caregiver child and the younger siblings. Separation of them may lead to lifelong grief.

In assessing sibling relationships the history and Family Life Graph can be used as a starting point. In addition, it is important to observe the siblings together. A final step includes discussing sibling realtionships with each child individually.

Advantages of placing brothers and sisters together include lessening separation trauma and enhancing identity formation. Additionally, there is less pressure on any one child to meet all of the parents' expectations. When caseworkers separate siblings, at some level they are accentuating the impression that family relationships are not really important.

There are, however, disadvantages to placing siblings together which must also be considered. As the McNamaras (1990) point out, when siblings are placed together the dynamics of the previous dysfunctional family are brought into the new home more strongly. They go on to note that some brothers and sisters who have experienced abuse may reinforce negative, dysfunctional, and pathologic patterns of behaviors. These behaviors can interfere with the children developing feelings of safety and attachment and ultimately interfere with healing.

There are some circumstances in which separation of siblings might be considered. There are situations in which a decision has to be made as to which is more important, a healthy parent-child bond or a sibling attachment. Ardith and Prentice present an example of this dilema. Others occur when the system creates new family ties by placing siblings separately for prolonged periods, not because it is in the children's best interests but because of the needs of adults.

When keeping siblings together means that one of them will not get his needs met, then separation might be considered. For example, if one member of a sibling group needs residential treatment, it is unlikely that all members of the group will be sent to the treatment facility. When it is impossible to provide adequate safety for one or more of the siblings, then separation will have to be considered. There are some cases, as the McNamaras point out, where siblings are so physically or sexually aggressive with each other that it is impossible to provide the level of supervision, within a family situation, which is necessary for safety. In a few cases, an extremely dependent relationship between siblings may prevent the development of healthier attachments. Banks and Kahn (1982) describe "Hansel and Gretel" children who are so intensely loyal and mutually protective of each other that they exclude others. They may share a special language and become very upset with even temporary separations. They view their relationship as more important than their individual selves.

274

Consider Separating Siblings when Keeping Them Together Would

> interrupt a normal parent-child relationship
> mean that one child would not get his needs met
> maintain a destructive relationship even after attempts to normalize it
> threaten someone's safety

According to Donley (1989) decisions to terminate attachments between brothers and sisters must be given as careful consideration as termination of the parent-child relationship. She feels that separation of siblings should be an exception to policy, rather than the rule as it is in many agencies.

If siblings are to be kept together it is important to identify families who are willing to provide care for them and capable of doing it well. LaPere et al (1986) identified characteristics of families that are likely to be successful with large sibling groups. A critical factor seemed to be for the parents, mother in particular, to have had experience living in a large family. The parent herself might be part of a large sibling group, or may have been raised in a household with extended family members, or she may already have several other children. A strong marriage and stable lifestyle are essential when one plans to parent sibling groups. Parents of large sibling groups need to be able to build and use a support system. They need to see sibling relationships as important. Although they should consider input from children, these parents must have confidence in their own decision-making abilities.

In general, in placing sibling groups for adoption—or possibly when reunifying them with their birth family after a prolonged separation—it makes sense to place the oldest or the most disturbed first. If one child is going to take considerably more time and energy than others, it makes sense to place that child first, when parents are in a high energy mode. Placement of the oldest child first recreates the birth order. This may be particularly important when the oldest child is the caregiver child. This child needs to have an opportunity to form a parent-child relationship with adoptive parents first.

Once the decision was made that Denise would not be remaining with Shelby, the latter requested that the child be moved within a month to six weeks.

Denise's caseworker, her supervisor, and members of the adoption unit met. A family requesting a sibling group had recently completed their group preparation homestudy. Cassie and Larry Osborn have been married for five years. It is a second marriage for both. Cassie's seventeen-year-old son, Curt, lives with her and Larry. Larry has two grown children. His daughter lived with her mom

Denise

during adolescence and visited Larry and Cassie. His son lived with Larry and Cassie for the four years prior to his emancipation.

When approached, the Osborns expressed an interest in the Gilbert children. Cassie had done some reading about child sexual abuse because her sister's teen-aged daughter had recently disclosed that her paternal grandfather had sexually abused her when she was between the ages of five and seven. After that age the niece had successfully avoided ever being alone with her grandfather. Both Cassie and Larry were more confident about their abilities to parent a girl who had been sexually abused than a boy. Neither had lived with emotionally disturbed children. However, both had first-hand knowledge of the importance of helping children cope with parent separation and loss and of the struggles associated with adding new members to a family. Both seemed to understand that Denise had not really dealt with her feelings about separation from her birth mother. They were concerned about this.

It was decided that instead of moving all three children into the Osborn home simultaneously, Denise would be moved first. Although it was recognized that she was not yet very accepting of having new parents on a permanent basis, she was very interested in being reunited with her younger brother and sister. She was told that as the older sister, she would have the opportunity to check out the placement and that she would then be part of the decision-making team as to the timing of the move for the younger children. She was asked to learn more about how Cassie and Larry would care for younger children.

Meantime, it was suggested to the adoptive parents that when Denise asked these questions they might sometimes demonstrate the caregiving, rather than just talk about it. For example, Cassie one evening said to Denise, "You know, I've had experience holding a little boy and reading bedtime stories to him but I've never done that for a little girl. I'd like to do a little practicing before Lily moves in. I know that you know her well and know what she likes. How about letting me practice with you and you can let me know what you think Lily will like."

Larry commented that it had been a long time since he had parented young children. He remembered about discipline but he thought he needed to brush up on the kinds of play that young children enjoyed. Denise commented that she didn't know much about that as she didn't remember having a dad play with her. Larry suggested that together they try a variety of activities.

LaPere (1989) suggests that adoptive families develop an understanding of the difficulties of removing the caregiver role from the child who was in that position when the sibling group lived in their birth family. It is important that this child be provided with a new role. She suggests that the caregiver child be given the role of consultant to the parents. That child probably knows more detail about the younger children than anyone else. It makes sense to make use of that knowledge. On the other hand, one never has to follow the advice of a consultant when it doesn't sound useful.

Exercise 5-1 has the reader use the Family Life Graph as a tool in decision making on the placement of a sibling group of three.

Using the Family Life Graph as a Case Planning Tool When Making Decisions about Sibling Placements

Romano
Carol
Tommy

Ramona, ten, Carol, eight, and Tommy, four, are legally free for adoption. Their mother, Susan, died in a car accident along with her husband, Tommy's father, three-and-a-half years ago. Up until that time all three children had lived continuously with their mother. Susan and John, who is the girls' father, divorced six years ago and Susan married Tom Sr. a year later.

Following Tom and Susan's death, the children were placed in interim care as there were no relatives available to care for them. Tommy was placed in one foster home, and the girls were placed together in a second foster home. Tommy has remained in the same foster home since his placement there.

After six months in foster care, Ramona and Carol went to live with their birth father, his new wife, and their baby. Ramona and her stepmother had many fights. After nine months, the stepmother gave her husband the ultimatum, "Either the girls go, or the baby and I go."

The girls were again placed in a foster home together. However, after about a year the foster parents requested that Ramona be moved since they"couldn't do a thing with her." She was characterized as "willful and stubborn." She lied, occasionally stole, and "argued all the time." The foster parents also stated that she constantly picked on Carol, who is characterized by the foster parents, with whom she continues to live, as a "quiet, good girl." Carol is very helpful and rarely misbehaves although she is sometimes slow to follow requests.

Ramona has been in a different foster home for the past year. In this home she seems to be doing "a little better." She and Carol see each other every two to three months. Carol's foster parents frequently do not follow through on tentatively scheduled visits. They see Ramona as a bad influence on Carol and would like to discontinue all contact. Furthermore, they state that Carol doesn't care about seeing Ramona and that the two girls aren't at all close.

Carol's foster parents have mentioned that they would like to adopt her. Carol indicates that she wants to remain in their home. Ramona, on the other hand, says that their mom would want them to all be together and that she wants an adoptive placement with both Carol and Tommy. She and Carol have recently had two visits with Tommy, whom they had seen only one to two times a year up until now. Tommy seems confused after the visits. His foster family views him as a permanent member of their family and are very interested in adopting him but are not interested in adopting his two birth sisters.

Using the Family Life Graph on page 250 note the following information.

1.   With whom did each child share times of trauma? (i.e. interruptions in parenting, moves, etc.)

2.   What percent of his/her life has each child spent with each set of parents?

3.   What percent of his/her lifetime has each child spent with each of the other siblings?

4.   What additional information would you want to gather before making a permanency plan for each child?

5.   In what ways might additional information change your plans?

Trans Racial Placements

Most people will agree that it is best for children to live with others of the same race and similar cultural background. Most will also agree that children need a permanent family. In the child welfare field unfortunately decisions frequently come down not to optimal but to least detrimental. When it is not possible for the child to have both—a permanent family, and grow up with people of the same race—which takes precedence? Indeed, how do we determine that it is not possible for a child to have both? What are the system barriers to recruitment of minority families as foster and adoptive resources? Agencies must be willing to look at these difficult questions and examine their own actions with a critical eye.

In the child welfare system, traditionally, more attention is paid to racial congruity at the time of permanency planning than when the child enters care. This, in itself, poses problems. Should a healthy relationship with essentially life-long caregivers be interrupted solely to preserve racial congruety? Does the underlying message to the child that skin color is more important than family ties encourage or discourage positive feelings about racial identity?

Currently, the federal government has chosen to take a stand in terms of placement of Native American children, but no other racial or ethnic group. The Indian Child Welfare Act of 1978 outlined guidelines for case decision making for children of Native American heritage on a federal, rather than state basis. Tribes must be notified of any state fostercare or adoption proceeding when Native American children are involved. Tribes can intervene in the proceedings if they choose. Indian parents and custodians must be given due process in the action, and tribes can request transfer of jurisdiction from the state to the tribal court. In general, the Indian Child Welfare Act has forced us to look at racial and cultural issues when the child enters care when a Native American child is involved, not only when the child is ready to leave it. However, this is not equally true with other races or ethnic groups.

Those concerned with children in the system need to know of the research that has been conducted on transracial placements and use this knowledge as they weigh the alternatives. Numerous studies have been conducted. However, many have focused on preadolescents and used only information from adoptive parents in determining "success" of placement.

278

Transracial placements were uncommon until after World War II. Since then, children from a variety of racial and ethnic heritages have been adopted by white parents. Japanese and Chinese children were placed with Caucasian families after World War II (Silverman, 1990). After the Korean conflict children from that country started to be placed in large numbers with white families, not only in North America, but also in Europe. In the late 1950's the Native American Indian Adoption Project placed about 700 Native children in white adoptive homes. In the 1960's there was a marked increase in black-white transracial placements which peaked in the early 1970's. Since then there has been an increase in children from India and from Central and South America placed in white adoptive homes, again both in the North America and in Europe.

Silverman and Feigleman (1990) report that none of the numerous studies done on interracial adoptive placements have reported widespread problems. They go on to summarize that non-white children raised in white homes for the most part identify with both white and non-white communities. This is true for black, Korean, and other children of color.

McRoy and Zurcher's study (1983) demonstrated that black children adopted by white families showed no significant differences in their self-esteem scores when compared with black children adopted by Afro-American families. They did note, however, that the attitudes of the children to some degree reflected those of their adoptive parents. Those parents who de-emphasized their children's racial identification and who isolated their families from the Afro-American community often raised children who accepted negative stereotypes about black people in American society. This confirms Grow and Shapiro's findings (1974) that indicated that the adjustment of the children was better when white parents regarded their children as Afro-American in appearance and did not try to minimize the importance of their racial heritage.

Simon and Altstein's study (1987) is one of the few that gathered information from the adopted individuals themselves, as opposed to depending only on parental reports. They followed the racial attitudes of a large number of transracially adopted black children until they were adults. In the early years of their study they noted that Afro-American children, ages three to eight, adopted by white families showed less ambivalence toward their own race than Afro-American children raised in black families. Young black children in white homes saw themselves as black and did not attach any negative evaluation to that assessment. These adopted persons, as adults, were firmly committed to their adoptive parents. Their self-esteem scores were as good as those of their nonadopted siblings. Friendship and dating patterns indicated that they maintained involvements with both races.

Feigelman and Silverman's 1983 study indicated that most of the emotional and developmental problems of black children who had joined white families by adoption were related to their preadoptive experiences, rather than to the transracial placement. The same was true of Asian and Latin-American placements in the same study. They noted that, in general, families who adopt black children are more open to children's interest in their birth families than white families who adopt white children.

Fanshel (1972) studied a large number of families five years after they had adopted Native American children who had been placed with them early in life, prior to age twenty-one months. About seventy-five percent were doing well in all spheres of life, according to their parents. However, it has been widely reported that many of these children had increasing problems in adolescence in the area of identity formation, feeling alienated both from their adoptive families and from their Native American heritage (Linkages, 1985). Since each tribe has its own culture and traditions, it is very difficult for a Euro-American family to provide an adopted child of Native American heritage with contact with his specific culture of origin.

Goodluck (1990) points out that traditionally Native American tribes have accepted and cared for children within the tribal system. Historically, out-of-home placements were open. Extended-family care has been a tradition. Prior to Americanizing the tribal court system in 1934, there was no provision for termination of parental right. Currently, guardianship is frequently the preferred option within the Native American culture.

(Readers should know that there is a Native American Adoption Resource Exchange. Mary Wood is the director. The address is 200 Charles Street; Dorseyville PA 15238. Some states, such as California and Washington also have state registers of Native children and families.)

Although there is little research data that indicates severe problems with transracial placements, America has a long-term history of racial discrimination and segregation which leads to minorities distrusting, with justification, that the white establishment will serve their children well. Increasingly, racial minority and ethnic groups are demanding that their children not be permanently placed with white families. Once again, it must be stressed that, to meet the child's needs, decisions must be made early on, before—not after—longtime caretaker relationships are formed.

Exercise 5-2, which follows, takes us back to the statements that introduced this chapter and has us consider the decision-making processes when it is not possible for one choice to encompass all of our basic beliefs. How are value conflicts resolved? Have agencies developed a protocol to help their caseworkers through the decision-making maze, or is each left to make decisions based upon their own biases? Does one unit (i.e. foster care) prioritize values differently than another (i.e. adoption)? Are there policies that could be implemented at the front end of the system, when children enter care, that would obviate the need for these difficult and damaging decisions later?

In looking at these difficult choices our own prejudices and beliefs will come to the fore. It is impossible to avoid this. Even if all readers were to agree on the original premises outlined on the first page of this chapter, caring persons still might prioritize the values in differing ways. Once again, the reader is asked to look both at the positive aspects of each decision and at the simultaneous damage that each will inevitably cause. How can the advantages be enhanced and the traumas be minimized? The goal must always be to try to determine which decision will be least detrimental to the child, or children involved.

Following the exercises is another case example in which the children gradually let adults know what they needed. In this case adult biases must be put aside if the sisters needs are to be met. Luckily, those responsible for decision making on their behalf were both committed and flexible in their approach.

5-2 *Exercise*

Prioritizing Values in Permanency Planning— Stephanie's Case Revisited, with Added Twists

Stephanie

Let us return to Stephanie, whom we met earlier in this chapter. You may remember that she is twenty-nine months old and has lived since age three months with a foster family who wants to adopt her. Because of system overload, permanency planning did not occur in a timely manner. As initally presented, the question was posed as to whether there would be less harm in legalizing this child's present placement or if she should, at the request of her imprisoned father, be placed with relatives whom she had never met. When we initially considered Stephanie's case we indicated that longtime parent-child relationships should take precedence over genetic ties alone.

Now let us add another feature to this case. Would we change our recommendations if Stephanie's birth mother is of Euro-American heritage while her father is Afro-American? Although we might agree that biracial children are best served by being raised by Afro-American families, what would be the message to Stephanie about the importance of relationships vs. racial identity if she were removed from the only family she knows to be placed with her Afro-American relatives? List the pro's and con's of each decision in this situation.

Let's stretch our value prioritizing by adding another factor. Let us say that Stephanie has a brother, Clayton, who is four-and-a-half. They are living together in their foster home. The foster parents want to adopt both children. Clayton has a different father, one of Euro-American descent. Will you opt to leave both children with the current family? Will you advocate that Clayton be adopted by the foster family, but that Stephanie be placed with the Afro-American relatives? List advantages and disadvantages for each decision. Which decision do you now think is least harmful?

What changes might there be in the process if, instead of Stephanie's father being of Afro-American descent, he is a registered member of a Native American tribe. The relatives being considered live on the reservation and could adequately meet the needs of both children. Should Clayton move with her to the reservation? Again, list the advantages and disadvantages, including the underlying messages that each decision conveys to the children.

Finally, to one last time encourage ourselves to look at our own prejudices, we are once again going to change the facts in Stephanie and Clayton's case. This time we are going to imagine that Stephanie's father is Afro-American while Clayton's father is Euro-American. The agency responsible for them is strongly committed to keeping siblings together and to placing children in same-race families. They have both black and white foster families available. In fact, they have a biracial couple with an Afro-American father and a Euro-American mother who provide foster care. Where do you place the children and why?

What have you learned about your own personal biases?

Carlita
Sharita

Carlita, ten, and her sister, Sherita, eight, are growing up in different adoptive homes. The adoption worker, who originally placed the children together in an adoptive home, has conflicted feelings about the decision that was subsequently made to move one of the girls. However, she realizes that these feelings reflect her own biases rather than the girls' needs.

The sisters were born to a biracial mother, Carla. Her long-term partner, Sherman, an Afro-American man, was listed as the father on the birth certificates of both girls. The family lived in a black neighborhood. Carla and Sherman were both using drugs. The girls entered interim care when they were six and four. They were quite dependent upon each other. They both thought of themselves as black. They were placed together in an Afro-American foster home.

Carlita physically resembles Sherman. However, by the time Sherita was three it became apparent to everyone that Sherman was not her birth father. Sherita has lighter skin than anyone else in the family and Euro-American, as opposed to Afro-American, features. Carla had had a brief liaison with a white man during a week-long separation from Sherman.

When Sherita started kindergarten a year after placement, she became quite confused. The Afro-American children at her school rejected her, viewing her as white. On visits with Carla and Sherman their preference for Carlita was evident. Sherita received a white doll at a Christmas party for foster children. Carla's comment, when Sherita was clinging to the doll during a visit, was, "Where did you get that ugly white doll?" Subsequently, Sherita told her caseworker, "I'm not pretty like my sister cause she's black."

When the girls became legally free for adoption, a racially mixed home with an Afro-American father and a Euro-American mother, was selected for Carlita and Sherita. The family had two children by birth. They lived in a middle class, racially integrated neighborhood.

Sherita and Shannon, the adoptive mother, quickly became very emotionally close. However, over the next year, Carlita became increasingly depressed. It was soon clear to all that she desparately wanted to live in an Afro-American neighborhood in a family with a black mother—even if it meant living apart from her sister. After an interim placment in a bridge family, Carlita was placed with an Afro-American adoptive family. Sherita has remained in the racially mixed adoptive family that had originally been selected for the girls.

The sisters see each other whenever they wish. They occasionally talk about missing each other. However, after three years, it is apparent to all that the decision to separate the sisters, to meet their differing needs in terms of racial heritage, is the one that is least detrimental for both girls.

"Everything youngsters do or say, either behaviorally or in words, signals to us why they're doing what they're doing. They do it because at some time it worked. We need to find out how they can have that need or feeling taken care of. We're not trying to change what they think or how they feel. We're not trying to tell them they shouldn't need what they need. All we're trying to do is tell them they deserve to not have a hard time getting their thoughts and needs and feelings addressed in an appropriate way."

Claudia Jewett-Jarrett
as quoted in Working with Older Adoptees
Eds. Coleman et al, 1988

In Chapter Six we will be looking at ways to go about decoding children's signals to us, and ways to help them get their needs met, and feelings addressed so that behavioral changes can be accompanied by continued psychological growth and maturation.

CHAPTER 6

Behavior Problems

Children in care demonstrate a wide variety of problems. Some have never learned to trust adults. Others have never learned appropriate autonomy. Some have developmental delays. Most give evidence of the underlying problems by their behavior. Birth parents, foster parents, and adoptive parents turn to professionals for help in handling difficult behaviors. This chapter addresses the management of behaviors that commonly occur in children in placement. The emphasis is on helping the child by creating an environment that meets his underlying needs. Many times this means providing the child with a variety of opportunities for re-education. Children in interim care frequently need to experience adult-child relationships different from those they have known in the past.

The impact of day-to-day experiences on a child's behavior is powerful. Perceptions of the world in general, of his own worth, and of the nature of parent-child relationships are all primarily gained through day in, day out interactions. Events, such as separation, loss, or illness that lead to emotional stress may modify or interfere with old pathways of learning and divert the child's energies.

This chapter has four major sections. The first describes an overall perspective on behavior management. It introduces the various child management techniques that will be implemented in more detail in the second section. Section II provides a framework for analyzing behavior problems. It is the heart of the chapter, and as such contains many examples. A variety of underlying causes of behavior problems are identified and paired with different behavior management approaches.

The Post Adoption Family Therapy study reported by Prew, et al (1990) lists the most common behavioral problems seen, following adoption, in children served by this project. Behaviors that were listed as occurring in over 70% of the population included: lack of cause and effect thinking, 83; superficially engaging and charming, 82; tunes out, withdraws, won't listen, 80; uses affection to manipulate, 75; lack of eye contact on parental terms, 74; and lies about the obvious, 74%.

These are representative of the behaviors discussed in Sections III and IV which look at some specific behavior problems that are particularly common among children in placement. Section III explores the behaviors commonly seen in children with attachment difficulties while Section IV looks at behavior problems secondary to problems processing information and learning.

I Principles of Behavior Management

Behavior problems in children have a variety of origins. Commonly, problem behaviors represent an expression, inappropriate though it may be, of underlying emotions. Others may be evidence of a child's delayed development. For example, a child of five may express negativism in a way that would have been appropriate at two but is problematic at five. Some behavior problems occur because of distortions in the child's perception of normal adult-child relationships, or because of unresolved separation or loss issues. These problems are common in fostercare, when children have in the past received uneven parenting and where important attachments are often abruptly severed.

Visual or auditory perceptual difficulties may underlie problem behaviors. A child may be in constant control issues with adults. This may come about either because of developmental or tempermental factors or they may be secondary to the child's basic perception of the adult-child relationship as adversarial in nature. Sometimes, behavior patterns that begin for any of the above reasons persist because they have become a habit. Finally, some children have serious psychiatric disturbances. Successful management of a particular behavior depends upon the underlying cause. For example, if the child's behavior occurs because he is "stuck" at a particular stage of development, then the sensible approach to managing his behavior is to meet these earlier developmental needs. This will free him up to continue to grow and change. On the other hand, if the behavior is an inappropriate expression of emotions, the child needs to learn new ways to express old feelings.

A behavior in one child does not necessarily have the same cause as the same behavior in another youngster. For example, running away may reflect a variety of underlying causes, such as unresolved loss or inappropriate expression of emotions. An intervention that is successful in one case may be ineffective, or even escalate the problem, in another child whose behavior stems from an entirely different cause. Or, a particular behavior pattern may stem from several interrelated factors. Caseworkers need to become expert in collaborating with families to accurately assess the roots of undesirable behaviors and select effective approaches for intervening.

In general, it doesn't help to ask a child why he was involved in any negative behavior. The child's reaction to this question is usually defensive. He will say whatever he thinks will get the adult off his back. Supportively said, "I wonder if you know why you did that," or, "Do you know why you did that?" are much better than accusatory, "Why did you do it?" If the child indicates that he doesn't know the reason behind his behavior the adult can suggest that neither she nor the child separately know but that by working together they can probably determine the cause.

In assessing any misbehavior it is important for adults to pay attention to specifics. When does this behavior occur? Frequency and intensity are important to note. Can any precursors to the specific behavior be identified? For example, some behaviors might be noted only after visits with a birth parent. As pointed out in an earlier chapter this does not necessarily mean that the visits should be discontinued, but it does provide a clue as to the area of concern—feelings about contact and separation and loss—that must be addressed. Is there an overall pattern to the behavioral problem? Who usually is present, or not present, at the time of the misbehavior? What is the reaction of others, particularly parents? Does this reaction seem to increase or decrease the problem behavior? Are there times when adults expected the undesired behavior to occur but it did not? The answers to these questions help clarify both the underlying causes of misbehaviors and suggest effective interventions.

General Environmental Needs

The most helpful intervention for children with any type of behavior problem, regardless of the cause, is providing a living environment which encourages growth. For this to occur, the child must feel physically and psychologically safe and his underlying needs must be met. The child's daily living experiences provide opportunities for him to have his needs met and to learn more about himself.

This does not negate the fact that many children may need other therapy as well. Some need psychotherapy, some need speech therapy, some need help in gross motor activities, and many need special academic programs.

All children, however, need love and nurturing from a family. They need a basic sense of safety. Additionally, they need parents to have appropriate expectations for them and to place controls on their behaviors. Finally, they look to their family for role modeling.

All children deserve to believe that they are loved. It is the everyday happenings in a child's life that provide this. When the child is hungry, someone feeds him. When he is tired, he is tucked in bed. He is comforted when troubled. He has opportunies to play. These things happen not because the child has been good, but because these things are good for children. Parents initiate many positive interactions with the child. When the child participates in spontaneous positive interactions, he feels worthwhile and lovable. It is precisely when adults and children alike least deserve love that they need it most.

A disadvantage to an overall behavior modification approach in raising children is that it depends on the child initiating interactions, either by his good or bad behaviors. The child is in charge of what happens to him. However, the child who is always misbehaving needs more positive interactions and show of affection the child who is usually well-behaved, and a behavior modification program does not provide for this. It poses special problems for the children in care who do not believe that they deserve to have good things happen to them. They are likely to convince adults that they are undeserving of love, affection, and positive gratification rather than vice versa.

Though one may think that children detest controls, according to one expert in child development, "No discipline feels like being on the wrong road without a map or directions" (Hymes, 1969). Reasonable limits are not only necessary, but indeed are welcomed by the child. Several years ago a preschool established a playground without visible boundaries. The staff did not want to inhibit the children. A small number of the children wandered off, determined to go until someone stopped them. However, the surprising result of the experiment was not that a few children went an unreasonable distance, but that most of the children seemed to fear going too far. They stayed much closer to the building than they would have had there been a fence.

Just as children are reassured by visible physical boundaries on the playground, so all children are reassured if they know the limits that adults are placing on their behaviors. Most children want to please their parents. They can't do this if they don't know what the expectations are. When appropriate limits are set, a great worry is removed from the child's shoulders. He can move about, explore, and try out new behaviors, knowing that if he gets out of line, his parents will tell him. He is made freer, rather that more inhibited by these limits.

In addition to needing love and limits, all children need to be exposed to adults who model appropriate behaviors. How can a child learn self-control from a parent who has not yet mastered this skill? Parents teach children by what they do, not what they say. The parent who makes a mistake with a child and says, "I goofed," teaches the child that it is not the end of the world when someone errs and that most mistakes can be rectified. The parent who models appropriate ways to deal with frustration teaches the child how to cope. The parent who demonstrates both positive and negative feelings in direct and appropriate ways teaches the child about expressing the range of emotions. The parent who shows his love for the child physically and verbally teaches the child what love is and how to love in return.

Children who have been abused, neglected, or have had other problems in their relationships with parents need extra doses of good parenting. They are more susceptible to further damage from poor parenting practices than the child who has experienced healthier parent-child relationships. For these children, when they enter care, we need to select families that provide optimum environments with both emotional nurturing and reasonable limits.

Children in placement have an opportunity to experience alternate forms of adult-child relationships. This is particularly important for the child who has unmet needs or who has experienced dysfunctional patterns of family interaction. In the new setting there is an opportunity for a re-education process to occur. Since reducing resistances to change and re-education are two major components of therapy, placement in an alternate setting indeed becomes a therapeutic tool for treatment of these children. Families become part of the healing process.

Families may, or may not, see this as a positive aspect of their role with children. However, the reality is that either opportunities for re-education occur or the old, unhealthy patterns will be reinforced in the new setting. Families are not neutral settings. The goal is for the family to help the child to change his perceptions of family life and develop healthier modes of relating. The alternative is that the young person will be successful in getting the family to accept and reinforce his dysfunctional behaviors. He will be successful in getting current caregivers to treat him in the manner of previous parents. They, too, will become either non-nurturing, neglectful, abusive, or rejecting. In order to avoid this, caregivers in the new setting need to have a clear picture of what they want in their relationship with this child. Then they must identify and implement strategies for the re-education process.

Abused and neglected children usually need relearning experiences in a variety of different areas. In many instances the children have perceived, for whatever reasons, the adult-child relationship as an adversarial one, in which there are winners and losers. From the child's viewpoint, parent-child relationships may be fraught with danger. They may have learned to view interpersonal interactions in terms of control. A major goal in placement is to help the young person recognize that adult-child relationships can be beneficial to both.

Many children in care do not perceive themselves as capable or worthy of success. Numerous opportunities for achievement and change must be provided to help these youngsters increase, and then internalize, feelings of self-worth. They may need to increase both their physical and psychological self-care skills. Emotionally and behaviorally these children may not have learned appropriate ways to have fun, or to experience positive feelings about themselves and others in this context.

The first step in the re-education process is for adults to sort out the child's psychological and developmental needs, to identify areas in which the youngster is "stuck," or fixated, in terms of emotional development, and to identify his misperceptions and maladaptive patterns. The second step is to devise strategies for overcoming resistances, meeting needs, and providing the relearning experiences. Many times caregivers will need help accomplishing both of these processes.

What Is Discipline? How Does It Work?

Discipline helps children stay within reasonable behavioral limitations and enhances self-esteem by helping a child meet expectations. The distinction between descipline and punishment is an important one. Punishment is usually initiated to alleviate the adult frustration while the primary goal of discipline is to help the child meet expectations.

Keith

Keith, eleven, had been repeatedly beaten by his birth father when he misbehaved. He joined the Kowalski family by adoption several months ago. His adoptive father has used a single swat on the buttocks as part of his disciplinary repertoire with his three birth children. He believes that it is important to treat his adopted son no differently than the birth children.

When Keith breaks a rule that he has previously demonstrated that he knows and understands, he gets a spanking. However, recently, his adoptive father noticed that when he went to spank Keith, the latter became nearly frozen, showing no affect. He did not seem to hear what his dad was saying.

Mr. Kowalski started thinking about why spankings had seemed to work with his birth children. He realized that, when successful, they interrupted misbehaviors and got the child's attention. This was not happening with Keith. He became less, rather than more, attentive. Mr. Kowalski recognized that the physical discipline was causing Keith's feelings about his birth father to echo once again. He now understood why the caseworker had recommended against physical discipline with Keith—not because it was wrong *per se* but because it was ineffective and harmful to the newly evolving relationship. He decided that it made sense to use different disciplinary strategies with Keith.

Discipline that works well with most children sometimes is ineffective when used with children with attachment problems. Most of the widely accepted child management techniques are based on two premises. The first is that the child has a normal attachment to his parents and wants to keep them emotionally close. He learns that he can do this by pleasing them. Second, most children, even those with poor self-esteem, believe, or at least hope, that they are deserving of good things happening to them. These premises have led to the development of a series of disciplinary techniques that are customarily used in our society. In general they create physical or emotional distance when the child misbehaves or provide rewards for good behaviors or take away privileges in response to misbehaviors. These techniques work quite well in children without severe attachment disorders and with reasonable feelings of self worth.

However, for many children in care closeness equals pain. Occasionally this reflects the pain of physical abuse. More frequently it signifies the psychological pain that accompanies separation experiences. A child may internalize, "Every time I start to love and trust, I move again." As protection from pain, these children create an emotional barrier between themselves and caregivers. Therefore, when parents use the techniques based on distancing children for their misbehaviors, such as sending them to their room or emotionally distancing them by ignoring or witholding affection, they may be giving the child precisely what he is seeking. Clearly, this is not going to encourage the child to change his behaviors. What the child is seeking—relief of pain—is not what is in his best interest. His long-term needs will be better met by learning that emotional connections do not universally lead to the pain of separation or loss.

Since many children in interim care have overwhelming feelings of rejection, it is important that the disciplinary techniques used with them do not reinforce these perceptions. The average child over four is not overwhelmed when sent to his room for discipline. However, for the child in foster care, being sent to his room may trigger and reinforce feelings of abandonment or rejection. They may interpret the discipline as, "This time you are being sent only as far as your room, but if you keep acting out you may be sent away from this home." Having these thoughts is enough to encourage some children to check out their perceptions by escalating misbehaviors. Messages that imply, "It's easier for you to be good and to be in control of yourself when you are close to me," work better than ones that imply, "No one wants a naughty child."

Some children with traumatic early life experiences do not believe that they deserve to have their basic needs met. They see themselves as undeserving of positive experiences and rewards. This is different than poor self-esteem. It reflects a real feeling of lack of self worth. Disciplines based on helping children earn rewards, such as, "You have to do your homework before you can go out with friends," or, "You must earn the privilege," are not effective with these children because they don't believe that they deserve good things. Some will start to earn the reward but then undermine it before completion. Others will give up before they even start.

What then are disciplines that do work with such children? Those who have not learned to be emotionally close respond best to having to remain physically close to an adult following misbehaviors. This might include restriction to a chair or specific area within the same room as the parent. In this way the emotional distance that these children seem to feel most comfortable with is not provided in response to misbehaviors. Instead, the message is, "No matter what you do, I want to be close and caring with you." Since most of these children also exhibit extremely poor self-control, adults are at the same time putting themselves in a position to provide the necessary external controls until the child can learn more self-discipline. The verbal focus should always be more on positive expectations than negative behaviors.

291

Children who see themselves as unworthy have never experienced the unconditional meeting of needs that teaches them that they are deserving. For these children, and particularly for adolescents with this problem, parents need to clearly identify the young person's legitimate needs and to provide unconditional giving in these areas. For example, teens cannot adequately accomplish the tasks of adolescence without peer relationships. Parents must insure that there are opportunities for this need to be met. Children who perceive themselves as unworthy need to learn that they do, indeed, deserve to have good things happen to them just because they are people, not because they have to earn it. At the same time, adults must help them learn that as grown-ups they will become totally responsible for making the good things happen for themselves. Islands of unearned gratification help achieve this balance. Some activities are protected. They are not used as a privilege to be denied following misbehaviors.

Ed

Ed, a seventh grader, had lived with his foster-adoptive family for two-and-a-half years. He was an A or F student. If he liked the subject and the teacher Ed got A's. Otherwise he refused to do any work and would get an F. Disruptive behaviors in the classroom were common. He was no longer allowed to ride the school bus because of physical fighting. At home, control issues occurred daily. Ed stole money from family members. He was on probation for shoplifting. The usual disciplinary techniques did not seem to work with Ed. If he was restricted his behaviors worsened. When programs were set up for him to earn privileges, he "blew it" just before attaining the goal.

In working with a therapist, a variety of strategies and consequences were devised for addressing the behavior problems. An island of strength for Ed was his athletic competence. He enjoyed sports and was not disruptive while involved in these activities. His family noted that sports provided a good outlet for his physical aggression and assertiveness. His behaviors while actively involved were not problematic. Parents and therapist agreed that this would be a protected area of gratification for Ed. No matter what his other behaviors in other settings were, he would be allowed to be involved in sports at the local recreation center. Athletic participation provided a physical outlet, an opportunity for peer interactions in a supervised setting with an acceptable peer group, and was an area in which Ed's feelings of capability and self worth were enhanced.

Sports participation remained a protected island of gratification throughout Ed's junior high years. However, when he reached high school he was able to maintain the grades and school related behaviors necessary for participation on school teams. By that time early life conflicts had resurfaced and been more successfully addressed. His foster-adoptive family had stuck with him through these very tumultuous years. Not only were there gains in behavioral control but academic performance had improved. Ed and his family were all ready to finalize his adoption.

Once a youth has experienced gratification and starts believing that he is deserving, adults can move to the more usual disciplinary techniques which involve some form of, "First you do this and then this will happen." Another approach is for the parent to align himself with the youth saying, "But you deserve to go to the dance—why don't you think you deserve it? How can we help you? Do you need help getting your homework done first? Could we, in the future, help you structure study time better? etc." This message combines the "first things first" approach with "you deserve good things and we will help you get them."

Methods of Managing Behavior Problems

In addition to providing an environment that enhances the child's growth, families of children in care need to be able to design specific approaches for addressing behavior problems. It is helpful for them to be familiar with a variety of approaches.

Good communication skills are invaluable to both caseworkers and parents. Parents need to be able to use "active listening," listening to feelings rather than to words (Gordon, 1971). The importance of using "I" messages rather than "you" messages to facilitate communication, raise self-esteem, and decrease defensiveness cannot be overstressed. Problem solving skills are mandatory for parents of children with behavioral problems. Conflict resolution methods are a life skill that children and adults alike need to master.

Although communications skills are important in child management, they are not sufficient for working with all problems. Those stemming from unmet developmental needs or those that have become habits need different interventions. The former need identification and support for meeting the needs and learning new, more mature, behaviors. Behavior modification approaches are most successful in interrupting habits. Behavior problems stemming from control issues must be addressed.

Logical consequences (Driekers, 1968) are especially useful with school age children and adolescents although variations can be used with younger children if the child's developmental capabilities and needs are kept in mind. Like logical consequences, providing the child with "two good choices" helps teach him responsibility for his actions. An example might be, "I would like it if you could go to the party Saturday, but our rule is schoolwork has priority. It is your choice. If you get your homework done before Saturday, then you can go to the party, or if you need more time to complete your assignments you can choose to skip the party."

Open-ended discipline fits with the concept of logical consequences. "You may not go out to play until your room is cleaned," is an example of open-ended discipline. It helps the child feel more autonomous. It makes him more responsible for his own behavior than does a statement such as, "Since you didn't clean your room, you are grounded for the day."

For the child in placement, we want to use disciplinary techniques that encourage relationship building, mutual trust, and increased self-esteem. Supportive control measures are designed to promote attachments, connect discipline with nurture and maintain behaviors within acceptable limits, while furthering self-control. Behaviors are viewed as helpful vs. non-helpful, in terms of the child being successful, rather than as good vs. bad *per se*. In general adults do not allow the child to use behaviors to maintain an emotional distance. Behavioral outbursts are seen as providing opportunities for the development of attachment rather than as something to be dreaded or avoided at all costs. The aim is to intervene early when problems are small and interventions can be low key. Individualization is connected to the needs of the child rather than to overt behaviors. When a child is out of control, adults will supply the necessary external controls until the child regains self-control. This is done not because adults want to take control of the child, but because it is too scary for anyone, adult or child, to feel out of control and have no one take charge.

Support and modeling for appropriate expression of feelings, as will be discussed further in the next section, is an example of a supportive control measure. Adults help the child articulate his emotions and learn to express them in ways that lead to his being in less, as opposed to more, trouble.

Rhythm and intensity control are other examples of supportive control measures. Individuals develop a characteristic rhythm to their responses to stress. Some slow down, becoming passive-aggressive or withdrawn, and may need help to get them more active, more in touch with their emotions, and better using their intellectual capacities. Others are so hyperactive that they cannot think or behave rationally. They may need brief periods of time-out to calm themselves and decide on a plan of action. Likewise with intensity. Some children seem oblivious to low-keyed interactions while others are paralyzed by loud, fast, or physically confrontive adult behaviors. To be effective with a child, the adult must recognize these traits and respond in a way that connects with the child and helps him become effective in managing his own behaviors.

Logical consequences and two good choices, as mentioned earlier, are two additional examples of supportive control measures. Environmental manipulation is frequently overlooked as a disciplinary measure, but can be very effective. It can involve simple things, such as providing a small stool for a child to climb on to reach a sink, or may involve more complex interventions, such as providing adequate supervision for the child who does not do well when out of sight of an adult.

Godfrey

Godfrey, six, pokes holes in furniture, draws on walls, and is otherwise destructive. His parents have labeled his behaviors as sneaky, since he does not indulge in them when an adult is present. His caseworker redefined the behaviors as seeking adequate supervision rather than as being sneaky. She helped the parents come up with an environmental intervention.

Together they talked to Godfrey about how things went for him when adults were not close by. He correctly identified these periods as not going well as he would get in trouble and his parents would become very angry with him. They then talked about how things went for him when adults were around. He acknowledged that he rarely got in trouble when parents were close by. The parents then told Godfrey that they liked it better when he wasn't in trouble and they weren't angry. Parents and child agreed that the easiest way to accomplish this was for them to remain within eyesight of one another.

Although environmental changes were made in the previous case, the social worker used an additional supportive control technique. For the parents she redefined Godfrey's negative behaviors (his destruction) as positive strivings (a desire and need to be physically close to an adult.) This technique is frequently combined with support for feelings while confronting behaviors. The negative behavior is redefined as an attempt to communicate an emotion. The affect is accepted and even praised, while the adult then helps the child acquire the skills necessary to express the feeling more productively.

Finally the One Minute Scolding, (Nelson,1984) is particularly well suited for children with attachment disorders, as it makes use of the theoretical concept in the arousal-relaxation cycle presented earlier. The one minute scolding combines confrontation of behaviors with affirmation of caring. For the first thirty seconds or so the adult states clearly and firmly, using an "I" message, that she does not approve of a specific behavior. This is combined, during the second half of the minute, with concern, caring, and optimism indicating that the adult wants to help the child find a better way of meeting his needs.

Brian and Joel, foster brothers, are doing the dishes together. Brian does his chores rapidly and well. Joel, on the other hand, has some organic impairment and is very disorganized. Brian is angry at Joel who is holding up completion of the task. Their foster father overhears Brian calling Joel a "stupid retard." Using a confronting tone, the foster father says to Brian, "I don't like it when you call Joel stupid. It sounds cruel and uncaring, as though you only care about yourself. I've tried to help you when you've had trouble with something like homework or talking to your birth mom about how you felt about being in care. It seems to me that I should be able to count on your help in doing the dishes with Joel without name calling. I get angry when I ask for something that simple and get no cooperation." Switching to a softer tone and more nurturing attitude, the foster dad goes on to say, "And you know, Brian, I think you can work cooperatively now. I've seen you make so much progress in other areas. You are always responsible about your chores. You do a great job looking good. I

Brian
Joel

enjoy being with you. I want to help you learn to get along better with other kids because I think it will help you make friends more easily. I know that's important to you and I want to help you with it. You mean a lot to me" (Fahlberg, et al, 1990).

Proponents of Brief Solution-Focused Therapy (Schaffer, 1988 and 1990) take a compatible approach when they focus on the times that the undesired behavior does not occur. The overriding principle of this form of therapy is a nonpathological view of families and children. It therefore focuses on the positives, rather than on negatives. Obviously, this helps raise both child and family's feelings of capability, and therefore their self-esteem.

A booklist for those particularly interested in behavior management techniques that are useful for the child in placement is at the end of this chapter.

II Selecting an Approach to Behavior Management

In selecting an approach to the management of behavior problems it is important to remember that the goal is to help the child. When children are successful in meeting expectations, parents will be less frustrated and less likely to become punitive. However, it is unlikely that any parent can always be therapeutic enough to use discipline, and never be frustrated enough to lapse into punishment. A reasonable goal is for parents to understand the difference between the two, and to work to maximize discipline and minimize punishment.

On the following page is a Discipline and Control Worksheet. This worksheet provides an outline for assessing the cause of behavior problems with responses. It is not meant to be used as a prescription. However, as adults are faced with specific behavioral problems, they can use the worksheet as a guide for assessing needs and determining the disciplinary techniques that have the best chance of success. Since a specific behavior may have different causes in different children, or even at varying times in the same child, errors in implementing disciplinary strategies are to be expected to occur on occasion. Mistakes in assessment usually become apparent when ineffective disciplinary techniques are instituted. If adults listen carefully to what a child says both verbally and behaviorally, the youngster will usually help clarify the disciplinary need.

Discipline & Control

Punishment is done to alleviate adult frustration.
Discipline is aimed at helping the childmeet expectations.
Supportive control defines the adult-child relationship as an alliance to the child's benefit.

Assess Disciplinary Need	Respond Appropriately
A. Inappropriate expression of feelings.	Permission to have feelings Modeling of appropriate expression Support the feelings Pushing for feelings when denial is used
1) unresolved separation issues	Go back over the facts and feelings about separation issues
B. Bad habits	Behavior modification approaches
C. Delayed development	Respond to developmental level- not chronological age
1) lack of experience	Teach Share Praise and support
D. Control issues	Sitting Two good choices Increase age- appropriate autonomy Holding
E. Lack of attachment (lack of trust, over- competence, over-affectionate, withdrawal, agression)	Working on building trust Re- parenting
1) delayed conscience	Use stages of normal conscience development
F. Behaviors secondary to misperceptions	Identify misperceptions and help child deal with these

Mina

Mina is 12. She is destructive, tearing up her own clothes and belongings. Her adoptive mother initially identified the behavior as an expression of anger. She started talking about anger, possible reasons for it, and more acceptable ways to discharge it. Mina's behaviors did not change and indeed she seemed to be becoming more emotionally distant. At this point, her mom asked herself about other possible causes of this behavior. She wondered if, instead of being angry, Mina believed that she did not deserve to have nice things. In retrospect, she realized that the destructive behaviors had more frequently followed shared good times, or success in some endeavor, than frustration and failure. At that point she switched her approach and focused instead on helping her daughter learn to accept good things and enjoy them.

Many behaviors have more than one possible cause and the possibility of more than one effective intervention. On the other hand, an approach that works well with one child might make no sense in the case of another. For example, bedwetting occurs for a variety of reasons. Many times it represents an unconscious reaction to anxiety or underlying fears and worries. During the denial stage of the grief process, when sleep disturbances are prominent, enuresis is frequently part of the pattern. However, many children with Attention Deficit Disorder are such sound sleepers that the sensation of a full bladder is not enough to awaken them. Other children have an entire symptom complex, discussed later in this chapter, indicating a lack of self awareness in a variety of areas. Occasionally, wetting might be secondary to the child's misperceptions as to the reasons for a previous separation or loss.

Charlotte

Charlotte is a developmentally delayed child who has lived with her current foster parents for four years. Although she is eight year -old, in general she is functioning at a four year level. Her foster parents have been having marital problems and Charlotte's case worker has decided that she is to be moved. Her foster mother is very opposed to the plan.

One day Charlotte wet her pants at school. This was very unusual for her. However, since some other students had fairly frequent accidents, the teachers were not particularly disconcerted. Charlotte, however, seemed very embarrassed, bursting out in tears. When she went home from school that day, her social worker was at the foster home. The latter told Charlotte that she would soon be moving. Later that evening, Charlotte, sobbing, came to her foster mother and said, "Honest, I promise I will never wet my pants again if only I can stay here." In Charlotte's mind the two events, the enuresis and the move, were cause and effect related. It will be important for the caseworker to help Charlotte in understanding that the move was not caused by the enuresis. Indeed, the wetting incident probably reflected the tension in the family.

Although some interventions may be effective no matter what the cause of the behavior, determining which of the underlying dynamics is present in the child may help us do a better job of addressing all of his needs.

Inappropriate Expression of Feelings

The single most common cause of undesirable behavior is an inappropriate expression of emotions. Children in care have many reasons to have feelings of anger, sadness, jealousy, fear, etc. Adults, as well as children, sometimes have difficulty discharging their feelings in ways that help, rather than hinder, them. Children in care frequently have been exposed to negative modeling from adults. The goal is to provide a relearning experience about the acceptability of feelings, but the unacceptability of certain behaviors.

It is possible to offer support for the child's underlying emotions while simultaneously confronting negative behaviors. For example, a child tears up a picture of his birth parent after he returns from a visit. If the foster parent says, "You shouldn't do that; that is naughty," the child receives the message that his feelings are bad. This response is quite likely to reinforce the child's thinking that he is bad and that it is his fault he is in foster care. On the other hand, if the foster parent accepts the child's feeling but not his behavior, she might respond, "I know that you are angry about not being able to be at home with your parents. That's understandable. I would be angry too. However, I think there might be some better ways to express your anger than by tearing up the photo. What would be some other things you could do when you are angry about not being at home?" This response gives the child permission to have strong feelings while helping him to explore alternative behaviors.

Adult modeling is a critical aspect of the child's learning. Parents need to look at their own modes of expressing emotions. Are only certain emotions openly expressed in the family and others covered over? Do adult males show anger but not sadness? What happens when a child does express anger openly to an adult? The view of most children is that when they get angry at an adult that adult gets more angry at them. Parents need to identify what it is that a child may say and do when he is angry at a parent—things that won't get him, the child, in more trouble.

Though one often thinks that a child who expresses his feelings with undesirable behaviors must be angry or frustrated, he is just as likely to be sad, lonely, or afraid. In fact, anger is frequently a cover for other more painful emotions, such as loneliness or fear (Gordon, 1971). Occasionally a child may even act out because of excitement or happiness. A variety of examples which demonstrate the range of emotions that can be expressed in problematic ways follows.

Behaviors associated with parental visits frequently indicate unresolved grief and many times are an indicator that contact should be maintained or increased rather than decreased. However, along with the continued contact foster parents and caseworkers need to help the child learn more appropriate behavioral outlets for their anger, sadness, and loyalty conflicts.

Exaggerating how wonderful life in the past was, or stealing from a foster family to give to birth family members, are two other behavior problems indicative of unresolved separation and loss issues. Running away, involving running back to someone and some place, is another behavioral indicator of unresolved grief.

However, sometimes both running away and stealing reflect different problems. Children run away for a variety of other reasons. Some children run away to express their feelings. They run when they become angry, or when they feel sad or lonely. Some children, particularly adolescents, in order to protect themselves and/or others, need to get away from people whenever they have strong feelings. In these cases the family and youngster can decide together where he can go and how long he can be gone, identifying it as "cooling off" rather than running away. Some children have run away so frequently that it has become a habit. Some children who run away are giving the parent a "love test." The test is, "Do you love me enough to come and get me? Do you really want me here?" For this reason parents of pre-teens should always try to retrieve the child, even if ultimately there will subsequently be a planned move because of the behavioral disturbances.

Most children in care have a time of day or night that they are particularly prone to thinking about the past and worrying about the future. To avoid the pain of these thoughts, it is common at this time for the child to become very active. These children need to learn an alternative that involves having them use the tension to facilitate building relationships with others. For many, their lonely time of day is at bedtime. These children come up with a variety of excuses not to go to bed and a variety of behaviors that frequently end up getting them in more trouble rather than providing relief for their loneliness. They end up feeling more, rather than less, distant from others. When there is a pattern of frequent bedtime problems, parents might want to use this period as a time for focused positive interactions with the child. They might want to develop a ritual which includes physical and emotional closeness as part of the bedtime routine.

For other children, their lonely time of day is early in the morning when they awaken ahead of others and start thinking about past and future. Again, a solution that keeps them busy in an acceptable way needs to be found. Some children awaken in the night, possibly to go to the bathroom, and then have trouble getting back to sleep. For some the loneliest time is right after school, as we will see in Stan's case later in this section.

The large number of children in out-of-home care who have problems coping with their own frustrations should not be surprising. Given their life histories, they have more reasons than most to be angry. In addition, in general they have had fewer opportunities to learn the life skills necessary for adequately coping with frustration. The birth parents of many children in care have problems in coping with frustration and anger in ways that are not harmful to themselves, their children, or relationship building. Many act out their anger and frustration, abusing children. Others, trying to escape strong emotions physically or emotionally, are unavailable to their children. Drugs and alcohol are frequently used to counteract anger and frustration.

Additional problem behaviors commonly seen in children in care also may reflect inappropriate expression of feelings. The child who is physically aggressive may need to learn new and more acceptable ways to show anger or frustration. On the other hand, this child might be using aggression to keep people distanced.

People have tantrums when they have a great need or desire, an inability to achieve this need, and are unable to appropriately express their frustration. Temper tantrums may occur in normal children between ages one and three, and again at ages five-and-a-half and six-and-a-half. At these ages the child's perceptions of the world and his ability to cope with it do not mesh well, and he experiences considerable frustration. The focus of the parent's efforts should be on helping the child learn to release his frustration appropriately.

When the child is in the middle of a tantrum, he cannot process sensory input well so it does little good to talk to him then. If he is not hurting himself or anyone else during the tantrum, the parent might ignore it. If he is hurting himself or someone else, then the parent must physically control him. However, no matter what is done during the tantrum, at the end of a it the child is open to being close and to learning new ways to express his frustration. This is the time for a parent to talk to the child about alternative behavior and then have the child practice the behavior right then and there. Some parents are hesitant to be close to a child at the end of a tantrum for fear of reinforcing negative behavior. However, this is precisely the time when the child has a desperate need for acceptance as a person.

A superficial smile is another example of inappropriate expression of an underlying feeling. Most often the fake smile expresses anxiousness, uncertainty, or embarrassment. Some children smile to cover up sadness or anger as well. These children need permission and encouragement to express their emotions more appropriately. Many of them are not yet truly aware of their underlying feelings, however, and they may need to be taught to identify as well as to express them.

Some children cope with strong emotions by denying them. These children may need to be given permission to express feelings in a structured situation such as a therapy session. Sometimes the worker or parent can make use of a time when the child can legitimately be angry in order to uncover his strong feelings. Children who strive to be perfect maintain their facade by working at a slow pace even in circumstances when they could be legitimately frustrated or angry. They frequently talk very softly, they may mumble, or leave out words. They may have difficulty expressing their own desires. Since one of the major defenses these children use is moving and talking at a slow pace, "rhythm" control is an effective way to interrupt their perfection. Adults talking rapidly with a demanding voice and getting them active by running or exercising with them frequently helps these children assert themselves so they can say "NO" or "I'm mad at you."

Tara

Tara was a child who never asserted herself. She got up in the morning and quickly made both her own and her brother's bed and straightened both rooms. When given choices, she always responded, "I don't know." She was so good that it was difficult for her adoptive mother to feel close to her.

Her younger brother started to dislike her because, in his words, "She never gets into trouble." Her teachers thought she was wonderful and had made "such a good adjustment" to her recent adoption. However, they were concerned that she worked so slowly in school that she was falling behind. Whenever her mother asked that Tara sit on her lap, she did so in a stiff manner, with a plastic smile on her face.

The goal in treatment was first to encourage Tara to express some appropriate anger toward the therapist in her parents' presence and subsequently some anger about the past events in her life as her Lifebook was reviewed, again with her parents' participation. In this way Tara had an opportunity to see that her parents could both accept and understand her underlying anger.

"Homework" was given. If Tara could show appropriate autonomy such as by saying, "I don't want to do that," she didn't have to. One parent would confront Tara, while the other would support her in asserting herself. On another occasion the parents would reverse roles, the one who previously confronted becoming the supporter.

Interestingly, her younger brother's behavior improved as Tara learned to be normally "naughty." He was delighted when he could report, "Guess what? Tara got in trouble for not picking up her room this week!"

To detemine the emotion underlying a behavior an adult might use visual imagery to help the child identify how he felt before a specific incident. The child is asked to close his eyes and imagine himself just before he misbehaved. Where was he? What was he doing? Who else was around? Once the adult is certain that the child is actively involved in the memory she asks, "Okay, right now, just before you (whatever the misbehavior was) how were you feeling, happy? sad? lonely? mad? scared?" If the child is really engrossed in the visual imagery, the word for the emotion usually pops out without the child taking time to think.

In the following case, visual imagery was used to try to determine the emotion underlying fire setting. Although traditionally this behavior has been linked to underlying anger or sexuality, young children are frequently lonely and depressed when they set fires.

Stan

Stan was eight. He had been in fostercare for several years. Parental rights had been terminated. His foster parents were considering adopting him, but they hesitated because of concern about his behavior problems. For instance, Stan had come home from school on several occasions and set small fires in the garage.

Stan had fairly severe learning problems. School was not very rewarding for him. His foster mother had a part-time job and was usually not present when he came home from school. An elderly woman babysat Stan after school. However, her favorite television program was on at the time that he returned home.

When Stan was led through visual imagery and asked about his feelings the last time he set a fire, the word that came forth was "lonely." He then looked very sad, started crying, and talked about how he "did not belong at school or home."

Once his foster mom found out that Stan was especially vunerable to feelings of loneliness right after school, she rearranged her work schedule so that she usually could be home at that time. On days that this was not possible, she gave Stan extra attention in the morning and left an, "I love you" note with a special after-school snack for his return. (Instead of changing her work schedule, she might have provided other care with focused high quality interactions after school.)

Stan set no more fires. Subsequently his foster parents adopted him. Since the family had been able to help Stan with this fairly serious problem, they felt confident in their ability to work together to overcome his other problems.

Habits

Behavior modification seems to be the most useful discipline for behaviors that have become habits. When the child himself sees a behavior as a problem and wants to change, a foundation for behavior modification efforts is laid. This approach is less useful when there is no desire on the child's part to change the behavior or when addressing problems reflective of unmet needs.

In general, behavior modification works better when used to increase, rather than decrease, a behavior. If a child is rewarded for a behavior, he has control over the amount of reinforcement he gets. On the other hand, using behavior modification to decrease a behavior requires establishing a time span during which a behavior is not to occur for a reward to be earned. It's easier for parents to praise a child's good behavior than to comment positively on the absence of a bad behavior. Frequently this means adults must be creative in devising a plan in which performance of a positive behavior automatically precludes a negative behavior.

Rachel lived in a foster home when she was between twelve and thirty months. Unfortunately, during this time her foster parents did not hold, carry, or rock her. She started to rock herself at any time and in any place.

Rachel

After Rachel joined her adoptive family, her parents tried to satisfy her unmet needs by providing her with lots of close physical contact. The rocking behavior disappeared during the daytime, but at bedtime she continued to get on her hands and knees and rock herself to sleep.

The behavior now seemed to be a habit and a behavior modification approach for the problem was designed. Rachel's parents rewarded her when she remembered to cuddle her favorite baby doll, rocking her to sleep in her arms. Cuddling the doll precluded her self-rocking on her hands and knees. A positive behavior was reinforced, and a negative behavior altered.

Bed wetting, as noted earlier, may be a habit or may indicate anxiety or lack of self-awareness, or there may be an underlying medical cause. Although behaviors such as whining, nailbiting, handwringing, hair twisting, or picking at face or fingers frequently start out as expressions of underlying anxiety, they soon become habits and usually respond well to behavior modification.

Jamie

Jamie, nine, whined when making requests of his parents, when reporting interactions with peers and when responding to questions. His parents found this to be a very irritating habit. Siblings and friends frequently imitated him, leading to an escalation in the problem. Jamie, himself, seemed totally oblivious to his own tone of voice.

The parents set up a behavior modification program. First they developed an alliance with their son around solving the problem. For the first few days of the program the parent would say, "Listen," each time Jamie whined. If he then repeated what he had said in a normal tone, he was awarded a point. Points were accumulated to be turned in for rewards that Jamie had selected. After a few days, the parents switched to a nonverbal cue, pulling on their ear lobe. Usually, with the cueing, Jamie was able to repeat his verbalization without whining. If he did not the parents ignored his comments or questions.

Within a couple of weeks, Jamie was able to move to the final step of the modification program. He was still awarded a single point each time he responded to the nonverbal cue. However, every time he caught himself and switched his tone on his own he received two points.

Clinging is an example of a behavior that commonly has two underlying causes. Although it usually reflects early unmet needs, the behavior itself has frequently become a habit. The child needs to learn that he will receive at least as much attention when he does not cling as when he does. To help him change, the parent may focus on one recurrent bothersome situation in which the behavior is prominent. For example, if a child clings to his mother whenever a neighbor comes over for a cup of coffee the mother might say to the child, "I know that you want attention when Mrs. Jones comes over. However, this is my time with her, and I find that I get angry with you when you cling and interrupt. I would rather spend fun time with you than time nagging you. How about making a bargain? When Mrs. Jones comes over, we will time how long you can go without clinging or interrupting? Then I will pay you back that time playing a game with you as soon as she leaves."

This approach allows the child to choose whether to get attention negatively or positively. The parent can help the child take responsiblility for the choice by asking, "Did you make a good choice or a bad choice about getting attention today?" or "How do you feel about the choice you made?" However, it should be remembered that preschoolers may not be able to delay as their needs are frequently too great to allow for postponing attention even this long.

Soiling is another behavior that usually needs a dual approach. In general, children with encopresis stain or soil their clothing rather than having an entire bowel movement. Encopresis commonly accompanies repressed anger. It occurs most frequently in children who tend to be stubborn or withholding. However, the child is usually unaware of the connection between fecal soiling and anger. He does not engage in the behavior "on purpose." The connection is usually unconscious rather than conscious. Soiling is seen with some frequency in children who have been sexually abused, particularly in those who have experienced anal intercourse. Some of these children have had physical damage to the sphincter muscles. Others defended themselves against pain by learning to block out sensory messages from that part of their body.

Behavior management techniques can be used to help the child overcome soiling. However, if the parent overreacts to the soiling this approach won't work. Frequently it needs to be someone other than the parent who gets the child to agree to work on the problem and cooperate with a behavioral program. Most children with encopresis desperately want to get over the problem, but most, because of adults implying that the behavior is purposeful, believe that change is unlikely.

Children with this problem frequently retain stool, become constipated, and leak around it. Foods such as raisins, prunes, or those high in fiber may make a significant difference in handling the problem. Physiologically, it is easiest for children to have a bowel movement right after eating. The child with encopresis needs to be encouraged to go the bathroom directly after each meal and sit on the toilet for a few minutes, say three to five. Positive reinforcement is provided every time there is any stool in the toilet. If he doesn't have a bowel movement nothing happens. If the child over five has an accident, he can be responsible for rinsing out his underwear and putting it in a specified place. For children between three and five, the parent can provide a diaper pail in which the child can place the soiled underwear.

If a parent can tell by smell that it is likely that the child has soiled underwear, it is more useful to ask him to go change clothes than to ask if he has soiled. Since it is common for a child with this problem to hide his soiled underwear, it is helpful if the parent asks the child each day if he remembered to put any soiled underwear into the wash. If the child perceives the parents as helping him to attain his goal of stopping soiling, it improves his relationship with his parents.

Developmental Delays

Although some children in foster care are significantly developmentally delayed, many more have uneven development. Although these children may be functioning at age level in some areas, in others they are "stuck" at earlier stages. Adults may label their immature behaviors as problems. Instead, parents need to respond to the child at the developmental level he exhibits rather than to his chronological age. This approach helps the child outgrow such problems by satisfying underlying needs.

Peer skills are a commonly seen example of a specific delay. Problems in this area occur most often when children have not had their early needs for dependency and autonomy met. They may not have learned to share, or to play with others. These children need to be actively taught how to relate to others. Parents can play games with the child who has difficulty losing. This is much more helpful than discussions about the virtue of being a graceful loser. Children who have difficulty making and keeping friends need practice in making those relationships, not protection from them. The helpful parent will encourage such a child to invite others over. She can then be watchful and, if things don't go well, can help the child alter his behavior to produce a desirable result. Some school social workers conduct groups with the primary purpose of teaching children relationship skills.

Fears which are common for an earlier age, but unusual at the child's current age, represent another common example of a problem behavior secondary to developmental issues.

Andrew

Ten-year-old Andrew had been in and out of foster care since he was four-years-old. He had recently moved to a new foster home. Andrew was fearful of monsters and the dark. His foster mother, recognizing that these fears typically occurred at a younger age, decided to address them as she would in a four or five-year-old. One evening at dinner she presented Andrew with a night light. He was embarrassed rather than reassured and refused to use it.

When the foster mother reported this to the caseworker, the latter suggested they review a summary of normal child development together. In the process, his foster mother realized that although Andrew had the fears of a four or five year old, he had the sensitivity about being singled out that is normal for a ten year old. Children this age are likely to be embarrassed when praised or reprimanded in front of others.

306

Subsequently his foster mom took Andrew aside and apologized for embarrassing him at the dinner table. She consulted privately with him about how she could help him cope with his fear of the dark. He decided that maybe the night light would help after all.

Developmental delays may be secondary to lack of experience. For example, although most children of ten understand very well what their parents mean when they say, "I want you to clean your room," children in foster care may never have been taught how to make a bed or where to put dirty clothes. When in doubt, the focus should be on teaching the child and on initially sharing responsibility with him. Positive behavior is praised and supported. After teaching the skills necessary for accomplishing the task a behavior modification approach may be instituted to reward performance of the desired behavior.

Young children who have been sexually abused in one home often attempt to interact with new parental figures in the same way that they interacted with the sexually abusive ones. This is particularly true if the child viewed sexual interactions as demonstrations of caring and affection. This child needs to learn ways to be physically close to parents in a non-sexual way. Once again, the focus needs to be on what the child needs to learn, rather than on what he should not do.

In Exercise 6-2 we will return to Dawn, the sexually abused child we met in an earlier chapter, and develop a plan of re-parenting that will address her sexually provocative behaviors in a non-judgemental way. The McNamara (1990) and Minshew (1990) resources listed in the bibliography provide further information on using family settings to facilitate the healing for the sexually abused child.

6-2 *Exercise*

Reparenting the Sexually Abused Pre-Schooler

Dawn

Dawn, four, and her mother lived with the maternal grandparents. Dawn was sexually abused by her grandfather. This was done primarily with enticement rather than threats or physical force. Grandpa told her she was the most special person in his life and that they could share some wonderful secrets. The sexual contact consisted initially of Grandpa fondling Dawn's genitals. It then progressed to her fondling Grandpa's penis and finally to oral-genital contact.

When Dawn was placed in foster care she was sexually provocative with her foster father. She would crawl up on his lap and masturbate against him; she would touch him in the genital area; she would try to unzip his fly. Dawn viewed these interactions as "normal." She had not learned any other ways for forming a relationship with an adult male. She would have to be reparented, actively taught new ways to interact.

1. Using the parent messages on pg 387-389, identify the messages that Dawn probably received from her grandfather.
2. What messages do adults want her to continue to receive? How might they provide them in a healthier way?
3. When she is sexually provocative with her foster father, what could he say and do that would be helpful to her growth? What role might the foster mom play?

Control Issues

The relationship between parent and child is supposed to be an alliance that benefits both rather than a competition for control. Parents are responsible for modeling this. Many disturbed families are very concerned with power. These families look at relationships in terms of who has power over whom, rather than seeing them as ways for two or more people each to get their individual needs met simultaneously.

Many children who enter foster care come from power-oriented families. Commonly these children have trouble with issues related to who is in control. Additionally, many of the children in care were separated from their parents during the toddler years. They may never have completed the normal developmental struggle for autonomy which is primary at this stage.

The supportive approach to control issues is twofold. First, the adult demonstrates to the child that he does not lose when he complies with reasonable demands, but instead that everyone wins. Second, the adult provides as many opportunities for the child to be autonomous as is appropriate, given the child's age.

Unfortunately, because these children tend to see encounters with parents as battles in which someone wins and someone loses, adults frequently end up seeing them in the same way. The parent may fall prey to the desire to gain more and more control over a child and see the child's every attempt to assert his autonomy as a challenge or an attempt to manipulate. In reality, in families if anyone feels like he has lost, everyone loses. The goal in families is for all to feel a measure of success.

Parents who know that they can take charge whenever the situation warrants are not threatened when their children make decisions that don't work out well. If a parent doesn't know how to take charge when a child is out of control, the youngster senses this and becomes frightened. He keeps setting up opportunities for the parent to learn to take charge. If the parent continues to be unable or unwilling to control the child in such a situation, the child's inappropriate behaviors usually escalate.

Throughout his twelve years, Juan has learned a variety of techniques for getting his own way. Aggression was a successful technique when he lived with his birth mom. He would hit, kick, or bite as a young child. By school age he had learned that just a raised fist or verbal threat usually worked as well.

These tactics were not successful with teachers. After several trips to the principal's office, Juan learned that, in general, a more passive approach worked better at school. He became verbally compliant with teachers, but just didn't do his work.

In his first interim care placement he learned that "poor me" usually worked with his foster mom. When he was ten he returned to his birth mother's care. He reverted to physical threats and she was unable to control his behaviors. Once again he is in placement.

In his current foster home he has developed new tactics for being in charge. If he argues long enough with his foster mom he can usually wear her down. He uses a totally different approach with his foster father. Juan approaches him when the foster mother is not around and, using a deferential tone, says, "I already checked with Mom, but I just thought I'd better ask you too." It works nearly every time. The foster father usually says, "If Mom says so, it sounds good to me." His foster father, who perceives Juan as a polite compliant child, can't understand why women can't control him.

Control battles are also seen as a reaction to parents who always have to be in charge. However, some children, faced with controlling parents, eventually give up and withdraw, never asserting age-appropriate autonomy. Many abused children become inhibited, fearful, and withdrawn as a way of avoiding overstepping the limits. Although this defense may help a young child avoid abuse, in the long run such withdrawn children have as many problems as children who are always engaged in control battles.

Since control issues are one of the prominent behavioral patterns seen in children with attachment disorders, further interventions are provided in Section III of this chapter.

Misperceptions

Some behavioral problems stem from misperceptions that the child holds about the way the world works. Misperceptions have two differing origins. Some are due to the visual and auditory perceptual problems that a large number of children in foster care have. A second type of misperception results from egocentric or magical thinking.

Kelly

Kelly's birth family considered her the bad child in the family. She and her mother got along very poorly. One day when Kelly was five and she misbehaved, her mother got very angry. Kelly got angry back. Later that day mother abandoned her children at the babysitter's. Mother did not follow through on any of the plans for reunification. Subsequently parental rights were terminated and adoption plans were made for Kelly and her siblings.

In her adoptive home Kelly never was openly angry at her adoptive mother. She was certain that her anger had caused her mother to abandon her, and she wasn't about to chance getting angry again. However, her underlying anger was manifested indirectly when she forgot to do her homework or her chores, and when she was overly dependent on her adoptive mother.

Identifying and correcting misperceptions are important. Comments that seem to make no sense may help us to identify misperceptions that result either from egocentric magical thinking or from visual or auditory perceptual problems. Careful observation and screening helps detect visual or auditory problems, speech delays, or other learning disabliities which will be discussed in more detail later in this chapter. The Lifebook can be a potent tool for clarifying magical thinking errors.

Psychotic Symptoms

Some children in foster care are very seriously disturbed and evidence symptoms of psychosis. These children are not just immature. They behave in a way that is different from normal children of any age. "The schizophrenic individual behaves either as though he were not interacting with another person or as though the interaction were not taking place at the present time and place" (Haley, 1963). Many times communications with psychotic children do not make sense. The child's responses have little to do with what is happening. Frequently, there is a predominant mood that is not appropriate to the situation. The normal range of feelings is not exhibited. Thought processes are not logical. These children may see or hear things that others do not.

Symptoms that are frequently seen in mentally ill children, were listed in Table 5-6 on page 255. Children with clusters of these symptoms should receive a full psychiatric or psychological evaluation.

Managing Behaviors
that Reflect Attachment Problems

Many children in the child placement system have not developed normal healthy attachments to parental figures. Problems frequently date back to their earliest experiences with birth parents. Unstable foster home placements and the multiple moves that many foster children experience add to their difficulties in developing trust for others as well as their attaining an appropriate sense of autonomy. Unresolved separations and losses can subseqeuntly interfere with the development of healthy attachments. Many attachment problems are signified by imbalances—between dependency and autonomy, awareness of surroundings and self, control vs. lack of control, and so on.

The signs and symptoms of attachment problems that a particular child exhibits are the result of the way parents behaved toward him, the environment, and his own particular psychological traits. In general, children who have been severely neglected are the most likely to suffer from a true lack of attachment. Children who have experienced less severe neglect, intermittent physical abuse, or cmotional abuse are more likely to exhibit attachment problems.

Most children with attachment problems do not trust that adults will be consistently available. They may believe that they do not deserve love and caretaking. Therefore, the underlying theme in the management of all of the behavioral problems stemming from attachment problems is building trust and attachment between the child and his parental figures.

Since some children with attachment problems have not learned to trust their own capabilities, everything that is done to correct the child's behavior must also help him succeed, thereby improving his self-esteem. Adults will not help these children by ignoring them, ridiculing them, or engaging in control battles over their behavior.

In working with attachment problems, as well as other difficult behaviors, it is useful to focus first on identifying an island of health in the behavior, or on understanding how the child learned the particular behavior. What purpose has it served? If the value of the purpose is acknowledged, then adults can help the child learn better, more adaptive, ways to meet the underlying needs. People, in general, resist and cling to either behaviors or possessions that others want to take from them. For this reason, rather than focusing on the undesirable behavior, it is more useful to actively help the child learn alternate or additional ways to get their needs met.

Since their mentally ill mother was rarely psychologically available for meeting their needs, Margaret, who is eight, learned to take responsibility for herself and for her younger sister, Miranda. In their current foster home, Margaret continues to parent Miranda. Both the caseworker and the foster parents are

Margaret

concerned about Margaret's behaviors. She frequently countermands the foster mom's verbal requests and continually suggests that the latter does not know how to take care of Miranda.

The goal is not to take away Margaret's independence and parenting abilities, but rather to acknowledge how important those skills were in her family of origin while teaching an additional skill, depending on others. With the foster parents present, the caseworker thanked Margaret for realizing that both she and Miranda deserved to be taken care of and for doing such a good job when their mother was unable to care for them. She then proceeded to advise Margaret that by the time children become adults they need to know two things—how to be taken care of and how to take care of themselves and others. Most children learn first to depend upon others and then to depend upon themselves. Margaret didn't have the opportunity to experience being taken care of by others but went right ahead and learned what is usually the more difficult task, relying on one's self.

"However, I don't think it would be fair if you were to be cheated out of ever having the experience of being taken care of. You have done such a good job of taking care of Miranda. Now, she needs to learn more about taking care of herself and you deserve an opportunity to be taken care of. How can your foster mom and I help you learn how to depend upon others?" An alliance is built. Margaret's self-esteem is enhanced by it being acknowledged that she recognized and met a need. At the same time she is told that she shouldn't have to miss out totally on life experiences just because she didn't have them at the same age as others do.

To further enhance her self-esteem and decrease the competitiveness in parenting Miranda, Margaret's foster mom told her, "You know your sister better than anyone. Many times you know what she wants and needs better than I do because you've had a lot of experience with her. On the other hand, I know a lot of different ways to take care of children and make them feel loved. You can teach me what you know about Miranda and I can teach you what I know. We both can learn from each other."

Withdrawal from Interactions

Because of lack of trust for adult availablity and fear of adult behaviors, many children with attachment problems withdraw from adult interactions. Withdrawal symptoms may range from the relatively mild but very frequent one of avoiding eye contact to children who physically or psychologically are not available at all.

Many children with attachment problems disengage from adults by avoiding eye contact. In general, the least intrusive means of reminding that is effective should be used. "I find that I can hear what people are telling me better when they are looking at me. It's important to me that I really listen to you. It will help me if we look at each other when we talk," may be all that is needed. All interventions need to be done in a supportive rather than controlling confrontive manner.

Some children behave acceptably for one parent but not for the other, or behave well at home but not at school. When this occurs, the child needs to be encouraged by the person for whom he usually behaves well to exhibit the same behavior in other situations. For example, the child who always minds his dad but not his mother needs to have his father tell him, "I want you to mind Mom!" Or, the father might overhear the child not minding his mother and ask, "What did your Mom just say? Well, then what do I think you should do?" These children frequently have lived in families where the child was used as a party to parental disagreements or where the child was given the message, "You don't have to mind anyone but me."

Other children perceive all three-party relationships as ones in which someone will be "odd man out". In their life experience, most commonly they have been the one to be left out or to have to leave a placement when there is a problem. From their viewpoint it makes sense that they will try, in a new setting, to develop a close enough relationship with one parent that if anyone is excluded it will be the other adult, not them. The goal in working with a child in this situation is to teach him that in most families everyone takes turns being "odd man out" with no one being consistently put in this position.

Jamal, who is nine, has no problems getting along with his foster dad. When the latter is present, Jamal obeys and is pleasant. He is appropriately affectionate with him. It is clear that he enjoys the attention his foster dad gives him. On the other hand, he is quite rebellious with his foster mother. He sasses her, doesn't obey, and is emotionally distant. The parents are starting to argue over how he should be treated. Dad says he can't understand why Mom has problems with Jamal as he doesn't. Mom says, "He's totally different when you're not around. You're not giving me any support."

Jamal's therapist helped the foster parents understand how earlier life experiences had led to his developing these behaviors as a protective device—if he pleased a dad no harm would come to him. The therapist then helped Dad expand his expectations for Jamal to include acceptable behavior with Mom when alone with her. As part of their therapy homework all three were to talk together on a daily basis about how Jamal was doing in learning to trust a mom enough to mind her and start developing an affectionate relationship with her.

Subsequently, therapy homework was given to address the "odd man out" triangle. Each week, Dad and Jamal were to do one activity together in which Mom was not involved. Likewise, Mom and Jamal were to be involved in a pleasurable activity not involving Dad. Jamal needed to learn that he could be "odd man out" for a short period of time without losing his dad's love and approval. Therefore, the parents were to go out once a week not including Jamal. Finally, the family as a whole was to be involved in at least one activity a week.

Some children pull away or cringe when adults reach out to them. They need to learn that nothing bad will happen when a parent touches them, and that

Jamal

they cannot control adult behavior by their cringing. Sometimes children try to prevent adult caregivers from showing them affection. They resist the adult's hugs and kisses. The child has the right to decide whether or not he loves adults or wants to hug or kiss them. However, he does not have the right to decide if his parents can show him affection. These children need many quick, physically affectionate exchanges during the course of the day. Children who do not trust adults, or do not feel worthy of adult attention and affection, may withdraw from interactions with them. When they start feeling emotionally close to parents, they may panic and start to misbehave. There is an unconscious desire to keep emotional or physical distance from the adult thereby decreasing the ultimate disaster—having to lose people one has learned to love.

Kevin

Kevin, nine, was in trouble frequently. In his foster home the usual form of discipline was for the children to be restricted to their bedrooms. This worked with the other children, but not with Kevin. The more he misbehaved, the more he was restricted. His behaviors did not change at all. When his caseworker asked specific questions, Kevin's foster dad told her that this child never seemed at all bothered by the restriction. In fact, he seemed to be quite comfortable in his room. The foster father concluded that Kevin needed to be restricted more frequently and for longer periods of time.

The caseworker suggested that they try a different form of discipline. She asked that the next time Kevin did something wrong, he be asked to take a seat in the living room until he was ready to talk about what he was thinking about or how he was feeling. The first time this was tried Kevin's foster father was most suprised when, within fifteen minutes, Kevin was looking very anxious and starting talk about his fears of never returning to his birth family.

Children who themselves withdraw need to learn that adults like them and value their company. They need gentle but persistent encouragement to be close to their parents. One might allow the child to earn time alone by first spending some time with a parent. For example, when a child who always withdraws protests that he wants to go to his room, the parent might say, "Well, I'd like to play a game with you; then you may play in your room by yourself."

Some children in placement withdraw because they are depressed about separation from their birth parents. They frequently seem to be preoccupied with their own thoughts, rarely sharing them with others. Other children do not necessarily shrink from physical contact but seem to have a shield protecting them emotionally. They are likely to need professional help. These children show little reaction to others' emotions and rarely share their own feelings. Rather than being preoccupied, they are emotionally disconnected from others. Frequently this emotional shield serves not only to "protect" the child from closeness with adults but also to "protect" himself from the intensity of his own feelings of sadness or rage. In other cases the presence of this emotional shield may indicate a severe psychological disturbance.

Aggressive and Hyperactive Behavior

If a parent is afraid of a child's strong feelings, the child learns to fear them himself. One of a parent's principal tasks is to help the child recognize and discharge his emotions in an age-appropriate manner. Children whose aggression comes from strong emotions need to learn more acceptable ways of expressing their emotions and desires. The family's rule about anger and aggression might be that people are not for hurting, neither child nor adult. Adults frequently become very angry when property is destroyed. Children need to be taught alternative ways, that do not involve physical pain to anyone or destruction of property, to discharge anger. If the child's automatic response is to hit, parents can usually help him identify a variety of objects which can be hit without breaking the rules. If the child's automatic response is to kick, again adults can help the youngster identify which objects in a room can be kicked without breaking the rules. The goal is to help children discharge anger, frustration, tension in a way that won't get them in more trouble.

Adolescents, once they have gone through the growth spurt, many times are very frightened by their own angry impulses. They realize that with their increased size, the parent no longer has the physical advantage. In general, adolescents when angry will storm off. This serves the purpose of diminishing the likelihood of physical confrontation. In fact, it is usually dangerous to have an angry adult and an angry adolescent in close physical proximity until one or the other has cooled down. Adults can model appropriate behavior in this situation by walking off while saying, "I need to cool down before I can talk rationally about this."

When a child is hyperactive but not out of control, he often may be helped by some form of time-out giving him a chance to calm down. Unless it is being used only to interrupt behaviors, the length of the time-out should not be arbitrarily chosen by the adult, but instead should be related to behaviors. For example, "You may get up (from a chair) when you are calmed down and have decided what you are going to do next." This helps the impulsive child focus on his next activity rather than the one that got him in trouble.

In attempting to protect themselves from the ultimate pain of losing those whom they have learned to love, some children use extreme aggression to distance adults. Once again the child is trying to protect himself from pain, an understandable goal. If an adult is hit, kicked, or scratched every time she approaches a child, she will probably learn to keep some distance between herself and the child. Hyperactivity also may serve as a distancing mechanism. It is difficult to get close to a child who is always on the move. In both of these situations the parents and the child usually need some professional counseling. The parents may need to learn ways to physically manage the child without anyone getting hurt.

Indiscriminate Affection

The child who is as affectionate with people outside his family as he is with those inside is saying by his behavior, "No one has special importance to me. I am equally close to everyone." It is difficult for parents to feel close to the child who acts equally affectionate with everyone. The closeness seems phony. Once again we can look for the island of health in the behavior and then focus on the next learning step. In this situation we have a child who wants physical closeness. This is positive. The new learning will center on identifying a small number of family members to whom the child is to turn when he needs to sit on a lap, or get a hug. Once again, the problem needs to be openly discussed with the child.

Nina

Nina, six, was overly friendly with non-family members. She would crawl up on the laps of anyone visiting in her adoptive home. At the store she would reach out and touch people she didn't know. Her adoptive parents were concerned about the possibility of her going off with strangers en route to school or when out playing. They consulted with their caseworker. The caseworker and adoptive parents together made a list of family members with whom they wanted to encourage attachment. They then sat down with Nina and told her that whenever she wanted to be close to someone she could seek out these particular people.

One day soon after this conversation, a neighbor was visiting and Nina started to crawl up on her lap. Her mother did not admonish her not to bother the neighbor. Instead, she held out her arm, non-verbally encouraging Nina to come and be close to her and said, "Nina, remember what we talked about the other day?" As Nina came to her, the mom said to the neighbor, "Nina knows a lot about being friendly to people. Right now, we are working on her learning to trust us. We're doing a lot of practice on getting close." In this way the focus remains on the positives and there is no implication that there is something wrong with the neighbor or with Nina.

Over-Competency or the Self-Parenting Child

Some children with attachment problems have learned, usually through necessity, to take care of themselves. When they are placed with a foster or adoptive family, they behave as though they do not need parents. When these children do need help, rather than asking for it, they give adults "permission" to help them. For example, "You may tie my shoes for me."

These children need parents who enjoy and feel comfortable parenting. A child should not be allowed to determine how much parents can parent him. If the parent says, "I didn't have a chance to do things for you when you were little and couldn't do them, and moms need to feel useful so I'm going to help you with this," the child's self-esteem does not suffer. This provides the message that helping others is fun, a message that these children have usually not received in the past.

When a child insists on giving parents permission there are several helpful responses. If the child says, "You may tie my shoes," in a demanding voice, the adult might respond, "I'd love to tie your shoes. I sure will be glad when you can just ask politely." If the child says, "You may sit here," the adult may react as she would with a toddler. If that is where she wanted to sit, she seats herself without comment. If it isn't where the adult wanted to sit, she might simply say, "No I'm planning to sit here."

Having discussions about whether the child has the "right" to boss the adult emphasizes, rather than diminishes, the control issue aspect of the problem. Although the behaviors rarely start for this reason, many children have learned that such comments are ways to upset or distance adults and subsequently use them with this as a goal.

Lack of Self-Awareness

Some abused children seem very aware of people in their environment, but nearly unaware of their own bodies. A balance between self- and other-awareness is not present. They may overeat to the point of bloating or vomiting. They may not react to pain or extremes of temperature in a normal manner. Problems with wetting are frequent and are as likely to occur in the daytime as at night. Occasionally there is soiling as well. These children frequently are not aware of their own symptoms of illness such as an earache or sore throat. It is as if they never learned to pay attention to the signals from their own bodies or to what alleviates discomfort.

We learned earlier that, with adequate parenting, infants learn which state of discomfort is alleviated by which form of relief. The infant gradually learns that there is a state of body discomfort that is alleviated by food. Later, he learns that the word for this is "hunger." As a toddler, he learns to recognize the discomfort caused by a full rectum or bladder. Early in toilet training, the child associates the feeling of discomfort with voiding only after he urinates. Gradually he becomes more aware of the feeling of a full bladder and learns to go to the toilet to void. However, learning these tasks depends upon the child developing the ability to pay attention to his own body. Again, he learns this when his parents pay attention to his discomfort and are able to help him again become comfortable.

In neglectful and abusive families, the child's unpleasure is not alleviated on a regular basis. He does not associate specific forms of discomfort with certain forms of relief. Indeed, in abusive families the child may learn that expressing discomfort may lead to additional pain. So the child learns to disregard his own needs and focus all his attention on others and their needs. These children become hypervigilent, always interested in the feelings and moods of the adults who take care of them, but not perceptive about themselves. They are frequently described as "sneaky and snoopy" or "wary and watchful."

The island of health in their behaviors is self-protection. The re-educational task for them is to learn to pay attention to their own bodily sensations. Parents can teach this. Comments such as, "It's nearly lunchtime, I'm hungry, are you?" or, "You ate a good meal; I bet you are full," help the child focus on his own stomach. When a child falls and hurts himself, parents might comment, "Gee, I bet that hurts. When I was a kid and skinned my knee, I would sometimes cry."

The child who overeats tends to gulp his food without chewing or savoring it. Parents might give this child several small servings instead of one large one. This slows the eating. Once the child starts to chew more slowly, the appetite usually decreases. It is best not to make chewing a power struggle. However, a parent might make a game of chewing slowly or focus on tastes and textures of the foods. Overall, the parent can be encouraged to allow the child to have a little more food than is reasonable and then when he still asks for more to say with big smile, "Well, you can't be hungry for more food. You must be hungry for more loving. Come here and get some."

The child who has daytime enuresis as part of this symptom complex needs to be toilet trained, no matter what his age. This means reminders need to be provided, just as they would have been had the child lived in this home as a toddler. The child is encouraged to think about how he feels before and after voiding. Sometimes these children do not even differentiate between a full bladder and an empty stomach.

Mike

Six-year-old Mike joined his adoptive family two months ago. Prior to his placement his caseworker, Ms. Alberts, had made suggestions to the family as to how they might work with his food gorging and insatiable appetite. During one of Ms. Albert's post placement visits in the adoptive home, Mike came in from outside complaining that his stomach hurt. He asked his mom if she thought he was hungry. The adoptive mother told Mike that since he had had a recent snack, she doubted the cause of the discomfort was hunger and suggested that maybe he needed to go to the bathroom.

After several minutes of moaning and groaning, his mom said, "Mike, I want you to go upstairs to the bathroom. If that's not what you need, that's okay, but I want you to try and see if that's the problem." After two minutes Mike returned with obvious relief on his face commenting, "That was it—needed to pee." He ran on out to the yard to play. Mother had been effective in her decoding of the problem and had offered a suggestion without making a control issue of it. Ms. Albert learned that children who overeat frequently have problems with other forms of body awareness as well.

_____

Control Issues

When reasonable parental requests lead to major confrontations a control issue exists. As Dobson defines it, "You have drawn a line in the dirt and the child has deliberately flopped his big hairy toe across it." (Dobson, 1972). Control issues are prevalent as children go through developmental periods when the surge for autonomy is great and there is an increase in stubborn and oppositional behavior. This means that control issues reflective of normal development are most noticeable during the toddler years, again at around age four, and during adolescence.

However, since the tasks to be accomplished at varying stages of development are so different, interventions with younger children need to differ from those with adolescents. With the preadolescent the emphasis can be on the child learning that meeting reasonable requests does not mean he has lost anything. With adolescents, the emphasis needs to be on what will help the young person build in self-control rather than others providing external controls.

With younger children in general, physical action works better than repeated verbal chastising in control issues. Most children who are prone to control issues have learned to manipulate parents by constant arguing or reasoning. Usually, they have learned these approaches from parental modeling. If a child is hassling a brother at the table, the parent might get up and lead the child who is misbehaving away from the table to a chair. "Let me know when you are ready to come back and eat instead of hassle," gives a clearer message than arguing about who started the hassle or reasoning about acceptable table behaviors.

Adults need to understand that the child's apparent need to control everything is usually a reflection of his feeling of not being in control of anything. If the parent feels threatened and needs to be in total control of the child, battles will escalate. On the other hand, if the parent backs off from the task of helping the child learn that "minding does not mean losing," problems will increase, and the child will rule the family. It is important that foster and adoptive parents not be re-educated by the child into behaving as though all family interactions are adversarial. The goal is for the child to learn reciprocity. Keeping this in mind, a variety of techniques can be used to address control issues.

When parents make a resonable request and a major battle ensues, they need to first stop, look, and listen. They must quickly assess: Is my request reasonable? Are there extenuating circumstances that prohibit the child from obeying the request? What is the real issue? If parents determine that a control issue exists, then they need to quickly devise a strategy that allows the child to obey the request without feeling that hc has lost.

Felicia

Six-year-old Felicia has just dropped her coat on the floor as she comes in from school. Her foster mother asks her to pick it up. Felicia, who has recently joined this family, stands her ground firmly and defiantly says, "You can't make me. You're not my real mother." The foster mother decides to handle the coat first and the feelings later. She does not use her mouth to pose further challenges. Instead, she approaches. and standing next to the child, reaches her arm around Felicia's shoulders placing her hand on top of the child's the coat is picked up and hung on the nearby hook. The foster mom then says, "Good. Now it's time for your after school snack." While Felicia is enjoying her fruit, the foster mom starts talking about Felicia's feelings about being away from her birth mother.

As in Felicia's case, sometimes the parents will quietly take charge to insure that the request is complied with. They may simultaneously be supportive of the child's underlying feelings. For example when a four year old is protesting going to bed, rather than arguing, the parent picks the child up, and heads off to the bedroom. However, en route the parent might in a supportive caring tone say, "I know you'd rather stay up and play, but it's bedtime now. I'll leave your cars all set up as they are now for you to play with in the morning." In general the take-charge approach works best when the child is not yet an adolescent, and when physical movement is involved, either from one location to another as in the above example, or when movement of an arm or hand is involved as in Felicia's case.

Both logical consequences and two good choices are supportive control measures that are useful in situations which involve more complex tasks, and with older children and adolescents. The child is refusing to make his bed. The parent gives him two equally acceptable choices. The child is given the choice of making it immediately or sitting in a chair until he is ready to make it. Choices must be given in a manner that conveys that the parent does not have strong need for the child to select one over the other, but that the choice is truly the child's. When there is a control issue, the parent should not give a good choice and a bad choice, the child will inevitably select the latter.

Trilby

Mrs. Appleton called distraught. Her ten-year-old foster daughter had run away. In trying to determine the cause of the behavior, the caseworker learned that Mrs. Appleton had inadvertently encouraged the behavior by giving a good choice and a poor choice. When Trilby had refused to do the dishes, Mrs. Appleton in frustration had said, "Either do the dishes or get out of here." Trilby was not disobeying by running away. In fact, she was obeying. This also explained why Mrs. Appleton was on the telephone seeking help rather than going after her foster daughter.

It is best for parents to avoid control battles from developing in certain areas. The Rule of Two Ends warns parents not to make a control issue out of anything that goes into or out of either end of the child. The child is much more in control of his two ends than the parent will ever be. A parent can say, "Yes, you will go to bed now," and enforce it by taking the child to bed, but to enforce, "You will not wet the bed," or, "You will eat all your peas," the parent might have to go to unacceptable extremes.

Establishing rules that have consistent and logical consequences is another useful way to handle control issues. "You must eat all your meat and vegetables before you can have dessert," is much more effective than a rule that says, "You must stay at the table until your plate is clean." In the latter case the child has merely to sit passively until the next meal to win. A few children will even eat and then vomit the food back onto their plates to control this situation.

Since children who frequently engage in power issues usually perceive themselves as having little real control over their lives, it is important that parents help them develop more age-appropriate autonomy by selecting areas they can legitimately manage. This can be done either by delegating an entire area to the child, for example, "You are in charge of your toys," or by defining limits within which the child does have sway. For example, "It is cold today, you need to wear a long sleeved shirt. Which of these would you prefer?"

If a parent notes that power issues are common at a certain time of day, such as bedtime, then it makes sense to give the child more feeling of authority, rather than less, at that time of day. Although bedtime itself is non-negotiable the child might be offered choices as to which pair of pajamas he prefers, which stuffed animal he wants to take to bed with him, whether he wants to walk or be carried to his bedroom, etc.

Delayed Conscience Development

In an earlier chapter it was noted that the foundation for conscience development is the child's trust in others and his attachment to someone. Thus, trust and attachment must be emphasized with children who are delayed in conscience development. With active work on the part of the parents and child, it is usually possible to accelerate conscience progression at least up to the age of ten and many times up to junior high years. This is especially true if the child will accept nurturance from parental figures.

The most common obstacle to conscience development in a family setting is the parents' notion that they have to be able to trust the child before they can really nurture him. This is the opposite of the truth. The child must first learn to trust that adults care enough about him to protect him from from making serious mistakes, enough to provide adequate supervision even when it is not easy to do so. He needs to learn to trust that the adult's limit-setting will be out of consideration for the needs of the child, not because the adult needs to be in control of everything. He needs to know that the parent will stick up for him when he needs adult support.

While the child builds up this sense of trust, parents need to know what the child is doing. If the child is in school, parents and teacher need to stay in frequent contact. The child needs to be under the supervision of an adult most of the time. If the child is enrolled in extra-curricular activities, parents need contact with the sponsors to know what is going on. Parents want to create an atmosphere of concern rather than distrust. The child learns to trust that parents care enough to know what he happening in his life. As much attention should be paid to behavior that indicates growth as to misbehaviors.

"Your Jared and another child are arguing over a dollar bill. Did Jared have a dollar when he left home?" The teacher who calls a parent to get this information can avoid hours of hassles and accusations at school. This teacher can go back to the classroom and say to the child, "Jared, I called your mother and she said she forgot to give you the money for the field trip. This money must belong to Taylor." The teacher can then drop the subject and let the parent pick up on it when the child returns home. This type of communication prevents the child who is being honest from being put in a defensive position.

If a teacher has called to report a problem, parents should not set the child up to lie by asking, "How did your day go at school?" The message behind this question is that the parent does not know how the child's day was. The parent who meets her child at the door with a no-nonsense attitude saying, "I got a call from Mrs. Bowen today about a dollar bill. I want you to tell me what happened," is making it easier, rather than more difficult, for the child to tell the truth.

Most preadolescent children with delayed conscience development give themselves away when they are lying. It is useful to ask parents, "How do you know when your child is lying?" Adults can then focus on the positive aspects of the child's body telling the truth even though the mouth may be having difficulty in this area.

Parents of children with delayed conscience development need not only to have "big eyes and big ears" but also to be exceptionally truthful themselves. Their expectations need to be clear. Being aware of the likelihood of concrete thinking on the part of the child, they are careful to give clear messages such as, "Is your room clean?" rather than, "Did you clean your room?" The latter could be truthfully answered yes if the child has ever cleaned his room. It has nothing to do with it's present state.

In facilitating conscience development, logical consequences are more meaningful than unrelated discipline. For example, working to repay stolen money makes more sense than does being restricted to the house for a week. It teaches an alternate way for the child to get his needs met. The solution when a child wants extra money is for him to find a way to earn it, not to be restricted to the house for a week.

Some adolescents who appear to have delayed conscience really have too much conscience rather than too little. These young people may sometimes lie and steal. However, they constantly promise themselves or others, "I'll never do it again." This is a very weighty promise. When they are unable to live up to their own expectations, they "dump" on themselves. They need help setting realistic goals for themselves. For example, "I'm not going to lie to my parents today," is a realistic goal which is likely to be achievable, enabling the youngster to build self-esteem.

Some children have problems that are more serious than delayed conscience development. The child who has true sociopathic tendencies may not give himself away when he lies. He may not only be deceiving adults by his lies but may be deceiving himself. This type of individual frequently convinces himself that his lies are the truth. Cognitive restructuring is the treatment of choice for these adolescents.

Although adults frequently label lying and stealing as delayed conscience development, many times they occur for other reasons. The single most common reason for lying is that the individual wants to avoid getting in trouble. This is the island of health in the misbehavior. It can be identified as a reasonable goal and the focus can then switch to alternate ways to achieve it.

Some adults describe a child's exaggeration as lying. Many children in foster care talk as though wishful thinking about themselves or their birth families were true. They need help building self-esteem and working on resolution of separation issues.

For some individuals lying about certain behaviors has become a habit. Helping the young person learn more about himself is useful. Asking, "How long after you say, 'No, not me,' do you think, 'Oh, boy am I ever in trouble now'?" can help identify these individuals. The emphasis then is put on thinking before answering. Parents might be advised to tell this child, "I need to ask you about something. It is important. I want you to take some time to think about it." The parent can then ask the question and tell the youngster that she will recheck with him about his answer in five minutes. Since she is stressing the importance of not answering impulsively, the adult needs to ignore anything—either the truth or a lie—coming from the child before the set time. Children who steal only from family members, particularly from parents, are usually demonstrating that they believe they are not receiving enough love and attention from the family. This reflects their perception, not necessarily reality. Other children steal when they are jealous of peers at school or when taking things has become a habit.

Suzanna, seven, usually comes home from school with a variety of objects in her pockets. These include pencils, hair clips, or small toys. When asked about them her usual response is, "I found them." Her foster mother and the teacher jointly come up with a plan for helping Suzanna. They openly acknowledge with her that she has a problem and that they want to help.

Suzanna

"Suzanna, you and I both know that many times you have other people's things in your pockets. You get in trouble when this happens. We don't like to see you in trouble and we want to help you with this problem. Therefore, I (foster mom) am going to help you check your pockets every day before you leave for school to make certain that you are taking only the things that are supposed to go to school. Mrs. Greenblatt (the teacher) is going to help you check your pockets once again before you leave school so that everything can be returned to its proper place or to its owner. That way you won't get in trouble."

Gradually both teacher and foster parent help Suzanna pay attention to her pockets on her own. If only her belongings are in her pockets she is praised. If she returns objects before leaving school she is praised.

One or two instances of shoplifting, especially between the ages of ten and thirteen, are common enough that they do not necessarily indicate a serious underlying problem. However, parents need to meet the misbehavior with disapproval and insist that the child return or pay double for the merchandise. Children then learn that purchasing on time, delaying payment, always costs more than earning the desired amount before making the purchase. More drastic measures need to be taken when an adolescent is involved in frequent shoplifting. Once again a clear message is given, "We know this is a problem for you and we are going to have to work together to make it easier for you not to be tempted to take things." This teen should not be allowed to borrow from friends. The parent might request that receipts accompany all new possessions. "It will be easier for both of us if you show me a receipt for everything you bring into this house. That way I won't unjustly accuse you when you buy things. It will be easier for me to trust you and for you to trust me."

Some children and adolescents steal because they want things and have no other way to obtain them. Even young children need an allowance to spend on things they want. Older children, and particularly adolescents, need opportunties to earn money so that they can purchase things for which they are willing to work.

Exercise 6-3 provides an opportunity to plan an overall behavior management program for a child who is moving to an adoptive home.

Exercise 6-3

Planning Strategies for Working with Behaviors Stemming from Attachment Problems

Sharon

In an exercise in the first chapter, you were asked to look at ways to encourage attachment between Sharon and her new family. In this exercise you have an opportunity to address all of her behavior problems, many of which stem from her attachment problems.

Sharon, age eight, will be moving from her foster home to an adoptive family within the next few weeks. She will be the youngest in a two parent family with three sons ranging in age from twelve to seventeen. Father is a clergyman;

mother is a teacher. Sharon's past history reveals considerable emotional and physical deprivation, rejection, and physical abuse. She has been in and out of foster care since she was four years old. Sharon has had seven moves, including two returns to her birth parents' care.

Behavioral problems noted in her current foster home include enuresis both at night and during the day. A medical workup was negative. Sharon has many fears including fear of the dark, sirens, and new situations. She is prone to nightmares. Sharon becomes very upset when family members tease each other or rough house. She is described as a demanding and manipulative child.

Although there is no known history of sexual abuse, Sharon demonstrates sexually provocative behaviors. She raises her dress in front of men and boys and asks them openly if they want to go to bed with her. Sharon has difficulty telling the truth. Sometimes she lies about her misbehaviors. Other times she tells meaningless lies, such as saying that peas are her favorite vegetable when, in fact, she does not like them at all. She frequently brings home small objects (i.e. pencils, hair clips, etc.) from school saying either that she "found" them or that, "a friend gave them to me."

Although academically Sharon is at grade level, she has many gaps in her basic fund of knowledge. She exhibits problems with logical thinking and basic cause and effect. She does not always complete her school work and may "forget" to turn in work she has completed. She is reading above grade level but has difficulty in math. Play skills are poor and she has difficulty keeping friends.

Sharon is physically attractive and demonstrates excellent self-care skills. She shows appropriate affect for the most part and is outgoing and affectionate. Sometimes she is inappropriately affectionate with relative strangers. However, she is able to talk openly about feelings and tells of many ways that she and her present foster parents have fun together.

1.   How would you go about helping her with her learning problems?
2.   How would you go about helping her with her problems with peer relationships.
3.   Make a list of Sharon's other problem behaviors. Identify a strategy to be used with each.

Children with Learning Problems   IV

The correlation between cognitive delays or problems and normal attachments in early life was discussed earlier. We noted that the symptoms noted in research studies of children raised without primarily caregivers were similar to those seen in children with Attention Deficit Disorder. The increased incidence of these symptoms in children in care most likely is the result of a variety of factors—genetic, prenatal abuse or neglect, birth trauma, and early life experiences. Many children in placement demonstrate the long-term effects of Fetal Alcohol Syndrome and Fetal Alcohol Effects (Streissguth et al, 1988.) Others are affected by their mother's prenatal drug use. Some suffer the effects of both alcohol and drug abuse on the part of their birth mother during the pregnancy with this child.

In working with a particular child, determining the underlying cause is probably less important than identifying the specific learning problems, and developing strategies which use his strengths to lessen the impact of the deficiencies. We must remember that learning problems affect not only school performance but also family and peer relationships as well as the acquisition of a variety of life skills usually learned within the family setting.

In this section we will briefly describe some of the learning difficulties commonly seen in children in care. At the end of this section you will find a list of books which are suggested for parents and others who are responsible for insuring that these children's needs are met.

Children who show any developmental delay or any behavioral problems should be screened for visual or auditory problems, speech difficulties, and gross motor delays. They are too common to ignore them as a possible cause of problem behaviors. The most effective interventions combine information gathered by formal assessments and the day-to-day observations made by parents and others routinely involved with the child.

Although it is unlikely that parents on their own will identify a child's perceptual and processing problems, once a professional helps them understand what to focus on in their observations, the adults who live with the child become important members of the treatment team.

Kristi

Her pediatrician had helped her parents determine the cause of Kristi's fussiness as a baby. Her parents learned that she had hyperacute hearing, was easily distracted by noises, and was overwhelmed in loud noisy environments. Being aware of these problems when she was an infant, they paid close attention to how she was learning when she became a toddler. Her mother noted that when Kristi was asking questions about the world around her, she was more likely to be listening than looking. Whenever she asked, "What's that?" her mother learned that Kristi was asking about things she heard rather than things she saw.

During her grade school years, Kristi was observed to have an excellent memory for information she heard, but a poorer memory for visual input. Initially she was taught to read out loud so she could auditorily process the information. Gradually, she was taught to listen to the words as she read without saying them. Soft background noise helped her screen out other sounds that might be distracting. In high school she was better able to focus on her assignments when there was background music than when there wasn't. In the latter situation, she was distracted by everything others in the house were saying or doing. She learned that when writing themes she did better if she "listened" to her thoughts before writing them down. An interesting aside is the fact that Kristi's memories of dreams are primarily auditory, rather than visual.

_____

The adults who are in day-to-day contact with these children are in the best position to help determine the gaps in the child's knowledge base. By understanding a child's problems in processing stimuli, an adult can help clarify misperceptions and aid the child in developing a better understanding of himself and his world. In general, children with perceptual problems have difficulty handling changes in their environments or routines. These children need a home life that is reasonably well organized, with parents who prefer to plan ahead and lead a rather scheduled life.

Auditory Problems
Children with auditory perceptual difficulties have normal, or even hyperacute hearing, but have difficulty processing the spoken word. They may have difficulty discriminating one sound from another. These misunderstandings frequently change the entire meaning of a sentence. Osman (1979) mentions in her book a child who misunderstood her father's shout from another room. He said, "Go to bed." She heard, "Your goat is dead," and became very upset. In situations like this adults may think the child is not paying attention or is manipulative when, in reality, they have misunderstood a request. When speaking, some of these children may have to struggle to find just the word they want. Some can use words fluently when speaking spontaneously, but have difficulty with word finding when asked questions that require short answers. Or, they may have problems with auditory memory, being able to retain only the last thing said, not a list of several. As Kristi demonstrated, children with auditory perceptual problems frequently suffer from auditory distractibility as well. They have problems focusing their attention on one input. They have difficulty discriminating between distant and nearby sounds. The world may be a very confusing place for them. Their processing problems will impact on all areas of their lives.

_____

Cory had been abused and neglected by his birth family. He had been in numerous foster homes prior to being hospitalized in a psychiatric facility. Sometimes he had violent temper tantrums during which he was self-abusive.

Cory

It became apparent to Cory's teacher at the psychiatric facility that he had problems with auditory distractibility and localizing sounds. Cory's hearing was hyperacute. He heard things others couldn't, such as a low rumble of thunder. If he said, "What's that?" his teacher soon learned to listen, rather than to look.

One day Cory was on an outing with his teacher. They were in a store which was very quiet. Cory commented, "It sure is noisy in here." The lady at the checkstand gave him a "smart aleck kid" look. His teacher knew she should listen. A jack-hammer a block away was pounding. "That jack-hammer sure does make a lot of noise," she commented. Cory replied, "Yeah, I wonder what they are building." At that point the clerk's expression changed from one of disapproval to one of admiration for his perceptiveness.

No wonder the world is a confusing place for Cory. Others don't share or understand his perceptions and react to him in what must seem to him to be very unpredictible ways.

Although most individuals with auditory processing problems are not psychotic, many children with childhood schizophrenia have extremely sensitive hearing.

Darren

Darren, a schizophrenic child, had strong fears of loud noises, especially vibrating sounds such as those made by vacuum cleaners, power mowers, and power saws. As he left his schizophrenic world and became part of "our world" more of the time, he was able to explain his perceptions to adults. When he was a toddler, Darren's family lived close to O'Hare Airport. When he was ten, he explained to his mother, "Everytime one of those planes went over, it was so loud that it felt like it was inside my head and was going to burst it open!" And so this child blocked out our world and withdrew into a world of his own.

Strategies can be devised to help these children both at home and at school.

Judy

As a result of Judy's language assessment, Marie Caldwell learned to make a list of chores for her foster daughter, rather than depending upon auditory memory. Judy was sometimes asked to repeat instructions, both to make certain that she had understood them and to reinforce auditory memory. Her teachers were advised that frequently Judy did not really understand verbal concepts in spite of parroting them. They needed to put extra steps into her directions, insuring that she did indeed understand what she was being taught.

Visual Perceptual Problems

These are the type of perceptual problem most readily picked up by teachers in the early school years when a child has trouble either reading or copying written work. The child may have difficulty differentiating between mirror letters (*b/d*, *p/q*) or those that are up-down reversals (*n/u*, *w/m*, etc). Again, these problems impact not only academic achievement but affect learning that usually occurs at home or play. These children frequently are ambidextrous and may have difficulty differentiating right from left. They are likely to have problems setting a table correctly, or doing other tasks that involve eye-hand coordination such as making a bed, doing jigsaw puzzles, coloring within the lines or drawing.

Making use of their other senses to compensate is necessary; explaining things auditorily is a possibility. When teaching the young child the alphabet, using his tactile sense by cutting out letters using sand paper, textured wallpaper, or constructing them with cotton may be helpful. Using bigger muscle movements such as drawing letters or numbers in the air using arm, rather than finger muscles is a common teaching tool.

Telling time is frequently difficult for these children. Using digital clocks is easier than face clocks. Those with visual memory problems may need to read aloud, thereby using auditory learning to enhance visual. A few need to have written materials put onto tape for auditory input. As with other problem areas, combining professional assessment and planning with the observations of parents and teachers is the approach most likely to lead to treatment strategies that can be implemented in all areas of the child's life.

Speech Problems

Children with speech problems need to learn to observe faces. Watching people talk and observing facial expressions help them hear and understand better. Children with speech delays often need parents who will provide speech stimulation, rather than formalized speech therapy, particularly during the preschool years.

Many children in care are either fearful of strangers or indiscriminant in their interactions with them. In general preschoolers are not used to talking in unfamiliar places with strangers on a one-to-one basis. Speech therapists who go to the child's home, observing speech there, will make a better assessment and be in a position to help parents encourage speech in the home. Or, a speech therapist might work with a child in an already familiar setting, such as home or day care center initially. Stimulation by family members provides the child with many more hours of speech therapy in a week than he can receive in individual therapy. Individual or group therapy becomes more useful as children become older and lose their fear of strangers.

Sense of Time

Many children in care lack an internal sense of time. In addition, some may have difficulty learning to tell time. Even learning the names of the days of the week or months of the year poses a problem for them. A sense of distance is often confusing to such children as well.

Most children begin to acquire a sense of time long before they are ever asked to tell time on a clock. They learn the sequence of the days of the week and gradually, between ages four and six, develop an internal awareness of how long a few minutes, an hour, or a half-day is.

How do most children learn this sense of time? Commonly, parents of preschool children talk about days of the week and help the child learn them by rote. Calendars that identify special events help the school-age child. When responding to the often-asked question, "How many days until my birthday?" using a calendar is much more helpful than simply saying, "Three months," or, "It's too early to start thinking about your birthday yet."

Parents teach a child about time by talking about it as they go about their daily business. For example they may say, "Come wash up, dinner will be ready in five minutes," or, "It's half an hour until bedtime." When children ask, "How long is half an hour?" the answer can be related to daily occurrences. A half hour can be equated to a favorite T.V. program, ten minutes to the length of time it takes to drive to the grocery store, and so on. Use of a timer helps a child to internalize a sense of time. If a parent says, "You have ten minutes to get dressed," and sets a buzzer, the child may even learn to "beat the clock" without looking at the timer.

Before a child can learn to tell time on a conventional clock, he must be able to count by fives. Until he learns this, he will only be able to identify the hour and the half hour. Devising games to use these skills is certainly more effective than either drilling or a parental response of disgust or ridicule in response to the child's early efforts.

Most children develop a sense of past and future through the type of conversation that occurs in the normal course of family living. Comments such as, "We moved to this house two years ago," or, "You can go to the roller rink without an adult when you become a teenager," provide the child with an understanding of past and future and help him gain a sense of continuity in life. For many children in interim care this type of time sense is poor even if they have no perceptual difficulties.

Two factors contribute to this. Too often foster parents do not have the information that helps the child sort out his past. They may know that the child was in another foster home, but not know where, when, or for how long. In addition, there is a tendency for foster, adoptive, and birth parents to feel uncomfortable when a child starts to talk about the past with which they are not familiar. The non-verbal message parents frequently give to the child in these situations is, "Don't talk about your past; I don't want to hear about it." The future poses even more of a problem for children in interim care. Foster parents, unable to answer the child's questions about what will happen when, may discourage talk of the future. The child in care may never learn how past impacts present and how both influence the future.

Attention Deficit Disorder

Many children with learning problems have Attention Deficit Disorder, characterized by problems paying attention, distractibility, impulsivity, and emotional over-reactions. Some are hyperactive as well. Others are not. For those who are easily distracted, an environment with less stimulation is helpful. This child usually does poorly in a household where there are many visual and auditory distractions, such as constant background noise from a T.V. Although he certainly needs a place to play with toys, he also needs a place that is not so stimulating to which he can retreat. This may be particularly important at bedtime. It makes sense to keep the toys for the easily distracted child in a box outside of his room or in another room of the house. Easily defined spaces help these children learn limits. A fence around the yard helps the child recognize the boundaries he must observe when his parents say, "Stay in the yard."

Since the child with Attention Deficit Disorder is frequently impulsive, it is useful to help him focus on what he is going to do next. With this kind of child a parent does well to say, "Sit down here a minute until you can decide what you want to do next." Once the child verbally commits himself to a specific activity, it is easier for him to focus on it. When parents give verbal instructions, it often helps to ask the child to repeat their request before he heads off. This provides parents with an opportunity to clarify instructions if the child is confused, or to give him positive reinforcement if he is clear about what is to happen.

Consistent daily routines help the child with Attention Deficit Disorder feel more secure. Islands of routine, such as those associated with meals or bedtimes are important. For these children attention to details, like putting out clothes for the next day at bedtime, are helpful. This provides an opportunity to talk briefly with the child about the next day's activities and expectations. In the morning there is an obvious visual focus of attention, the clothes, rather than having the child have to make choices immediately on awakening, or face the distractions posed by open drawers or closets.

For a child with learning disabilities it is frequently necessary to break learning tasks into parts that the child can understand and achieve more easily. An important component of treating children with learning disabilities is to provide day-to-day experiences at home and at school that enhance the child's self-esteem.

Brent is in second grade. He is having difficulty with math, in spite of knowing his basic addition and subtraction facts well. His class is learning to regroup and to subtract double digit numbers by borrowing. His dad is helping him with his homework. He notices that Brent correctly completed a page where he was asked to regroup each number. However, when asked to do a page of problems, every one was wrong. Dad decided to introduce an additional step. He asked Brent to first regroup the top number in each problem and only after completing two rows that way, to go back and subtract. This time the answers were correct. Brent was beaming. He then did a single row that way and by the final row on the page was able to regroup, subtract, regroup, subtract. He had the basic skills. He needed an additional step in learning to coordinate the two skills involved.

Brent

331

There is considerable controversy about the use of medication with ADD children. When the child's primary problem is one of short attention span, medication may be helpful. Such children are in constant motion. They are frequently out of their seats at school or are very fidgety. These children may be helped, particularly during their early school years, by medications such as Ritalin or Cylert. Caseworkers should make a point of knowing doctors with expertise in working with children with Attention Deficit Disorder to whom they can refer families.

Some parents prefer to try the dietary restrictions suggested in the Kaiser-Permanente diet for their hyperactive children. This diet restricts the intake of food colorings and food additives (Osman, 1979). Although double blind studies attempting to demonstrate the efficacy of this approach have not, to date, yielded conclusive results, some families have felt that the diet significantly helped their children.

There are some children who seem to become more hyperactive after eating sweets. In such cases, foods containing simple sugars called glucose, should be limited. Fructose, the sugar contained in fruits, and more complex carbohydrates do not seem to cause the same problem for these children. Snacks of fruit, nuts, popcorn, and natural fruit juices can be substituted for glucose-rich snacks like cookies, candy, cake, or Kool Aid.

Exercise 6-4 describes the behaviors of Chad, a seven-year-old with typical ADD symptoms.

Exercise 6-4

Developing Strategies for Helping the Child with Attention Deficit Disorder

Chad

Chad is seven years old and is in the second grade. He reads at grade level or above and does well in math when he completes his work. His handwriting, however, is poor. Although he rarely gets out of his seat at school unless it is appropriate, he constantly twists, turns, drops things, and picks them up. Chad also frequently talks out in class.

He has great difficulty switching from one subject to another particularly if he hasn't completed the work. He is apt to direct a verbal outburst at the teacher when this happens.

Chad has difficulty getting along with his peers. If someone accidently brushes against him, he is likely to verbally, and possibly physically, lash out at that person. He seems socially immature.

His foster parents state that Chad is very messy at the table. He never sits still and frequently drops food from his fork. He falls asleep promptly at night and is a very sound sleeper. He wets the bed two or three times a week.

Chad wakes up early and promptly goes to the kitchen where he gets into whatever food is available, leaving the kitchen a mess. He occasionally has daytime wetting problems. This occurs most frequently on weekends or on outings. Chad is very hard on his clothes, and frequently misplaces or loses coats, hats, and sweaters.

Chad is very good at gross motor activities. He is a very agile child. He much prefers outdoor to indoor activities. Although he does like playing with small cars and trucks, he dislikes models and other arts and crafts activities.

1.   Make a list of Chad's behavioral problems. Group together the ones that are indicative of Attention Deficit Disorder
2.   Outline a plan for initiating behavioral management of these problems.
3.   Outline a plan for initiating behavioral management of Ronnie's behavioral problems that are not indicative of ADD.

Resource List

Although there are many excellent parenting books on the market, most do not address the specific types of problems frequently exhibited by children in placement. The techniques offered in many books "backfire" when used with children who have poor attachments or little feeling of self worth. The following books are selected because they describe techniques that can be used effectively with children in placment, or because they offer basic parenting skills that no parent should be without.

Growing Up Again by Clarke and Dawson (1989) presents an excellent framework for providing structure and nurture—the two primary components of—parenting and looks at the dangers of too much or too little of either.

Self-Esteem: A Family Affair, an earlier book by Jean Clarke, again provides many excellent ideas. I adapted many of the ideas from this book in developing tools to use with children and adults in therapy. Jean is always respectful of the parents' needs, as well as the child's.

Foster Cline's *Understanding and Treating the Difficult Child* looks at some very difficult behavior patterns and ways to intervene with them. Foster writes with as much humor and compassion as he speaks.

Dreikers' many books such as *Logical Consequences* and *Children The Challenge* focus on using consequences and the family conference to solve problems.

The Foster Parent Training Project of Eastern Michigan University has produced a series of workbooks written by Patricia Ryan. They include topics such as *Training Foster Parents to Handle Lying and Stealing* and *Training Foster Parents to Handle Destructive Behavior.*

Parent Effectiveness Training by Thomas Gordon is an easy-to-read book that explains basic communication skills without using any psychological jargon.

The One Minute Scolding is by Gerald Nelson, a psychiatrist who has worked extensively with children in the foster care system. This technique encourages relationship building by making use of the arousal-relaxation cyle in discipline.

Books that are useful for those working with children with cognitive problems:

Betty Osman's two books, *Learning Disabilities: A Family Affair* and *No One to Play With*, are very useful in helping parents understand how their children's learning problems affect home and family life as well as academic performance.

Other books that the reader might find helpful are *Your Hyperactive Child, A Parents Guide to Coping with Attention Deficit Disorder* by Barbara Ingersoll and *The Hyperactive Child, Adolescent, and Adult* by Paul Wender. *Maybe You Know My Kid: A Parent's Guide to Identifying, Understanding and Helping Your Child with Attention Deficit Hyperactive Disorder* by Mary Gahill from Carol Publishing Group.

The Broken Cord by Michael Dorris, an adoptive father of a child (now young adult) who suffers from Fetal Alcohol Effects. This best seller, award winning book, provides a poignant account of the frustrations of living with, and providing educationally for, children with this disorder.

Pulling up his sleeve and pointing to his arm, the child said, "Look, Lady, do you see the color of my skin? People are supposed to live with people who have the same color skin."

**Gilbert, seven,
during discussion of adoption plans**

"The pieces are all starting to come together. I'm starting to feel like a real person!"

**Trevor, fourteen,
upon receiving a letter with
information about his birth family**

To become effective advocates for the children for whom they are responsible, adults need to understand the child's perceptions. Additionally, they must be able to help children understand what has happened to them in the past and what the plans are for the future.

This chapter is about direct work with children in care.

CHAPTER 7

Direct Work with Children

Direct work with children is undertaken in a variety of circumstances and with several different objectives. If we are to intervene effectively in their current lives and make the least detrimental decisions on their behalf, we must understand the child's perceptions of his life experiences. In addition, as the youngster matures, it is the obligation of the adults responsible for him to help the young person expand his understanding of his own earlier life history and to become aware of the impact it may have on his future decision making. Direct work can also be used to facilitate changes in the child's current functioning. Finally, it is used to prepare the child for upcoming changes.

Direct work with the child may be done by many different people. For the purpose of this chapter, we will center on the work undertaken primarily by caseworkers. Although some of the examples will include therapists working with children, the focus will be on the tasks for which social workers share responsibility. The work can, as we shall see, take place in a variety of locations. It should not be limited to an office setting. In fact, in many situations, this is the least effective site. Direct work does not have to be done on a one-to-one basis. Indeed, in most circumstances it is important to involve members of the child's current family. This is, as we have seen in previous chapters, especially true when we are trying to understand the child's current behaviors and helping him to find alternate, more effective, ways for him to express his feelings and get his needs met.

Sometimes members of the young person's previous families will need to be included as well. This is especially true when we are undertaking the "disengagement" work which is frequently a precursor to having the child be willing and able to firmly commit himself to a new permanent legal family. Other times, as the youngster matures, reconnecting with important people from his past may help him solidify his sense of identity.

In some cases, the goals will be most effectively accomplished by group work. For example, to help a child improve his interactions with peers there must be an arena in which he can practice the skills being taught. Or, children who have been sexually abused may find it easier to talk about their history when in the presence of others who have had similar experiences.

A variety of examples, using many different communication tools, will be offered throughout the chapter. It is necessary to stress the importance of being creative and flexible when working with children. Using a child's area of greatest interest as an inroad for the direct work is usually more productive than trying to duplicate what worked with another child.

In Section I we will, using a developmental framework, explore further some of the general uses of direct work. Section II provides information on general principles for communicating with children. Section III will provide additional communication tools, presented along a developmental continuum. The Lifebook, which can be used in a variety of ways in direct work with children, is the topic of Section IV. The final section will be devoted to exploring the role of direct work during adolescence as we come full circle and try to help youth develop the skills they need to overcome the legacies of the past and interrupt the intergenerational cycle of abuse and neglect.

I   The Scope of Direct Work

According to Hapgood (1988) direct work is used to enable the child to understand significant events in the past, confront the feelings that are secondary to these events, and become more fully involved in the future planning of their lives. However, the first step in direct work is frequently to increase our own understanding of the child's perceptions of his life. Table 7-1 lists the uses the direct work.

Table 7-1

Direct work is used for

> gaining an understanding of the child's perceptions of his life
> disengagement work
> explaining plans for the future
> addressing current areas of concern
> enhancing attachments in current family
> facilitating identity formation
> increasing the child's knowledge of self
> reintegration of early life events
> focusing on life-long issues

A major aspect of direct work is listening for the child's perceptions. Until we do this, we won't know if we are to expand their information or correct their misperceptions.

Gene

Gene, age six, was legally free for adoption. His parents had divorced when he was two and he had had minimal contact with his dad subsequently. His birth mother had died quite suddenly when he was four. He then lived with maternal relatives. Although they cared deeply about him, they saw their mission as being to "save" Gene from the Devil, whom they likened to his birth father. Because Gene needed to be helped, not saved, he was moved to a foster home to be prepared for adoption by non-relatives.

Gene refused to talk with his caseworker about either parent, his relatives, or his thoughts or feelings about adoption. She had completed a Life Story Book with him, but knew that he had not really involved himself in it. It had been a compilation of information, not a tool for expressing emotions or sharing his perceptions with her.

The caseworker was concerned about moving Gene to an adoptive family while he was still in denial about his past. She was seeking help in getting Gene to share information. A consultant saw the caseworker and Gene together. He told Gene that he could either answer questions himself or that the caseworker, Ms. Weber, would answer for him if he preferred. Gene easily gave his name, told where he was living, and provided other current information. However, as soon as the consultant asked how he had come to be in interim care, Gene got up and started running around the playroom in a seemingly meaningless fashion. The consultant commented, "I think Gene is telling us that this is a very difficult subject for him to talk about. Maybe you can help him, Ms. Weber, by answering for him."

At this point, the consultant directed the questions about Gene's past to his caseworker, who told of the mother's death, of his minimal contact with his father, and of the relatives' strong negative feelings about Gene's father. She indicated that she thought Gene was really confused about his own feelings about his dad and what they should be.

As she had started talking of his father, Gene had taken some large pillows from a corner of the office and placed them around him in the center of the floor, with one on top of him. The consultant commented, "I think Gene has put himself in a coffin." At this point, the child removed the top pillow, sat up erect and said, "That's it. I have a black heart and am on the way to Hell."

This was the opening that Ms. Weber needed for further conversations with Gene. She subsequently used his coding, and they drew pictures of hearts which they painted in various colors. She had him assign different colored hearts to various people he knew and they talked of what that meant. During subsequent conversations Ms. Weber clarified some of Gene's misperceptions, including his magical thinking that he had been the cause of his mother's death because he had not called 911, but had run to a neighbor after spending considerable time trying to awaken his comatose mother.

Understanding Gene's perceptions was the first step in helping him to disengage from his past and look ahead to his future. Disengagement work is comprised of five steps according to Kay Donley, as reported by Cipolla *et al* (1990). The first step is to accurately reconstruct the child's placement history. The second is to identify various attachment figures in the child's life. Next, one must decide who were the most powerful of these figures in influencing the child's perceptions of self and others. The fourth step involves gaining the cooperation of the most significant attachment figure available so that the fifth step, having that person give the child permission to become a member of another family can transpire. The permission may be given in a face-to-face contact, via video or audio tape, or by written communication. What is important is that it come directly from the family members. This work is particularly important with children of school age who are joining an adoptive family.

Brad

Brad, six, is a Deprivational Dwarf. This is a condition in which a child develops, in response to attachment difficulties, hormonal changes which lead to the body size and proportions of dwarfism. Brad has had several out-of-home placements and returns to his parent's care. Consistently, when he is placed away from his family, his eating problems cease and he starts to grow. Although he is attached to his father, he actively rejects his mother to the extremes of refusing to talk to her, to acknowledge her presence, and most pertinently in refusing to eat if she is in the same room. A variety of home-based services have been supplied to Brad and his family. None have been successful. Finally, the parents decide that an adoption plan for Brad is the only viable solution.

In planning for a good-bye session between Brad, his parents, and his siblings, the caseworker knows that it will be important for Dad to give Brad permission to form close connections with an adoptive family. Dad is very sad about the circumstances in his family, but understands the importance of the task which has been designated to him.

At the time of his last contact with his son, Dad gets down on his knees in front of Brad and says, "I am so sad that it has not worked for you to live at home with us. I wanted that so much for all of us. However, since it isn't possible, more than anything else in the world right now I hope that you will have a family that you will learn to love and that will love you in return.

Even when parents agree to a face-to-face good-bye with their child, it is helpful to also have a letter which addresses three basic facts. The first is that the parent cares about the child. The second indicates that the parent either can't or won't be taking care of the child on a day-to-day basis. The final part gives the child permission to join another family, becoming emotionally close to another set of parents, so that his needs will be met. An example of such a letter was given on pag 265-266. Written communications are particularly helpful in disengagement work. Each time the letter is read, the child is likely to understand the message in a slightly different way, reflecting his current intellectual abilities and psychological needs. Yet, the basic message is always the same.

Horne (1983) identifies the caseworker as having the task of "building a bridge for the child" as he moves from one placement to the next. One of the major aspects of direct work is preparing children for new relationships. We have already seen how important preplacement preparation and attention to detail during the transition are. Several communication tools, such as the Aspects of Parenting on pg 159 have already been discussed. Other techniques, such as The Life Path will be discussed later in this chapter. The Child's EcoMap, a tool which is particularly useful when working with the preadolescent school-aged-child, is introduced in Exercise 7-1, which follows. The map, developed by members of the Branch County Department of Social Services in Coldwater, Michigan, was originally designed as an interviewing tool to open communication between the child of school age and social worker. Simultaneously, it can be used to assist the child in understanding his placement in interim care and the reasons he was removed from the birth home. It also provides an opportunity to clarify the caseworker's job and the role of the court. The EcoMap can be included in the child's Lifebook.

7-1 *Exercise*

Learning to Use the Child's EcoMap

The instructions are written with a child entering care in mind. They can be modified to fit other situations. Instructions: Select a child of grade school age, preferably a child whom you do not know well. Give the child a copy of the EcoMap and crayons or markers. Encourage the child to do the writing and coloring himself as the various areas of the map are discussed. The EcoMap is designed to alternate less psychologically loaded questions with those that are more difficult.

1.   Fill in the informational blanks.

2.   *Why am I here?* Encourage the child to share his own explanation to himself as to why he is in fostercare. If the child says something such as, "Well you put me here; you answer the question," the worker might

respond by saying, " It is important for you to understand why we made the placement decision, but I'm also interested in your thoughts. We will discuss both."

3.   *Social worker:* Children are often confused about this new person in their life.Let the child know what your job is--i.e.to work with him and his parents toward his return home.

4.   *Courthouse:* Briefly describe the hearing process and the role of the judge.

5 & 6.   *Homes:* Encourage the child to identify one of the homes as his birth home and one as the foster home with pathways to both. A third home can be added when necessary (i.e. if the child has contact with two birth parents who do not live together). Encourage the child to talk about similarities and differences in the two homes and parenting styles. Although children commonly initially focus on the physical attributes, let them know that through time the two of you will be comparing them in terms of the interactions. Describe the role of foster parents.

7.   *Siblings:* Finding out about sibling relationships is important whether brothers and sisters are placed together or not. As we have already observed, for many children separation from siblings may be as painful, or even more so, than separation from birth parents.

8.   *I feel* ————-*:* Encourage spontaneous verbalization from the child.

9.   *Things that bug me:* Let the child complete this. Younger children frequently respond to the visual cue by indicating that bugs bug them, but will usually expand on their dislikes if encouraged to do so.

10.   *School:* Encourage the child to talk about previous school experiences and the feelings he has about going to a new school while he is in foster care.

11.   *I worry about* ———-*:* Encourage spontaneous responses.

12.   *Things I like to do:* Let the child talk both of the things he enjoys and things that others do that make him happy. The responses can be used to help foster parents initiate positive interactions with the child

13.   *Dreams:* These can be either night time dreams or daydreams. The former frequently help identify fears and worries; the latter, hopes and dreams.

14.   *Friends:* Talk with the child about friends and how he might keep contact with them as well as discussing how he might go about making new friends in the new neighborhood and school.

Child's EcoMap

1.Me

Today is _____

by _____ I am _____ years old

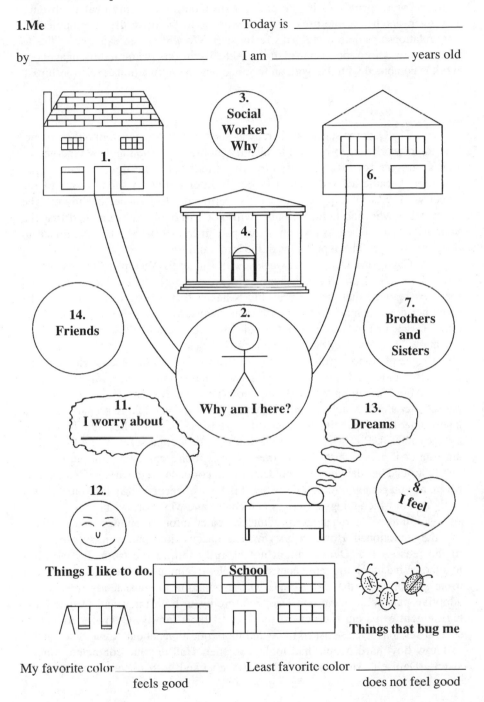

Things I like to do.

My favorite color _____
feels good

Least favorite color _____
does not feel good

A variety of examples of using direct work to address current areas of concern were provided in the chapter on Common Behavioral Problems. However, another of the uses of direct work is to facilitate the development of new relationships before problems really start. We will see an example of this as Denise moves into the Osborn family. Actually in this example, disengagement work is combined with the work on forming new, more functional, relationships.

Denise

The Osborns started in therapy as soon as Denise moved into their home. The direct work was to be used to identify problems as soon as they emerged so that strategies for effectively addressing them could be devised before the problems became a fixed pattern in family interactions. A second goal of the direct work was to help Denise face the permanent loss of her birthmom. The caseworker who had helped Denise with her Lifebook had indicated that the youngster had refused to take an active part in the work. She had continued to deny that there had been problems in the birth family.

Cassie and Denise met weekly with Linda, the therapist. Because of his work schedule, Larry joined them only every other week. The parents and therapist realized that Denise probably believed that others were trying to take away her good memories of her birth mom, Anna. Since Denise didn't yet know either Cassie or Linda well, it was decided that they would work together to earn her trust. They told Denise that although the social workers had told them both about some of Anna's problems, they felt that they didn't know enough about her positive qualities and strengths. Could Denise share some of this information with them? After coming up with several enjoyable memories and comments, Denise paused, her affect switched, and she then rattled off several more scenarios. Using a soft tone, Linda verbally confronted Denise by saying, "I believe the first set of things you said. But, what I don't know about the second set is if you think they are true or if you wish they were true." Cassie didn't comment, but put her arm gently around her daughter's shoulders. Linda commented to Cassie, "You know, Mom, as you get to know Denise better, I bet it will become easy for you and Dad to figure out which things are errors in memory and which are wishes."

In these interchanges the adults separated information they believed from that they questioned. However, they made no accusations and were supportive as to the reasons that Denise might not be fully telling the truth. By working together, Linda took the more confronting role, freeing up the new adoptive mom to be supportive to the child. Linda was also careful to consistently refer to the adoptive parents as Mom and Dad, reinforcing to both them and Denise their entitlement to parent the newest member of their family. Over the course of several sessions, Denise asked more and more questions about Anna. She wanted to know how hard people had looked for her. Had anyone contacted Anna's sister—Denise's Aunt Shirley? Had they checked with hospitals and police?

Linda suggested that they ask Denise's original caseworker to come in for an interview one day. Denise and her parents were asked to come up with a list of questions for Mr. Dawson. When they met with the CPS caseworker, Mr. Dawson, he told them that Anna had been in jail six months for forging checks to get money for drugs. After she was released from jail, she disappeared. Her parole officer had been unable to locate her.

Linda asked Denise if she would like Mr.Dawson to recontact the parole officer to see if he had any more recent information on Anna. She said yes. It was suggested that Denise and her parents, in the meantime, work on a letter to the aunt. Although Denise did not know her aunt's address, she did know her last name and what city and state she lived in. Larry was able to track down the address. Initially, Denise asked to call her Aunt Shirley. However after a thorough discussion, looking at the pros and cons of this course, it was decided that it might be best to first write a letter. Then, if Aunt Shirley responded, all four of them— Denise, her parents, and Linda—would decide, based on the contents of the letter, if a phone call was in order.

Their aligning with Denise in her search for information about her birth mother, helped the girl develop trust for her parents and therapist. Strong emotions started to resurface. Instead of the therapist being the primary support person for these feelings, Denise's parents were there to provide physical support and comfort. Meanwhile, at home, work on positive interactions continued. Attachments and bonds were being forged. Cassie and Larry felt effective and emotionally close to Denise. The decision was made that the weekly contact with the younger children should proceed to active preplacement planning. Denise agreed.

Denise had not yet acknowledged any sexual abuse in her family of origin. Since she was showing no signs of sexually reactive behaviors, it was decided to postpone addressing this area until after the younger children were settled in the family. Linda and the Osborns hoped that there would be a group for preadolescent girls who had been sexually abused, that Denise might join.

When a child has moved to a new home, particularly if this is to be a permanent placement—including returns to the birth family or to other relatives— active work with the child and family throughout the initial adjustment period should be provided. Commonly, an initial adjustment will be made within the first three months. However, it is nearly as common for there to be some sort of resurfacing of issues, sometimes with nearly explosive behaviors, between six and nine months. In the older child this seems to reflect the emotions they have as genuine feelings of closeness develop and their unconscious fears of subsequent pain surface. For parents, it may reflect the true extent of commitment that must be made on their part. They are no longer just excited about the child living with them. They have a clearer understanding of the depth of the problems and of the energy it will take to work with them. The caseworker's—or therapist's—commitment must be to the parent-child relationship, not to either the child or parent as individuals. (Katz, 1977).

When moving to a new permanent placement, the child may benefit from directions about things that he can do to start feeling emotionally connected to his new parents. Children from the age of four and up understand the concept of "practicing" as a way to learn a new skill. Situations in which the child may "practice" getting close to the new permanent caregivers can be defined. For example, after a move to adoption, the child might be asked to practice calling his new parents "Mom" and "Dad" right away; to practice giving hugs and kisses at bedtime; or to practice sitting on Mom's and Dad's lap; or to practice having fun together by playing games, or sitting close while reading a story, etc. Parents are given similar instructions, primarily so that the child understands that learning to be close involves both children and adults working at it. Variations of these practice sessions can be used when children return to birth parents after a lengthy absence.

Duke
Lily

When Duke and Lily joined the Osborn family, the direct work included them. In addition to the younger children practicing using the names Mom and Dad, and sitting on laps, they were encouraged to practice looking to the new parents for direction, even when Denise was present.

An additional aspect of the work was directed at creating an environment in which there was adequate supervision to diminish the likelihood of the sexually reactive behaviors resurfacing. Privacy in bathrooms and bedrooms was stressed. When children were dressing or undressing, doors were to be closed. When more than one child was in a bedroom, playing or talking, the door was to always be left open. Intercoms were placed in the younger childrens' bedrooms. The verbal message provided was, "We know that scary things have happened to you in bedrooms in the past. A parent's job is to know what is happening with their children and to keep them safe. If you need us at night, you can call to us from your rooms, you don't even need to get out of bed."

Over the course of the young person's growing up years, repeated intervals of direct work may be necessary to help him learn more about himself, integrate early life experiences with his current perceptions of himself and other, and to help him identify the life-long issues he will face as a result of early life events.

Looking at the Tasks of Direct Work Within a Developmental Framework

At every age, direct work can be used to help strengthen current relationships, to understand the child's needs and perceptions, and to prepare him for transitions. However, when it comes to coping with the effects of earlier traumas and parental separations and losses, the child's cognitive abilities will strongly influence what can be accomplished. Direct work by a caseworker with the child under age three-and-a-half to four is relatively rare. However, as we saw in Martin's case, a professional—in this case, Jane Paulson, a psychiatric nurse with training in infant mental health—may work with the primary caregivers—in this case, the LaBelles—to complete the goals of the direct work. For children of these tender years, these objectives usually center around facilitating relationships with current caregivers and helping the child process his sensory input. The more problematic the youngster's relationships with caregivers, the more important it is that helping professionals insure that all of their interventions are supportive of, not competitive with, the child's attachments to family members. Although we can work at minimizing the trauma of separations and losses, we cannot help the child of these years understand them.

Earlier chapters explained that children from ages four to eight have little capacity for abstract thinking. Magical and egocentric thinking are especially prominent in the early years of this period. These factors influence the nature of the direct work to be done during this period, as well as the modalities that will be used.

Because of his immature cognitive abilities, it is unlikely that adults will be able to change the child's perceptions of past events during this period. However, adults can be gathering information as to how the child explains the past to himself and to others. Adults need to capture the child's memories before they fade and go underground into the unconscious. This information will be useful in later work with the child. Much of the focus of direct work during the years four to eight or nine will be on facilitating new relationships, developing strategies for working with problem behaviors, and teaching new ways to express emotions and get needs met. As in all periods, direct work will also be used to minimize the truama of transitions. The child's perceptions of his life, being very difficult to counteract via an intellectual approach at these ages, may influence decision making about the future.

We met seven-year-old Gilbert at the beginning of this chapter. Gilbert's birth mother, of Euro-American descent, was addicted to cocaine. She neglected and occasionally abused him. When he was three, he was placed in interim care with a white couple. Gilbert had never had contact with his Afro-American birth father.

Currently, Gilbert is awaiting placement with an adoptive family. Although his caseworker believes that, in general, biracial children should be placed with families that are of their minority heritage, she is having difficulty

Gilbert

finding a black family for Gilbert. She also recognizes that he has never lived with an Afro-American family. She decides that she needs to learn more about Gilbert's views on race and his thoughts about an adoptive family.

In completing a Life Path for Gilbert's Lifebook, Ms. Waters learns that his memories of his birth mother are realistic. He can remember some good times, but also remembers the neglect and abuse. There does not seem to be a need for further disengagement work at this time. She uses the Life Path to talk about her desire that he have just one more move, a move to permanency with an adoptive family.

Ms. Waters then asks Gilbert to join her in thinking ahead to the type of family in which he envisions himself living. She takes out a series of envelopes. One contains pictures, cut from magazines, of women of all different sizes, shapes, and racial heritages. She spreads them out on the table and asks Gilbert to select the one that is most like the picture he has in mind of a "growing up with" mom. Gilbert selects a picture of an Afro-American woman. Ms. Waters then takes out her envelope with pictures of adult males. Gilbert selects an Afro-American man. Ms. Waters comments, "What if someone decided you should grow up in a family like this?" as she replaces the mother figure with one of Euro-American features, leaving the black father (recreating the circumstances of Gilbert's family of origin). Gilbert said no and replaced the mother with a another Afro-American woman. No matter how Ms. Waters rearranged the pictures, Gilbert was consistent in his representation of a family with a black father and a black mother. Finally, pulling up his sleeve and pointing to his arm, he said, "Look, Lady, do you see the color of my skin? People are supposed to live with people who have the same color skin." It really doesn't matter why Gilbert believes what he believes. What is important is that Ms. Waters take his views seriously. It is unlikely that he will be able to commit himself to a white family. He needs, and deserves, to have an Afro-American family to grow up with.

Around age eight or nine, children make a considerable leap in their cognitive abilities. This will affect their perceptions of life events and may influence the direction of the direct work to be undertaken with them. Brodzinsky (1990) points out that the child's understanding of the significance of the events that took place earlier in his life deepens during the school years. He goes on to point out that this increased understanding is likely to lead to behavioral changes that may be of concern to parents and teachers. These changes are likely to be the result of the normal process of adaptive grieving.

Colin

You may remember Merideth, a little girl we met in an earlier chapter. At age four she was leaving a foster family to whom she was strongly attached. You will remember that she had returned to the Faraday foster home after a previous disrupted adoptive placement. She did not want to leave the Faradays. You were

348

asked to outline a plan to help the transition process and decrease the likelihood of a second disruption. That second move to adoption was successful, and Merideth has been living with her adoptive family for five years now. She is nine.

Recently, the post adoption worker received a call from Merideth's mother. Her daughter had run away from school the day before. Mother described the run as a response to Merideth having become very upset when she was not allowed to be in charge during a game at recess. The post adoption worker set up an appointment for Merideth and her parents, but before hanging up the telephone she asked, "What game were they playing?" The response was, "Orphanage."

Glancing through the paper that night, the social worker noted that the movie *Annie* was playing at a local theater. Aha, it was starting to make sense. When Ms. MacNeice met with Merideth, she asked about the game. Close to tears, Merideth replied, "but they wouldn't let me be the Orphan Lady." That meant she had to be an orphan. Half-memories that were already bubbling in her unconscious memory had finally erupted to the surface, and the feelings were overwhelming. She knew that she had another mother before moving to the Faradays. What ever had happened to her? Was she dead? Was Merideth really an orphan?

Merideth had a Lifebook that described her early life history. However, she hadn't looked at it for years. It had been put up in a safe place. At the time of her move to her adoptive home, her feelings of separation centered on the loss of her foster family. Her birth family was only a distant memory, and not very important at that moment in time. Now, with her increasing awareness of life processes—of birth and conception, of past and present—the birth family had become more important to Merideth.

It was time to help her reconnect with her own history, through information provided both in the Lifebook and in the case records, so that she could better understand her life and mesh her past with her present.

Disengagement work is usually a priority in the direct work with children this age. This is just as true when the loss is in the distant past, as in Merideth's case, as when it is in the more recent past, as in Denise's. In both situations, there is the potential for the strong emotions that resurface during the disengagement work to be used to facilitate new relationships. As at all other stages of development, direct work may center on working with problem behaviors in the here-and-now as we saw in the numerous case examples in Chapter Six. The child's increased intellectual capabilities now make it possible to use inductive and deductive reasoning to help him overcome the legacies of earlier magical and egocentric thinking.

For example, if Ms. Waters had been seeing a ten-year-old Gilbert instead of a seven-year-old, she might have focused more on how he had arrived at his conclusions and might even have made attempts to expand his thinking. She might have pointed out that although people do usually grow up with families of the same race, there are exceptions. At ten, Gilbert would have the cognitive skills to explore looking at positive and negative attributes of people—beyond skin color. At seven, his concrete thinking prevents this. At either age, the best placement decision would most likely be an African-American family.

During the years eight to twelve, a common component of direct work is helping the child develop a "cover story", particularly if he has recently joined a new family. Children in care need a way to explain to others why they do not live with their birth family. The cover story is a shortened, not too revealing version of the truth. "They had so many problems of their own that they couldn't take care of me," is an example of a cover story that might be used by a child in foster care for any reason. "I needed a family to grow up with," might be a shortened explanation for a move from foster to adoptive home. A helping adult might provide a variety of short explanations that a child could use and then help him select, modify, or develop the one with which he feels most comfortable. If he has practiced his cover story with a trusted adult, it will be easier for him when someone else asks him, "Why aren't you living with your real parents?"

Sometimes adults or peers are dissatisfied with the child's responses, and they may continue to ask probing questions. Children need to be given permission to politely refuse to provide strangers or mere acquaintances with answers to personal questions. They need to learn to ask themselves, "Is this someone who really needs this information?" If not, they might say, "I'd rather not talk about it," or, "That's very personal information," or to give the Ann Landers response, "Why would you ask a question like that?" Again, providing the young person with opportunities to practice responses ahead of time will help him not to be caught off guard.

Colin

Colin, nine, following a previous adoption disruption, had recently joined another adoptive family in the same town in which his previous adoptive family, the Lees, lived. Although the two families lived in different neighborhoods, it was likely that at some time he might see his previous parents on the street or in a store. Mr. Lambert, his caseworker, wanted Colin to be prepared for the event. They talked about the possibility and rehearsed a variety of scenarios.

Sure enough, one day when he was at a large department store with his new adoptive family, Colin saw Mr. Lee. Although he was somewhat anxious, he greeted Mr. Lee and told him that he was getting along well in his new family and school. He then asked how things were with the Lee family and in the old neighborhood. Mr. Lee, caught totally off guard, stammered, stuttered, and looked very uncomfortable. Colin came away from the experience believing, rightly so, that he had handled it better than Mr. Lee. It was a tremendous boost to his self-esteem.

Although children need to know that it is okay not to answer everyone's personal questions, they also need to recognize that other children may be asking questions because they genuinely want information, not because they are trying to tease or to be mean. Grade schoolers in particular may be worried and wondering if someone is going to take them away from their family. The child in care might be able, in that circumstance, to talk about the variety of reasons that children enter care without identifying his own circumstances.

It is particularly common for teen-age girls to share too much personal information with their best friends. Unfortunately, adolescent friendships are not always permanent, and best friends may become worst enemies. Teens may need help and direction on deciding when and how to reveal personal information about themselves.

In working with adolescents it is useful to help them look ahead at the relationships they may form with others. When in the course of dating are they going to share information about their past? How much will they tell? These questions cannot necessarily be answered in advance. However, if they are raised in early adolescence, the teen will at least recognize that they must be considered and addressed in the future.

Once the young person has reached adolescence, his abilities for hypothetical thinking expand the possibilities and content of direct work. Brodzinsky (1990) observes that the adolescent not only must grieve for the loss of unknown (in the case of infant adoptions) birth parents, but he must also grieve the loss of part of himself. In solidifying his own identity, the adolescent that has been separated from his family of origin will realize that he has lost access to at least some aspects of his personal history.

Adolescents may need help in developing a strong sense of self that is not dependent on being either a victim or a victimizer in interpersonal relationships. Most importantly, the young person must learn to see himself as deserving of love and of good things happening to and for him. He needs to find ways to "fill up" the internal emptiness that will recur with stressful or hurtful here and now occurrences. The major long range goal is that hurts in the here and now should not have to lead to a reliving or acting out of all the hurts of the past (Beyer).

Triseliotis (1983) has identified three important areas which contribute to identity building in adolescence. The first is having a childhood experience of feeling wanted and loved. The second is knowledge about one's own personal history and the third is the experience of being perceived by others as a worthwhile person. With direct work we can insure at least two of these three areas.

As we will see later in this chapter, because of adolescents' increased cognitive abilities they can be helped to integrate information about their early life events with their current perceptions of themselves and others. They may then, with help, be able to forgive their birth parents and surpass them without feeling guilt about doing so.

Communicating with Children

Communication occurs via a variety of senses. It should not be thought of as limited to verbal interchanges. Adults need to be flexible and willing to try a variety of communication techniques with the goal being to find the ones that a particular child can most easily use to share information.

Adults are responsible for setting the stage for communicating with children, for knowing the type of information they desire to elicit or share, and for developing both overt and covert goals. Children are unique individuals. It is impossible for an adult to adequately represent them in making decisions on their behalf without knowing the child well. A primary goal of all communications with a child is to convey the dual message, "You are an important person. The more I know about you, the better I can act on your behalf." During all interchanges we want to facilitate alliance building between the child and adult and diminish the adversarial or power-based aspects that many children see as the norm for adult-child relationships.

Attention to detail pays off in setting the stage for communicating with children. Site selection, who is present, tools used, etc. all are dependent upon the child's age and stage of development as well as the particular details of his case. In general, for a very young child, it is likely that useful information will only be obtained if the child is seen in his home environment. The under-three is not likely to communicate much to adults who are strangers to him unless he is in a familiar environment or has a known adult close by.

The preschooler can usually tolerate short separations from caregivers without undue distress. However, this is only likely to happen if parental figures indicate that it is acceptable for the child to be with the non-family member. Children of this age will communicate most if in a setting with familiar type toys. They do not do well in a typical office for adults or in a small interview room with only one or two toys.

School-aged children, too, do not commonly communicate well when seen in a traditional office setting. However, in other settings, such as a playroom, they may be very expressive. Many caseworkers and parents have learned that school-aged children talk more freely when traveling in cars. However, talking with them in public, such as on an outing to a park or restaurant, carries some risk. Distractions are many, and the conversation may be interrupted by others at a crucial point. Difficult subjects that are likely to be accompanied by tears or angry outbursts are not good topics for public places. However, sometimes it makes sense to plan an outing to a specific place that is likely to trigger memories for the child.

Fran
Camille

Fran, thirteen, and Camille, eleven, have been in fostercare for a long time. Their mother was killed six years ago, several months after the girls had entered foster care because of neglect and repeated family violence. Their current behaviors are indicative of a resurfacing of the loss issues associated with

Mother's death. Although they were told at the time of its occurrence about Mother's death, they had not attended the funeral, and, because of their young ages, details were not shared with them.

A therapist was working with them on re-integrating earlier life experiences into their current sense of self. She was seeing the two girls together. Initially she asked them to draw a picture of the home where they had lived with their mother prior to entering care. Fran drew a detailed floor plan, while Camille drew a picture of the outside of the home. As they talked, each started to remember small details about the house and yard. Each memory seemed to trigger another. They were able to recall both some pleasant and unpleasant events.

The therapist asked what they remembered about their mother's death. What had they been told? At this point both girls became silent and denied any knowledge other than knowing the date of the death. Their change in affect was pronounced. Their therapist focused on whom they might talk to if they wanted more information. It was clear from their responses that they needed some time to process the memories that had already resurfaced before going further with the discussion of Mother's death.

At the outset of the next session, Fran suggested that there might be a record of their mother's death in the local newspaper. Since the public library was only two blocks away, the therapist and girls walked there during the therapy session. As the girls were scanning the microfiche copies of the newspaper, Fran noted a small item mentioning that an unknown woman's body had been found in a field. Both became involved in detailed scanning of subsequent editions of the paper. They found the article that identified the body as that of their mother. The obituary was located and the girls learned where their mother's body had been buried. Camille suggested that they make a trip to the cemetery.

The next therapy session involved a trip to the cemetery. The girls, with their therapist, talked with the caretaker who helped them locate their mother's burial plot. As they sat on the grave, the girls talked both about memories of their mother and about their feelings about her death.

In general, when interviews of school-aged children are being conducted in an office setting, using a table and chairs and some structured paper and pencil tasks or using play materials or games seems to put children more at ease than just sitting talking. Sitting at a kitchen or dining room table can be used when the school aged child is being seen in his home. When adolescents are seen in their homes, they usually communicate more openly when sitting in their rooms than in other areas of the house.

With older children, it is particularly important to help them in fully exploring issues, seeing that there are at least two sides to every issue. The child beyond the age of eight or nine, now capable of inductive and deductive reasoning, should be encouraged to look at all the ways a particular decision might be good for him and all the ways it might not work out well. By inviting children's input into both sides of the equation the adult models good decision making.

In general, people will share more with those who not only ask questions but who also disclose information about themselves. Especially with adolescents, it is important to enter into an alliance in which the young person is able to teach adults and influence their perceptions of the world just as much as adults try to change teens. A goal of all adult interactions with adolescents is to help expand their thinking from either/or to include a variety of options which fall between the two extremes. In working with adolescents, we are preparing them to take on the responsibilities of adulthood. Therefore, another of our objectives should be to help the young person understand himself. For information to be of any lasting value, everything we learn about the teen must be shared with him. He needs to know as much about himself as we do. Our task is to help him become aware of his choices. His task is to become responsible for the choices he ultimately makes.

Although adults need to be supportive of the youngster's underlying feelings, they should also feel comfortable supportively confronting problematic behaviors. Children are most likely to signal behaviorally either their unwillingness or inability to cope with information or their emotions. We saw an example of this with Gene, who hid under the pillow. Physical complaints may mask emotions. "Listening" to these symptoms will aid communication. For example, when a difficult topic of conversation is raised, children may say they are too tired to talk further or they have a headache or stomachache. The adult might respond with, "I know it would be much easier just to block everything out like we do when we are asleep, but I don't think that will help you cope with your feelings. They are too important to ignore." Or, "Lots of people get stomach aches when they are anxious. Thanks for letting me know that that's one of the ways I can tell when we're talking about something difficult. How could I make it easier for you to talk about this?"

Charmaine

Charmaine, twelve, would literally run and bury herself under a stack of large pillows in her therapist's office whenever a difficult topic was raised. Initially, the therapist tried in a supportive tone to verbally confront her about her long-standing defense of running away from problems. This didn't seem to work.

Charmaine continued to hide until the end of the session. One day, her therapist "decoded" the hiding behavior in a different way. This time she said, "I know sometimes it's really hard to talk about painful things. Lots of times people haven't waited until you were ready. It probably seems to you like adults are always in a hurry and don't really want to hear what you have to say. I'm just going to sit here with you until you are ready to come out. I really care about you and want to know what you are thinking." She accompanied her words with a gentle touch on Charmaine's shoulder under the pillows. Within a few minutes, Charmaine started crying and gradually emerged from under the pillow.

In listening to behaviors, adults must risk verbalizing what they think the children are trying to say about their thoughts or feelings, while continuing to give permission for disagreement, either verbally or behaviorally, about the interpretation.

Latency-aged children, particularly from age eight or nine, and adolescents may share more information in a semi-structured group setting than on an individual basis. Being involved in a therapy group can address basic social skills interpersonal communication skills, as well as specific issues such as divorce, parent loss, sexual abuse, etc. The younger the children, the more important it is that adults provide structure for the group.

Adults working with children who have experienced abuse, neglect, or parental separation and loss must be able to accept a variety of strong emotions without either minimizing them or feeling overwhelmed by them. However, they must also be careful that their own feelings about the child's situation do not exceed or contradict the child's perceptions. To be successful in this work, it is necessary for adults to come to grips with their own personal histories. Everyone has experienced life events which are likely to resurface as we work with children. Sometimes the boundary between adult helper issues and child issues is unclear, as we saw in the case of Mrs. Green, the caseworker in an exercise in an earlier chapter.

Additional Communication Tools   III

Again, the avenues that are most useful for communication will vary with the child's age. Many have already been mentioned throughout this book. Although an exhaustive list will not be supplied, several additional specific tools that we have found to be particularly useful in communicating with children in placement will be mentioned here.

From age three or four to eight or nine, toys are frequently used to facilitate communication. Two toy telephones, a couple of puppets or stuffed animals, and maybe some dollhouse figures are useful supplies. Photographs of family members can be very useful adjuncts in helping both child and adult be certain they are talking about the same people.

Table 7-2

Some Communication Tools Useful with Ages Four to Ten

> toy telephones, puppets, and dolls
> joint storytelling
> books, workbooks, games
> art activities
> "little pitchers have big ears"
> Feeling Faces/lists of emotions
> "listening" to behaviors
> Child's EcoMap
> Life Path
> Lifebook
> "who do you go to for what?" cards

Toy telephones, when combined with photographs of adults from whom they are separated, are useful in gathering information about the child's impressions of previous relationships. The interviewer initially might give the child a choice as to whether he wants to be himself or the adult in the picture during a conversation. The examiner will take the other role. The child can be encouraged to ask questions or say whatever he wants, no matter which role he initially takes. However, it is useful to eventually have both the child and examiner take each role. This technique is equally useful whether the adult is trying to gather information or dispense it.

Brenda

Brenda, five, had left her birth mother's care two years ago. At that time the mother was hospitalized with a brain tumor. Using the toy telephones, Brenda pretended she was calling her birth mom. Brenda asked what she had done that had made her mother ill. She asked if her mother was still angry at her. The caseworker, taking the role of Mom, said, "I know that I was frequently angry when we were together. But it wasn't you that made me mad; it was my sickness. I hope things are going well with you now. I hope you have a mommy who is not sick and can take good care of you. You deserve that."

In this situation, the caseworker not only learned more about Brenda's situation, but she provided some corrective information, and attempted to do some disengagement work. In general, preschoolers will communicate more information when not asked direct questions. Using puppets or stuffed animals and joint storytelling facilitate active participation on the part of the child. The puppets or stuffed animals ask the questions or make the comments. Children of these ages will reveal much more to a puppet than directly to the adult asking the same questions. Likewise, they will listen more carefully to puppets than to adults.

Joint storytelling (Gardner, 1971) is a useful technique with children from ages three to twelve. The child is asked to choose a favorite animal and name him. The adult then starts telling a story about the animal. The story reflects the child's history. After several sentences, the adult asks the child to continue the story. In this way the child has the opportunity to share emotional reactions to life events as well as his perceptions and desires for the future. Since the adult once again takes up the story after several sentences from the child, the examiner has the opportunity to lead the story line into areas where she desires information.

Benjamin, age four, had been living in interim care for close to a year because of being severely physically abused by his mother's boyfriend. He had developed a close, loving relationship with his foster parents. Benjie had weekly visits with his teen-aged birth mother who was no longer with the same boyfriend. The plan was for him to be returned to Mother's care shortly. His caseworker, Mrs. Shields, wanted to know more about how Benjamin viewed the past abuse and whether or not he perceived his mom as now able to provide adequate physical safety. She decided to use joint story telling to facilitate her communications with Benjie. She knew that with the younger child it is frequently necessary for the adult to ask some leading questions during the story telling.

Benjamin

Mrs. S: Once upon a time there was a bunny named Ben. When he was just a baby, Bunny Ben lived with his mommy and his grandma. How do you think things went for Bunny Ben when he was a baby?

B: Bunny Ben was happy with his mommy and grandmother.

Mrs. S: Then what do you think happened?

B: Then they moved.

Mrs. S: One day Bunny Ben's mommy and grandmother had an argument and Ben and his mommy moved. They moved in with some friends of Bunny Ben's mother. How do you think things went for Bunny Ben then?

B: Sad.

Mrs. S: Was Ben sad a lot? Was he missing someone?

B: He was *very* sad for his grandma. There was a mean man.

Mrs. S: When Bunny Ben was very sad, he cried a lot. Mommy's friends did not like to hear crying. One of them would get so frustrated that he would spank Bunny Ben so hard that it really hurt him. It is not okay for adults to hurt children. One day some neighbors heard Bunny Ben crying very hard. They called some adults who help bunny families who are having problems. One of the adults came to visit Bunny Ben's family.

357

Bunny Ben had lots of bruises on his bottom. The man who had spanked him was very angry at everyone. Bunny Ben needed to be in a safe place where he wouldn't be hurt. How do you think Bunny Ben felt when he moved to a new place?

By continuing the story, Mrs. Shields encouraged Benjie to talk about his feelings in interim care and about his thoughts and feelings about the upcoming move back to Mother's care. She learned that he missed his mom and wanted to spend more time with her. However, Mrs S. also learned that he was less worried about physical harm in the future than sad about anticipating the separation from his foster family. Like most children his age, the story solution he chose was for Mommy Bunny to move in with Bunny Ben and his foster family.

Mrs. S. then modified the ending to the story, acknowledging that Bunny Ben would like one ending, but that none of the adults thought it would work out for them. Instead, they decided that he should go live with Mommy Bunny but frequently visit with his foster family so he wouldn't miss them so much.

The "Little Pitchers Have Big Ears" technique is effective with a wide variety of ages. Many times children will listen to what adults are saying *about* them, but have difficulty hearing what is said directly *to* them. A combination of this technique and "listening" to behaviors was used with Gene—the child who believed he had a black heart—a few pages ago.

With older preschoolers and grade-school-aged children a variety of books, workbooks, and games can be used to facilitate communication. Books or printed fill-in-the-blanks handouts help children understand that others have experienced similar life events, and that talking about them is acceptable. Non-competitive communication games are useful. They are usually dependent upon the adult, as well as the child, sharing feelings. They can be used either with one adult and the child, with an entire family, or in a group of children.

Story books that talk about the events that are common for the child in placement— such as separation from parents, sexual abuse, divorce, birth, and various emotions—can be used to introduce specific topics of conversation. It is worthwhile to periodically check the children's section in a large bookstore for new story books or workbooks that might be useful. Some books and games are listed in the resource list at the end of this chapter.

In the first chapter we mentioned a series of cards developed by E. James Anthony, M.D. which can be used for helping the young child share information about family interactions. They are equally useful with the child between four and eight and the preadolescent. The Feeling Faces cards, shown in Figure 7-1 on the page 360, can be used when talking with children about either current or past events. The cards are spread out on the floor or on a table and the child is asked to select the ones that show how he felt at the time of specific events, such as entering care, visiting with parents, before the fight with his brother, etc.

Once children are able to read, cards each with a single emotion written on them, may be used. These can be used in a variety of ways. Most commonly they are spread out on a table and the child is asked to select the ones that represent his feelings about specific events that are being discussed. Seeing the words, as well as giving permission to have any of a variety of emotions, frequently triggers the child's memory. Sometimes it becomes apparent that a certain combination of feelings leads to a predictable behavioral reaction.

7-3 *Table*

Common Emotions

confused	discouraged	blamed
pleased	depressed	loved
comfortable	unloved	cheated
frustrated	resigned	lost
furious	abandoned	rejected
proud	worried	uncomfortable
numb	empty	embarrassed
lonely	anxious	powerless
stubborn	triumphant	angry
happy	hopeful	sad
mad	satisfied	ashamed
scared	concerned	jealous
guilty	excited	unlovable
loss	hopeless	relieved

Figure 7-1

Happy

Sad

Scared

Angry

Lonely or Left Out

Confused

In the following case, the feeling cards were used to facilitate communication with parents and children at the time of an adoptive disruption.

The adoptive parents of Jim, thirteen, and his sister Karen, eleven, decided to disrupt the placement after twelve months. As part of trying to minimize the trauma of the disruption, they were meeting with a therapist. The therapist insisted that the parents themselves tell Jim and Karen that they have decided to disrupt the placement. However, this was done in the therapist's office. The children were not surprised, as there had been many problems and they both had said frequently that maybe they should just move.

After Jim and Karen were told of the decision, the therapist handed out copies of a list of emotions and asked that each circle the feelings they were currently experiencing. All four family members—both parents, Jim, and Karen—circled "guilty" and "sad." Each had a couple of additional emotions which were dissimilar from those of other family members. The therapist helped each to talk about his own feelings of guilt. Each was able to take responsibility for his part of the relationship without anyone becoming a scapegoat. They then focused on the sadness that each would feel, both in reaction to missing each other and also in having to give up a fantasy that each had had about what their relationship might have become.

Other times the cards are used in a gamelike manner, particularly in groups. The cards are spread face down and each child is asked to select three or four and then to write or tell a story that involves each of the emotions on the cards they drew.

Jim
Karen

7-4 _Table_

Some Communication Tools Helpful with Ages Eight to Twelve

list of feelings
parent messages
art activities
board games
books and workbooks
printed fill-in sheets
using visual ways to explain concepts
one to ten scale
Life Path
Lifebook
advantages/disadvantages lists
Aspects of Parenting circles
Joint Storytelling

Beyond the age of nine or ten, children may use their abilities for more abstract thinking in their drawings. Frequently they can share complex information in this way—information that is difficult to put into words. Examples include drawing a circle that represents all of a child's feelings about a particular event and then asking the child to divide the circle into sectors representing the percentages of various feelings. Figure 7-2 provides an example.

_____ *Figure*   7-2

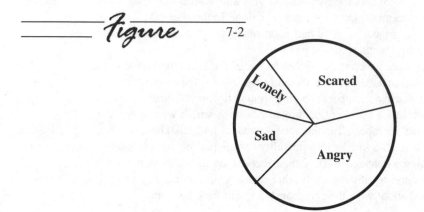

Drawing a circle that represents the family as a whole and then having the child draw a circle that represents themselves is another example. Earlier, Judy used this method for sharing how she felt in the Haslett family through time. Another example is given in Figure 7-3.

_____ *Figure*   7-3

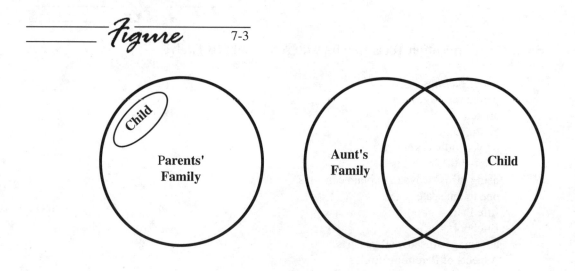

362

Fifteen-year-old Mario is living with an aunt and uncle. He was placed with them a year ago after his parents were sentenced to prison for selling drugs. The circle on the left represents his perception of himself in his family of origin. He felt like he was an insider, but not very significant. In his aunt's family, where he currently lives, the drawing on the right indicates that he sees himself as having more influence and power, but as being not totally included in the family. The drawings confirmed information gained by the history. When living with his parents, he knew of their illegal activities but was threatened with bodily harm if he ever told anyone. His aunt spends considerable time with this adolescent and has helped him become involved in a variety of extracurricular activities. However, the uncle is fearful that his acting-out behaviors and school problems will have an adverse effect on the younger children in the family. He is resentful of this teen's presence in his home and is not very involved with him.

Mario

A Life Path may be used with children five and up both to help them understand and reintegrate earlier life events and to aid communication about possible alternative plans for the future. A sample Life Path is shown in Figure 7-4 on the following page.

This Life Path summarizes the major events in ten-year-old Craig's life. His parents divorced when he was three and he has had minimal contact with his father since then. Craig lived with his birth mother until he was four, when he entered interim care after being sexually abused by mother's boyfriend. Mother did not believe the allegations and ran off with the boyfriend, abandoning her son in foster care. Craig has lived in two different foster homes. His current foster parents would like to adopt him. A maternal aunt and uncle, whom he has visited about twice a year, have expressed a desire for guardianship. Birth father retains his parental rights but has only visited Craig once in the past year. However, he has sent birthday and Christmas gifts consistently.

Craig

Craig's caseworker, Ms. Brown, is interested in knowing how the youngster would view each of the alternative plans for permanency. Ms. Brown initiates the conversation by talking about Craig being on the path to adulthood. There is more than one road that can be taken. The various paths involve Craig living with different families during the remainder of his growing up years. She then introduces the idea of one path involving adoption by the foster family, another having Craig living with his aunt and uncle, and the third having him live with his birth dad. Ms. Brown seeks input from Craig as to what he sees as the good parts and not so good parts of each path. How would he feel if Ms. Brown and the judge decided he was to be placed on this path? On this one? Or on this one?

Figure 7-4

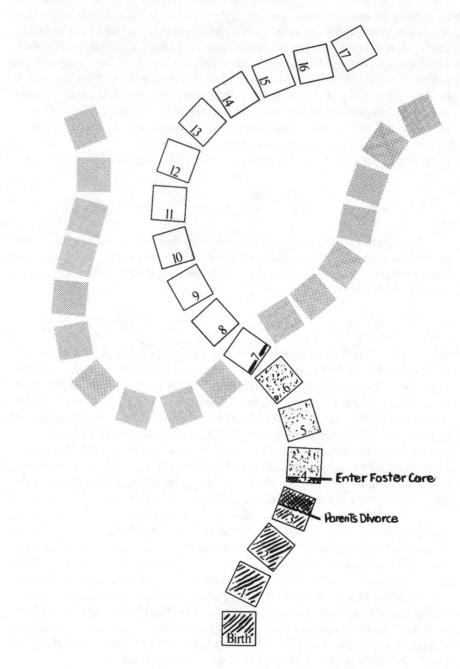

+	-

Actually, in this example Mr. Brown was using a combination of the life path and the plus and minus chart shown in Figure 7-5.

The purpose of this chart is to help the young person look at both sides of any issue. In general the adult helps the child focus first on the decision she thinks the child hopes will be made, for example a return to the birth parent's care. The adult then asks the child to help list all of the ways that decision would be good for him. She makes certain that she, too, lists at least one advantage while they are exploring the positives. Then the adult comments that every decision has pluses and minuses and that it is important to look at both. She then switches to the ways that the particular decision being contemplated might not work out well. By adult and child working together on both sides of the list, it helps to avoid a situation in which a child lists all of the advantages and the adult lists all of the disadvantages or vice versa. It models that two people working together will usually come up with more ideas than one, and that by cooperating they frequently will agree upon which plan has more advantages than disadvantages. Even if an agreement cannot be reached, the adult will know more about how the child feels and why he feels that way. Avenues for maximizing all advantages and minimizing the disadvantages that accompany a decision are more likely to become apparent.

Once they are old enough to use abstract thinking, both children and adolescents may make use of codes for sharing information. For example, an adult might ask how things are going at school on a scale of one to ten. This type of scaling can be used in a wide variety of ways. Both child and parent might be asked to scale how he did on chores during the past week. In this way we can determine if children and parents agree on performance levels. Scaling can also be used to describe the intensity of both an event and the reaction to it. Many children in care seem to over-react to minor stimuli—for example, physically hitting a child who accidently brushed against them in the hall—while under-reacting to major events—i.e. showing no reaction when a parent does not show up for a scheduled visit on the child's birthday.

Some Communication Tools Which are Useful with Adolescents

writing journals or letters	parent messages
one to ten scales	communication games
drawings	fill-in worksheets
gestalt techniques (i.e. two	advantages/disadvantages lists
chair, personal fairy tales,	Lifebook
or guided fantasies)	Aspects of Parenting circles
lists of emotions	

       Although adolescents may sometimes refuse to talk directly to an adult, we find that they will frequently interrupt if adults are talking to each other, in the teen's presence, about what they think he is trying to tell them with his behaviors. Adolescents have the conceptual abilities necessary for making use of the wide variety of communication techniques that have been developed for working with adults.

Parent message, are useful in communicating with children nine and older. A sample list of parent messages is given in Table 7-9 on pages 387 to 389. Again, they can be used in a variety of ways. Young people can share their interpretations of the expectations of previous parents. They can be used to identify new and healthier messages and ways to get them across. They can, as we will see a little later in this chapter, be used to determine how successful our reparenting strategies are.

IV   The Life Story Book

       Traditionally, the family is the repository of knowledge about the child. Children who do not live with their families of origin do not have daily access to this source of information about their own personal history. When children are repeatedly separated by multiple moves from those individuals with whom they have shared life experiences, their personal history becomes fragmented. It becomes more difficult for them to develop a strong sense of self and for them to understand how the past influences present behaviors. It is less likely that they will understand the patterns of either their family or personal history. Without this awareness, it will be more difficult for them to make conscious choices and take responsibility for their own behaviors. Our past history confirms who we are and provides us with a sense of identity.

Every individual is entitled to his own history. For that reason, we believe that a Lifebook should be started for each child in the child welfare system at the time he first enters care. The Lifebook needs to accompany him, and to be added to, as he journeys through life, whether that includes reunification with the birth parents, a placement with relatives, joining a family by adoption, or emancipating from the system.

If a child becomes legally free for adoption and a Lifebook has not been initiated by the protective service or foster care workers, it falls to the adoption worker to seek out the information and pictures necessary for the book as part of the preparation for adoption. For children who are already in their adoptive home without a Lifebook, compiling one may enhance the attachment to the adoptive family if they are involved with the professional in gathering information and completing the book. It is never too late to do a Lifebook nor too early to start one.

It is difficult to grow up as a psychologically healthy adult if one is denied access to one's own history. The very fact that adults hesitate to share with a child information about his past implies that it is so bad that the youngster won't be able to cope with it. Whatever the past was, the child has lived through it and survived. He has already demonstrated his survival skills. However, facts can be presented either in a way that helps the child understand and accept his past while raising self-esteem, or in a way that lowers feelings of self worth. With experience, helping adults can learn to reframe even negative life experiences as positive strivings that went astray.

Successful completion of a Lifebook is dependent upon the development of good communication between an adult and the child. In general, the adult must prove herself to be trustworthy and dependable before the child is likely to share his innermost thoughts and feelings. Once again the goal of the interchanges between the adult and child should be to convey the message, "You are important. Your thoughts and feelings are important in my decision making." Ryan (1985) comments, "In working with a child your essential task is to learn how he explains himself to himself, and what he understands his situation to be."

Many abusive and neglectful parents themselves have gaps in their self-knowledge. Some protective service caseworkers have helped birth parents compile their own Lifebooks, helping the parents understand their own past. The worker who is willing to help them fill in these gaps will be trusted more than the worker who ignores the past. If parents have experienced the usefulness of a Lifebook, Genogram, or EcoMap in understanding themselves, they are more likely to help provide information for their child in care.

Purposes of a Lifebook

Basically, the Lifebook provides a chronology of the child's life, helping the young person understand and remember what has happened to him in the past. Additionally, the Lifebook can be used to enhance self-esteem and identity formation. Therapeutically, it can be used as a tool for resolution of strong emotions about past events, especially those related to separation or loss experiences. There will be many opportunities for the adult to separate feelings from behaviors, being accepting of the former while confronting inappropriate behaviors that either the child, his parents, or other adults may have demonstrated. A Lifebook can link the past to the present by helping the child understand how earlier life events affect current perceptions and behaviors. It can be used as a tool to help the child understand his past, what is currently happening to his family, and what it means to be in the child welfare system. It can also be used in preparing a child for an upcoming move. This history provides a vehicle for sharing information with significant others in the child's life, such as new parent figures.

Table 7-6

A Lifebook Can-

> provide a chronology of the child's life.
> enhance self-esteem and identity formation.
> help a child share his history with others.
> assist in resolving separation issues.
> identify connections between past, present, and future.
> facilitate attachment
> increase trust for adults
> help the child recognize and resolve strong emotions
>   related to past life events
> separate reality from fantasy or magical thinking
> identify positives, as well as negatives, about the family of origin

Later in this section we will look at how the Lifebook can be used for a variety of objectives in working directly with children throughout their growing up years. We will see that it is used to clarify the child's understanding of what has happened, to help him and his family understand what underlies current behaviors, and to help him understand himself through time.

What Goes into a Lifebook?

The Lifebook is an account of the child's life conveyed by words, pictures, photographs, and documents. Every Lifebook should mention the child's birth mother and birth father. "We have no information about your birth father," at least acknowledges that he exists and that it is acceptable to talk about him.

Children like to have information about their own birth, including how much they weighed, how long they were, what day of the week they were born, and at which hospital. A baby picture should be included if one is available. Some hospitals can refer the worker to the photographer who did the infant photos when the child was born, and a picture may still be available. Health problems or abnormalities observed at birth should be noted as well.

Each book should explain why and how the child entered the foster care system and how subsequent decisions were made. Children come into foster care because of abuse, neglect, or because their parents ask for help. Many times adults helping the child with his book gloss over the reasons he entered care. This can pose long range problems.

Cheryl

Cheryl, who is twelve, demonstrates many behaviors that are commonly seen in children with a history of sexual abuse. Before she joined their family, the adoptive parents were advised that the agency had strong suspicions the Cheryl had been sexually abused while living with her birth family. However, no attempt had been made to either substantiate or prosecute the allegations. In Cheryl's Lifebook the reason given for her leaving her family of origin was that her parents were very young. Although the birth parents had not asked that she be placed in foster care, there was no mention of abuse or neglect in the book.

Currently, Cheryl strongly denies any memories of sexual abuse. When either adoptive parent or therapist confronts her with the possibility of this having happened, she becomes very angry, shouting, "I left them because they were young. The social worker said so. You don't know anything. You weren't there."

In this case, the caseworker who helped Cheryl with her Lifebook did a major disservice by joining in the denial defense and not mentioning any form of abuse, neglect, or the possibility of sexual abuse. The only way that Cheryl will be able to face the reality of her situation is if someone can open the records and show her documentation of events and why the original casworkers suspected that she had been sexually abused.

Photographs of the birth parents should be included when the child comes into placement. One-of-a-kind photos should be duplicated before being put in the Lifebook, with a copy being put away for safekeeping. Information about parents and siblings should be gathered as soon as possible. If a Genogram has been completed as part of the assessment of the birth family, a copy should be included. Information about developmental milestones and the youngster's behavior in the home should be presented in words the child understands and should be accompanied by pictures whenever possible. While a child is in a foster family, additional information is added to the Lifebook. Information that foster families should compile is listed in Table 7-7.

Table 7-7

Information to be Compiled by Foster Parents

developmental milestones
common childhood diseases
immunizations
information about injuries, illnesses, or hospitalizaion
ways the child showed affection
what he did when he was happy or excited
what things he was afraid of
favorite friends, activities and toys
birthday and religious celebrations
trips taken with the foster family
members of the foster parent's extended family
   who were important to the child
cute things the child did
nicknames
family pets
visits with birth relatives
names of teachers and schools attended
report cards
special activities, such as scouting, clubs, or camping experiences.
church and Sunday school experiences
pictures of each foster family, their home, and their pets

Most toddlers and preschoolers do some things that upset their parents at the time, but seem humorous in retrospect and become the basis of family stories. Talking about such behaviors gives the child a clear indication that he can and will change. Even though there are frequently no pictures of these incidents, they usually elicit strong visual images. For example, one child as a toddler loved to sit on the sack of dogfood, feeding a piece first to the dog and then to himself. Another child washed her hair in a mud puddle twice in one day as her mother tried to get her ready to go to a party. These behaviors are unique to each child but are ones that usually lead to shared laughter when the youngster outgrows that conduct, and they should be included in the Lifebook.

Letters obtained as part of the disengagment work may be included. As children reach adolescence, they want additional information about their birth parents. This additional information can either be put in the Lifebook itself, or handed on separately to the permanent caregivers for sharing later with with adolescent.

Many times a child needs basic information about his life ("How old was I when I left my birthfamily?") but does not want to deal with all of the difficult emotions. For that reason, as well as for others, it is advisable to put a copy of the child's Life Path either at the front or at the back of the Lifebook. It provides a summary of major life events and comparisons of lengths of time the child lived with various families.

Sources of Information

There are a wide variety of sources of information to be explored when one is completing a Lifebook. Obviously the social service record is the primary one used by most caseworkers. Sometimes previous caseworkers can provide considerable information that might be important to the child, but that was not incorporated into the case record. Records from other agencies that have had contact with the child or other family members may also be a source of information. These might include hospitals, well baby, or mental health clinics. Day care personnel may have pictures, as well as information about the child's development and peer skills. Specific teachers, as well as school records, might be utilized. Usually, classroom pictures are available, even if the individual photographs are not.

Birth family members are an obvious source for pictures, mementos, and a variety of other information as well. It is easiest to access this source when one is doing the initial assessment. However, even if a Lifebook is not done until long after the child has left the family, caseworkers have sometimes had success obtaining information and pictures by contacting the birth parents even several years after termination of parental rights or a voluntary release of legal rights. The message to the birth parents in such cases is that they still have something to offer the child even though they will not be parenting him. Requests from the adoptive parents for pictures or information reassures the birth parents of their importance in the child's life. If the caseworker makes such contacts, there are minimal problems with confidentiality.

——— *Table* ——— 7-8

Sources of Information

the child himself	school records*
case records	health records
birth parents*	court records
other relatives*	police reports
neighbors	adult sponsors of activities*
previous caregivers*	

Sometimes grandparents or other relatives may have the desired pictures or information. Past and present foster families, as mentioned earlier, should provide information. Other adults who have come in contact with children in foster care might be utilized in gathering information. Examples might include Sunday School teachers, church group or Scout leaders, or coaches.

Police reports from the time of the original contacts with the family are particularly useful, as they are usually written in a very factual manner, clearly differentiating between observations and impressions. Sometimes individual policemen have extensive information about specific families or situations. They may even have pictures obtained for Missing Persons files.

Phillipa

Twelve-year-old Phillipa wanted more information about her mother who had disappeared eight years ago. Phillipa remembered that there had been a police investigation and that mother's boyfriend had been suspected of murdering her. Her case record contained the name of the police detective who had been assigned to the case.

Phillipa's therapist contacted the policeman. He remembered the case well. He confirmed that the boyfriend had been under suspicion of murder. However, two years later, friends of the mother had received a letter from her. Handwriting experts had determined that it had, indeed, been written by her.

The detective had pictures of the mother—from the missing person posters made at the time of the disappearance—and a copy of the letter on file. He sent both to the therapist and offered to meet with Phillipa herself.

* items may also be sources of photographs of the child

Newspapers may provide birth announcements, marriage or divorce announcements, or obituaries, sometimes again with pictures. In searching, it is always worthwhile to ask the child for ideas as to where pictures or additional information might be obtained. Many times children themselves know of relatives, neighbors, or others who might have either pictures or facts.

How To

There is no right or wrong way to do a Life Story Book. Just as each child and his history is unique, so will each Life Story be one of a kind. Some children like to start at the beginning, with their birth or even before, with how their birth parents met, etc. Others are not ready to think or talk about the past until they learn to trust the adult who is helping them with their book. They may do better starting with the present, talking about current family, school, friends, likes, and dislikes. Some even want to start out talking about future plans. There are advantages to each of these approaches.

Some caseworkers use a book with construction paper pages. Although to many children the idea of a scrapbook is pleasurable, to the child in foster care who may have poor self-esteem, the term "scrap" may have a negative connotation. Therefore, we prefer to avoid the term scrapbook. Loose leaf photo albums with plastic protecting the individual pages may be used. Some adults use prepared books, others make up their own. Some include photocopied or printed pages to be filled in. The resource list at the end of the chapter provides some further ideas.

The particular words used in a Lifebook are often very important. The use of "natural" or "real" parents should be avoided because of the connotation that adoptive, foster, or step parents are either "unnatural" or "unreal." We also purposefully avoid the term "forever" which may sound overwhelming to the child. The terms "keeping" or "growing up with" explain equally well the permanency that we are seeking for children when we make adoption plans for the child.

Although the child usually contributes, not only in terms of content, but also in terms of production, we have learned that through time children will most use the books that have the history itself in neat legible script, as opposed to it being entirely composed of the child's early writing. If they themselves have done all of the writing at young ages, they tend to see the book as "for little kids." Alternatively a worker might want to include samples of the child's writing or pictures, but other documentation as well.

Children are very concrete in their thought processes, particularly when it comes to emotionally-laden material. For this reason, it is important that the helping adult be careful in selecting the words used. Differentiating emotions and desires from actual behaviors, as we will see in Sarah Ann's Life story, is particularly helpful in describing why adults did harmful things to children.

When children are resistant to being an active participant in working on their Lifebook, adults have to become more creative. Trips, with a camera, to an old neighborhood, to the hospital where the child was born, or to the courthouse where decisions were made on his behalf are examples. A caseworker from Delaware told of a technique she had used with an especially resistant preadolescent who was being prepared for adoption. This particular boy wanted to perform on television when he grew up. She used his interest to involve him. She asked him to conduct a series of videotaped interviews. The child's original protective services worker was the first to be interviewed. At the end of the taping session, the current caseworker asked a few additional questions and took a picture. A previous foster parent was invited to another interview. After talking extensively about the child's likes and dislikes when he was in her home, she mentioned that she had met the birth parents during some of the visits. Although the child did not ask questions about the parents, he did not protest when his adoption worker did so.

Miles Hapgood (1988) relates a wonderful story about Craig, an adolescent. Mr. Hapgood, a social worker, had tried a variety of techniques, suggested by this author and others, to involve Craig in Life Story work. All were to no avail. Craig was not interested in learning about his past. He was only interested in computers. Finally, Mr. Hapgood decided to go with Craig's interest. He helped him get the money for his own computer—Craig saved half the money, social services came up with the other half. The social worker suggested that Craig develop a game for children in foster care. Craig came up with his own idea—remember, he is an adolescent. He designed a computer program for use with children and adolescents who were entering foster care.

For pre-school aged children, caseworkers themselves frequently write the child's Life Story, hopefully with some input from the child. For children this age, the story may be written in the second or third person. Obviously the words chosen reflect the child's abilities to understand and communicate at the time the story is written.

Sarah Ann Jensen's Life Story

This is a Life Story written for a four-and-one-half-year-old child. Since many of the most important events in Sarah's life occurred before the age of three, the caseworker chose to write the story in the third person. She and Sarah Ann talked about what was being written. Using the Feeling Faces cards, the caseworker helped Sarah identify the emotions that she might have had at various times in her life. This Life Story was written by the caseworker for Sarah's Lifebook as part of the preparation process for an adoptive placement.

Sara Ann

Sarah Ann Jensen was born on Sunday, November 10, 1986, at Memorial Hospital in Denver, Colorado. She was a beautiful healthy baby who weighed 6 lbs. 3 oz. and was 19 1/2 inches long. Her birth parents, Janet and Joe, were

374

excited and proud of Sarah. However, soon after she was born, her daddy lost his job. Sometimes her family did not have enough to eat. Sometimes they didn't have enough money to pay the rent.

Mommy Janet and Daddy Joe were worried. Sometimes when they were worried and Sarah cried, like all babies cry, Mommy Janet and Daddy Joe didn't know what to do. Sometimes when they were worried about other things, they spanked Sarah too hard instead of picking her up and loving her.

Sarah's birth parents started having lots of problems. They were mad at each other much of the time. Sometimes they got angry at Sarah even though she didn't cause the problems. One day Mommy Janet got so angry she spanked Sarah much harder than babies should ever be spanked. Afterwards she was sorry. Sarah's leg was badly hurt, and she had to stay in the hospital for many days. This happened when Sarah was nine months old.

In the hospital Sarah was scared and hurting, so she cried a lot. When her mommy and daddy came to see her, Sarah would cry like most babies do after they have been away from their mom and dad for a while. However, Mommy Janet and Daddy Joe didn't know that that was just how babies act. They thought that the crying meant that Sarah was mad at them. Pretty soon they stopped coming to visit.

When Sarah's leg was well enough so that she could leave the hospital she was eleven months old. Sarah's Mommy Janet and Daddy Joe were still having problems. Sometimes when grownups are having lots of problems, they cannot take care of babies. Sarah went to live in a foster home with Mr. and Mrs. Jones and their three children — Sam who was nine, Virginia who was seven, and Veronica who was five.

Sarah learned to love Mommy and Daddy Jones and Sam, Virginia, and Veronica. When she was about sixteen months old, she learned to walk. She already could say ten words. She had a favorite stuffed animal named Teddy that she took everywhere with her. Mommy Jones had brought Teddy as a present for Sarah the first time she came to visit her in the hospital. Sam enjoyed giving Sarah piggy back rides. Virginia liked to read stories to her. Veronica, whom Sarah called "Wonnie" taught her to turn somersaults.

When Sarah was two-and-a-half her first mommy and daddy—Mommy Janet and Daddy Joe—thought that they were ready to take care of her. While Sarah was living with the Jones family, her Mommy Janet and Daddy Joe had had a baby boy whom they named Jeffery. They had moved to a new apartment.

When Sarah started having visits with her Mommy Janet, Daddy Joe, and baby Jeffery, she was confused. She didn't remember her first mommy and daddy and she didn't know Jeffery. Nothing looked familiar. She didn't understand— two-and-a-half-year-olds don't understand lots of things yet—why everyone said this was her "real" mommy and daddy. She though that Mommy and Daddy Jones were her "real" parents because they took care of her the same way they took care of Sam, Virginia, and Veronica.

At first she thought that Sam, Virginia, and "Wonnie" would be moving with her, but she found out she was wrong. Sarah was confused. She was scared of moving to a "new" house. She was sad about leaving the Jones' home. She was angry. In fact, she was so mad and sad that when she went to live with Mommy Janet and Daddy Joe she cried and cried. She was so mad that she didn't want to mind. Sometimes she felt scared and would hide. When she especially missed the Jones family, she would sometimes hit Jeffery. Maybe she thought that then Mommy Janet and Daddy Joe would send her back to the Jones' home; maybe she just didn't know what to do with all of those feelings.

Mommy Janet and Daddy Joe didn't know what to do when Sarah cried. They didn't understand that Sarah was scared, lonely, sad, and mad and that she needed extra loving. They sent her to her room whenever she cried, but that just made Sarah feel more lonely and scared. She cried harder and harder. That made Mommy Janet and Daddy Joe really mad, and they started to spank her too hard again, and sometimes they told her she was a bad girl. Sarah believed them, but they were wrong. She wasn't "bad." She was scared, lonely and sad.

One day Mommy Janet called Mr. Dunlap, the caseworker, and said it wasn't working out with Sarah at home and that she would have to go back into foster care. Mommy Janet and Daddy Joe packed up all of Sarah's clothes, and Mr. Dunlap came and got her. Sarah had been "home" for two months. She still missed the Jones family. But Mr. Dunlap didn't take her back to the their home. He took her to the Robinson foster home. Sarah was still confused and sad. She missed Mommy and Daddy Jones and their children.

The Robinsons had a baby boy named James and two big foster boys, Richard and Ronny. Sarah didn't know how Ronny could be a boy when in the Jones home "Ronnie" was a girl. Every time Sarah heard Ronny's name she thought of "Wonnie" and missed her. She didn't like Ronny, and sometimes she would sneak his toys and hide them when he was at school. Baby James reminded her of baby Jeffery and she would remember Mommy Janet calling her a "bad" girl.

Sometimes Sarah wished that she was a baby again. Then she would take Jamie's bottle and suck on it. That made Mrs. Robinson angry, and she would put Sarah in time-out. She didn't understand how confused Sarah was. Sarah wouldn't call Mr. and Mrs. Robinson "Daddy" and "Mommy." She would pull away from them. She was a very unhappy girl.

Mr. Dunlap saw how unhappy Sarah was. He tried to explain to Mrs. Robinson how Sarah felt, but she had trouble understanding. Finally, just before Sarah's third birthday, Mr. Dunlap decided that Sarah was just too sad at the Robinson home so he moved her. This time she got to go back to the Jones' home.

At first she was happy to be there, but part of her kept being mad and scared that she might have to move again. Another foster girl, Heather, who was four-and-a-half, was also living there. Heather, and Veronica played together lots of the time so sometimes Sarah felt left out.

Sarah had a special clown cake for her third birthday, and got her very own tricycle. It was a fun day. Mama Jones decorated the house with balloons. The other kids gave her books and clay. She was happy and felt very loved that day. She kept saying, "I love you Mommy. I'm going to have all my birthdays at your house." Mommy Jones told Sarah that she loved her too. Sarah asked, "Can I have all my birthdays here?" Mommy Jones told her that Mr. Dunlap would decide how many birthdays she would have with the Jones family.

Whenever Mr. Dunlap came to visit Sarah was careful to be extra special good hoping that Mr. Dunlap would let her stay with the Jones family. Mr. Dunlap was working with Mommy Janet and Daddy Joe to help them understand how Sarah felt. When Sarah was three years and four months old, she started having visits every week with Mommy Janet and Daddy Joe. Sometimes they went to the park for a picnic or to the zoo. Sarah would have a good time on those days. But sometimes they went "home" for visits. When that happened, all the old, scared, sad and mad feelings would come back, and Sarah would cry and have a hard time minding

Mommy Janet and Daddy Joe wanted things to work out well for them all, but it seemed no matter how hard they tried, Sarah and they didn't feel loving toward each other. Finally Mommy Janet and Daddy Joe decided that maybe it would never work out well for them and Sarah. Sarah stopped having visits. She wasn't sure why the visits stopped.

Part of her was glad that she didn't have to go "home" anymore, but part of her was sad about it. She really didn't understand the mixed up feelings so she just "forgot" about Mommy Janet, Daddy Joe, and baby Jeffrey. Whenever anybody asked about her family she would talk about the Jones family. If anyone talked about Mommy Janet and Daddy Joe she wouldn't listen. She would just think her own private thoughts and wouldn't talk.

Sarah was still with the Jones family for her fourth birthday. She got a new dolly, whom she named Melody. She had a special ice cream cake that looked like a doll and her best friend, Tammy, came for her birthday dinner. Even Oscar the dog enjoyed some cake.

Soon after her fourth birthday, Mr. Dunlap, Mommy Janet, and Daddy Joe went to talk to the judge. They all decided together that Sarah would not ever go back to live with Mommy Janet and Daddy Joe. They decided that she should get a new set of "keeping" parents with whom she would grow up. Sarah said she already had a family—the Jones family. However, Mommy and Daddy Jones and Mr. Dunlap explained that the Jones family is a foster family. Children live with foster families until they can either go back to their birth families or until they get an adoptive family, which is another name for a "growing up with" family. Sarah got a new caseworker. Her name is Mrs. Small. Her job will be to find Sarah's "growing up with" family.

Sarah still doesn't like the idea of moving to a new family. She wants to stay with the Jones family. When she thinks of moving, she gets sad and mad. Sometimes she does naughty things. Mommy Jones doesn't like the naughty things, but she understands how Sarah feels, and she tells her that when she is sad or scared, she should come and be close to her. Mommy and Daddy Jones will miss Sarah because they love her. Sam, Virginia, Veronica, and Heather will miss her too. However, Mommy and Daddy Jones are happy, too, because Sarah will be getting an adoptive family and won't have to keep moving. Even big people sometimes feel happy and sad at the same time.

Mrs. Small talked to Sarah's first mommy and daddy and got pictures of them and pictures of Sarah when she was a baby. Sarah will get to keep those pictures as well as lot of pictures of the Jones family. Since all of her birthdays were with the Jones family, she has pictures of every birthday. Birthdays are special days. Mrs. Small even got a picture of the Robinson family to put in Sarah's book, but Sarah says she doesn't much care about that picture she says. Sometimes Sarah likes to look at her pictures; sometimes she doesn't.

At bedtime, Sarah and Melody, her special doll, talk to each other about what kind of "keeping family" they dream of. Mrs. Small has told Sarah and Melody that they will have a chance to meet the adoptive family before Mrs. Small decides for sure if it is the right family for them. Mrs. Small says that lots of families want children who will grow up in their family. Lots of children need families to grow up with. Her job is to help children meet the family that is right for them. She says that she will be sure to tell Sarah's adoptive family about how much Sarah loves Mommy and Daddy Jones and Sam, Virginia, Veronica, and Heather.

Mrs. Small will tell them that sometimes when Sarah gets sad, mad, or lonely she forgets and does naughty things instead of remembering to come be close to a mommy and daddy and talk about her feelings. Sarah's adoptive family will help her with that. When Melody gets lonely, or if she is naughty, Sarah says she will be sure to hug her, because she knows that Melody is going to miss the Jones family too.

Mrs. Small says that Sarah will be celebrating her fifth birthday with her "keeping family." Sarah wonders what kind of cake she will have. She hopes it is chocolate. Sarah hopes that she will be able to invite the Jones family to her birthday party. She and Melody are planning to talk to their new parents about that when they meet them. Sarah thinks she will have Melody ask them about that instead of asking herself.

Using the Lifebook throughTime

There are many times, in the course of direct work, when reviewing the Lifebook will be useful. Or, it may be used in treatment to identify earlier life events which are echoing in the present

Aaron

Ten-year-old Aaron first moved to his adoptive family as a foster child when he was five. A year later he had a brief return to his mother's care. Subsequent to his return to foster care, his mother decided that she was not able to parent Aaron. She made an adoption plan for her son, requesting that he be adopted by his foster family if at all possible.

Aaron's entry into the foster care system initially had come about when his parents were having severe marital problems, and the child had become the brunt of all of their frustrations and anger. He was severely abused. After he was placed in foster care his parents divorced. When he returned to mother's care she had a new live-in partner. Once again the cycle of adults' problems leading to child abuse was repeated.

Although Aaron had many behavioral and learning problems, he had made gradual improvement throughout his years in his adoptive family. Therapy was discontinued when he was eight. When he was ten, his adoptive mom called the therapist and said that Aaron was again talking in school about his early abuse. An appointment was set up. The therapist asked that they bring Aaron's Lifebook to the session.

As they were reviewing the book and came to the description of his entering foster care because of his parents' marriage problems, Aaron's effect changed. He stopped reading. The therapist looked at his mom and said, "There is something that Aaron doesn't think he should talk about. Do you know what it is?" The adoptive mom got tears in her eyes and said, "Now I understand." She then went on to say that she and her husband had recently separated and were contemplating a divorce.

This led to an echoing of Aaron's fears of having to move because of adult problems. Mother's reassurance that he would remain a member of the family, even if there was a divorce, led to a cessation of the symptoms at school.

The Lifebook can be used to differentiate between reality and fantasy. It is important that the helping adult listen to the child's memories and contradict them only if she has information that indicates that the child's perceptions were incorrect. If, inadvertently, an adult contradicts a child's correct reading of a situation, she will have given the message, "Don't trust your own perceptions." On the other hand, if information contrary to the child's memories is available, it needs to be shared with the young person.

Michelle, eleven, had been a member of her adoptive family for four years. In her family of origin she had been the scapegoated child. Her birth mother had recognized when Michelle was very young that she was having difficulty feeling the same love for her that she felt for her older daughter, Mary. On several occasions she had sought advice from the local department of social services because of her feelings about her daughter.

Michelle

At age eleven Michelle was reviewing her Lifebook with her therapist. In a pensive tone, she commented, "You know, I feel like my first mom never loved me as much as she loved my sister Mary." The therapist, who had seen the original social service agency records replied, "I think you are right about that." Michelle looked at her with great surprise. Evidently, someone in the past had reassured her that her birth mother had loved both daughters equally. The reassurance was not helpful because it did not reflect the truth. The therapist brought out the record and shared with Michelle her birth mother's comments and concerns about her own parenting abilities. They discussed possible reasons that parents might feel differently about each of their children.

The therapist then asked Michelle if she thought that her adoptive parents loved both her and her older adoptive sister, Sally, equally well. Michelle was surprised at the question and quickly responded, "Yes." The therapist agreed with her and then reassurred her that it seemed like Michelle could certainly count on her own perceptions as to how people felt about her. Her views had been right in the past and were correct now.

If the adult working with the child does not have complete information, as is so often the case when a child makes a statement such as Michelle's about it seeming as though her birth mom had not loved her as much as her sister, the helper might respond along the lines of, "That is possible. Some parents have difficulty loving all of their children. I don't have any information as to whether or not that was so in your case. Can you think of some other reasons it might not have been working out well for you and your parents when you lived together?" This allows for a hypothetical exploration of a variety of reasons that parents and children have problems living together and expands the young person's thinking.

When children face another move, old emotions rise from the unconscious to the conscious. Reviewing the Lifebook near the time of the transition provides opportunities to identify and clarify the child's memories of the past and to help him look at ways this move is both similar to, yet differs from, the previous ones.

Exercise 7-2, which follows, gives the reader an opportunity to construct a Life Path for Sarah Ann Jensen and to think about helping her adoptive parents share information throughout their daughter's growing up years, information that Sarah cannot yet really understand.

Constructing a Life Path and Gathering Information for Later Sharing.

1. Fill in a blank Life Path to be included in Sarah Ann Jensen's Life Story, reflecting her moves.
2. What additional information will Sarah Ann and her adoptive family need to help her understand her past, develop a strong sense of identity, and clarify her choices in interrupting the cycle of abuse and neglect.
3. Identify the sources of the information you want to gather..
4. Outline a plan for explaining to the adoptive parents the importance of sharing information, ages at which is is important, and ways to reframe Sarah Ann's negative life experiences without being judgemental of her birth parents, foster families or caseworkers.
5. What skills will Sarah need to learn if she is to break the cycle of abuse. How might her parents help her learn these skills?

Coming Full Circle   V

In working with adolescents, we have the opportunity to look into the future and try to break the cycle of abuse from one generation to the next. Adolescents have the capacity for hypothetical thinking. By thinking ahead, they can identify and prepare themselves for the times when the effects of the traumas of the past are most likely to resurface. They can start to identify the skills that they need to develop so that they will have choices that their birth parents may never have had. They can look more realistically at the choices others involved in their lives have made and be encouraged to take responsibility for the choices they will ultimately make for themselves.

The effects of early childhood traumas become more evident during early adolescence as separation/individuation tasks are recycled. The psychological tasks of early adolescence are very similar to those of years one through five. This is both good news and bad. The bad news is that unmet early needs come back to haunt the adolescent in exaggereated form; the good news is that there is potential to readdress these earlier needs and meet them more appropriately, thereby leading to true lifelong change for the young person.

Rutter (1981) observed that although early life experiences may have a permanent influence for some, the effects may be overcome by adolescent experiences. Main et al (1985) point out that although in childhood it is likely that perceptions of relationships can only be changed by actual experiences, in

381

adolescence it is possible for the views they formed earlier to be altered. This is what happens in therapies that depend upon gaining insight. It is possible to facilitate these changes by providing the adolescent with a combination of information from the past and an educational approach about how children think and perceive what is happening. This helps them understand why they have thought whatever it is they thought and makes it more likely that they will be able to use their improved intellectual skills to reorder earlier life experiences.

Adolescence provides opportunities for decreasing the lifelong effects of negative early life experiences and minimizing the emotional scarring secondary to these. Although adults cannot undo the psychological damage of early life experiences, they can help the young person learn compensatory skills (Beyer, 1990). Adults can help the young person look ahead, identifying times that the feelings of early life experiences might echo.

Maria

Maria is thirteen. She has been living with her adoptive family for a year-and-a-half. In her family of origin, Maria was the oldest of six. Not only had she been a caregiver for the younger children in general, but from ages six to nine she had been expected to be her father's sexual partner.

Maria has been working hard in therapy. She had received excellent therapeutic interventions when she first entered care. However, her current parents had been advised that with the onset of the normal sexual feelings that accompany puberty, Maria would be likely to re-experience old thoughts and emotions. As part of looking at the abuse, Maria's Lifebook, with pictures of her birth parents, had been used. She had drawn floor plans of the house she had lived in during the abuse and, using Groth and Stevenson's (1984) anatomical drawings, she shared detailed information about the abuse with her therapist. She had asked many questions about the sexual words she had heard, but not understood, as a child. Because her body had been responsive to the sexual overtures, she felt an increased sense of shame about her responsibility. She was assured that adults, not children, must always bear the responsibility for their sexual behaviors with minors. She was also advised that the fact that her body was responsive indicated that it was normal.

Using the list of parent messages, Maria identified those that she had received from her birth parents and talked of how they had been conveyed. She then identified those she was currently getting from her adoptive parents. It was clear that their reparenting was successful.

However, the therapist believed that it was also important that she help the teen to understand that the legacy of early sexual abuse would continue to influence Maria's decisions and reactions in the future. When, in the course of normal dating, was she likely to have the old feelings retriggered? During adolescence and young adult years, how much would she decide to tell? To whom? When and how might she share information with a male partner? These were not questions to be answered now, but she was certain to have to face them in the future. How would she decide when she might need help and from whom would she seek it? In identifying additional times that the traumas of the past were likely to echo again, Maria summed it up with the statement, "And if I ever have a daughter, when she is six it will be hard for me." Understanding this before the feelings flooded over her would be Maria's best line of defense. Although it was important that the sexual abuse not be incorporated as the most important aspect of her life, its effects would need to be addressed repeatedly as she continued her life. She was using her improved self-esteem and newly acquired intellectual skills to help herself feel powerful in facing the future.

The young teen must not only separate from his current parents, but must also psychologically separate from all other significant parenting figures. This may include a birth parent with whom the child no longer lives and/or past foster parents. To psychologically separate and individuate the adolescent must know from whom he is separating. If he is living away from his birth parents, he must reconnect with them at some level. Beyer (1990) notes that the adolescent's search for an independent identity drives him to reassert the original connection, no matter how inadequate the birth parents may be, or how loving the current caregivers are. Many times the young person's current parent figures view this as reflecting negatively on themselves. It does not. The adolescent is trying to accomplish the developmental challenge at hand. The parents' job, as always, is to act as facilitators.

When Judy was fourteen, she started thinking more about her birth mother. When had she started her periods? What did she look like? Why had she abandoned Judy? What would Judy's own life be like if she had grown up in Korea? Would she feel like she belonged there if she ever went to visit? The questions kept popping into her head.

Judy

Unfortunately for Judy, she had no way to obtain information about her birth parents. She had to create a fantasy to separate from. Ms. Silver used Han's (1984) book, *Understanding My Child's Korean Origins* to help Judy learn more about Korean culture and the history of adoption, including why Korean children, with some frequency, are abandoned in train stations. If Judy had lived in either Oregon or Minnesota she would have been able to have met in a group setting with other children of similar heritage.* Although this service was not available where Judy lived, she was encouraged to go to the Korean church in her town and to meet some of the children of immigrants from Korea.

(Holt of Oregon supports a summer camp for children from other cultures placed in adoptive families. Children's Home Society of Minnesota has extensive postplacement support services which include groups for children from other countries.)

Because a Lifebook is written with, or for, the child at whatever age the youngster is when it is initially compiled, information in it may be accurate but incomplete. For example, the book may say that the birth dad sometimes touched the child in ways that adults should only touch other adults. However, eventually the child will need more specific information as to the type of sexual abuse experienced. If the youngster is still in foster care, the current caseworker will have the records available to share with him. However, because in most states records are sealed once the child is adopted, we believe that adoptive parents should be provided with all additional information, in written form, that would have been put in the Lifebook if it were being completed with an adolescent. Adoptive parents deserve to have accurate information to share with their children, as well as advice as to how and when to share it. If the information will be difficult for them to share on their own, they should be encouraged to ask a postplacement caseworker or therapist to help them.

Although the adolescent must, at some level, reconnect with his birth family as we saw in both Maria's and Judy's cases, this does not necessarily mean face-to-face contact. The connection may take place only in the youth's mind. However, accurate information about parents facilitates the process of psychological separation. It is more difficult when a child has to create a fantasy, as Judy did.

In general, abused or neglected youth will combine their rage against birthparents for what they did not receive, with protectiveness for these same parents who are a major source of their identity. Although they themselves may be very critical of their parents, they do not tolerate even implied criticism by others (Beyer, 1990).

If birth parents consistently made poor choices and had few long-range goals, following in their path serves a dual purpose. It is protective of the birth family ("If it was good enough for them it is good enough for me") while, at the same time, it expresses anger toward all adults. ("You can't make me be like you want me to be.") A major goal of intervention with previously abused or neglected teens is to help them be willing to surpass their parents without viewing it as a criticism of them.

Because of improved cognition, teens whose current needs are being met and who have at some time formed trusting secure relationships with adults may during adolescence not only acknowledge their past anger and hurt, but may also be able to truly "forgive" their abusive or neglectful parent. To do this, the youth first needs to see parents as individuals (not just parent figures) with individualized needs and problems. The forgiveness usually comes about through acceptance of the fact that the parents were unable to love or care for the child in healthier ways because of their own unmet needs and problems, not because of any deficits on the part of the child. As the adolescent understands the effects of his early life experiences and develops compenstory skills, he may see that he has more choices open to him for long-term adjustment than his birth parents had. This child may have had opportunies to learn to discharge his emotions more appropriately; he may have a family who will continue to be available as an emotional resource; he may have learned to trust his current caregivers and himself. Although adults cannot force an adolescent to make good choices on his own behalf, they can help him identify the choices that he has, and can facilitate his developing specific skills that will help break the cycle of abuse or neglect.

Ricks (1985) observed that those individuals who had experienced early life abuse and rejection but who were able to forgive the rejecting parent and/or speak coherently about an unhappy childhood were more likely to themselves as adults have securely attached children. How do we help adolescents come to the point of forgiveness? How do we know if they have?

Let us return to Trevor, whom we met at the beginning of this chapter. After spending five years moving from one home to another, from one group care placement to another, he has been in his current placement for two years now. Although Trevor is still a very demanding teen, he has been able to form close interpersonal relationships with two adults. Currently, he is working hard on understanding his past history. He has a Lifebook filled with photos and information. Recently, he reestablished contact with distant relatives. They are providing him with information about his birth father, who had abandoned his family when Trevor was two. Trevor learned that his father, Will, had himself been abandoned by his father when he was two. As this information was filled in on the Genogram that was part of his Lifebook, Trevor commented, "There's a pattern in this family. I want it to stop with me." Knowing the pattern provides Trevor with an opportunity to make conscious, rather than unconscious, choices.

Trevor's mother had voluntarily released her parental rights when Trevor was eight. He had seen her only once during the interim. However, when he went to visit relatives who were in the area where she also lived, he met her again. On his return, his caseworker asked if he had seen his mother and how she was doing. Trevor replied, "You've got to understand. She has all the same problems I have had, but she's never had any help with them. We'll just have to be patient. I don't know if she'll ever make it." Trevor has clearly moved to forgiveness. This, combined with his information about family patterns, may encourage him to make choices that will help him surpass his birth parents without being judgemental.

Trevor

Viorst (1986) points out that although each person has a long history by the time he reaches adolescence, the sense of self takes on a new quality and a new clarity during this period. Dockar-Drysdale (1967) has observed that to develop a stable sense of self, the young person must pass through a series of steps. First, he must have experienced a positive relationship. He must truly feel that good has happened to him at some point in his journey through childhood. Then he must find a way of storing the good experiences inside of him by symbolizing them. Conceptualization is the final step. He must be able to understand intellectually what has happened to him. It is only of value if it is retrospective—ideas must be a sequel to experience.

Using this concept, let us analyze what has happened for Trevor. After many years of turmoil, he finally has acheived not only some stability, but has had a series of positive experiences with his current caregivers. He does not have trouble enjoying the memories of these experiences. When he is down, he can pull up an enjoyable memory to help himself. Finally, he has now learned to conceptualize some of the changes in his life, and contrast them with his mother's experiences. He is developing, in adolescence, a stable sense of self.

Thoburn (1988) points out that to be able to develop new and satisfying relationships as an adult, the young person needs the security of a permanent placement—with the security, sense of belonging, being loved and loving that go with it—combined with knowledge about his family of origin, past relationships, and the interconnections between the past and present. This is our goal as helping adults, either as parents or professionals, in helping the young person not only complete his journey through placement, but embark on his journey to adulthood.

Resources

This list is not meant to be exhaustive, but it will provide the reader with some starting points. The books are all listed in the bibliography for this chapter. The coloring books are not.

Three books that will be particularly useful to individuals desiring a variety of ideas as to ways to communicate with children include Claudia Jewett's *Helping Children Cope with Separation and Loss*, Cipoella, Mcgown, and Yanulis' *Using Play Techniques to Assess and Prepare Older Children for Adoption,* and Ryan and Walker's *Making Life Story Books*. All contain many examples of direct work with children of a variety of ages, in a variety of circumstances. *Post Adoption Family Therapy* (Prew); *After Adoption* (Bourguignon); *Working with Older Adoptees* (Coleman), and *Adoption Resources for Mental Health Professionals* (Grabe) all provide useful ideas for ways to work with adoptive families and their children. Lois Melina's book *Making Sense of Adoption* provides information on what children understand at different ages, and provides ideas as to how to convey difficult information in positive ways. *How It Feels To Be Adopted* by Jill Krementz is a series of stories written by children who joined their families by adoption. They can be used for encouraging others to agree or disagree in their perceptions. *Filling in the Blanks: A Guided Look at Growing up Adopted* by Susan Gabel is meant to be used directly with the child but it also provides a wealth of ideas for the professional working with children. *Choices and Challenges* are workbooks that look at universal adolescent conflicts, issues, and skills to be developed.

The Ungame, Reunion, and *Social Security* are all available from Talicor Inc., 190 Arovista Circle; Brea, CA 92621, tel. 714-255-7900. They can frequently be found in stores with a large selection of games as well. *The Talking,*

Feeling, Doing Game designed by Richard Gardner and put out by Creative Therapeutics is another useful way to encourage communication. *The Storytelling Therapeutics* by Richard Gardner, M.M., is from creative Therapeutics (155 County Rd., Cresskill, NJ 07626-0317, tel. 1-800-544-6164). *The Changing Family Game*, distributed by Cognitive Behavioral Resources in Canterbury, Ohio, is a game about divorce.

Two divorce workbooks are Ken Magid's, *Divorce is............:* and *A Kid's Coloring Book* and *Divorce is a Grown Up Problem* by Sinberg.

A variety of workbooks and other tools have been developed for communicating about child sexual abuse. *My Own Special Book About Me*, developed and distributed by Lutheran Social Services of Spokane, Washington, is excellent for use with the grade-school-aged child. Material is presented in a non-threatening, hypothetical manner. It focuses primarily on sexual contact with known people, as opposed to strangers, and has a scenario involving a boy being touched by a favorite male teen babysitter. In general, anatomical drawings, (Groth) are less stimulating, less embarrassing, and easier to use than anatomically correct dolls for communicating with children about the particulars of child sexual abuse.

Kahn's *Pathways* and McClarty's *Superkid*s workbooks, also listed in the bibliography, have many suggestions for activities to be used in group therapy with sexual abuse victims or pre-adult perpetrators.

There are many children's books about emotions. *It's Okay to be Angry (Afraid. Different, etc.)*, a series from Colony books by Creative Pathways are especially useful with the four to eight.

7-9 — *Table* —

Sample Parent Messages

You're smart	You act wild
You're stupid	Be successful
Be Happy	You klutz
Feelings are okay	You're crazy
You're unlovable	You're so slow
My needs come first	Teen-agers are the pits
I knew you could do it	You come last
Don't have fun	Parents are consistent
I love you	Why can't you do anything right?
I'm glad you're a girl	I'm glad you're a boy
Please others	You can trust your own feelings
I like your hugs	I don't have time for you

You're my favorite child
Solve your own problems
Boys are better than girls
It's okay to ask for help
You're just like me
I like to touch you
I'm afraid of your anger
It's okay to be scared
You are lovable
Parents *never* make mistakes
Girls are better than boys
Problem Child
I want you to stay young
You'll never succeed
Don't trust anyone
You can succeed
You're perfect
Don't brag
It's okay to make mistakes
Are you still here?
Work before play
You're messy
Nothing is secret
Don't feel
Why can't you learn to do
    things for yourself?
I'll be glad when you grow up
    and get out of here
You can trust yourself to know
    what you need
I (parent) need to know how you
    feel so I can make the best
    decisions for the family
I need you to help take care
    of_____
It's sinful to be angry at
    your parents
I won't pay attention to you
    no matter what you do
I wish you were a boy rather
    than a girl
I'm glad you're part of our family

When you're lonely come be close
I enjoy you
You come first
I like you to touch me
Poor thing
I like parenting
It's okay to be angry
You're in charge
I'm glad you're my child
Work can be fun
You meet my needs
I need you to comfort me
Make me look good as a parent
You're driving me crazy
You can trust me
You never learn
I hate you
Play before work
You have a big mouth
Dummy
You're a neat kid
Drop dead
Goofed again
Mind your own business
You're beautiful
Why don't you find something
    to do?
If something goes wrong it must
    be you fault
If it's fun it must be immoral
I'll pay more attention to you if
    you're bad than if you're good
I wish you were a girl rather
    than a boy
If you lie you can get out of things
Why can't you be more like your
    _____(brother, sister, etc)
If you beg or whine you can
    usually get your own way
You drive me to drink(drugs,etc.)
You don't have to be perfect
I wish you hadn't been born

You never can pay me back for all
   I've done for you-but keep trying
Expect others, not me, to take
   care of you
Don't tell your_____
   (mother, father)
Parenting is a difficult and
   unrewarding job
It's okay for parents to
   hurt children
Think the way I tell you to think
Anything worthwhile is worth
   suffering for
It at first you don't succeed,
   try, try again
You can count on me to know
   what is happening
I'll pay more attention to you if
   you're bad than if you're good
If only you'd learn to think
You're a busy child
He (she) is our slow one
I like to watch you try new things
I like the way you mind
There's no excuse for a bad mood
Bring all of your problems to me
   I'll solve them

Hurry up and grow up
Your needs aren't important. Don't
   expect others to take care of you.
Children are to be seen and not heard
Everyone makes mistakes sometimes
You keep on like that and you'll
   end up in prison
I wish someone else were my
   child instead of you
Money is more important than love
If something goes wrong it must
   be your fault
Girls don't have to be smart
I don't want to know what you
   are doing
You have to cheat to get anything
   out of life
Parents are inconsistent
I never have time for you
Won't you ever learn?
I always have time for you
I have time enough for all of you
I'm scared of your sadness
I enjoy watching you grow up

Post-Script

Let's look into the future. The children in the four ongoing cases have all completed their journeys through placement. However, the legacies of every decision made while they were in care continue to influence their ongoing journeys through life. There have been some rough times for these children. However, each has a family who has remained firmly committed to them. Their families would be the first to admit that these children have helped their parents learn more about themselves, acquire new skills, become more flexible in their thinking, and become strong advocates on behalf of their children.

Ardith is now close to twelve. Her strong early attachment to Rose, combined with her resiliency in the face of adversity , have stood her in good stead. When Ardith was four, Rose had a brief relapse into substance abuse. While she was again in treatment, Ardith lived with Kelly, Wayne, and Prentice for a few months. Two years later Rose married Sal. They have established a stable home life for themselves, Ardith, and two younger children, born subsequently.

Ardith
Prentice

Prentice, now fourteen, has had to learn to live with the fact that his relationship with his birth mom is so different from Ardith's. His sister's temporary placement with Prentice's family, followed by her return to Rose's care, led to the resurfacing of the feelings associated with his early separations and losses.

Kelly and Wayne are concerned that their son may experiment with drugs and alcohol during adolescence. Given his probable genetic predisposition for addictive behaviors, they worry. They have openly shared their concerns with Prentice. Rose, too, has talked with him and his parents about the long-term effects of the choices she, herself, made as an adolescent.

There have been times when the open relationship between Prentice's birth and adoptive families has posed problems. On balance, however, Kelly and

Wayne believe that it has helped them face the true issues and feelings that Prentice has had to cope with throughout the years.

Martin

Martin is eleven and in fifth grade. He seems to be well attached to his family. The legacies of his past are evident in his academic performance and his peer relationships. Concrete thinking is still prominent. Sequencing and determining cause and effect are problematic. He misreads cues from peers, seems immature in social skills, and is easily frustrated.

Although he has none of the facial features that accompany Fetal Alchohol Syndrome, it is quite likely that Martin suffers from Fetal Alcohol Effects. His adoptive parents know that the future will continue to provide both Martin and themselves with a series of challenges.

Judy

Judy is now twenty-two. When she was fourteen, she and the Caldwells decided to pursue legal guardianship. The agency attorney did not think that it was worth the legal effort. However, psychologically it was important and Ms. Silver kept pushing for it. With the change in status to legal guardianship, Judy legally changed her last name from Haslett to Caldwell.

In early adolescence, Judy became increasingly conscious of her Asian features. There were times when she felt alienated from her peers. It would have been good if she could have had contact with other Asian children adopted by American families, but that didn't happen. Her problems with self-esteem were further increased by her academic problems secondary to the language processing difficulties. Judy's relationship with Marie Caldwell continued to be strong as mother supported daughter through these difficult years.

As Judy approached emancipation, she became more provocative and belligerent. She left the Caldwell home during a stormy argument. Within months she was pregnant. When she gave birth to her daughter, Marie was there. Judy had difficulty deciding if she should care for her daughter, or if she should make an adoption plan for her. She and Marie agreed that it would not work for them to have Judy live at the Caldwell home with the baby. However, Marie was willing to either provide child care, if Judy decided to raise her daughter, or to emotionally support her during the legalities of making an adoption plan.

Judy decided to try to raise her daughter. The child's father was no longer part of Judy's life. Within months, Judy was again questioning her plan to raise her daughter. She asked if her parents would keep the baby for her while she decided. This was a very difficult time for Marie and Neal. Finally, they agreed to care for their grandaughter for up to four months. However, they were firm that by then a permanent plan for the baby had to be made. The four months posed a series of one problem after another. Judy did eventually decide on an adoption plan. She hoped it could be an open adoption, but the agency was not supportive of this plan. During the relinquishment and placement, Judy and the Caldwells mended their relationship.

Currently, Judy shares an apartment with a friend, works full time, and is taking evening classes in computer technology at the local community college. She spends holidays with the Caldwells and visits them once or twice a month.

Cassie and Larry Osborn have had to actively advocate for services for their children throughout the years. They have been the prime movers in their community in advocating for therapy groups for child survivors of sexual abuse.

Denise
Duke
Lily

Denise is nineteen and a senior in high school. As her early life experiences resurfaced in adolescence, there were many difficult times. Between the ages of thirteen and fifteen she became very ambivalent about remaining with her adoptive family. She was still denying her abusive background. She ran away repeatedly, became involved with peers who were in difficulty at school and with the law, and experimented with drugs and alcohol. Her parents were persistent in their commitment to her, even though she was ambivalent about her commitment to them. They continued to advocate for services for her.

Denise became a member of a group for adolescent girls who had been sexually abused. After finally confronting her own history, she worked hard in the group. By the time she started high school, her antisocial behaviors had subsided. She has become a peer counselor at her high school. She participates as a guest co-leader intermittently with the current groups for sexually abused adolescent girls. As a child she excelled in school. In junior high she did little academic work. She was held back a year. However, in high school she has worked hard. She has just received a university scholarship. She hopes to major in psychology.

Duke is now sixteen. In the late grade school and early adolescent years, his aggressive behaviors resurfaced. Once more he became involved in sexual interactions with peers. He seemed to be the instigator. Although he would verbally cajole others into participating, he did not actively pursue those who refused. The Osborns were instumental in advocating for services for adolescent male victim-perpetrators. He, too, worked hard in group therapy and made many positive changes.

A year ago Duke became very ambivalent about his first name. Although he was comfortable with his family and close friends calling him Duke, he had trouble imagining himself using this name when applying for jobs. Teachers, thinking Duke was his nickname, frequently asked him for his "real" name. He and his parents talked extensively about the possiblity of changing his first name. Six months ago they decided to legally change his first name to Lorren. His sisters usually still call him Duke. Cassie and Larry use both names. His teachers call him Lorren. Old friends call him Duke, new ones, Lorren. He feels comfortable with both.

393

The most surprising thing about Lorren's adjustment is that since ninth grade he has been able to set positive goals for himself, both in terms of academics and employment. He is no longer so easily frustrated. He is persistent in school work. He has consistently followed through on the goals he has set for himself. The Osborns are hopeful about his future.

At age fourteen, Lily is in the midst of early adolescence. Her parents recognize that this has been the most difficult period for each of their adopted children. Lily has some learning difficulties. The parents suspect that she may have some long-term effects from Gloria's use of drugs or alcohol during her pregancy with Lily. She seems to be having more academic problems in junior high than she had during the grade school years. Currently, the Osborns are seeking a full neuropsychological evaluation for her.

However, Larry and Cassie's biggest concern is that Lily is very anxious to please friends. She is a follower and seems to be easily led by peers. They are concerned that she may become a ready victim or scapegoat for others.

Glossary

Active listening, a communication technique in which the emphasis is "listening" to the behavioral or emotional undercurrent rather than to the words per se.

Attachment, The close interpersonal connections that children form with others. These connections are strong enough to last through time and space, even without the benefit of direct day-to-day contact currently. In this book the term is used in the direction of child to others.

Bonding, The close interpersonal connections that adults, especially primary caregivers, form with children in their care. Others use it to describe only the connection with the birth mother or to describe the connecting process that occurs immediately after birth. In this book, it is used to describe the reciprocal aspects of attachment—in the direction of adult to child.

Claiming, When parents claim the child, they come to accept the child as their own and as a full fledged member of the family, according to Bourguignon and Watson (1987). In claiming, the focus is on similarities rather than differences. In this book we recognize that children, also, claim families as their own

Cover story, A brief, not fully revealing, response that a child can give to others to explain why he is not living with his birth parents.

Disengagement work, The work that is done with the child, so that he feels free to become a member of a family other than the one he was born to. It allows him to believe he is entitled to form new attachments with current caregivers.

Empowerment, Similar to entitlement. However, true empowerment develops as relationships strengthen and have the ability to influence others' behaviors.

Entitlement, The right to parent a child. It includes both legal and emotional components and may be affected by either external or internal factors. For example, although adoptive parents are legally entitled to parent the child, society frequently implies that they are not the real parents.

Lifebook or Life Story Book, Since children in care are separated from their families, the usual source of information about one's personal history, they need an alternate source of information. A Lifebook is a chronicle that contains the child's personal history. He can use it to share the parts of his life that were not spent together with his current parents. He can use it to facilitate his own identity formation.

Mothering, A term used to describe the day-in, day-out caregiving of the young child that leads to the building of primary attachments. Although most commonly provided by birth mothers, it can be provided by foster or adoptive mothers, fathers, or even siblings.

Reframing, A basic strategy of psychotherapy and reparenting in which negative behaviors are identified as positive strivings.

Sexually reactive behaviors, A term to describe the sexualized behaviors that are commonly seen in children who have been sexually abused, or exposed to inappropriate for age adult sexuality, but are uncommonly seen in other children.

Uneven parenting, A term coined by Clarke and Dawson to describe the condition of the many children who have had some, but not all, of their needs met by their caregivers.

Unpleasure, A term coined by Spitz to describe the generalized discomfort that the newborn infant experiences when he has a physical need.

Bibliography by Chapter

Chapter 1: Attachment

Aldgate, J. and Simmonds, J. Eds. *Direct Work with Children*. London: B.T. Batsford Ltd. 1988.

Allan, J. "Identification and Treatment of Difficult Babies." *Canadian Nurse*. Vol 72 (12) pp 11-16, 1976.

Allan, J. "The Body in Child Psychotherapy" in Schwartz-Salant, N. and Stein, M. (Eds) *The Body in Analysis*, pp 145-166. Wilmette, IL: Chiron Publ, 1986.

Ainsworth, M.D.S. Infancy in Uganda: *Infant Care and the Growth of Love*. Baltimore: Johns Hopkins University Press, 1967.

Anderson, J. "Holding Therapy: A Way of helping Unattached Children." *Adoption Resources for Mental Health Professionals*. Eds. Grabe. New Brunswick, CT: Transaction Publishers, 1990.

Anthony, E. J., "Treating Children and Adolescents: Opening Moves." A paper presented at the San Francisco Psychiatric Symposium, September, 1983. Dr. Anthony has written a series of publications through the years. They are part of *The Child in His Family*, published by John Wiley and Sons, New York.

Bretherton, Inge and Waters, Everett: *Growing Points of Attachment Theory and Research*. Monographs of the Society for Research in Child Development. Vo. 50, Nos 1-2, 1985.

Bourguignon, J.P. and Watson, K.W.: *After Adoption: A Manual for Professionals Working with Adoptive Families*. Springfield, Ill.: Illinois Department of Children and Family Services, 1987.

Bowlby, J. *Attachment and Loss, Volume II Separation: Anxiety and Anger.* New York: Basic Books, 1973.

Castner, Ames, Amatruda. *Life: The Preschool Years.* New York: Harper and Row, 1940.

Cline, F. "Understanding and Treating the Severely Disturbed Child." *Adoption Resources for Mental Health Professionals.* Grabe, P. Ed. New Brunswick, CT: Transaction Publishers, 1990.

Cruger, Martin J. Personal communication, 1989. Mr. Cruger can be contacted through Rational Point of View; 288 E. Maple, Suite 220; Birmingham, MI 48011.

Delcato, C.H. *The Ultimate Stranger.* New York: Doubleday and Co., Inc., 1974.

Deutsch, D.K., Swanson, J.M., Bruell, J.H., Cantwell, D.P., Weinberg, F., & Baren, M. "Overrepresentation of Adoptees in Children with the Attention Deficit Disorder." *Behavior Genetics*, 12, 231-238, 1982.

Elmer, Elizabeth: *Fragile Families, Troubled Children*: *The Aftermath of Infant Trauma.* Pittsburgh: University of Pittsburgh Press, 1977.

Erikson, E.H.: *Childhood and Society.* New York: W.W. Norton and Co., Inc. 1950.

Foley, G.M. "An Assessment Scale-Family Attachment to the High Risk Infant." A paper presented in Denver, Co., in May 1980.

Fraiberg, Selma. *Every Child's Birthright: In Defense of Mothering.* New York: Basic Books, 1977

Freud, A. and Dann, S. "An Experiment in Group Upbringing." *Psychoanal. Study Child* 6, 127-68, 1951.

Gesell, A., Halverson, Ilg, Thompson. *The First Five Years of Life*: The Preschool Years. New York: Harper and Row, 1940.

Gesell, A. and Ilg, F. *The Child from Five to Ten.* New York: Harper and Row. 1946.

Goldfarb. " Emotional and Intellectual Consequence of Psychological Deprivation in Infancy—A Re-Evaluation". *Psychopathology of Children*, 1954.

Goldstein, J. Freud, A. and Solnit, A.J. *Beyond the Best Interests of the Child.* New York, Macmillan Publishing 1973

Gordon, Sol. *Facts About Sex: A Basic Guide.* New York: John Day Co., 1969.

Greenspan, S, and Greenspan, N.T. *First Feelings: Milestones in the Emotional Development of Your Baby and Child from Birth to Age Four.* New York: Viking Penguin Inc., 1985.

Greenspan, S. and Greenspan, N.T. The Essential Partnership: How Parents and *Children Can Meet the Emotional Challenges of Infancy and Childhood.* New York: Viking Penguin Inc., 1989.

Group for Advancement of Psychiatry, Committee on Adolescence. *Normal Adolescence: Its Dynamics and Impact.* Report No. 68. New York, 1968.

Hymes, J. L. *The Child Under Six.* Englewood Cliffs, N.J.: Prentice-Hall, 1969.

Jernberg, Ann M. In "Attachment Enhancing for Adopted Children." *Adoption Resources for Mental Health Professionals.* Grabe, P. Ed. New Brunswick CT: Transaction Publishers, 1990.

Jernberg, Ann M. *Theraplay.* San Francisco CA: Jossey-Bass, 1979.

Klaus, M.H. and Kennell, J.H. *Maternal-Infant Bonding.* St. Louis: C.V. Mosby Company, 1976.

Lorenz, Konrad. *On Aggression.* New York: Harcourt Brace and World, 1966.

MacFarlane, J.S.: *In Parent-infant interaction,* Ciba Foundation Symposium 33, Amsterdam: Elsevier Publishing Co., 1975.

Massie, H.N., MD and Campbell, B.K.,MD. The AIDS Scale in The *Special Infant*, Jack M. Stack, MD, Editor. New York: Human Sciences Press, 1982.

McNamara, J. and McNamara, B. *Adoption and the Sexually Abused Child.* Human Services Development Institute, University of Southern Maine. 1990.

Moscy, A.C., Foley, G.M.,McCrae, M., and Evaul, T. *Attachment-Separation-Individuation.* 1980.

Nova Series on PBS television. *Life's First Feelings* narrated by Tom Cottle, 1986.

Polansky, N.A., Chalmers, M.A., Buttenvieser, E, and Williams, D.P.: *Damaged Parents: An Anatomy of Neglect.* Chicago and London: Chicago University Press, 1981.

Rutter, Michael. *Maternal Deprivation Reassessed.* London: Penguin Books, 1981.

Schneider, J.W., Chasnoff, I.J. "Cocaine Abuse during Pregnancy: Its Effects on Infant Motor Development—A Clinical Perspective."*Topics in Acute Care and Trauma Rehabilitation* 2(1):59-69, 1987.

Sheffield, M. *Where Do Babies Come From?* New York: Alfred A. Knopf, 1975.

Smith, D.W., and Sherwin, L.N.: *Mothers and Their Adopted Children: The Bonding Process.* New York: Tiersias Press, 1983.

Spitz, R. *The First Year of Life.* New York: International Universities Press, 1965.

Stroufe, L.A., Fox, N.E. and Pancake, V.R. "Attachment and Dependency in Developmental Perspective." *Child Development* 54, 1615-1627, 1983.

Tizard, Barbara: *The Care of Young Children: Implications of Recent Research.* London: University of London Institute of Education, 1986.

White, Michael. *Selected Papers.* Adelaide, Australia: Dulwich Centre Publications, 1989.

Winnicott, D.W. *Collected Papers.* New York: Basic Books, Inc. 1958.

Wolff, P.H. *The Causes, Controls and Organization of Behavior in the Neonate.* New York: International Universities Press, 1966.

Yogman, M. "Development of the Father-Infant Relationship." Fitzgerald, Lester, Yogman, eds. *Theory and Research in Behavioral Pediatrics*, Vol. 1. New York: Plenum Publishing Corporation.

Chapter Two: Child Development

Bernstein, A. *The Flight of the Stork.* New York: Delacorte Press, 1978.

Beyer, M. Emotional Problems of Neglected Children. In *Adoption Resources for Mental Health Professionals*, edited by Grabe, P., 1986.

Blos, P. *On Adolescence: A Psychoanalytic Interpretation.* New York: The Free Press, 1962.

Calderone, M.S. and Ramey, J. *Talking with Your Child about Sex: Questions and Answers for Children from Birth to Puberty.* New York: Random House, 1982.

Erikson, E.H.(Ed): *The Challenge of Youth.* New York: Basic Books, 1963.

Fraiberg, Selma. *The Magic Years.* New York: Charles Scribner and Son, 1959

Gesell, A., Halverson, Ilg, Thompson. *The First Five Years of Life: The Preschool Years.* New York: Harper and Row, 1940.

Gesell, A. and Ilg, F. *The Child from Five to Ten.* New York: Harper and Row. 1946.

Green, A. "Developmental Factors Associated with Child Abuse." Presented at Keystone conference on Child Abuse and Neglect, May 1980.

Greenspan, S, and Greenspan, N.T. *First Feelings: Milestones in the Emotional Development of Your Baby and Child from Birth to Age Four.* New York: Viking Penguin Inc, 1985.

Greenspan, S. and Greenspan, N.T. *The Essential Partnership: How Parents and Children Can Meet the Emotional Challenges of Infancy and Childhood.* New York: Viking Penguin Inc., 1989.

Group for Advancement of Psychiatry, Committee on Adolescence. *Normal Adolescence: Its Dynamics and Impact.* Report No. 68. New York, 1968.

Hagens, K.B., Case, J. *When Your Child Has Been Molested: A Parents Guide to Healing and Recovery.* Lexington Books.

Hymes, J. L. *The Child Under Six.* Englewood Cliffs, N.J.: Prentice-Hall, 1969.

Jewett, Claudia. Workshop on Adolescent Development presented in Golden, Colorado, in 1980.

Johnson, T.C. "Children Who Act Out Sexually" in *Adoption and the Sexually Abused Child* ed. McNamara and McNamara. Human Services Development Institute, University of Southern Maine, 1990.

Kagan, Jerome. *The Growth of the Child: Reflections on Human Development.* New York: W.W. Norton and Co. Inc., 1978.

Lewis, H.R. and Lewis, M.E. *Sex Education Begins at Home.* Norwalk, Connecticut: Appleton-Century-Crofts, 1983.

McNamara, J. and McNamara, B. *Adoption and the Sexually Abused Child.* Human Services Development Institute, University of Southern Maine. 1990.

Moss, H.A. and Robson, J.S., "Maternal Influences in Early Social Visual Behavior," *Child Development,* 39: 401-403, 1968.

Pulaski, M.A.S. *Your Baby's Mind and How It Grows: Piaget's Theory for Parents.* New York: Harper and Row, 1978.

Scherz, F.H. *Maturational Crises and Parent-Child Interaction.* Social Casework: June, 1971, pp. 362-369.

Stoller, R. "Primary Femininity." *Journal of the Americal Psychoanalytic Association,* Vol. 24, No. 5. 1976.

Viorst, Judith. *Necessary Losses.* New York: Simon and Schuster, 1986.

Whiting, B.B. and Whiting, J.W.M. *Children of Six Cultures.* Cambridge, Mass: Harvard University Press, 1975.

Wolff, P.H. *The Causes, Controls and Organization of Behavior in the Neonate.* New York: International Universities Press, 1966.

Chapter Three: Separation

Aldgate, J. and Simmonds, J. Eds. *Direct Work with Children.* London: B.T. Batsford Ltd. 1988.

Bowlby, J. *Attachment and Loss, Vol I Attachment.* New York: Basic Books, 1970.

Bowlby, J. *Attachment and Loss Volume III Loss*: Sadness and Depression. New York: Basic Books, 1980.

Breier, A., et al. "Early Parental Loss and Development of Adult Psychopathology" *Archives of General Psychiatry,* 45:987-993, 1988.

Fraiberg, Selma. *Every Child's Birthright: In Defense of Mothering.* New York: Basic Books, 1977

Freud, A. and Burlingham, D. *War and Children.* New York: International Universities Press, Inc. 1943.

Goldstein, J. Freud, A. and Solnit, A.J. *Beyond the Best Interests of the Child.* New York: Macmillan Publishing 1973

Hill, O.W. "Childhood Bereavement and Adult Psychiatric Disturbance." *Journal Psychosom. Res.*, Vol. 16. pp. 357-60.

Jewett-Jarrett, C. Workshop on Separation and Loss, presented in Manchester, England, 1988.

Kubler-Ross, E., *Death: The Final Stage of Growth.*Cliffs, New Jersey: Prentice-Hall, Inc. Englewood, 1975

Rutter, Michael. *Maternal Deprivation Reassessed.* London: Penguin Books, 1981.

Schoenberg, Carr, Peretz, Kutcher Ed. *Loss and Grief.* New York: Columbia University Press, 1970.

Spencer, Marietta, of the Children's Home Society of Minnestota. From presentation at Child Welfare League of America offices in New York City. 1978.

Stoller, R. "Primary Femininity." *Journal of the American Psychoanalytic Association*, Vol. 24, No. 5. 1976.

Viorst, Judith. *Necessary Losses.* New York: Simon and Schuster, 1986.

Wallerstein, J.S. and Kelly, J.B. Surviving the Breakup: *How Children and Parents Cope with Divorce.* New York: Basic Books, 1980.

Wallinga, J. F. "Foster Placement and Separation Trauma." *Public Welfare*, Vol. 24, No. 4.

Winnicott, Clare. "Face to Face with Children." *Working with Children.* London: The British Agencies for Adoption and Fostering, 1986.

Chapter Four: Minimizing the Trauma of Moves

Clarke, J.I. and Dawson, C: *Growing Up Again.* Harper and Row, San Francisco, 1989.

Dobson, W. *Dare to Discipline.* Wheaton, Ill and Glendale CA: Tyndate Hourse and Regal Books, 1972.

Dreikurs, R. and Green, L. *Logical Consequences.* New York: Meredith Press, 1968.

Gordon, Thomas. *Parent Effectiveness Training.* New York: Peter Wyden Inc., 1971.

Haley, Jay. *Strategies of Psychotherapy.* New York: Greene and Straton, 1963.

Hymes, J.L. *The Child Under Six.* Englewood, N.J.: Prentice Hall, 1969.

McNamara, J. and McNamara, B. *Adoption and the Sexually Abused Child.* Human Services Development Institute, University of Southern Maine. 1990.

Minshew, D and Hooper, C. *The Adoptive Family as a Healing Resource for the Sexually Abused Child. A Training Manual.* Child Welfare League of America. Washington D.C. 1990.

Nelson, G. *The One Minute Scolding.* Shambhala Publications 1984.

Schaffer, J. and Lindstrom, C. "Brief Solution-Focused Therapy with Adoptive Families". In *The Psychology of Adoption.* Brodzinsky and Schecter Eds. New York: Oxford Univ. Press, 1990.

Stewart, M. *Raising a Hyperactive Child.* New York: Harper and Row, 1973.

Chapter Five: Case Planning

Adcock, M. "Assessment: a Summary" in Adcock, M. and White, R., ed., *Good-Enough Parenting: a Framework for Assessment*, London. British Agencies for Adoption and Fostering, 1985.

Banks, S.P. and Kahn, M.D. *The Sibling Bond.* New York: Basic Books, Inc. 1982.

Barth, R., Berry, M, Goodfield, R. and Carson, M.L. *Older Child Adoption and Disruption.* Washington D.C.: The Children's Bureau, 1987.

Department of Health: *Protecting Children: A Guide for Social Workers undertaking a Comprehensive Assessment.* London: Her Majesty's Stationery Office, 1988.

Donley, K. S. "Sibling Attachments and Adoption" Paper presented at Family Builders by Adoption conference in Charleston, S.C. in May 1989. Available from National Resource Center for Special Needs Adoption; P.O. Box 337, Chelsea, MI 48118.

Dunn, J. "Sibling Relationships in Early Childhood." *Child Development*, 54: 787-811. 1983.

Fanshel, David. *Far From the Reservations: The Transracial Adoption of American Indian Children.* New York: Scarecrow Press, 1972.

Feigelman, W. and Silverman, A.R. *Chosen Children.* New York: Praeger, 1983.

Goldstein, J. Freud, A. and Solnit, A.J. *Before the Best Interests of the Child.* New York: Macmillan Publishing, 1979.

Goldstein, J. Freud, A. and Solnit, A.J. *Beyond the Best Interests of the Child.* New York: Macmillan Publishing, 1973.

Goodluck, C. "Mental Health Issues of Native American Transracial Adoptions." *Adoption Resources for Mental Health Professionals.* Ed. Grabe. New Brunswick, CT: Transaction Publishers, 1990.

Gordon, Thomas. *Parent Effectiveness Training.* New York: Peter Wyden Inc., 1971.

Grow, L.J. and Shapiro, D. *Black Children—White Parents.* New York: Child Welfare League of America, 1974.

Hartman, A.: *Finding Families: An Ecological Approach to Family Assessment in Adoption.* Beverly Hills: Sage Publications, 1979.

Horejsi, C.; Bertsche, A., and Clark, F. *Parents with Children in Foster Care: A Guide to Social Work Practice.* Springfield, Illinois: Charles C. Thomas, 1981.

Jones, David: The Untreatable Family. *Child Abuse and Neglect,* Vol. 11 pp 409-420, 1987.

LaPere, D. W., Davis, L.E.., Courve, J, and McDonald, M. *Large Sibling Groups.* Washington D.C.: Child Welfare League of America, Inc. 1986.

LaPere, D. "Placing Sibling Groups for Adoption." Paper presented at the Family Builder by Adoption Conference in Charleston, S.C. 1989.

Lawson A. and Ingleby, J.D. "Daily Routines of Preschool Children." *Psychological Medicine,* 4: 399-415, 1974.

Linkages Project of the National American Indian Court Judges Association. "Adoption and the American Indian Child." Boulder, CO: National Indian Law Library, August 1985. Published by TCI Inc.; 3410 Garfield Street, N.W., Washington, D.C. 20007.

Maluccio, A.N. and Fine, E. "Permanency Planning: A Redefinition." *Child Welfare*, 63 (May-June) 1983, p 197.

McNamara, J. and McNamara, B. *Adoption and the Sexually Abused Child.* Human Services Development Institute, University of Southern Maine. 1990.

McRoy, R.G. and Zurcher, L. *Transracial and Inracial Adoptees.* Charles C. Thomas: Springfield IL, 1983.

Melina, Lois. " Parents Attitudes and Expectations Influence Sibling Realtionships." *Adopted Child* 9:6, June 1990.

Pike, V. et al, *Permanent Planning for Children in Foster Care: A Handbook for Social Workers.* Washington DC: US Department of Health, Education, and Welfare, 1977.

Rutter, Michael. *Maternal Deprivation Reassessed.* London. Penguin Books, 1981.

Silverman, A.R. and Feigelman, W. "Adjustment in Interracial Adoptees: An Overview." in *The Psychology of Adoption* Eds. Brodzinsky and Schechter. New York: Oxford University Press, 1990.

Simon, R. and Altstein, H. *Transracial Adoptees and Their Families: A Study of Identity and Commitment.* New York: Praeger, 1987.

Stein, T.J. *Social Work Practice in Child Welfare.* Englewood Cliffs, NJ: Prentice-Hall, Inc. 1981.

Tizard, Barbara: *The Care of Young Children*: Implications of Recent Research. London: University of London Institute of Education, 1986.

Viorst, Judith. *Necessary Losses.* Simon and Schuster, New York, 1986.

Chapter Six: Behavior Problems

Clarke, J.I. *Self-Esteem: A Family Affair.* Minneapolis MN: Winston Press, 1978.

Clarke, J.I. and Dawson, C: *Growing Up Again.* San Francisco: Harper and Row, 1989.

Cline, Foster W. Understanding and Treating the Difficult Child. Evergreen CO: Evergreen Consultants on Human Behavior, 1981.

Coleman, L; Tilbor, K.; Hornby, H.; Boggis, C. Eds. *Working With Older Adoptees*. Portland Maine: Univeristy of Southern Maine, 1988.

Dobson, W. *Dare to Discipline*. Wheaton, Ill and Glendale CA: Tyngate House and Regal Books, 1972.

Dorris, Michael. *The Broken Cord*. New York: HarperCollins Publishers, 1990.

Dreikurs, R. and Green, L. *Logical Consequences*. New York: Meredith Press, 1968.

Fahlberg, V. and Staff of Forest Heights Lodge: *Residential Treatment: A Tapestry of Many Therapies*. Indianapolis: Perspectives Press, 1990.

Gordon, Thomas. *Parent Effectiveness Training*. New York: Peter Wyden Inc., 1971.

Haley, Jay. *Strategies of Psychotherapy*. New York: Grune and Stratton, Inc. 1963.

Hymes, J. L. *The Child under Six*. Englewood Cliffs, N.J.: Prentice-Hall, 1969.

Ingersoll, B. *Your Hyperactive Child, A Parents Guide to Coping with Attention Deficit Disorder*. New York: Doubleday, 1988.

Jewett, Claudia. "Treating Older Adoptees: An Interview With" inColeman, L; Tilbor, K.; Hornby, H.; Boggis, C. Eds. *Working With Older Adoptees*. Portland Maine: Univeristy of Southern Maine, 1988.

McNamara, J. and McNamara, B. *Adoption and the Sexually Abused Child*. Human Services Development Institute, University of Southern Maine. 1990.

Minshew, D and Hooper, C. *The Adoptive Family as a Healing Resource for the Sexually Abused Child. A Training Manual*. Washington D.C.: Child Welfare League of America, 1990.

Nelson, G. *The One Minute Scolding*. Shambhala Publications, 1984.

Osman, Betty. *Learning Disabilities: A Family Affair*. New York: Warner Books, 1979.

Osman, Betty. *No One to Play With*. New York: Random House, 1982.
Prew, Suter, Carrington. *Post-Adoption Family Therapy: A Practice Manual*. Available from Children's Services Division, 198 Commercial Street, S.E. Salem, OR 97310-0450

Schaffer, J. and Kral, R. "Brief Solution-Focused Therapy with Adoptive Families." *Working with Older Adoptees*. Coleman et al, Eds. Portland Maine: University of Southern Maine, 1988.

Schaffer, J. and Lindstrom, C. "Brief Solution-Focused Therapy with Adoptive Families". In *The Psychology of Adoption*. Brodzinsky and Schecter Eds. New York: Oxford Univ. Press, 1990.

Ryan, P. Ed: *Training Foster Parents to Handle Destructive Behavior*. Ypsilanti, MI: The Foster Parent Training Project, Eastern Michigan University. 1978

Ryan, P. Ed: *Training Foster Parents to Handle Lying and Stealing*. Ypsilanti, MI: The Foster Parent Training Project, Eastern Michigan University. 1978

Streissguth, A.P. and Randels, S. "Long Term Effects of Fetal Alcohol Syndrome" in *Alcohol and Child/Family Health*. Robinson, G.C. and Armstrong, R.W. (Eds.) Vancouver, B.C.: University of British Columbia, 1988.

Wender, Paul. *Hyperactive Child, Adolelescent, and Adult: Ateention Deficit Disorder through the Lifespan*. 3rd ed. New York: Oxford Univ. Press, 1987.

Chapter Seven: Direct Work

Aldgate, J. and Simmonds, J. Eds. *Direct Work with Children*. London: B.T. Batsford Ltd. 1988.

Beyer, M. "Emotional Problems of Neglected Children." In *Adoption Resources for Mental Health Professionals*, edited by Grabe, P., 1986.

Bourguignon, J.P. and Watson, K.W.: *After Adoption: A manual for Professionals Working with Adoptive Families*. Springfield, Ill. Illinois Department of Children and Family Services, 1987.

Brodzinsky, D. and Schechter, M.D. *The Psychology of Adoption*. New York: Oxford University Press, 1990.

Cipolla J., McGown, D.B., and Yanulis, M.A. *Using Play Techniques to Assess and Prepare Older Children for Adoption*. Chelsea, Michigan, National Resource Center for Special Needs Adoption. 1990.

Coleman, L; Tilbor, K.; Hornby, H.; Boggis, C. Eds. *Working With Older Adoptees*. Portland Maine: Univeristy of Southern Maine, 1988.

Dockar-Drysdale, B. E., "The Process of Symbolization Observed Amoung Emotionally Deprived Children in Therapeutic School," in TOD, R.J.N., Eds, *Disturbed Children*, London: Longmans, 1967.

Gabel, S. *Filling in the Blanks: A Guided Look at Growing Up Adopted.* Indianapolis IN: Perspectives Press, 1988.

Han, Hyun Sook. *Understanding My Child's Korean Origins.* Minneapolis MN: Children's Home Society of Minnesota, 1984

Hapgood, M. "Older Child Adoption and the Knowledge Base of Adoption Practice," in Bean, P., ed. *Adoption: Essays in Social Policy, Law, and Sociology,* Tavistock Publishing, 1984.

Hapgood, M. "Creative Direct Work with Adolescents: the Story of Craig Brooks," in Aldgate, J. and Simmonds, J. Eds. *Direct Work with Children.* London: B.T. Batsford Ltd. 1988.

Horne J."When the Social Worker is a Bridge," in Sawbridge, P., Ed. *Parents for Children*, British Agencies for Adoption and Fostering (BAAF), 1983.

Jewett, Claudia, *Helping Children Cope With Separation and Loss*. Harvard Mass: Harvard Common Press, 1982.

Kahn, Timothy J., *Pathways: A Guided Workbook for Youth Beginning* Treatment. The Safer Society Press, Shoreham Depot Road, RR 1, Box 24-B, Orwell, VT, 1990.

Katz, L. "Older Child Adoptive Placment: A Time of Family Crisis." *Child Welfare*, 56(3) March, 1977.

Krementz, J. *How It Feels To Be Adopted.* New York: Alfred A. Knopf, 1988.

Main, M, Kaplan, N and Cassidy, J. "Security in Infancy, Childhood, and Adulthood: A Move to the Level of Representation" in *Growing Points of Attachment Theory and Research.* Bretherton and Waters (Eds). Chicago IL: University of Chicago Press. 1985.

McClarty, Joanne. *Superkids: A Boys Group About Abuse.* Portland, OR: Waverly Children's Home, 1990.

Melina, L. R. *Making Sense of Adoption.* New York: Harper and Row, 1989.

Prew, Suter, Carrington. *Post-Adoption Family Therapy: A Practice Manual.* Available from Children's Services Division, 198 Commercial Street, S.E. Salem, OR 97310-0450

Ricks, M.H. "The Social Transmission of Parental Behavior: Attachment Across Generations" in *Growing Points of Attachment Theory and Research.* Bretherton and Waters (Eds). Chicago IL: University of Chicago Press. 1985.

Ryan, Ryan, T and Walker, R. *Making Life Story Books.* British Agencies for Adoption and Fostering, 11 Southwark Street, London SE1 1RQ, 1985.

Thoburn, J. *Child Placement: Principles and Practice.* London: Wildwood, 1988.

Triseliotis, J.P. "Identity and Security in Adoption and Long-Term Fostering. *Adoption and Fostering*, 7:1, 22-31, 1983.

Viorst, Judith. *Necessary Losses.* New York: Simon and Schuster, 1986.

Bibliography

Adcock, M. "Assessment: a Summary" in Adcock, M. and White, R., ed., *Good-Enough Parenting: a Framework for Assessment*, London: British Agencies for Adoption and Fostering, 1985.

Ainsworth, M.D.S. Infancy in Uganda: *Infant Care and the Growth of Love.* Baltimore: Johns Hopkins University Press, 1967.

Aldgate, J. and Simmonds, J. Eds. *Direct Work with Children*. London: B.T. Batsford Ltd. 1988.

Anderson, J. "Holding Therapy: A Way of Helping Unattached Children." *Adoption Resources for Mental Health Professionals*. Eds. Grabe. New Brunswick, CT: Transaction Publishers, 1990.

Anthony, E. J. "Treating Children and Adolescents: Opening Moves." A paper presented at the San Francisco Psychiatric Symposium, September, 1983. Dr. Anthony has written a series of publications through the years. They are part of *The Child in His Family*, published by John Wiley and Sons, New York.

Banks, S.P. and Kahn, M.D. *The Sibling Bond*. New York: Basic Books, Inc. 1982.

Barth, R., Berry, M, Goodfield, R. and Carson, M.L. *Older Child Adoption and Disruption*. Washington D.C.: The Children's Bureau, 1987.

Beyer, M. "Emotional Problems of Neglected Children." In *Adoption Resources for Mental Health Professionals*, edited by Grabe, P., 1986.

Blos, P. *On Adolescence: A Psychoanalytic Interpretation.* New York: The Free Press, 1962.

Blos, P. The Second Individuation Process of Adolescence. *Psycholanalytic Study of the Child* Vol 22, New York: International Universities Press, 1967.

Bourguignon, J.P. and Watson, K.W.: *After Adoption: A Manual for Professionals Working with Adoptive Families.* Springfield, Ill. Illinois Department of Children and Family Services, 1987.

Bowlby, J. *Attachment and Loss, Vol I Attachment.* New York: Basic Books, 1970.

Bowlby, J. *Attachment and Loss, Volume II Separation: Anxiety and Anger.* New York: Basic Books, 1973.

Bowlby, J. *Attachment and Loss Volume III Loss: Sadness and Depression.* New York: Basic Books, 1980.

Breier, A., et al. "Early Parental Loss and Development of Adult Psychopathology" Archives of General Psychiatry, 45:987-993, 1988.

Bretherton, Inge and Waters, Everett: *Growing Points of Attachment Theory and Research.* Monographs of the Society for Research in Child Development. Vo. 50, Nos 1-2, 1985.

Bretherton, I. "Young Children in Stressful Situations: The Supporting Role of Attachment Figures." In G.V. Coelho & P. Ahmed (Eds) *Uprooting and Development.* New York: Plenum. 1980.

Calderone, M.S. and Ramey, J. *Talking With Your Child About Sex: Questions and Answers for Children from Birth to Puberty.* Random House, New York, 1982.

Carswell, John. "Preparation of Children and Youth in Residential Treatment for Adoptive Placement." Paper presented annual meeting of the American Association of Children's Residential Centers, 1980.

Chennells, Prue. *Explaining Adoption To Your Adopted Child.* London: British Agencies for Adoption and Fostering, 1987.

Cipolla J., McGown, D.B., and Yanulis, M.A. *Using Play Techniques to Assess and Prepare Older Children for Adoption.* Chelsea, Michigan: National Resource Center for Special Needs Adoption. 1990.

Clarke, J.I. *Self-Esteem: A Family Affair.* Minneapolis MN: Winston Press, 1978.

Clarke, J.I. and Dawson, C: *Growing Up Again.* San Francisco: Harper and Row, 1989.

Cline, Foster W. *Understanding and Treating the Difficult Child.* Evergreen CO: Evergreen Consultants on Human Behavior, 1981.

Coleman, L; Tilbor, K.; Hornby, H.; Boggis, C. Eds. *Working with Older Adoptees.* Portland Maine: Univeristy of Southern Maine, 1988.

Delcato, C.H. *The Ultimate Stranger.* New York: Doubleday and Co., Inc., 1974.

Department of Health: Protecting Children: *A Guide for Social Workers undertaking a Comprehensive Assessment.* London: Her Majesty's Stationery Office, 1988.

Deutsch, D.K., Swanson, J.M., Bruell, J.H., Cantwell, D.P., Weinberg, F., & Baren, M. "Overrepresentation of Adoptees in Children with the Attention Deficit Disorder." *Behavior Genetics*, 12, 231-238, 1982.

Dobson, W. *Dare to Discipline.* Wheaton, Ill and Glendale CA: Tyndate Hourse and Regal Books, 1972.

Donley, K. S. "Sibling Attachments and Adoption" Paper presented at Family Builders by Adoption conference in Charleston, S.C. in May 1989. Available from National Resource Center for Special Needs Adoption; P.O. Box 337, Chelsea, MI 48118.

Dockar-Drysdale, B. E., "The Process of Symbolization Observed Amoung Emotionally Deprived Children in Therapeutic School," in TOD, R.J.N., Eds, *Disturbed Children*, London: Longmans, 1967.

Dorris, Michael. *The Broken Cord.* New York: HarperCollins Publishers, 1990.

Dreikurs, R. and Green, L. *Logical Consequences.* New York: Meredith Press, 1968.
Dunn, J. "Sibling Relationships in Early Childhood." *Child Development*, 54: 787-811. 1983.

Elmer, Elizabeth: *Fragile Families, Troubled Children: The Aftermath of Infant Trauma.* Pittsburgh: University of Pittsburgh Press, 1977.

Erikson, E.H.: *Childhood and Society.* New York: W.W. Norton and Co., Inc. 1950.

Erikson, E.H.(Ed): *The Challenge of Youth*. New York: Basic Books, 1963.

Fahlberg, V. and Staff of Forest Heights Lodge: *Residential Treatment: A Tapestry of Many Therapies*. Indianapolis: Perspectives Press, 1990.

Fanshel, David. *Far From the Reservations: The Transracial Adoption of American Indian Children*. New York: Scarecrow Press, 1972.

Feigelman, W. and Silverman, A.R. *Chosen Children*. New York: Praeger, 1983.

Foley, G.M. "An Assessment Scale-Family Attachment to the High risk Infant." A paper presented in Denver Co in May 1980.

Fraiberg, Selma. *The Magic Years*. New York: Charles Scribner and Son, 1959

Fraiberg, Selma. *Every Child's Birthright: In Defense of Mothering*. New York: Basic Books, 1977

Freud, A. and Burlingham, D. *War and Children*. New York: International Universities Press, Inc. 1943.

Freud, A. and Dann, S. "An Experiment in Group Upbringing." *Psychoanalytic Study of Children* 6, 127-68, 1951.

Gabel, S. *Filling in the Blanks: A Guided Look at Growing Up Adopted*. Indianapolis IN: Perspectives Press, 1988.

Gardner, R.A. *Therapuetic Communication with Children: The Mutual Storytelling Technique*. New York: Jason Aronson, Inc., 1971.

Gesell, A., Halverson, Ilg, Thompson. *The First Five Years of Life: The Preschool Years*. New York: Harper and Row, 1940.

Gesell, A. and Ilg, F. *The Child from Five to Ten*. New York: Harper and Row. 1946.

Ginott, Haim: *Between Parent and Child: New solution to old problems*. New York: MacMillan Co., 1965.

Goldfarb. Emotional and Intellectual Consequence of Psychological Deprivation in Infancy—A Re-Evaluation. *Psychopathology of Children*, 1954.

Goldstein, J. Freud, A. and Solnit, A.J. *Before the Best Interests of the Child*. New York: Macmillan Publishing 1979

Goldstein, J. Freud, A. and Solnit, A.J. *Beyond the Best Interests of the Child.* New York: Macmillan Publishing 1973

Goodluck, C. "Mental Health Issues of Native American Transracial Adoptions." *Adoption Resources for Mental Health Professionals.* Ed. Grabe. New Brunswick, CT: Transaction Publishers, 1990.

Gordon, Thomas. *Parent Effectiveness Training.* New York: Peter Wyden Inc., 1971.

Gordon, Sol and Gordon, Judith. *Raising a Child Conservatively in a Sexually Permissive World.* New York: Simon and Schuster, 1983.

Grabe, P.V., editor: *Adoption Resources for Mental Health Professionals.* New Brunswick: Transaction Publishers, 1990.

Green, A. "Developmental Factors Associated with Child Abuse." Presented at Keystone Conference on Child Abuse and Neglect, May 1980.

Greenspan, S, and Greenspan, N.T. *First Feelings: Milestones in the Emotional Development of Your Baby and Child from Birth to Age Four.* New York: Viking Penguin Inc., 1985.

Greenspan, S. and Greenspan, N.T. *The Essential Partnership: How Parents and Children Can Meet the Emotional Challenges of Infancy and Childhood.* New York: Viking Penguin Inc., 1989.

Groth, N. and Sevenson, T.M. *Anatomical Drawings.* Newton Center, MA: Forensic Mental Health Associates, Inc., 1984.

Group for Advancement of Psychiatry, Committee on Adolescence. *Normal Adolescence: Its Dynamics and Impact.* Report No. 68. New York, 1968.

Grow, L.J. and Shapiro, D. *Black Children—White Parents.* New York: Child Welfare League of America, 1974.

Hagens, K.B., Case, J. *When Your Child Has Been Molested: A Parents Guide to Healing and Recovery.* Lexington, MA: Lexington Books., 1988.

Haley, Jay. *Strategies of Psychotherapy.* New York: Grune and Stratton, Inc. 1963.

Han, Hyun Sook. *Understanding My Child's Korean Origins.* Minneapolis MN: Children's Home Society of Minnesota, 1984

Hapgood, M. "Older Child Adoption and the Knowledge Base of Adoption Practice," in Bean, P., ed. *Adoption: Essays in Social Policy, Law, and Sociology,* Tavistock Publishing, 1984.

Hapgood, M. "Creative Direct Work with Adolescents: the Story of Craig Brooks," in Aldgate, J. and Simmonds, J. Eds. *Direct Work with Children.* London: B.T. Batsford Ltd. 1988.

Hartman, A.: *Finding Families: An Ecological Approach to Family Assessment in Adoption.* Beverly Hills: Sage Publications, 1979.

Hill, O.W. "Childhood Bereavement and Adult Psychiatric Disturbance." *Journal Psychosom.* Res., Vol. 16. pp. 357-60.

Horejsi, C.; Bertsche, A., and Clark, F. *Parents with Children in Foster Care: A Guide to Social Work Practice.* Springfield, Illinois: Charles C. Thomas, 1981.

Horne J."When the Social Worker is a Bridge," in Sawbridge, P., Ed. *Parents for Children*, London: British Agencies for Adoption and Fostering (BAAF), 1983.

Hymes, J. L. *The Child Under Six.* Englewood Cliffs, N.J.: Prentice-Hall, 1969.

Ingersoll, B. *Your Hyperactive Child, A Parents Guide to Coping With Attention Deficit Disorder.* New York: Doubleday, 1988.

Jewett, Claudia. *Adopting the Older Child.* Harvard, Mass: Harvard Common Press, 1978.

Jewett, Claudia, *Helping Children Cope With Separation and Loss.* Harvard Mass: Harvard Common Press, 1982.

Jewett, Claudia. "Treating Older Adoptees: An Interview With" inColeman, L; Tilbor, K.; Hornby, H.; Boggis, C. Eds. *Working With Older Adoptees.* Portland Maine: Univeristy of Southern Maine, 1988.

Jewett, Claudia. Workshop on Adolescent Development presented in Golden, Colorado, in 1980.

Jewett-Jarrett, C. Workshop on Separation and Loss, presented in Manchester, England, 1988.

Johnson, T.C. "Children Who Act Out Sexually" in *Adoption and the Sexually Abused Child* ed. McNamara and McNamara. Human services Development Institute, University of Southern Maine, 1990.

Jolowicz, A. R. "The Hidden Parent: Some Effects of the Concealment of the Parent's Life Upon the Child's Use of a Foster Home" Presented before the New York State Conference of Social Welfare, New York City, Nov., 1947.

Jones, David: "The Untreatable Family". *Child Abuse and Neglect*, Vol. 11 pp 409-420, 1987.

Kagan, Jerome. *The Growth of the Child: Reflections on Human Development.* New York: W.W. Norton and Co. Inc., 1978.

Kahn, Timothy J., Pathways: *A Guided Workbook for Youth Beginning Treatment.* The Safer Society Press, Shoreham Depot Road, RR 1, Box 24-B, Orwell, VT, 1990.

Karen, R. "Becoming Attached". *The Atlantic Monthly*, January 1990.

Kinney, J., Madsen, B, Fleming, T. and Haapala, D., "Homebuilders: Keeping Families Together" J. *Consulting and Clinical Psychology.* 1977.

Klaus, M.H. and Kennell, J.H. *Maternal-Infant Bonding.* St. Louis: C.V. Mosby Company, 1976.

Krementz, J. *How It Feels To Be Adopted.* New York: Alfred A. Knopf, 1988.

Krugman, D.C. "Working With Separation". *Child Welfare* Vol I., No. 9, pgs. 528-537, 1971.

Kubler-Ross, E., Death: *The Final Stage of Growth.* Englewood Cliffs, NJ: Prentice-Hall, Inc., 1975

LaPere, D. W., Davis, L.E.., Courve, J, and McDonald, M. *Large Sibling Groups.* Washington D.C.: Child Welfare League of America, Inc. 1986.

Lawson A. and Ingleby, J.D. "Daily Routines of Preschool Children." *Psychological Medicine*, 4: 399-415, 1974.

Lewis, H.R. and Lewis, M.E. *Sex Education Begins at Home.* Appleton-Century-Crofts, Norwalk, Connecticut, 1983.

Lindenauer N. and Selmon, E.G. *I Am Me.* New York: Grosset and Dunlap, 1979.

Linkages Project of the National American Indian Court Judges Association. "Adoption and the American Indian Child." Boulder, CO: National Indian Law Library, August 1985. Published by TCI Inc.; 3410 Garfield Street, N.W., Washington, D.C. 20007.

Littner, Ner, "The Importance of the Natural Parents to the Child in Placement", *Child Welfare*, vol. LIV, 54, March, 1975.

Lorenz, Konrad. *On Aggression*. New York: Harcourt Brace and World., 1966.

MacFarlane, J.S.: I*n Parent-infant Interaction, Ciba Foundation Symposium 33*, Amsterdam: Elsevier Publishing Co., 1975.

Magid, K. and Schreibman, W. *Divorce Is.........: A Kid's Coloring Book*. Gretna, LA: Pelican Publishing Co., 1980.

Main, M, Kaplan, N and Cassidy, J. "Security in Infancy, Childhood, and Adulthood: A Move to the Level of Representation" in *Growing Points of Attachment Theory and Research*. Bretherton and Waters (Eds). Chicago IL: University of Chicago Press. 1985.

Maluccio, A.N. and Fine, E. Permanency Planning: A Redefinition." *Child Welfare*, 63 (May-June) 1983, p 197.

Massie, H.N., MD and Campbell, B.K.,MD. The AIDS Scale in *The Special Infant*, Jack M. Stack, MD, Editor. New York: Human Sciences Press, 1982.

McClarty, Joanne. *Superkids: A Boys Group About Abuse*. Portland, OR: Waverly Children's Home, 1990.

McNamara, J. and McNamara, B. *Adoption and the Sexually Abused Child*. Human Services Development Institute, University of Southern Maine. 1990.

McRoy, R.G. and Zurcher, L. *Transracial and Inracial Adoptees*. Springfield IL: Charles C. Thomas, 1983.
Melina, Lois. " Parents Attitudes and Expectations Influence Sibling Realtionships." *Adopted Child* 9:6, June 1990.

Melina, L. R. *Making Sense of Adoption*. New York: Harper and Row, 1989.

Minshew, D and Hooper, C. *The Adoptive Family as a Healing Resource for the Sexually Abused Child. A Training Manual*. Washington D.C.: Child Welfare League of America., 1990.

Mosey, A.C., Foley, G.M.,McCrae, M., and Evaul, T. *Attachment-Separation-Individuation*. 1980.

Moss, H.A. and Robson, J.S., "Maternal Influences in Early Social Visual Behavior," *Child Development*, 39: 401-403, 1968.

Nelson, G. *The One Minute Scolding*. Shambhala Publications 1984.

Nova Series on PBS television. *Life's First Feelings* narrated by Tom Cottle, 1986.

Osman, Betty. *Learning Disabilities: A Family Affair*. New York: Warner Books, 1979.

Osman, Betty. *No One to Play With*. New York: Random House, 1982.

Pike, V. et al, *Permanent Planning for Children in Foster Care: A Handbook for Social Workers*. Washington DC: US Department of Health, Education, and Welfare, 1977.

Polansky, N.A., Chalmers, M.A., Buttenvieser, E, and Williams, D.P.: *Damaged Parents: An Anatomy of Neglect,* Chicago and London: Chicago University Press, 1981.

Prew, Suter, Carrington. *Post-Adoption Family Therapy: A Practice Manual*. Available from Children's Services Division, 198 Commercial Street, S.E. Salem, OR 97310-0450

Pulaski, M.A.S. *Your Baby's Mind and How It Grows: Piaget's Theory for Parents*. New York: Harper and Row, 1978.

Ricks, M.H." The Social Transmission of Parental Behavior: Attachment across Generations". *Growing Points of Attachment Theory and Research* edited by Bretherton and Waters. Monographs of the Society for Research in Child Development. Vo. 50, Nos 1-2, 1985.

Rutter, Michael. *Maternal Deprivation Reassessed*. London. Penguin Books, 1981.

Rutter, Michael. "Resilience in the Face of Adversity: Protective Factors and Reistance of Psychiatric Disorder." *British Journal of Psychiatry* (1985), 147, 598-611.

Ryan, P. Ed: *Training Foster Parents to Handle Destructive Behavior*. Ypsilanti, MI: The Foster Parent Training Project, Eastern Michigan University. 1978

Ryan, P. Ed: *Training Foster Parents to Handle Lying and Stealing.* Ypsilanti, MI: The Foster Parent Training Project, Eastern Michigan University. 1978

Ryan, T and Walker, R. *Making Life Story Books.* British Agencies for Adoption and Fostering, 11 Southwark Street, London SE1 1RQ, 1985.

Schaffer, J. and Kral, R. "Brief Solution-Focused Therapy with Adoptive Families." *Working with Older Adoptees.* Coleman et al, Eds. Portland Maine: University of Southern Maine, 1988.

Schaffer, J. and Lindstrom, C. Brief Solution-Focused Therapy with Adoptive Families. *In The Psychology of Adoption.* Brodzinsky and Schecter Eds. New York: Oxford Univ. Press, 1990.

Scherz, F.H. Maturational Crises and Parent-Child Interaction. *Social Casework*: June, 1971, pp. 362-369.

Schoenberg, Carr, Peretz, Kutcher Ed. *Loss and Grief.* New York: Columbia University Press, 1970.

Silber, K. and Dorner, P.M. *Children of Open Adoption.* San Antonio, TX: Corona Publishing Co., 1989.

Silverman, A.R. and Feigelman, W. "Adjustment in Interracial Adoptees: An Overview." in *The Psychology of Adoption* Eds. Brondzinsky and Schechter. New York: Oxford University Press, 1990.

Simon, R. and Altstein, H. *Transracial Adoptees and Their Families: A Study of Identity and Commitment.* New York: Praeger, 1987.

Smith, D.W., and Sherwin, L.N.: *Mothers and Their Adopted Children: The Bonding Process.* New York: Tiersias Press, 1983.

Spencer, Marietta, of the Children's Home Society of Minnestota. From presentation at Child Welfare League of America offices in New York City. 1978. Spitz, R. *The First Year of Life.* New York: International Universities Press, 1965.

Stein, Hoopes: *Identity Formation in the Adopted Adolescent*: *The Delaware Family Study.* Child Welfare League of America, N.Y. 1985.

Stein, T.J. *Social Work Practice in Child Welfare.* Englewood Cliffs, NJ: Prentice-Hall, Inc. 1981.

Streissguth, A.P. and Randels, S. "Long Term Effects of Fetal Alcohol Syndrome" in *Alcohol and Child/Family Health.* Robinson, G.C. and Armstrong, R.W. (Eds.) Vancouver, B.C.: University of British Columbia, 1988.

Stewart, M. *Raising a Hyperactive Child.* New York: Harper and Row, 1973. Stoller, R. "Primary Femininity." Journal of the American Psychoanalytic Association, Vol. 24, No. 5. 1976.

Stroufe, L.A., Fox, N.E. and Pancake, V.R. "Attachment and Dependency in Developmental Perspective." *Child Development* 54, 1615-1627, 1983.

Thoburn, J. *Child Placement: Principles and Practice.* London: Wildwood, 1988.

Tizard, Barbara: *The Care of Young Children: Implications of Recent Research.* London: University of London Institute of Education, 1986.

Triseliotis, J.P. "Identity and Security in Adoption and Long-Term Fostering. *Adoption and Fostering*, 7:1, 22-31, 1983.

Viorst, Judith. *Necessary Losses.* Simon and Schuster, New York, 1986.

Wallerstein, J.S. and Kelly, J.B. *Surviving the Breakup: How Children and Parents Cope with Divorce.* New York: Basic Books, 1980.

Wallinga, J. F. *Foster Placement and Separation Trauma. Public Welfare*, Vol. 24, No. 4.

Wender, Paul. *Hyperactive Child, Adolelescent, and Adult: Attention Deficit Disorder through the Lifespan.* 3rd ed. New York: Oxford Univ. Press, 1987.

Whiting, B.B. and Whiting, J.W.M. *Children of Six Cultures.* Cambridge, MA: Harvard University Press, 1975.

Winnicott, D.W. *Collected Papers.* New York: Basic Books, Inc. 1958.

Winnicott, Clare. "Face to Face with Children." *Working with Children.* London: The British Agencies for Adoption and Fostering, 1986.

Winter, Alice. "Only People Cry" *Women's Day Magazine*, Diamandis Communications, Inc.: 1963.

Index

importance of, 103, 248
role of, 22, 116
security in, 104
as support unit, 23, 25, 147,
    232, 266, 270
traditions, 59
Family Life Graph, 249-50, 274, 276-8
failure to thrive, 14, 27, 51, 70, 247-8
fears, 63, 73, 82, 126, 166-7, 187, 193,
    206-7, 306, 324. See also
    anxiety
  in adolescence, 116
  and attachment, 155
  in childhood, 103-4, 121
  lack of, 255
  due to moving, 189
  preschool, 84
  and separation, 141
  of strangers, 76
  in toddlers, 78
  of unknown, 154
feelings. See emotions
Fetal Alcohol Syndrome, 259, 325,
    334, 392
fire setting, 302
food problems. See eating disorders
foster care
  effects of, 49
  for families affected by HIV,
    266-7
  limitations of, 60-61
  long term, 263, 268-9
  strengths and weaknesses, 236
  as therapy, 289
foster parents
  adoption by. See adoption, by
    foster parents
  birth children of, 202-3
  contact with, 208
  and emancipated adolescents,
    231-2
  emotions of, 181, 198-9, 201-3,
    212
  role of, 24, 25, 192, 198, 200,

207, 215, 217, 210-11,
    213-14, 219, 222, 223, 228
  as source of information, 370

Genogram, 247-8, 367, 369
goals, 255, 394. See also permanency
    planning
  personal, 115
  of placement, 190, 192
  planning, 185
good/bad split, 80, 145-6, 270
grief, 24-5, 38, 141-4, 149, 153,
    160, 162-4, 169-71, 173,
    180, 183, 192-3, 195, 206,
    210, 221-2, 225, 228-9,
    230, 246, 267, 298, 351
  adaptive, 348
  and emotions, 184
  resolution of, 166, 178
  stages of, 164-6
  unresolved, 299-300
group work, 337, 355, 393
guardianship, legal, 180, 259, 263-5,
    392
guilt, 102, 120, 135, 167

hallucinations, 255
HIV virus, 266-7
holding therapy, 65
homosexuality, 135
honesty, 187
hygiene, poor, 16
hyperactivity, 294, 314-15, 330,
    334. See also Attention
    Deficit Disorder
hyperacute hearing. See perceptual
    problems, auditory
hypersensitivity, 32, 35

identity, 22, 31, 75, 106, 108, 112,
    114, 118, 145, 260, 273,
    274, 280, 338, 346, 350-1,
    366-7, 383-4. See also
    Lifebook

and attachment, 23
racial, 279
sexual, 83, 128-9, 132
imaginary friends, 81
independence, 23, 31, 74, 76, 81, 83,
107, 112, 117, 119, 144-5,
184, 239, 246, 311. *See
also* autonomy
individuation, 184
institutionalization, effects of, 49-50

legal parents, 158-9, 208, 217, 263
legal system, 159, 207, 257, 264-5,
270 341-2
Lifebook, 106, 145, 154, 207, 302,
310,339, 341, 344, 348-9,
356, 361, 366-71, 373-80,
382, 384-6. *See also* identity;
past history
Life Path, 217, 348, 356, 363, 364, 381
Life Story Book. *See* Lifebook
loss. *See* separation
love, need for, 292. *See also* affection
loyalty conflict, 149, 179-2, 179-81,
186, 190-91, 195, 205-7,
219, 228, 270. 299
lying, 16, 55, 63, 127, 246, 277, 285,
322-3, 333, 344

magical thinking, 80, 84, 108, 123,
146-8, 150, 165, 167, 179-
80, 183, 208, 224-5, 229-
30, 247, 340, 349, 368
masturbation, 85, 106, 128, 130, 231,
243, 307
misperceptions, 309-10. *See also*
magical thinking
"mothering", 28, 181. *See also*
caregiver, primary
moving of children. *See also*
separation
abrupt, 175
adjustment to, 345
in adolescence, 184, 202

from adoption to foster care,
154, 196
to adoption, 23, 176, 207-9,
216, 225, 349
child's perception of, 167-8, 182
to emancipation, 232-33
and fear, 156
from foster care, 177, 198
from foster care to adoption, 63,
151-2, 160, 163, 183,
210-15, 223, 268, 363 377
from foster care to birth family,
163, 375.*See also*
reunification
to foster care, 154, 176, 185-8,
194, 197, 204
within foster care system, 199-
203
multiple moves, 146, 150, 210,
310
packing for, 186
parting message, 153
to permanency, 229, 346, 348,
363
postplacement contact, 25,
179-81, 183,185, 189, 193,
213, 228
preplacement contact and
preparation for, 152, 175, 177-
8, 181-2, 184-5, 187-90,
193-4, 197-8, 200, 203-5,
207, 209-210, 212-16,
219-223, 226, 230-31, 236,
341,
reasons for, 151, 158
to receiving home, 200
record of, 182
sibling reaction, 162
welcoming message, 153

name
changes in, 145-6, 217, 223-4,
393
and identity, 76

importance of, 60
of parents, 172
nailbiting, 304
Native American Children in placement,
278-80
neglect. See abuse, physical
nightmares, 63, 126, 165, 193, 324

"odd man out", 312-13
Oedipal stage, 83, 128, 131-2, 147
overcompliance, 145-46

parent-child interaction, 252
parental rights, termination of, 15, 159,
259, 261, 264, 266, 309, 377
parentification, 311-12
parenting, 195
aspects of, 159
interruption of, 21
positive, 238-40
skills, 238
uneven, 48
parenting parents, 158-9, 178, 217
parents. *See also* birth parents;
caregivers,
primary; legal parents;
parenting
parents
role of, 58, 73, 78-80, 84-5, 104,
117-19, 121, 136, 158-9,
271
as role models, 288, 319
past history, 25, 58, 101, 106 242-4,
247-9, 270, 330, 347, 349,
351-3, 355, 366-7, 369-70,
372-3, 380, 282-5, 393.
See also Lifebook
racial heritage, 383, 392
peer interaction, 15, 55, 102, 107, 109-
10,112-13, 137, 148-9,
227, 231, 246, 252, 255,
292, 306, 323, 326, 332,
337, 342, 392-3

perceptual problems
auditory, 326-8
visual, 328-9
permanency planning, 196, 236, 241,
256-9, 261-2, 266-9. *See
also* goals play, 80-82, 246
and psychological development,
85
positive interaction cycle, 36-7, 40,
54-7, 60, 62-3
pregnancy, psychological, 38
prenatal care, lack of, 14
psychotic symptoms, 255, 310, 314.
See also schizophrenia
punishment. *See* behavior
modification;
discipline

racial congruity, 236, 260, 269, 278-
81,283, 336, 347-8, 350
reciprocity, 32, 40, 50, 144, 150-51,
190, 273, 289
reframing, 191-2
regression. *See* under development
rejection, 291
relative placement, 236, 262, 270-71,
See also adoption, by
relatives
reparenting, 237, 243, 245, 247, 307
reunification, 23, 180-81, 193, 195-6,
201, 205, 217, 230, 241,
248, 261, 267, 271, 275,
309
barriers to, 258, 260
plans for, 204-5
rituals, 227
rocking, 303
running away, 300

scaling, 365
scapegoated child, 27, 145, 379
schizophrenia, 85-6, 328

About the Author

Vera I. Fahlberg, M.D., is a pediatrician and psychotherapist who has worked with disturbed children and their families since 1964. Much of Dr. Fahlberg's work has been focused on attachment and separation problems, with special emphasis on children in out-of-home placements.

Dr. Fahlberg has completed over 400 evaluations of children in placement for public and private agencies throughout the U.S., as well as having seen numerous children in out-patient therapy, and serving as an expert witness in child welfare-related cases. For thirteen years she was medical director of Forest Heights Lodge, a residential treatment facility in Evergreen, Colorado. She continues to serve as a consultant and trainer for Forest Heights, though she is now based in the Seattle area.

A trainer and consultant of international reputation, Dr. Fahlberg has conducted workshops in over 40 states as well as in Canada, England, Scotland, Ireland, Sweden, Greece, Israel and Australia, and has contributed to a variety of child welfare related training curricula, including written materials, films and videotapes. Her publications include the workbook series *Fitting the Pieces Together*, which served as the adaptable basis for updating, revising, expanding in order to create this book, *A Child's Journey through Placement*, and *Residential Treatment: A Tapestry of Many Therapies* (Perspectives Press, 1990.)

Let Us Introduce Ourselves

Perspectives Press is a narrowly focused publishing company. The materials we produce or distribute all speak to issues related to infertility or to child welfare issues. Our purpose is to promote understanding of these issues and to educate and sensitize those personally experiencing these life situations, professionals who work in infertility adoption and fostercare, and the public at large. Perspectives Press titles are never duplicative. We seek out and publish materials that are currently unavailable through traditional sources. Our titles include . . .

Perspectives on a Grafted Tree

An Adoptor's Advocate

Understanding: A Guide to Impaired Fertility for Family and Friends

Our Baby: A Birth and Adoption Story

The Mulberry Bird: Story of an Adoption

Real For Sure Sister

Filling in the Blanks: A Guided Look at Growing Up Adopted

Sweet Grapes: How to Stop Being Infertile and Start Living Again

Where the Sun Kisses the Sea

Residential Treatment: A Tapestry of Many Therapies

William Is My Brother

Our authors have special credentials: they are people whose personal and professional lives provide an interwoven pattern for what they write. If **you** are writing about these issues, we invite you to contact us with a query letter and stamped, self addressed envelope so that we can send you our writers guidelines and help you determine whether your materials might fit into our publishing plans.

 Perspectives Press
P.O. Box 90318
Indianapolis, IN 46290-0318